ABOUT THE AUTHOR

 **N**ick Redfern works full time as an author, lecturer, and journalist. He writes about a wide range of unsolved mysteries, including Bigfoot, UFOs, the Loch Ness Monster, alien encounters, and government conspiracies. His many books include *The Zombie Book* (co-written with Brad Steiger); *Close Encounters of the Fatal Kind*; and *Monster Diary*. He writes regularly for *Cryptomundo.com*, the *Mutual UFO Network Journal*, and *Mysterious Universe*. He has appeared on numerous television shows, including Fox News; History Channel's *Ancient Aliens*, *Monster Quest*, and *UFO Hunters*; VH1's *Legend Hunters*; National Geographic Channel's *The Truth about UFOs* and *Paranatural*; BBC's *Out of This World*; MSNBC's *Countdown*; and SyFy Channel's *Proof Positive*. Nick lives just a few miles from Dallas, Texas' infamous Grassy Knoll and can be contacted at his blog: http://nickredfernfortean.blogspot.com.

D1225529

ALSO FROM VISIBLE INK PRESS

Alien Mysteries, Conspiracies, and Cover-Ups
by Kevin D. Randle
ISBN: 978-1-57859-418-4

Ancient Gods: Lost Histories, Hidden Truths, and the Conspiracy of Silence
by Jim Willis
ISBN: 978-1-57859-614-0

Angels A to Z, 2nd edition
by Evelyn Dorothy Oliver, Ph.D., and James R Lewis, Ph.D.
ISBN: 978-1-57859-212-8

Armageddon Now: The End of the World A to Z
by Jim Willis and Barbara Willis
ISBN: 978-1-57859-168-8

The Astrology Book: The Encyclopedia of Heavenly Influences, 2nd edition
by James R. Lewis
ISBN: 978-1-57859-144-2

The Bigfoot Book: The Encyclopedia of Sasquatch, Yeti, and Cryptid Primates
by Nick Redfern
ISBN: 978-1-57859-561-7

Conspiracies and Secret Societies: The Complete Dossier, 2nd edition
by Brad Steiger and Sherry Hansen Steiger
ISBN: 978-1-57859-368-2

The Dream Encyclopedia, 2nd edition
by James R Lewis, Ph.D., and Evelyn Dorothy Oliver, Ph.D.
ISBN: 978-1-57859-216-6

The Dream Interpretation Dictionary: Symbols, Signs, and Meanings
By J. M. DeBord
ISBN: 978-1-57859-637-9

The Encyclopedia of Religious Phenomena
by J. Gordon Melton
ISBN: 978-1-57859-209-8

The Fortune-Telling Book: The Encyclopedia of Divination and Soothsaying
by Raymond Buckland
ISBN: 978-1-57859-147-3

The Government UFO Files: The Conspiracy of Cover-Up
By Kevin D. Randle
ISBN: 978-1-57859-477-1

Hidden Realms, Lost Civilizations, and Beings from Other Worlds
by Jerome Clark
ISBN: 978-1-57859-175-6

The Horror Show Guide: The Ultimate Frightfest of Movies
By Mike May
ISBN: 978-1-57859-420-7

The Illuminati: The Secret Society That Hijacked the World
By Jim Marrs
ISBN: 978-1-57859-619-5

The Monster Book: Creatures, Beasts, and Fiends of Nature
By Nick Redfern
ISBN: 978-1-57859-575-4

Real Aliens, Space Beings, and Creatures from Other Worlds,
by Brad Steiger and Sherry Hansen Steiger
ISBN: 978-1-57859-333-0

Real Encounters, Different Dimensions, and Otherworldly Beings
by Brad Steiger with Sherry Hansen Steiger
ISBN: 978-1-57859-455-9

Real Ghosts, Restless Spirits, and Haunted Places, 2nd edition
by Brad Steiger
ISBN: 978-1-57859-401-6

Real Miracles, Divine Intervention, and Feats of Incredible Survival
by Brad Steiger and Sherry Hansen Steiger
ISBN: 978-1-57859-214-2

Real Monsters, Gruesome Critters, and Beasts from the Darkside
by Brad Steiger and Sherry Hansen Steiger
ISBN: 978-1-57859-220-3

Real Vampires, Night Stalkers, and Creatures from the Darkside
by Brad Steiger
ISBN: 978-1-57859-255-5

Real Visitors, Voices from Beyond, and Parallel Dimensions
By Brad Steiger and Sherry Hansen Steiger
ISBN: 978-1-57859-541-9

Real Zombies, the Living Dead, and Creatures of the Apocalypse
by Brad Steiger
ISBN: 978-1-57859-296-8

The Religion Book: Places, Prophets, Saints, and Seers
by Jim Willis
ISBN: 978-1-57859-151-0

The Sci-Fi Movie Guide: The Universe of Film from Alien to Zardoz
By Chris Barsanti
ISBN: 978-1-57859-503-7

Secret History: Conspiracies from Ancient Aliens to the New World Order
By Nick Redfern
ISBN: 978-1-57859-479-5

The Spirit Book: The Encyclopedia of Clairvoyance, Channeling, and Spirit Communication
by Raymond Buckland
ISBN: 978-1-57859-172-5

UFO Dossier: 100 Years of Government Secrets, Conspiracies, and Cover-Ups
By Kevin D. Randle
ISBN: 978-1-57859-564-8

Unexplained! Strange Sightings, Incredible Occurrences, and Puzzling Physical Phenomena, 3rd edition
by Jerome Clark
ISBN: 978-1-57859-344-6

The Vampire Book: The Encyclopedia of the Undead, 3rd edition
by J. Gordon Melton
ISBN: 978-1-57859-281-4

The Werewolf Book: The Encyclopedia of Shape-Shifting Beings, 2nd edition
by Brad Steiger
ISBN: 978-1-57859-367-5

The Witch Book: The Encyclopedia of Witchcraft, Wicca, and Neo-paganism
by Raymond Buckland
ISBN: 978-1-57859-114-5

The Zombie Book: The Encyclopedia of the Living Dead
By Nick Redfern and Brad Steiger
ISBN: 978-1-57859-504-4

"REAL NIGHTMARES" E-BOOKS BY BRAD STEIGER

Book 1: *True and Truly Scary Unexplained Phenomenon*

Book 2: *The Unexplained Phenomena and Tales of the Unknown*

Book 3: *Things That Go Bump in the Night*

Book 4: *Things That Prowl and Growl in the Night*

Book 5: *Fiends That Want Your Blood*

Book 6: *Unexpected Visitors and Unwanted Guests*

Book 7: *Dark and Deadly Demons*

Book 8: *Phantoms, Apparitions, and Ghosts*

PLEASE VISIT US AT VISIBLEINKPRESS.COM

SECRET SOCIETIES:
THE COMPLETE GUIDE TO
HISTORIES, RITES, AND RITUALS

Copyright © 2017 by Visible Ink Press®

This publication is a creative work fully protected by all applicable copyright laws, as well as by misappropriation, trade secret, unfair competition, and other applicable laws.

No part of this book may be reproduced in any form without permission in writing from the publisher, except by a reviewer who wishes to quote brief passages in connection with a review written for inclusion in a magazine, newspaper, or website.

All rights to this publication will be vigorously defended.

Visible Ink Press®
43311 Joy Rd., #414
Canton, MI 48187-2075

Visible Ink Press is a registered trademark of Visible Ink Press LLC.

Most Visible Ink Press books are available at special quantity discounts when purchased in bulk by corporations, organizations, or groups. Customized printings, special imprints, messages, and excerpts can be produced to meet your needs. For more information, contact Special Markets Director, Visible Ink Press, www.visibleink.com, or 734-667-3211.

Managing Editor: Kevin S. Hile
Art Director: Mary Claire Krzewinski
Typesetting: Marco DiVita
Proofreaders: Larry Baker and Janet Hile
Indexer: Shoshana Hurwitz

Cover images: Thule symbol by NsMn (Wikicommons), Rosy Cross of the Golden Dawn (public domain); all others, Shutterstock.

Cataloging-in-Publication Data is on file at the Library of Congress.

10 9 8 7 6 5 4 3 2 1

LA CROSSE COUNTY LIBRARY

SECRET SOCIETIES

THE COMPLETE GUIDE TO HISTORIES, RITES, AND RITUALS

Nick Redfern

VISIBLE
I N K
PRESS

Detroit

366
Re

Acknowledgments

I would like to say a big "thank you" to everyone at Visible Ink Press—and particularly publisher Roger Jänecke and editor Kevin Hile—and to my agent, Lisa Hagan, for all her hard work. Thanks, also, to VIP typesetter Marco DiVita, page and cover designer Mary Claire Krzewinski, indexer Shoshana Hurwitz, and proofreaders Larry Baker and Janet Hile.

TABLE OF CONTENTS

Photo Sources [xi]

Introduction [xiii]

Contents

M

N—O

P

R

S

T—U

V, W, Z

Photo Sources

Bdm25 (Wikicommons): p. 251.
Beinecke Rare Book & Manuscript Library, Yale University: p. 376.
Boy Scouts of America: p. 279.
Bundesarchiv: pp. 289, 336.
Carl Van Vechten Photographs collection, Library of Congress: p. 124.
Carol M. Highsmith Archive, Library of Congress: p. 24.
Central Intelligence Agency: p. 226.
Coolcaesar (Wikicommons): p. 266.
Kim Dent-Brown: p. 223.
DietG (Wikicommons): p. 127.
Franzfoto (Wikicommons): p. 59.
Theodor Fritsch: p. 122.
George Grantham Bain collection, Library of Congress: p. 75.
Gryffindor (Wikicommons): p. 84.
Gustavo89 (Wikicommons): p. 68.
Simon Harriyott (Fabian Society): p. 114.
Henrygb (English Wikipedia): p. 253.
HMman (Wikicommons): p. 71.
Indytnt (Wikicommons): p. 241.
International Institute of Social History, Amsterdam, Netherlands: p. 173.
LuxAmber (Wikicommons): p. 323.
Macieklew (Wikicommons): p. 348.
Malyszkz (talk) (Wikicommons): p. 9.
Michiel1972 (Wikicommons): p. 39.
NASA: pp. 295. 333.
NASA/JPL-Caltech: p. 247.
NASA/JPL/Malin Space Science Systems: p. 199.
National Portrait Gallery, London: pp. 201, 378.
NBC Television: p. 327.

NsMn (Wikicommons): p. 358.

nutsandroutes-co-uk (Wikicommons): p. 3.

Ordo Aurum Solis: p. 228.

Serge Ottaviani: p. 210.

Poliphilo (Wikicommons): p. 244.

Rafaelomondini (Wikicommons): p. 190.

Rick (Wikicommons): p. 101.

Jorge Royan: p. 298.

Shutterstock: pp. 7, 11, 25, 27, 30, 32, 38, 42, 44, 46, 63, 64, 73, 76, 79, 83, 86, 90, 92, 94, 105, 118, 144, 157, 181, 184, 194, 203, 206, 222, 238, 258, 277, 301, 303, 320, 330, 338, 345, 352, 356, 366, 372, 374, 386, 387, 395.

Susan Skaar: p. 198.

Carmen Slade: p. 262.

Adam Smith: p. 306.

John Thaxter: p. 132.

U.S. Air Force: pp. 33, 196, 340.

U.S. Army Air Corps: p. 19.

U.S. Department of Defense: p. 383.

U.S. National Archives and Records Administration: pp. 139, 278.

U.S. Navy: p. 14.

Krishna Venta: p. 116.

Daniel Villafruela: p. 165.

Wikophile1 (Wikicommons): p. 49.

Wonder Stories: p. 97.

Ziff-Davis Publishing Company: p. 98.

Public domain: pp. 12, 16, 21, 51, 53, 81, 102, 107, 112, 128, 134, 137, 141, 142, 149, 153, 154, 168, 169, 177, 192, 213, 215, 234, 269, 283, 292, 297, 311, 315, 317, 322, 326, 341, 361, 393.

INTRODUCTION

Sir Thomas Moore: "Everywhere do I perceive a certain conspiracy of rich men seeking their own advantage under that name and pretext of commonwealth."

President Woodrow Wilson: "Some of the biggest men in the United States, in the field of commerce and manufacture, are afraid of somebody, afraid of something. They know there is a power somewhere so organized, so subtle, so watchful, so interlocked, so complete, so pervasive, that they better not speak above their breath when they speak of condemnation of it."

Senator Daniel K. Inouye: "There exists a shadowy government with its own Air Force, its own Navy, its own fund raising mechanism, and the ability to pursue its own ideas of national interest, free from all checks and balances; free from law itself."

Duke of Brunswick, Grand Master of World Freemasonry: "I have been convinced that we, as an order, have come under the power of some very evil occult order, profoundly versed in Science, both occult and otherwise, though not infallible, their methods being black magic, that is to say, electromagnetic power, hypnotism, and powerful suggestion. We are convinced that the order is being controlled by some Sun Order, after the nature of the Illuminati, if not by that order itself."

As the words above demonstrate, secret societies are everywhere. They are within the worlds of government, business, politics, the military, religion, the intelligence community, and even Hollywood. Their names include the Bohemian Club, the Freemasons, the Bilderbergers, and the Illuminati. They thrive on power, on manipulation, and on shaping and controlling world events. They are here. They are there. They are just about *everywhere*. They often profess to be benevolent and nonthreatening. Wrong. They claim to have no covert agenda. Wrong. They say they are our friends. Wrong again.

The history of humankind is filled with secret orders, clandestine groups, and shadowy organizations that have sculpted and molded society on a global scale since time immemorial. Some of them parade their power in our faces, despite their secret affiliations and actions. Others prefer to lurk in the darkness, pulling planet-wide strings as they see fit. They have killed to protect their members and to ensure their end-games are not derailed.

The book you are about to read will take you on a sinister, eye-opening journey from the earliest years of civilization to the present day. It demonstrates how, to a shocking degree, the world as we know it is the product of an almost omnipotent elite. From ancient Egypt to the palaces of Rome, from hired assassins of the Middle Ages to witchcraft cults that engage in human sacrifice for political and financial gain, and from the heart of the British Royal Family to the Oval Office, secret societies abound.

Ace of Spades Group

History has shown that military agencies and the world of clandestine, secret activity go together hand in glove. A perfect example can be found in a May 1967 file with the intriguing title of *Vietnam: PSYOP Directive: The Use of Superstitions in Psychological Operations in Vietnam*. While the file covers a wealth of previously classified U.S. Army operations, one particular section really stands out from all of the rest. It is focused upon a near-elite band of warriors who chose to scare North Vietnamese personnel with the imagery of the ace of spades from a deck of cards. As for the reasons, consider the following words from the file in question:

"A strong superstition or a deeply held belief shared by a substantial number of the enemy target audience can be used as a psychological weapon because it permits with some degree of probability the prediction of individual or group behavior under a given set of conditions. To use an enemy superstition as a starting point for psychological operations, however, one must be sure of the conditions and control the stimuli that trigger the desired behavior.

"The first step in the manipulation of a superstition as an enemy vulnerability is its exact identification and detailed definition of its spread and intensity among the target audience. The second step is to insure friendly control of the stimuli and the capability to create a situation that will trigger the desired superstitious behavior. Both conditions must be met or the psyops [psychological operations] effort will not yield the desired results; it might even backfire.

"As an illustration, one can cite the recent notion spread among combat troops in the First Corps area that VC and NVN troops were deathly afraid of the 'Ace of Spades' as an omen of death. In consequence soldiers, turned psy-warriors with the assistance of playing card manufacturers, began leaving the ominous card in battle areas and on patrols into enemy-held territory. The notion was based on isolated instances of behavior among Montagnard tribes-men familiar from French days with the Western deck of cards. A subsequent survey determined that the ace of spades does not trigger substantial fear reactions among most Vietnamese because the various local playing cards have their own set of symbols, generally of Chinese derivation.

"Here then was an incorrect identification of a superstition coupled with a friendly capability to exploit the presumed condition. It did not work.

"In summary, the manipulation of superstitions is a delicate affair. Tampering with deeply held beliefs, seeking to turn them to your advantage means in effect playing God, and it should only be attempted if one can get away with it and the game is indeed worth the candle. Failure can lead to ridicule, charges of clumsiness and callousness that can blacken the reputation of psychological operations in general. It is a weapon to be employed selectively and with utmost skill and deftness. There can be no excuse for failure."

The file makes it very clear that the strange operation did not have the effect that the military was hoping for. Nevertheless, the data most assuredly does reveal that when waging war Uncle Sam employed some very strange tools.

Aerial Phenomena Enquiry Network

Most people have heard of the alleged UFO crash at Roswell, New Mexico, in the summer of 1947. Far fewer, however, have likely heard the story of a similar such crash in the Berwyn Mountains of North Wales, United Kingdom. No one knows more about the controversial story—which revolves around claims that a wrecked alien spacecraft and its crew were recovered by the British military in January 1974—than UFO investigator and author Andy Roberts, whose book on the subject, *UFO Down?*, is essential reading. He says: "The claim was that a UFO piloted by extraterrestrials crashed, or was shot down, on the mountain known as Cader Berwyn and that the alien crew, some still alive, were whisked off to a secret military installation in the south of England for study."

As Roberts also notes, however, it wasn't long before a mysterious, and even dangerous, group surfaced and immersed itself in the strange story. Back to

A path along the Berwyn Mountains in Wales, where a UFO is said to have crashed in 1974.

Roberts: "Within months of the event, UFO investigators in the north of England began to receive official-looking documents from a group called the Aerial Phenomena Enquiry Network (APEN). These documents claimed that an extraterrestrial craft had come down on the Berwyns and was retrieved for study by an APEN crash retrieval team [that] had been on the scene within hours of the event. Some researchers have speculated that APEN may have been part of a government cover up, using UFO mythology to spread disinformation."

It's not at all out of the question that APEN's agenda was centered upon provoking within the UFO research community paranoia, fear, distrust and confusion. Indeed, history has shown that APEN's members had more than a few dirty tricks up their collective sleeves. One person of many who felt the sinister brunt of APEN's wrath was veteran U.K. UFO researcher/writer Jenny Randles. In early 1997, I interviewed Randles about her experiences with the mysterious members of the Aerial Phenomena Enquiry Network.

She told me: "At about the same time as [the alleged UFO crash on the Berwyn Mountains] occurred, I was involved in setting up an organization known as the Northern UFO Network, or NUFON. The original concept of NUFON was to be kind of a liaison scheme to bring local groups up and down the North and the Midlands together."

It's illuminating to note that APEN was intent on meddling in the world of NUFON, and most definitely not for positive reasons, as Randles readily admitted to me: "You do have to wonder if some of the sinister things that [APEN] did would really have been perpetrated just for the sake of it. I think that the most serious aspect was that it did attempt to destabilize NUFON. I've no doubt whatsoever that that was the case. At the time, when BUFORA [the British UFO Research Organization] were attempting a similar initiative—trying to bring in local groups, a group liaison system that they operated—they also started to get similar APEN letters, basically telling them not to contact BUFORA, and also in the late seventies, when BUFORA, through their then-chairman, Roger Stanway, attempted a direct liaison with *Flying Saucer Review*, exactly the same thing happened vis-à-vis *Flying Saucer Review*."

To this very day, more than forty years after the curious incident on the Berwyn Mountains occurred, the saga of APEN has still not been unraveled. They were never identified, outed, or revealed. And anyone who tried to get close to them was soon on the receiving end of threats, intimidation, and hang-up phone calls in the middle of the night. Even mail interference, on a few occasions, was reported. Given the scale and activities of APEN—and particularly so regarding the group's ability to interfere with the delivery of mail to certain UFO researchers—the idea that APEN was a group from within the field of ufology is slim in the extreme. Far more likely, APEN was a secret group from within the British government or military, a group intent on disrupting research into the matter of whatever it was that came crashing down on the Berwyn Mountains, Wales, late one night in January 1974.

Aetherius Society

The website of the Aetherius Society tells us: "The Aetherius Society is an international spiritual organization dedicated to spreading, and acting upon, the teachings of advanced extraterrestrial intelligences. In great compassion, these beings recognize the extent of suffering on Earth and have made countless sacrifices in their mission to help us to create a better world.

"The Society was founded in the mid-1950s by an Englishman named George King shortly after he was contacted in London by an extraterrestrial intelligence known as 'Aetherius.' The main body of the Society's teachings consists of the wisdom given through the mediumship of Dr. King by the Master Aetherius and other advanced intelligences from this world and beyond. The single greatest aspect of the Society's teachings is the importance of selfless service to others."

There is, however, far more to the Aetherius Society, such as its stance on matters relative to politics and issues concerning nuclear weaponry. We know this because back in the 1950s, an arm of the British Police Force—an elite group known as Special Branch—clandestinely opened a file on the Aetherius Society. Special Branch was not particularly interested in, or bothered by, the UFO beliefs of the society. Its big concern was that the Aetherius Society was trying to sway the public's attitudes on nuclear bombs and towards the realm of complete disarmament of the U.K.'s atomic arsenal.

Thanks to the work of an English UFO investigator, Dr. David Clarke, Special Branch agreed to declassify its file on George King and the Aetherius Society. Its contents make for notable reading. So far as can be determined, the very first inkling that Special Branch was interested in the activities of the Aetherius Society surfaced in 1957. It was all thanks to the probing of the United Kingdom's *Empire News* newspaper that fragmentary parts of the story began to surface, and it all began in late May 1957. On May 26, the *Empire News* ran an article below the following banner: "Flying Saucer Clubs Probe."

> "**T**he Society was founded in the mid-1950s by an Englishman named George King shortly after he was contacted in London by an extraterrestrial intelligence known as 'Aetherius.'"

The story provided the following to the readers of the newspaper: "'Warnings' from outer space against Britain's H-Bomb tests published in a flying saucer magazine take a similar line to Moscow-inspired propaganda. The 'warning'—in a special issue of the magazine—is being scrutinized by Scotland Yard's Special Branch. It is suspected that a number of flying saucer clubs—and some spiritualists as well—are unwittingly being used by the communists. The warning appears in the magazine of the Aetherius Society, which circulates widely among flying saucer enthusiasts."

As this shows, Special Branch's detectives were clearly digging deep into the world of the Aetherius Society. However, that the U.K. did not have a Freedom of Information Act at the time meant that Special Branch was under no obligation to release its files, and it didn't. At least, not until 2005, when the aforementioned Dr. David Clarke managed to secure a copy of the file via newly implemented FOIA rules. The documents in question make it very clear that Special Branch knew all about the inner workings of the Aetherius Society. One particular section of the length file notes that "King is obviously a crank.... Since 1st June 1957, the date of the last report about the Aetherius

Society, this organization has remained active in its campaign against nuclear weapons tests, and in this respect its policy is closely allied with that of the Communist Party. However, there is still no evidence of open communist association with the Society."

The detectives of Special Branch even went so far as to tail the members of the Aetherius Society, and—in undercover fashion—mingled with them at their anti-nuke rallies. After monitoring a gathering at Trafalgar Square, London, one Special Branch officer recorded the following in an official, secret report: The gathering was "devoted to almost incomprehensible rubbish about Venusians and Martians, and how the Aetherius Society was in touch with superior beings from Galactic Space.... It appears that the Aetherius Society is pacifist insofar as war is abhorrent to the 'Cosmic Parliament,' and in like manner is aligning itself with the demand for a cessation of nuclear tests and the abolition of nuclear weapons."

As all of the above shows, it was not UFOs, flying saucers, and aliens that worried Special Branch when it came to the matter of the Aetherius Society. Rather, it was the concern that its followers—and, perhaps, even sizeable numbers of the British public—would demand an end to the arms race and offer their support to the idea of unilateral disarmament in the U.K.

> "The detectives of Special Branch even went so far as to tail the members of the Aetherius Society, and—in undercover fashion—mingled with them at their anti-nuke rallies."

Africa's Secret Criminal Enterprises

The Federal Bureau of Investigation (FBI) has taken extensive note of all manner of secret groups—whether definitive secret societies or underground, organized criminal activity. A particular target for special agents of the FBI is the continent of Africa. Of specific concern to the FBI is Nigeria. Under Freedom of Information legislation, the FBI has released the following summary of its careful study of what's afoot at an underground level in the world of Nigeria's criminal bodies: African criminal enterprises have developed quickly since the 1980s due to the globalization of the world's economies and the great advances in communications technology. Easier international travel, expanded world trade, and financial transactions that cross national borders have enabled them to branch out of local and regional crime to target international victims and develop criminal networks within more prosperous countries and regions. The political, social, and economic conditions in African countries like Nigeria, Ghana, and Liberia also have helped some enterprises

Heroin and opium come from harvesting, and then processing, the milky sap of poppy seed pods. Growing poppies is a profitable farming business for many impoverished regions of the world.

expand globally. African criminal enterprises have been identified in several major metropolitan areas in the United States, but are most prevalent in Atlanta, Baltimore, Chicago, Dallas, Houston, Milwaukee, Newark, New York, and Washington, D.C.

The FBI reports that Nigerian criminal bodies are the most significant of these groups and operate in dozens of countries around the world. They are among the most aggressive and expansionist international criminal groups and are primarily engaged in drug trafficking and financial frauds. The most profitable activity of the Nigerian groups is drug trafficking: delivering heroin from southeast and southwest Asia into Europe and the United States and cocaine from South America into Europe and South Africa. Large populations of ethnic Nigerians in India, Pakistan, and Thailand have given these enterprises direct access to ninety percent of the world's heroin production. The associated money laundering has helped establish Nigerian criminal enterprises in every populated continent of the world.

And, finally, we have this from the FBI: "Nigerian groups are famous globally for their financial frauds, which cost the United States alone an estimated $1 billion to $2 billion each year. Schemes are diverse, targeting individuals, businesses, and government offices. Here's just a partial list of their fraudulent activities: insurance fraud involving auto accidents; healthcare billing scams; life insurance schemes; bank, check, and credit card fraud; advance-fee schemes known as 4-1-9 letters; and document fraud to develop false identities. The advent of the Internet and e-mail have made their crimes more profitable and prevalent."

Ahnenerbe

Although World War II came to a decisive and bloody conclusion way back in the summer of 1945, it was a six-year-long and carnage-filled event that still provokes major discussion and commentary to this very day. One of the many notable reasons for that same commentary relates to the secret, wartime actions of senior Nazis in relation to: (a) priceless historical treasures plundered by Adolf Hitler's hordes as a means to fund their war effort, and (b) Nazi Germany's overriding fascination with religious and priceless artifacts.

Just like the maniacal Hitler himself, a significant body of high-ranking Nazis, such as Richard Walther Darré, Rudolf Hess, Otto Rahn, and Heinrich Himmler, had major, unsettling obsessions with matters of a supernatural and mystical nature. Rahn, for example, who made his mark in a wing of Nazi Germany's greatly feared SS, spent a significant period of time deeply engaged in a quest to find the so-called Holy Grail, which, according to Christian teachings, was the dish, plate, or cup used by Jesus at the legendary Last Supper.

That the Grail was said to possess awesome and devastating powers spurred the Nazis on even more in their attempts to locate it, and then utilize those same powers as weapons of war against the Allies. Thankfully, the plans of the Nazis did not come to fruition, and the Allies were not pummeled into the ground by the mighty fists of God.

Acknowledged by many historians with being the ultimate driving force behind such research, Himmler was, perhaps, the one high-ranking official in the Third Reich, more than any other, most obsessed with the occult. In 1935, Himmler became a key player in the establishment of the Ahnenerbe, which was basically the ancestral heritage division of the SS.

With its work largely coordinated according to the visions of one Dr. Hermann Wirth, the chief motivation of the Ahnenerbe was to conduct research into the realm of religious-themed archaeology; however, its work also spilled over into areas such as the occult—primarily, from the perspective of determining if it was a tool that, like the Holy Grail, could be useful to further strengthen the Nazi war machine.

Then there is Trevor Ravenscroft's book *The Spear of Destiny*, which detailed a particularly odd fascination Hitler had with the fabled spear, or lance, that supposedly pierced the body of Jesus during the crucifixion. Ravenscroft's book maintained that Hitler deliberately started World War II with the intention of trying to secure the spear—again as a weapon to be used against the Allies—and with which he was said to be overwhelmingly obsessed.

So the account went, however, that Hitler utterly failed in his weird aim. Ravenscroft suggested that as the conflict of 1939 to 1945 came to its end, the spear came into the hands of U.S. general George Patton. According to legend, losing the spear would result in nothing less than death—a prophecy that was said to have been definitively fulfilled when Hitler, fortunately for the Allies, committed suicide.

But, perhaps, not every ancient artifact remained quite so elusive to Hitler. One rumor suggests that an attempt on the part of the Nazis to locate the remains—or, at least, some of the remains—of nothing less than the legendary Ark of Noah was actually, and incredibly, successful. It's a strange and secret story indeed.

The Bible states: "God said unto Noah.… Make thee an ark of gopher wood.… and this is the fashion which thou shalt make it of: The length of the ark shall be three hundred cubits, the breadth of it fifty cubits, and the height of it thirty cubits." A cubit roughly equates to twenty inches—thus making the Ark five hundred feet in length, eighty-three feet in width and fifty feet in height. In addition, it is said the Ark was powerful enough to withstand the cataclysmic flood that allegedly overtook the globe and lasted for forty terrible days and nights. So the legend has it, when the flood waters finally receded, the Ark came to rest on Mount Ararat.

Precisely why Hitler was apparently hot on the trail of the Ark is tantalizingly unclear; however, that he was certainly after it is not a matter of doubt. Intelligence files generated by Britain's highly secret MI6 in 1948 state that,

The logo of the Deutches Ahnenerbe, a branch of the Nazi SS that specialized in researching religious antiquities such as the Holy Grail and Noah's Ark.

in the closing stages of the war, rumors were coming out of Turkey to the effect that German military personnel were then engaged in a secret program that involved flying a sophisticated spy balloon—based upon radical, Japanese designs—over Mount Ararat, as part of an attempt to photograph the area.

And, if the operation proved successful in locating the Ark, and recovering it, or whatever remains still might be left given the lengthy passage of time and the harsh conditions that exist on the permanently snowcapped mountain, the secrets of the ancient past and the Ahnenerbe may be only a locked vault away.

AIDS Secret Group

Did a secret U.S. group—buried deep in the heart of the military—create the AIDS virus? No. But, in the 1980s, the then-Soviet Union's secret police, the KGB, was determined to spread just such a controversial rumor. A January 2005 U.S. Department of State document—titled "AIDS as a Biological Weapon" and declassified under the terms of the Freedom of Information Act—reveals the strange story of how the rumors began and were ultimately quashed. The document begins: "When the AIDS disease was first recognized in the early 1980s, its origins were a mystery. A deadly new disease had suddenly appeared, with no obvious explanation of what had caused it. In such a situation, false rumors and misinformation naturally arose, and Soviet disinformation specialists exploited this situation as well as the musings of conspiracy theorists to help shape their brief but highly effective disinformation campaign on this issue."

The Department of State continued: "In March 1992, then-Russian intelligence chief and later Russian Prime Minister Yevgeni Primakov admitted that the disinformation service of the Soviet KGB had concocted the false story that the AIDS virus had been created in a U.S. military laboratory as a biological weapon. The Russian newspaper *Izvestiya* reported on March 19, 1992: '[Primakov] mentioned the well-known articles printed a few years ago in our central newspapers about AIDS supposedly originating from secret Pentagon laboratories.'"

According to Primakov, the articles exposing U.S. scientists' "crafty" plots were fabricated in KGB offices. The Soviets eventually abandoned the AIDS disinformation campaign in their media under pressure from the U.S. government in August 1987.

It was not just the KGB, however, who were spreading rumors of a secret U.S. group creating the AIDS virus, as the Department of State knew all too well:

In addition to the Soviet disinformation specialists, a tiny handful of fringe-group conspiracy theorists also espoused the false charge that the AIDS virus had been created as a biological weapon. One of them was Mr. Theodore Strecker, an attorney in the United States, who had a brother, Robert, who was a physician in Los Angeles. Theodore wrote a manifesto, "This Is a Bio-Attack Alert," on March 28, 1986. He imagined that traitorous American doctors, United Nations bureaucrats, and Soviet officials were involved in a gigantic conspiracy to destroy the United States with biological warfare. He wrote, "We have allowed the United Nations World Health Organization to combine with traitors in the United States National Institutes of Health to start a Soviet Union attack."

The document continues: "Mr. Strecker claimed that the 'War on Cancer' led by the U.S. National Institutes of Health (NIH) was a cover for developing AIDS. He wrote, 'the virologists of WHO [the World Health Organization], NCI [the U.S. National Institute of Cancer], and the NIH, have written in plain English their plan for conquest of America and are presently executing it disguised as cancer research.'

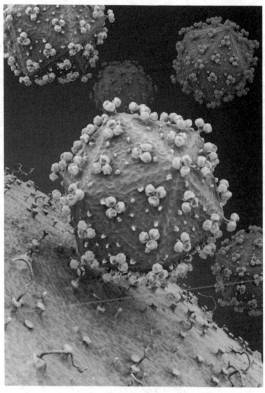

The KGB spread rumors that HIV was deliberately created by a secret U.S. government program.

"Mr. Strecker," said the Department of State, "saw the Soviet Union at the heart of this alleged conspiracy."

Indeed, Strecker himself said: "This is an attempt to exhaust America with hatred, struggle, want, confusion, and inoculation of disease. The enemy intends to control our population with disease, make us dependent upon their remedies, engineer each birth, and reduce America to a servant of the Supreme Soviet."

The Department of State added: "Mr. Strecker sent his manifesto to the president and vice president of the United States, governors of several states, and various U.S. government departments, urging them to 'retake the virus labs using force if necessary' and other dramatic emergency measures. It did not have the galvanizing effect he had hoped."

As for the real origins of AIDS, the Department of State said: "In the mid-1980s, there was still considerable confusion about how AIDS had developed, although scientists universally agreed that it was a naturally occurring disease, not one that was man-made. In the intervening years, science has done much to solve this mystery. There is now strong scientific evidence that the AIDS virus originated as a subspecies of a virus that commonly infects the western equatorial African chimpanzee."

Alchemists

Author Brad Steiger, who has a particular fascination for alchemy, says: "Helvetius, the grandfather of the celebrated philosopher of the same name, was an alchemist who labored ceaselessly to fathom the mystery of the 'philosopher's stone,' the legendary catalyst that would transmute base metals into gold. One day in 1666 when he was working in his laboratory at the Hague, a stranger attired all in black, as befitted a respectable burgher of North Holland, appeared and informed him that he would remove all the alchemist's doubts about the existence of the philosopher's stone, for he himself possessed such an object."

In 1852, Charles Mackay wrote of this affair that the Man in Black "asked Helvetius if he thought he should know that rare gem if he saw it. To which Helvetius replied, that he certainly should not. The burgher immediately drew from his pocket a small ivory box, containing three pieces of metal, of the color of brimstone, and extremely heavy; and assured Helvetius, that of them he could make as much as twenty tons of gold. Helvetius informs us, that he examined them very attentively; and seeing that they were very brittle, he took the opportunity to scrape off a small portion with his thumb-nail. He then returned to the stranger, with an entreaty that he would perform the process of transmutation before him. The stranger replied, that he was not allowed to do so, and went away."

Mackay continued that several weeks later the mysterious character in black was back. Helvetius implored the MIB to share with him the secrets of alchemy, which, apparently, he did: "Helvetius repeated the experiment alone, and converted six ounces of lead into very pure gold."

The story of the philosopher's stone—a magical rock able to change ordinary metals to gold—dates back to the Middle Ages.

Such was the fame that surrounded this event, said Mackay, "all of the notable persons of the town flocked to the study of Helvetius to convince themselves of the fact. Helvetius performed the experiment again, in the presence of the Prince of Orange, and several times afterwards, until he exhausted the whole of the powder he had received from the stranger, from whom it is necessary to state, he never received another visit; nor did he ever discover his name or condition."

In 1677, Leopold I, the Holy Roman Emperor and King of Austria, suffered something terrible: his precious supply of gold finally became exhausted. This was utterly disastrous, as it was gold, specifically, that Leopold relied upon to pay his troops, as they sought to keep at bay the marauding attacks of the Turks. Help, however, was soon at hand, and in a decidedly curious fashion.

Late one night, in November 1672, Leopold was visited by a monk of the Order of St. Augustine, one Johann Wenzel Seiler. Interestingly, it has been suggested that "Johann Wenzel Seiler" was actually a pseudonym that the dark-garbed, cloaked, and hooded character had adopted. Whatever the truth, Seiler confidently said he could banish all of the king's problems in an instant. The king, who already had an interest in all things alchemical, listened carefully to what Seiler had to say.

The monk motioned Leopold to follow him to the steps of the palace, which he did. It was on the steps that Seiler did something remarkable. He took a silver medallion, placed into a cauldron of magical liquid, and then extracted it. Lo and behold, it had been transformed into gold. The king was delighted, Austria's gold problem (or, rather, the sudden lack of it) was solved.

In 1880, Dr. Franz Hartmann, who carefully and deeply studied the controversy surrounding alchemy, said that "it is stated that this medal, consisting originally of silver, has been partly transformed into gold, by alchemical means, by the same Wenzel Seiler who was afterwards made a knight by the Emperor Leopold I and given the title Wenzeslaus Ritter von Reinburg."

Interestingly, Hartmann pointed out that many came to believe Seiler was not who he claimed to be, and was soon "regarded as an impostor." Specifically, this was with regard to claims that Seiler had merely coated the medallion with a gold-colored substance, rather than having literally transformed it into gold. Nevertheless, and despite exiling Seiler shortly afterwards, Leopold—seemingly entranced by Seiler—continued to eagerly employ the skills of this mysterious character, time and again.

American Nazi Party

Established in 1959 by a man named George Lincoln Rockwell, the American Nazi Party was a highly controversial body that had its base of operations in Arlington, Virginia. It was originally known by the far less inflammatory name of the World Union of Free Enterprise National Socialists. That, however, was apparently not enough for Rockwell. In fact, it was nowhere near enough. Within a year of its creation, Rockwell decided that he needed to make it clear to potential followers the ideology that his group adhered to. As a result, the ANP—the American Nazi Party—came into being.

To say that the ANP held controversial views is an understatement of epic proportions. Its members followed—to a tee—the teachings of Adolf Hitler and were taught that the Holocaust—which led to the deaths of millions of Jews—did not occur. That Rockwell created what was distastefully termed a "Stormtrooper barracks," and that members were encouraged to pledge their allegiance via nothing less than a "Sieg, Heil!" demonstrates the nature of just how closely the ANP was allied to the world of Adolf Hitler.

As the 1960s progressed, Rockwell chose to make a number of significant changes to the American Nazi Party. "Sieg Heil" was replaced by the equally controversial "White Power," and the placing of potential candidates into U.S. elections became a firm goal of the party. There was yet another name change, too. As 1967 dawned, Rockwell opted to rename the ANP as the National Socialist White People's Party (NSWPP). The title might have been

George Lincoln Rockwell established the American Nazi Party in 1959.

different, but very little else was altered. Not all of the members of the newly christened NSWPP were happy with the change in name, however. The result was that there was very soon dissent in the ranks—major dissent, in fact. As a demonstration of just how dissenting some of the members were, one of them—a man named John Patler—shot and killed Rockwell on August 25, 1967. This was not, however, the first attempt on Rockwell's life.

On June 28, 1967, as he drove to the group's Arlington headquarters, Rockwell found that the driveway was blocked by a tree. Not a fallen tree, however: one that had apparently been deliberately chopped down and placed there. As a colleague of Rockwell's began the task of clearing a path, two shots rang out, one of which narrowly missed Rockwell's head. Enraged, Rockwell raced after the gunman. It was to no avail, however. But, it was clear that Rockwell was now a marked man and time was running out for him. Cue the entrance of the aforementioned John Patler.

Approximately two months after the first attempt on his life, Rockwell finally bit the bullet. It was August 25, 1967, when Patler—strategically positioned on the roof of the Dominion Hills Shopping Center—put a bullet in Rockwell's chest, damaging his heart to a fatal degree. Rockwell, in his final moments, managed to crawl out of the car and waved his hand in the direction of the roof. It turns out that Patler was disgruntled by Rockwell's attempts to bring the NSWPP more in line with the teachings of Karl Marx. Patler received a two-decades-long jail sentence.

With Rockwell dead, the running of the group was handed over to a man named Matt Koehl, who was Rockwell's second in command. Koehl was a devotee of the teachings of Adolf Hitler, a believer in a Caucasian-only future, and someone who ensured that Hitler's infamous swastika had pride of place on the NSWPP publications. As the 1960s became the 1970s, there was even more noticeable dissention in the ranks. One if its members, Frank Collin, had had enough and established a splinter organization, the National Socialist Party of America. It, too, was dominated by controversy: in 1979, Collin was jailed for child molestation, something that fortunately brought his plans for a Nazi-driven United States to a sudden end.

> **K**oehl came to believe that Adolf Hitler's suicide (or, at least, his reported suicide) in 1945 was, in essence, an act of martyrdom.

Things became even more fraught and tension-filled for the NSWPP when Koehl began to take the group in a somewhat new direction. Koehl came to believe that Adolf Hitler's suicide (or, at least, his reported suicide) in 1945 was, in essence, an act of martyrdom. Kohl also came to believe that Hitler's act had nothing less than a spiritual aspect to it: that his self-sacrifice would, one day, provoke a supernatural-driven resurrection of Hitler's National Socialism. This was way too much for many of the NSWPP, who saw the group specifically as a political group. Koehl's ideas, however, were taking things down a significantly different pathway: religion and even matters of an occult nature were now a major part of the NSWPP. It was this issue that provoked yet further divisions, leading to major changes. Today, the NSWPP is the decidedly low-key New Order. Group members state: "We are the movement of Adolf Hitler. We are his heirs."

As for Koehl, he died in 2014.

American Protective Association

Established thirteen years before the beginning of the twentieth century, the American Protective Association was a secret group dedicated to extinguishing what it perceived as the sweeping powers and influence of the Catholic Church in the United States. It was an organization destined not to last. March 13, 1887, was the date on which the APA came into being. The location: Clinton, Iowa, and it all went down in the office of a man named Henry F. Bowers, who promptly designated himself the group's "supreme president." His followers (all six of them) would help to further the goal to significantly lessen what they saw as the iron grip that Catholicism had on the nation and its people. Their approach was hardly surprising, since all of the members were ardent Protestants.

Indeed, *New Advent* notes: "Of the A.P.A. ritual and obligations there was frequent publication during the years 1893–94, now divulged by spies, and now admitted by ex-members. What purports to be a full exhibit of these oaths may be found in the 'Congressional Record,' 31 October, 1893, in the petition of H. M. Youmans for the unseating of Representative-in-Congress William S. Linton. These oaths bound members 'at all times to endeavor to place the political position of this government in the hands of Protestants to the entire exclusion of the Roman Catholics.'"

Published by the APA in 1894 and written by Scott Funk Hershey, *Errors of the Roman Catholic Church* (from which this illustration was taken) excoriated the history of Catholicism.

In 1893, the APA fell into the hands of one W. J. H. Traynor, who became the new "supreme president." He was a Protestant of Irish descent, originally from Ontario, Canada. Traynor was someone who had a deep understanding of secret societies, and for one specific reason: he was a member of more than a few of them. The list included the Illustrious Order of the Knights of Malta, the Royal Black Knights of the Camp of Israel, the Knights of the Maccabees, and the American Patriot League.

Although the APA had a fair degree of visibility in the 1894 presidential election, its members were primarily involved in promoting those local candidates who, it was believed, could further the aims and goals of the APA. In other words, the APA did not have, itself, a candidate who had major pulling power: its members were much more concerned about ensuring that whoever got elected would be beneficial to the APA. To say that the APA had some profound influence is not a matter of doubt or exaggeration. For example, in the late 1800s, no fewer than twenty members of Congress were also members of the APA.

It should be noted that the American Protective Association did not have anything specifically against the teachings of the Catholic Church. Rather, the APA feared that the church was trying to flex its muscles within the world of the U.S. government—even to the point of having some degree of "hold" over it. The separation of church and state was paramount to the teachings of the APA.

The profile of the APA increased majorly in 1895. In December of that year, at a Conference of Patriotic Societies, the APA allied itself with a large number of like-minded groups, including the Orangemen, the Society for the Protection of American Institutions, and the Junior Order of United American Mechanics. The combined approximately three million people called for the curbing of immigrants to the United States and the preventing of non-citizens from voting. Ultimately, the APA found itself eclipsed by the far more dominant and regular world of politics, its members drifted away, and—largely as a result of well-publicized attacks by the Democrats—its public image suffered badly. By the end of the nineteenth century, it was all over for the American Protective Association.

American Vision

The brainchild of a man named Steve Schiffman, American Vision was established in 1978 and operates out of Powder Springs, Georgia. Essentially, its mandate, in its own words, is focused upon "equipping and empowering Christians to restore America's foundation." It's a relatively small group: today, it's overseen by its current president, Gary DeMar, and a staff of just one dozen. Its primary approach is to fly the flag of Christian Reconstructionism and Postmillennialism. It believes in "developing family oriented biblical worldviews" and holds a yearly conference, the Worldview Conference.

The teachings of American Vision are steeped in controversy: Gary DeMar has gone on record as stating that with a "reconstructed government," the periodic execution of what he terms "sodomites" would actually benefit U.S. society. His warped justification reads like this: "The law that requires the death penalty for homosexual acts effectively drives the perversion of homosexuality underground, back into the closet."

Given this very disturbing stance—namely, suggesting that it's perfectly fine to execute American citizens because of

American Vision believes that one goal that should be strived for, in particular, is "the execution of abortionists and parents who hire them."

their sexual preferences—it's worrying to note that American Vision provides its reading material for "Christian schools and home schoolers," something that exposes more and more impressionable minds to DeMar's ideas. Equally controversial, American Vision believes that one goal that should be strived for, in particular, is "the execution of abortionists and parents who hire them."

To say that the United States, living under the type of control that DeMar envisions, would be a grim world is not an exaggeration. American Vision calls for the end of its current political structure. In its place will exist, as author Brad Steiger notes, "a theocratic government completely dominated by Christians who will strictly enforce Old Testament prohibitions."

America's Secret Nazi Scientists

Immediately after World War II came to an end in 1945, certain elements of the American military and intelligence community clandestinely sought to bring some of the most brilliant figures within the German medical and scientific communities into the United States to continue research—and at times highly controversial research—they had undertaken at the height of the war. It was research that included studies of human anatomy and physiology in relation to aerospace medicine, high-altitude exposure, and what was then termed "space biology." The startling fact that some of these scientists were ardent Nazis, and even members of the notorious and feared SS, proved not a problem at all to the government of the time. Thus was born the notorious Operation Paperclip, so named because the recruit's papers were clipped to regular American immigration forms.

In January 1994, President Bill Clinton appointed an Advisory Committee on Human Radiation Experiments (ACHRE) that was tasked with investigating unethical medical experimentation undertaken on human beings from the mid-1940s onwards. The ACHRE was quick to realize that Paperclip personnel played a considerable role in postwar human experimentation on American soil. According to an April 5, 1995, memorandum, from the Advisory Committee Staff (ACS) to the Members of the ACHRE:

"The Air Force's School of Aviation Medicine (SAM) at Brooks Air Force Base in Texas conducted dozens of human radiation experiments during the Cold War, among them flash-blindness studies in connection with atomic weapons tests, and data gathering for total-body irradiation studies conducted in Houston. Because of the extensive postwar recruiting of German scientists for the SAM and other U.S. defense installations, and in light of the central

The School of Aviation Medicine at Brooks Air Force Base was the site of human radiation experiments during the Cold War.

importance of the Nuremberg prosecutions to the Advisory Committee's work, members of the staff have collected documentary evidence about Project Paperclip from the National Archives and Department of Defense records.

"The experiments for which Nazi investigators were tried included many related to aviation research. These were mainly high-altitude exposure studies, oxygen deprivation experiments, and cold studies related to air-sea rescue operations. This information about aircrew hazards was important to both sides, and, of course, continued to be important to military organizations in the Cold War."

The ACHRE memorandum then detailed the background and scope of the project: "Project Paperclip was a postwar and Cold War operation carried out by the Joint Intelligence Objectives Agency (JIOA) [Author's Note: the JIOA was a special intelligence office that reported to the Director of Intelligence in the War Department, comparable to the intelligence chief of today's Joint Chiefs of Staff.] Paperclip had two aims: to exploit German scientists for American research, and to deny these intellectual resources to the Soviet Union. At least 1,600 scientists and their dependents were recruited and brought to the United States by Paperclip and its successor projects through the early 1970s."

ACHRE continued: "In recent years, it has been alleged that many of these individuals were brought to the United States in violation of American government policy not to permit the entrance of 'ardent Nazis' into the country, that many were security risks, and that at least some were implicated in Holocaust-related activities.

"At the time of its inception," said ACHRE, "Paperclip was a matter of controversy in the War Department, as demonstrated by a November 27, 1946 memorandum from General Groves, director of the Manhattan Project, relating to the bringing to the United States of the eminent physicist Otto Hahn. Groves wrote that the Manhattan Project 'does not desire to utilize the services of foreign scientists in the United States, either directly with the Project or with any affiliated organization. This has consistently been my views [sic]. I should like to make it clear, however, that I see no objection to bringing to the United States such carefully screened physicists as would contribute materially to the welfare of the United States and would remain permanently in the United States as naturalized citizens. I strongly recommend against foreign physicists coming in contact with our atomic energy program in any way. If they are allowed to see or discuss the work of the Project the security of our information would get out of control.'"

Experiments there included total-body irradiation, space medicine and biology studies, and flash-blindness studies.

The Advisory Committee Staff also revealed: "A number of military research sites recruited Paperclip scientists with backgrounds in aero-medicine, radiobiology and ophthalmology. These institutions included the SAM, where radiation experiments were conducted, and other military sites, particularly the Edgewood Arsenal of the Army's Chemical Corps.

"The portfolio of experiments at the SAM was one that would particularly benefit from the Paperclip recruits. Experiments there included total-body irradiation, space medicine and biology studies, and flash-blindness studies. Herbert Gerstner, a principal investigator in TBI experiments at the SAM, was acting director of the Institute of Physiology at the University of Leipzig: he became a radiobiologist at the SAM.

"The Air Force Surgeon General and SAM officials welcomed the Paperclip scientists. In March 1951, the school's Commandant, O. O. Benson Jr., wrote to the Surgeon General to seek more 'first class scientists and highly qualified technologists from Germany. The first group of Paperclip personnel contained a number of scientists that have proved to be of real value to the Air Force. The weaker and less gifted ones have been culled to a considerable extent. The second group reporting here in 1949 were, in general, less competent than the original Paperclip personnel, and culling process will again be in order.'

"General Benson's adjutant solicited resumes from a Paperclip list, including a number of radiation biology and physics specialists. The qualifications of a few scientists were said to be known, so curricula vitae were waived. The adjutant wrote, also in March 1951: 'In order to systematically benefit from this program this headquarters believes that the employment of competent personnel who fit into our research program is a most important consideration.'"

"Most important" was right: it was this secret body of Nazi scientists who significantly boosted the United States' rocket-based programs, and without whom, and in all likelihood, NASA would not have been able to land men on the Moon by 1969.

Ancient Egyptian Arabic Order Nobles Mystic Shrine

❝The Ancient Egyptian Arabic Order Nobles Mystic Shrine of North and South America and Its Jurisdictions, Inc. has a long and colorful history," its members state.

It is an order that was created—as an "Imperial Council of Prince Hall Shriners"—on June 3, 1893, in Chicago, Illinois, by thirteen Prince Hall Masons, all under the leadership of one John George Jones. Their place of meeting was the Apollo Hall on State Street, where the Palestine Temple was organized. Precisely one week after the initial meeting, Jones and his colleagues formulated the Imperial Grand Council of Prince Hall Shriners. It was, however, seven years later that the group took on the name it still has to this very day, as the order itself notes:

"On December 12, 1900, a meeting was held in Philadelphia with officers and members attending from Temples in Philadelphia, Pittsburgh, and

The first Shriner's auditorium was constructed in 1910 in Los Angeles, California.

from Alexandria, Virginia. At this meeting the Imperial Council was reorganized and the order adopted a new name: Imperial Council of the Ancient Egyptian Arabic Order Nobles Mystic Shrine of North and South America and its Jurisdiction, Incorporated."

Further notable data on the "Shriners," as they are known, can be found in a U.S. court document of 1929: "From early times there have been two distinct Masonic fraternities in the United States, one confined to white men and the other to Negroes. Each has had its local lodges, grand lodges, and Supreme Lodge, and also several component bodies, including Knights Templar and Scottish Rite consistories. Both have existed in the same territory and have had similar names, rituals, and emblems, and yet have been independent and without any interrelation. The white fraternity's existence in this country reaches back to early colonial times. The Negro fraternity was organized in Boston in 1784, and afterwards was extended to other sections.

"The orders called 'Nobles of the Mystic Shrine' are relatively modern, originated in the United States, and are outgrowths of the Masonic fraternities just described. They were founded by Masons, and their membership is restricted to Masons—white in one case and Negro in the other—who have become Knights Templars or have received the thirty-second degree in a Scottish Rite consistory. The white Masons were the first to establish an order of Nobles of the Mystic Shrine. They organized one in New York in 1872 for fraternal and charitable purposes. The order grew rapidly and soon came to have local lodges, called temples, in most of the states, and also to have a national governing body called its Imperial Council. The Negro Masons imitatively organized a like order for like purposes in Chicago in 1893."

As of 2016, the group notes, the "Worldwide Fraternal Shrine Family" has more than thirty thousand members in "some 227 Shrine Temples and 200 Courts."

Ancient Noble Order of the Gormogons

The Grand Lodge of British Columbia and Yukon tells us: "The Ancient Noble Order of the Gormogons was a short-lived eighteenth century society; leaving no records or accomplishments to indicate its true goal and purpose. From the few published advertisements and notices, it would appear that its sole objective was to hold up Freemasonry to ridicule."

It was the creation of a man named Philip Wharton, the 1st Duke of Wharton—a Jacobite and an expelled Freemason who was born in 1698. The

London Daily Post of September 3, 1724, made what is believed to have been the very first reference to the Gormogons. It told its readers: "Whereas the truly ANCIENT NOBLE ORDER of the Gormogons, instituted by Chin-Qua Ky-Po, the first Emperor of China (according to their account), many thousand years before Adam, and of which the great philosopher Confucious was Oecumenicae Volgee, has lately been brought into England by a Mandarin, and he having admitted several Gentlemen of Honor into the mystery of that most illustrious order, they have determined to hold a Chapter at the Castle Tavern in Fleet Street, at the particular request of several persons of quality. This is to inform the public, that there will be no drawn sword at the Door, nor Ladder in a dark Room, nor will any Mason be received as a member till he has renounced his Novel Order and been properly degraded. N.B.—The Grand Mogul, the Czar of Muscovy, and Prince Tochmas are entered into this Hon. Society; but it has been refused to the Rebel Meriweys, to his great Mortification. The Mandarin will shortly set out for Rome, having a particular Commission to make a Present of the Ancient Order to his Holiness, and it is believ'd the whole Sacred College of Cardinals will commence Gormogons. Notice will be given in the Gazette the Day the Chapter will be held."

In 1953, Fred L. Pick and G. Norman Knight—acknowledged experts on the history of Freemasonry—wrote: "When exactly the Gormogons died out is not known, but two considerations seem to render untenable Gould's theory that 'the Order is said to have become extinct in 1738.' In the first place the existence of a Lancashire Gormogon in the person of John Collier, better known as Tim Bobbin (1708–86) was revealed by the chance stumbling upon a poem of his, *The Goose*, by one of the present authors. The first appearance of the poem known to the authors is in *Tim Bobbin's Collected Poems* of 1757 and in any case very little of his verse is ascribed to a period before the last forty years of his life. *The Goose* has a dedication: 'As I have the honor to be a member of the ancient and venerable order of the Gormogons, I am obliged by the laws of the great Chin-Quaiw-Ki-Po, emperor of China, to read, yearly, some part of the ancient records of that country.'"

Archaeology Office

Within the heart of the Central Intelligence Agency at Langley, Virginia, there exists a secret group with the name of the Archaeology Office. At least, that's its informal title. Rumor suggests it has a highly classified secret title. That it exists, however, is not in any doubt. Its involvement in studying

An aerial view of the Central Intelligence Agency in Langley, Virginia, which houses the secretive Archaeology Office.

numerous ancient mysteries has been revealed, all thanks to the Freedom of Information Act.

In the 1981 blockbuster movie *Raiders of the Lost Ark*, which starred Harrison Ford as archaeologist/adventurer Indiana Jones, the Nazi hordes of Adolf Hitler were in hot pursuit of the legendary Ark of the Covenant. It was a mysterious chest said to have housed the Ten Commandments as allegedly provided to Moses by God on Mount Sinai. Given that the Ark was supposed to possess powers both awesome and devastating, Hitler's intention was to harness those same powers, use them against anyone and everyone who might stand in his way, and then take control of the entire world. Fortunately for us, things did not go Hitler's way.

After a wild adventure that took him from Peru to the United States and from Egypt to an island in the Aegean Sea, Indiana Jones saved the day, wrestled the Ark out of the clutches of Hitler's minions, got the girl, and all was good. But, it's the final moments of the movie that are the most memorable.

As *Raiders of the Lost Ark* told it, after the Nazis were defeated, the Ark of the Covenant was transferred to the United States, where U.S. military intelligence personnel assured a pleased and satisfied Jones that the priceless artifact would be studied carefully by the finest minds and scholars available. That assurance, however, was nothing less than a brazen lie. Instead, something very different happened.

Unbeknownst to Jones, the Ark was not studied. The U.S. government, perhaps fearful of unleashing the incredible forces the Ark possessed, took what it considered to be the wisest and safest course of action: the Ark was placed into a wooden crate, which was then carefully and firmly sealed, and taken to a huge, secure warehouse away from any and all prying eyes and inquiring minds. The government was intent on keeping the genie firmly in the bottle, so to speak, never again to be released.

Raiders of the Lost Ark was, and close to forty years after its release still is, a work of highly entertaining, onscreen fiction. The deep and secret involvement of the U.S. government in the study of ancient artifacts, religious relics, and numerous archaeological wonders, however, is most assuredly not fiction. As far back as 1947, the Pentagon has dug very deeply, and under cover of overwhelming secrecy, into such controversial areas.

The discovery of the Dead Sea Scrolls, the origin and final resting place of Noah's Ark, the incredible question of whether or not the pyramids of Egypt may have been built via the use of levitation, the reasons for the construction of England's famous Stonehenge, rumors that ancient nuclear warfare was fought by an advanced civilization in India in the very distant past, a highly thought provoking Mars–Egypt connection, and even the controversy concerning the Mayan prophecies and 2012 are all issues that have attracted the lengthy, and highly secret, attention of the Pentagon's finest minds for nothing less than decades.

Not surprisingly, this has collectively led to an absolute plethora of very significant questions at an official, classified level, including: Are some of our oldest and most cherished religions actually based upon visitations not from gods, but aliens in the distant past? Was Noah's Ark not just a huge vessel of the waters designed to survive a mighty flood, but actually a highly advanced spacecraft from another world?

And the questions go on and on: Did the pharaohs of Egypt possess secret, arcane knowledge of how to move massive, multi-ton stones using what, today, we might call anti-gravity? Is there a connection between the pyramids of Egypt and the very similar structures that have been photographed on the surface of the planet Mars?

From the mysterious depths of ancient Egypt to the standing-stones of old England, from the now long-gone cultures of the Maya and the Inca to the heart of India, and from Mars to the Middle East, the Pentagon has spent decades carefully and clandestinely studying the very foundations of our civilization as it exists today, and has come to a shocking, paradigm-changing conclusion: our history is not at all what it appears to be. It's actually much stranger. Perhaps, "out of this world" would be a far better, and much more appropriate, term to use.

Indeed, the CIA has a file (portions of which remain classified) on Noah's Ark titled "The Ararat Anomaly." In 1947, a highly regarded CIA employee, Miles Copeland, became embroiled in a conspiracy-tinged affair involving the Dead Sea Scrolls. Official files were opened on "ancient astronaut" researchers/authors Morris Jessup and Bruce Cathie. None other than Edgar Cayce became a target of what might be termed "official inter-

A reproduction of Noah's Ark sits on Mount Ararat. Not only is there the biblical version of the ark, but some speculate that it might have been a spacecraft of some kind.

est." The reason: his theories on Atlantis, no less, and the list—and the attendant ancient mysteries—goes on and on.

Millennia old visitations from alleged extraterrestrials, highly advanced and devastating technologies in the hands of early civilizations, mysterious artifacts displaying incredible powers, and aliens perceived as gods are just a few of the controversial issues that have, for years, kept the finest minds in the CIA secretly, and worriedly, focused on times, people and eras long gone.

Aryan Nations

Aryan Nations is one of the most well-known of the many and varied "white supremacist"-based groups in the United States. There's no doubt that the group would not have existed—at least, not how it exists today—had it not been for a man named Wesley A. Swift. A Christian who embraced anti-Semitism, he had a fiery and controversial radio show, and established his very own church, which ultimately became known as the Church of Jesus Christ-Christian—the name adopted by Aryan Nations' churches.

As for the Aryan Nations group itself, it was created in the mid-1970s by the Reverend Richard Girnt Butler. Its initial headquarters was at Hayden Lake, Idaho, which became infamously and controversially known as the "international headquarters of the White Race." In Butler's personal history of the world, it was the Anglo-Saxons—rather than the Jewish people—who were the "chosen" ones, and a lot of people came to hang on every word that Butler spoke to the extent that the Aryan Nations held a yearly conference at the lake: the World Congress of Aryan Nations.

> **I**n Butler's personal history of the world, it was the Anglo-Saxons— rather than the Jewish people— who were the "chosen" ones....

It should be noted that when he established the Aryan Nations, Butler was hardly a young man, and time inevitably took its toll. By the latter part of the 1990s, Butler—then in his eighties—was in failing health. As a result, in 1998, the reins were taken over by one Neuman Britton. Three years later, however, Harold Ray Redfeairn became the head honcho. Not everyone in the Aryan Nations was happy with Redfeairn, however, and particularly so after he revealed certain illegalities within the group. Redfeairn and one of the Aryan Nations' ministers—August Kreis III—soon jumped ship and created their own group. It was not to last, however: Redfeairn died in 2003.

Today, the Aryan Nations is no longer unified. First, there is the group run by the aforementioned Richard Girnt Butler. Very controversially, in 2005 Butler sought to make itself allied to al Qaeda. That Butler had no problems with the Islamic faith and that of Wiccans led some within the Aryan Nations to leave the group, and they created the New York City-based Aryan Nations Revival. Among its members were violent vigilantes from the Holy Order of the Phineas Priesthood. Its radio show soon had an audience in excess of one hundred thousand. Some of those members have been identified by the FBI as domestic terrorists. As for Kreis, as a pedophile, he got his just desserts: in November 2015 he received a decades-long sentence for child molestation.

Asian Organized Crime

Their names include the Triads, the Tongs, and the Yakuza. And, they have all attracted the deep attention of the FBI, whose files on such groups have now been declassified under Freedom of Information legislation.

The FBI says: "Asian criminal enterprises have been operating in the United States since the early 1900s. The first of these groups evolved from Chinese Tongs—social organizations formed by early Chinese-American immigrants. A century later, the criminalized Tongs are thriving and have been joined by similar organizations with ties to East and Southeast Asia. Members of the most dominant Asian criminal enterprises affecting the United States have ties—either directly or culturally—to China, Korea, Japan, Thailand, the Philippines, Cambodia, Laos, and Vietnam. Other enterprises are emerging as threats, however, including groups from the South Pacific island nations."

These enterprises rely on extensive networks of national and international criminal associates that are fluid and extremely mobile. They adapt easily to the changes around them, have multilingual abilities, can be highly sophisticated in their criminal operations, and have extensive financial capabilities. Some

Globalization of the economy and world travel have helped gangs from Asia prosper in the West.

enterprises have commercialized their criminal activities and can be considered business firms of various sizes, from small family run operations to large corporations.

Asian criminal enterprises have prospered thanks largely to the globalization of the world economies and to communications technology and international travel. Generous immigration policies have provided many members of Asian criminal enterprises the ability to enter and live on every populated continent in the world today undetected.

There are two categories of Asian criminal enterprises. Traditional criminal enterprises include the Chinese triads (or underground societies) based in Hong Kong, Taiwan, and Macau as well as the Japanese Yakuza or Boryokudan. Nontraditional criminal enterprises include groups such as Chinese criminally influenced tongs, triad affiliates, and other ethnic Asian street gangs found in several countries with sizeable Asian communities.

Asian criminal enterprises conduct traditional racketeering activities normally associated with organized crime: extortion, murder, kidnaping, illegal gambling, prostitution, and loansharking. They also smuggle aliens, traffic heroin and methamphetamine, commit financial frauds, steal autos and computer chips, counterfeit computer and clothing products, and launder money.

There are several trends among Asian criminal enterprises. First, it is more common to see criminal groups cooperate across ethnic and racial heritage lines. Also, some gangs and criminal enterprises have begun to structure their groups in a hierarchical fashion to be more competitive, and the criminal activities they engage in have become globalized. Finally, more of these criminal enterprises are engaging in white-collar crimes and are comingling their illegal activities with legitimate business ventures.

In the United States, Asian criminal enterprises have been identified in more than fifty metropolitan areas. They are more prevalent in Boston, Chicago, Honolulu, Las Vegas, Los Angeles, New Orleans, New York, Newark, Philadelphia, Portland, San Francisco, Seattle, and Washington, D.C.

Assassins

Assassins have played significant roles in the history of secret societies, as this book demonstrates on more than a few occasions. Few people know more about the ancient art of assassination, however, than the CIA. How can we be so sure? The answer is quite astonishing: in the early 1950s, the CIA drafted a document for those personnel working undercover, and in the field, and whose work involved "taking out of circulation" certain people deemed by the CIA to be undesirables. We're talking about foreign leaders, dangerous dictators, and more.

The document is appropriately titled "A Study of Assassination." The CIA has been very careful to delete from the available pages the name of the author. But, the content is largely uncensored.

The unknown author of the document states: "Assassination is a term thought to be derived from 'Hashish,' a drug similar to marijuana, said to have been used by Hasan-Dan-Sabah to induce motivation in his followers, who were assigned to carry out political and other murders, usually at the cost of their lives. It is here used to describe the planned killing of a person who is not under the legal jurisdiction of the killer, who is not physically in the hands of the killer, who has been selected by a resistance organization for death, and whose death provides positive advantages to that organization."

The document also offers the following: "Assassination is an extreme measure not normally used in clandestine operations. It should be assumed that it will never be ordered or authorized by any U.S. headquarters, though the latter may in rare instances agree to its execution by members of an associated foreign service. This reticence is partly due to the necessity for committing communications to paper. No assassination instructions should ever be written or recorded. Consequently, the decision to employ this technique must nearly always be reached in the field, at the area where the act will take place. Decision and instructions should be confined to an absolute minimum of persons. Ideally, only one person will be involved. No report may be made, but usually the act will be properly covered by normal news services, whose output is available to all concerned."

> "**A**ssassination is a term thought to be derived from 'Hashish,' a drug similar to marijuana, said to have been used by Hasan-Dan-Sabah to induce motivation in his followers...."

The clearly well-informed CIA figure who penned the document then stated: "Murder is not morally justifiable. Self-defense may be argued if the victim has knowledge which may destroy the resistance organization if divulged. Assassination of persons responsible for atrocities or reprisals may be regarded as just punishment. Killing a political leader whose burgeoning career is a clear and present danger to the cause of freedom may be held necessary. But assassination can seldom be employed with a clear conscience. Persons who are morally squeamish should not attempt it."

As for the assassin himself or herself, there's this: "The techniques employed will vary according to whether the subject is unaware of his danger, aware but unguarded, or guarded. They will also be affected by whether or not

The CIA has used assassination (or, as they call it, taking someone "out of circulation") when it has suited the U.S. agenda.

the assassin is to be killed with the subject hereafter, assassinations in which the subject is unaware will be termed 'simple'; those where the subject is aware but unguarded will be termed 'chase'; those where the victim is guarded will be termed 'guarded.' If the assassin is to die with the subject, the act will be called 'lost.'"

Moving on: "If the assassin is to escape, the adjective will be 'safe.' It should be noted that no compromises should exist here. The assassin must not fall alive into enemy hands. A further type division is caused by the need to conceal the fact that the subject was actually the victim of assassination, rather than an accident or natural causes. If such concealment is desirable the operation will be called 'secret'; if concealment is immaterial, the act will be called 'open'; while if the assassination requires publicity to be effective it will be termed 'terroristic.'"

Of course, when dealing with such a controversial topic it's vital that agents of the CIA know exactly how to kill a person, how to do so quickly, and how to make it look like anything but an assassination: "The essential point of assassination is the death of the subject. A human being may be killed in many ways but sureness is often overlooked by those who may be emotionally unstrung by the seriousness of this act they intend to commit. The specific technique employed will depend upon a large number of variables, but should be constant in one point: Death must be absolutely certain. The attempt on Hitler's life failed because the conspiracy did not give this matter proper attention."

The author had more to say on this matter, which makes one wonder if he, himself, had experience as an "in the field" assassin: "It is possible to kill a man with the bare hands, but very few are skillful enough to do it well. Even a highly trained Judo expert will hesitate to risk killing by hand unless he has absolutely no alternative. However, the simplest local tools are often much the most efficient means of assassination. A hammer, axe, wrench, screw driver, fire poker, kitchen knife, lamp stand, or anything hard, heavy and handy will suffice. A length of rope or wire or a belt will do if the assassin is strong and agile. All such improvised weapons have the important advantage of availability and apparent innocence. The obviously lethal machine gun failed to kill Trotsky where an item of sporting goods succeeded."

Would-be killers for hire were told that "for secret assassination, either simple or chase, the contrived accident is the most effective technique. When successfully executed, it causes little excitement and is only casually investigated. The most efficient accident, in simple assassination, is a fall of seventy-five feet or more onto a hard surface. Elevator shafts, stair wells, unscreened windows and bridges will serve. Bridge falls into water are not reliable. In simple cases a private meeting with the subject may be arranged at a properly cased location. The act may be executed by sudden, vigorous [deleted] of the ankles, tipping the subject over the edge. If the assassin immediately sets up an outcry, playing the 'horrified witness,' no alibi or surreptitious withdrawal is necessary. In chase cases it will usually be necessary to stun or drug the subject before dropping him. Care is required to insure that no wound or condition not attributable to the fall is discernible after death."

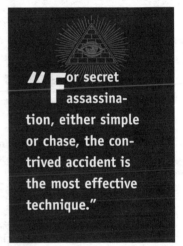

"**F**or secret assassination, either simple or chase, the contrived accident is the most effective technique."

And the deadly list went on and on: "Falls into the sea or swiftly flowing rivers may suffice if the subject cannot swim. It will be more reliable if the assassin can arrange to attempt rescue, as he can thus be sure of the subject's death and at the same time establish a workable alibi. If the subject's personal habits make it feasible, alcohol may be used [several words deleted] to prepare him for a contrived accident of any kind. Falls before trains or subway cars are usually effective, but require exact timing and can seldom be free from unexpected observation."

As for assassinations involving cars and even trucks, the CIA had that area covered, too: "Automobile accidents are a less satisfactory means of assassination. If the subject is deliberately run down, very exact timing is necessary and investigation is likely to be thorough. If the subject's car is tampered with, reliability is very low. The subject may be stunned or drugged and then placed in the car, but this is only reliable when the car can be run off a high cliff or into deep water without observation. Arson can cause accidental death if the subject is drugged and left in a burning building. Reliability is not satisfactory unless the building is isolated and highly combustible."

Drugs and medicines all played a role in the early, formative years of the CIA's assassins: "In all types of assassination except terroristic, drugs can be very effective. If the assassin is trained as a doctor or nurse and the subject is under medical care, this is an easy and rare method. An overdose of morphine administered as a sedative will cause death without disturbance and is difficult to detect. The size of the dose will depend upon whether the subject has been using narcotics regularly. If not, two grains will suffice. If the subject drinks heavily, morphine or a similar narcotic can be injected at the passing out stage, and the cause of death will often be held to be acute alcoholism. Specific poisons, such as arsenic or strychnine, are effective but their possession or procurement is incrim-

Another time-honored method of assassination is the use of poison, often in a drink or food. In 2006, for example, former Russian spy Alexander Litvinenko was poisoned by his own government, which used radioactive polonium-210.

inating, and accurate dosage is problematical. Poison was used unsuccessfully in the assassination of Rasputin and Holokan, though the latter case is more accurately described as a murder."

It should be noted that the author made an error when referencing "Holokan." The name should actually be "Holohan," as in Major William Holohan, who, in World War II, was attached to the U.S. Office of Strategic Services in Italy and who came to a fatal end as the victim of assassination.

Then, we get to see how guns played major roles in the matter of death by the CIA: "Firearms are often used in assassination, often very ineffectively. The assassin usually has insufficient technical knowledge of the limitations of weapons, and expects more range, accuracy and killing power than can be provided with reliability. Since certainty of death is the major requirement, firearms should be used which can provide destructive power at least 100% in excess of that thought to be necessary, and ranges should be half that considered practical for the weapon. Firearms have other drawbacks. Their possession is often incriminating. They may be difficult to obtain.... However, there are many cases in which firearms are probably more efficient than any other means."

Explosives, said the CIA, were also valuable tools when it came to getting rid of the enemy:

Bombs and demolition charges of various sorts have been used frequently in assassination. Such devices, in terroristic and open assassination, can provide safety and overcome guard barriers, but it is curious that bombs have often been the implement of lost assassinations. The major factor which affects reliability is the use of explosives for assassination. The charge must be very large and the detonation must be controlled exactly as to time by the assassin who can observe the subject. A small or moderate explosive charge is highly unreliable as a cause of death, and time delay or booby-trap devices are extremely prone to kill the wrong man. In addition to the moral aspects of indiscriminate killing, the death of casual bystanders can often produce public reactions unfavorable to the cause for which the assassination is carried out.

Could there be a more dangerous document than "A Study of Assassination?" Probably not.

Aswang Plot

Edward Lansdale was a man highly skilled in the field of what is known, in military circles, as psychological warfare. Back in the early 1950s, Lansdale—who rose to prominence during World War II, while working with the Office of Strategic Services, a forerunner of the CIA—spread rumors throughout the Philippines that a deadly vampire was wildly on the loose. Its name was the Aswang, a bloodsucking monstrosity, of which the people of the Philippines lived in complete dread. The reason for Lansdale's actions was as bizarre as it was simple.

At the time, specifically 1952, the Philippines were in turmoil and chaos, as a result of an uprising by the Hukbalahap—or Huks, as they were also known. They were vehemently anti-government rebels and did their very best to oust the president of the Philippines, Elpidio Rivera Quirino, with whom Lansdale was friends, and when the major general was asked by Quirino to help end the reign of terror that the Hukbalahap had generated, he quickly came on board.

One of the first things that Lansdale noted was that the rebels were deathly afraid of the vampiric Aswang and its nocturnal, blood-drinking activities. So, he came up with a plan, albeit a grisly one. It was a deception that was kept secret for decades, until Lansdale finally went public with it himself, long after his prestigious military career was finally over. As the major general recalled: "To the superstitious, the Huk battleground was a haunted place filled with ghosts and eerie creatures. A combat psywar squad was brought in. It planted stories among town residents of an Aswang living on the hill where the Huks were based. Two nights later, after giving the stories time to make their way up to the hill camp, the psywar squad set up an ambush along the trail used by the Huks."

U.S. Air Force major general Edward Lansdale came up with the plot to scare Philippino rebels with stories of the blood-sucking Aswang.

That same psywar squad then did something that was very alternative, but which proved to be extremely effective. They silently grabbed one of the Hukbalahap rebels, snapped his neck, and then—using a specially created, metallic device—left two, deep, vicious-looking puncture marks on the neck of the man. But that was barely the start of things: they then quietly tied a rope around the man's ankles, hung his body from a nearby tree, and let just about as much blood as possible drain out of the body. After several hours, the corpse was lowered to the ground and left close to the Hukbalahap camp, specifically to ensure it was found by his comrades. They *did* find it.

The result, as Lansdale noted, was overwhelmingly positive, from the perspective of the Philippine government, at least: "When the Huks returned to look for the missing man and found their bloodless comrade, every member of the patrol believed that the Aswang had got him and that one of them would be next if they remained on that hill. When daylight came, the whole Huk squadron moved out of the vicinity."

It was an ingenious, and spectacularly successful, tactic, one that was reportedly utilized on more than fifteen occasions to take back strategic ground from the Hukbalahap soldiers. A vampire of legend was now one of reality—or so the rebels believed.

The Atticus Institute

A film made in 2015, *The Atticus Institute* is a fictional production focused on a secret group within the U.S. military that attempts to understand—and weaponize—paranormal phenomena, including nothing less than dangerous and deadly demons. Although this book is focused on secret groups and societies in the real world, it's important to note that the Atticus Institute of the movie's title has its very own, real-life equivalent, as will readily become apparent.

The Atticus Institute is set in the present day but flashes back extensively to the 1970s. That's when the institute's Dr. Henry West (actor William Mapother) is hard at work trying to understand the nature of supernatural activity, and how it might even be harnessed and utilized. Much of West's work revolves around a particularly gifted psychic named Judith Winstead (played by Rya Kihlstedt). There's a problem, however. And it's a big one: Winstead is not exactly herself. In fact, she is well and truly possessed by a manipulative and menacing demon. Cue the entry of the U.S. military, who are very interested in knowing if such a demon might be controlled and used against hostile individuals.

Not even the military strength of Uncle Sam is a match for the terrifying creature, however. Things go very wrong—and very quickly. The entire team is plunged into states of fear as the demonic presence provokes an air of hostility. People fall sick, others die. Bad luck is everywhere. As one might imagine, the story builds up to a full-blown confrontation between the powers of evil and the might of the American military.

The real-life equivalent of the Atticus Institute is known as the Collins Elite, a well-hidden group within the U.S. government that has spent a great deal of time trying to contact demonic entities and understanding their powers—for military purposes, of course. And, just as is the case in *The Atticus Institute*, the Collins Elite experienced death and tragedy when they called forth the demons that they stupidly thought they could control and utilize. In late 1991, in Lincoln, Nebraska, an Anglican priest named Ray Boeche met with a pair of fear-filled members of the Collins Elite who were looking for ways to escape from the demonic presence that had established such an icy grip on the group. They did not find those ways. Instead, the Collins Elite still believes that the doorway it opened remains open—to the cost of all of us (see Collins Elite).

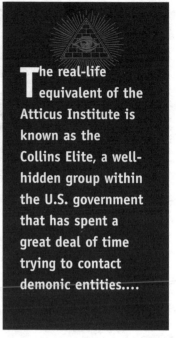

The real-life equivalent of the Atticus Institute is known as the Collins Elite, a well-hidden group within the U.S. government that has spent a great deal of time trying to contact demonic entities....

Aum Shinrikyo

In 1995, terrorists wreaked havoc and death in Tokyo, Japan. They were members of a group known as Aum Shinrikyo. The U.S. Department of State prepared an extensive report on the catastrophic event, the summary of which outlines the shocking series of events: "Aum Shinrikyo (Aum) was designated as a Foreign Terrorist Organization on October 8, 1997. Jailed leader Shoko Asahara established Aum in 1987, and the organization received legal status in Japan as a religious entity in 1989. The Japanese government revoked its recognition of Aum as a religious organization following Aum's deadly sarin gas attack in Tokyo in March 1995. Despite claims of renunciation of violence and Asahara's teachings, members of the group continue to adhere to the violent and apocalyptic teachings of its founder."

In March 1995, Aum members simultaneously released the chemical nerve agent sarin on several Tokyo subway trains, killing twelve people and causing up to six thousand to seek medical treatment. Subsequent investigations by the Japanese government revealed the group was responsible for other

Logo of the Aum Shinrikyo, a doomsday cult and terrorist organization later called Aleph.

mysterious chemical incidents in Japan in 1994, including a sarin gas attack on a residential neighborhood in Matsumoto that killed seven and hospitalized approximately five hundred. Japanese police arrested Asahara in May 1995; in February 2004, authorities sentenced him to death for his role in the 1995 attacks. In September 2006, Asahara lost his final appeal against the death penalty and the Japanese Supreme Court upheld the decision in October 2007. In February 2010, the death sentence for senior Aum member Tomomitsu Miimi was finalized by Japan's Supreme Court. In 2011, the death sentences of Masami Tsuchiya, Tomomasa Nakagawa, and Seiichi Endo were affirmed by Japanese courts, bringing the number of Aum members on death row to thirteen.

Since 1997, the group has recruited new members, engaged in commercial enterprises, and acquired property, although it scaled back these activities significantly in 2001 in response to a public outcry. In July 2001, Russian authorities arrested a group of Russian Aum followers who had planned to detonate bombs near the Imperial Palace in Tokyo as part of an operation to free Asahara from jail and smuggle him to Russia.

Although Aum has not conducted a terrorist attack since 1995, concerns remain regarding its continued adherence to the violent teachings of founder Asahara that led Aum to carry out the 1995 sarin gas attack. According to a study by the Japanese government issued in December 2009, Aum Shinrikyo/Aleph membership in Japan is approximately 1,500, with another two hundred in Russia. As of November 2011, Aum continues to maintain thirty-two facilities in fifteen prefectures in Japan and may continue to possess a few facilities in Russia. At the time of the Tokyo subway attack, the group claimed to have as many as forty thousand members worldwide, including nine thousand in Japan and thirty thousand members in Russia. Aum's principal membership is located in Japan; a residual branch of about two hundred followers live in Russia.

Benandanti

In English, Benandanti means "Good Walkers." Benandanti was a society that flourished in the 1500s and that came to an end in the following century. Based in northeast Italy, they were a group that claimed the ability to leave their physical bodies and travel by night in what we might call an astral plane or another dimension. There was a particular reason for this: namely, to wage war upon deadly, evil witches who roamed the area. The primary goal was to ensure those same witches did not blight their crops. Despite their good intentions, a number of the Benandanti—during the witchcraft trials of the Middle Ages—found themselves accused of being witches and of engaging in both Satanism and sorcery. Some were tortured, others were burned at the stake.

Daniil Leiderman says of the Benandanti that they "were of peasant stock, poor and largely illiterate, they spoke almost exclusively the friuli dialect, and at times had trouble communicating with their judges. However, several statements reappear throughout the entire length of a study by Italian historian Carlo Ginzburg. All Benandanti insist they were chosen by being born with a caul.

"Superstition ascribed an unusual destiny for children born with a caul, a piece of the amniotic sac on their head. This was true throughout Europe and even the Middle East, however the specifics of the superstition; whether it was a good or bad omen, tended to vary from region to region. For several defendants in Ginzburg's study, the caul was a lifetime protective talisman worn in

Based in Italy, the Benandanti was a mystical society in the 1500s; its members sometimes were mistaken for bad witches and burned at the stake.

a pouch around the neck. It was the caul that identified a potential Benandanti to his or her recruiters.

"After the age of approximately twenty each Benandanti said another Benandanti came to them during the night and led them out, riding cocks or goats beyond the village and into the woods. On the way the Benandanti would drink wine from their neighbor's casks, invisible and flying. All Benandanti insisted their bodies were left behind on their journeys."

Academics tell us: "Four times a year, on holidays associated with the planting and harvesting of crops, the Benandanti were called to Gatherings. It was at these Gatherings that the major battles with 'Malandanti' (loosely translates to 'evil-doers') or 'Strigoni' were fought. The Benandanti fought with fennel stalks, the Malandanti with sorghum. These Gatherings, in spite of their evident seriousness, had a kind of festive air about them. They were to become, along with the Equinoxes and Solstices, the basis of the 'Pagan' year."

Bilderberg Group

Whenever a discussion or debate occurs on the matter of secret societies, seldom is the Bilderberg Group left out of the equation. In fact, the exact opposite is the case: it's likely to be near the top of the list of talking points, and there are very good reasons for that, too.

SourceWatch says of the Bilderberg Group: "The name came from the group's first meeting place at the Hotel de Bilderberg, in the small Dutch town of Oosterbeek. Bilderberg was founded by Joseph Retinger, Prince Bernhard of the Netherlands and Belgian Prime Minister Paul Van Zeeland and is composed of representatives from North America and Western Europe. Since 1954, the secret meetings have included most of the top ruling class players from Western Europe and America. Until he was implicated in the Lockheed bribery scandal in 1976, Prince Bernhard served as chairman. Now, Bilderberg is a symbol of world management by Atlanticist elites. Some observers feel that it borders on the conspiratorial, while others are primarily interested in its implications for power structure research. Bilderberg participants from the United States are almost always members of the Council on Foreign Relations (CFR). Since 1973, Japanese elites have been brought into the fold through a third overlapping group, the Trilateral Commission."

According to Richard J. Aldrich, a political lecturer at Nottingham University, the Bilderberg Group is an "informal secretive transatlantic council of key decision makers, developed between 1952 and 1954.... It brought leading European and American personalities together once a year for informal discussions of their differences.... The formation of the American branch was entrusted to General Dwight D. Eisenhower's psychological warfare coordinator, C. D. Jackson and the first meeting was funded by the Central Intelligence Agency (CIA)."

When, in 2004, the Bilderberg Group celebrated its fiftieth anniversary, the BBC profiled the organization. In doing so, it significantly noted the aura of

The Bilderberg Group was named after this hotel in Oosterbeek, the Netherlands, where members had their first meeting in 1954.

mystery surrounding both the group and its members. The BBC didn't shy away from discussing the issue of alleged Bilderberg-orchestrated conspiracies, either:

"What sets Bilderberg apart from other high-powered get-togethers, such as the annual World Economic Forum (WEF), is its mystique. Not a word of what is said at Bilderberg meetings can be breathed outside. No reporters are invited in and while confidential minutes of meetings are taken, names are not noted. In the void created by such aloofness, an extraordinary conspiracy theory has grown up around the group that alleges the fate of the world is largely decided by Bilderberg. In Yugoslavia, leading Serbs have blamed Bilderberg for triggering the war which led to the downfall of Slobodan Milosevic. The Oklahoma City bomber Timothy McVeigh, the London nail-bomber David Copeland and Osama Bin Laden are all said to have bought into the theory that Bilderberg pulls the strings that make national governments dance."

Daniel Estulin, who has deeply and carefully studied the work and history of Bilderberg, says: "Slowly, one by one, I have penetrated the layers of secrecy surrounding the Bilderberg Group, but I could not have done this without help of 'conscientious objectors' from inside, as well as outside, the Group's membership. Imagine a private club where presidents, prime ministers, international bankers and generals rub shoulders, where gracious royal chaperones ensure everyone gets along, and where the people running the wars, markets, and Europe (and America) say what they never dare say in public."

Perhaps most chilling of all are the following words of Henry Kissinger, which were said at the Bilderberg Group Meeting in 1992: "Today, Americans would be outraged if UN troops entered Los Angeles to restore order; tomorrow, they will be grateful. This is especially true if they were told there was an outside threat from beyond, whether real or promulgated, that threatened our very existence. It is then that all people of the world will plead with world leaders to deliver them from this evil … individual rights will be willingly relinquished for the guarantee of their well-being granted to them by their world government."

For the sake of everyone, let's hope that Henry Kissinger is way off the mark.

Bird Flu

A secret group determined to spread bird flu in the first decade of the twenty-first century? Don't bet against it. In 2005, President George W. Bush stated that with regard to the fears of bird flu erupting in the United States, and erupting big time: "If we had an outbreak somewhere in the United States, do we not then quarantine that part of the country? And how do you, then, enforce a quarantine? It's one thing to shut down airplanes. It's another thing to prevent people from coming in to get exposed to the avian flu, and who best to be able to effect a quarantine? One option is the use of a military that's able to plan and move."

Bush's words raised eyebrows in both the mainstream media and the domain of conspiracy theorizing. For the former, it was a case of the media suggesting Bush was overreacting by making semi-veiled allusions to martial law and military occupations of infected zones. For the latter, suspicions rose to the effect that a secret cabal within the Bush administration (and, as we shall see, with alleged links to the Trilateral Commission and the Bilderberg Group) was planning on using fears of avian flu breaking out all across America as a means to invoke martial law at a whim and possibly even keep it in place for an extensive time, maybe even near-permanently. Before we get to the conspiracy angles, let's first take a look at what avian flu actually is.

Bush's words raised eyebrows in both the mainstream media and the domain of conspiracy theorizing.

There is no better source to turn to for information on bird flu than the Centers for Disease Control and Prevention, which has its headquarters in Atlanta, Georgia. The CDC is at the forefront of helping to lessen, and ultimately stop, any and all threats posed by deadly viruses. "Category A" viruses, for the CDC, are considered to be the most serious ones of all. They are those specific viruses that, says the CDC, "can be easily spread or transmitted from person to person," that "result in high death rates and have the potential for major public health impact," that "might cause panic and social disruption," and that would "require special action for public health preparedness."

Moreover, and by the CDC's very own admission, its work is "a critical component of overall U.S. national security." The U.S. government most assuredly recognizes the profound importance of the CDC from that very same national security perspective. Currently, the CDC receives yearly funding of around $1.3 billion to "build and strengthen national preparedness for public health emergencies caused by natural, accidental, or intentional events." It also works closely with the Department of Homeland Security, and with FEMA, the Federal Emergency Management Agency.

In February 2008, an extraordinary story surfaced out of Indonesia. The nation's health minister, Dr. Siti Fadilah Supari, hit the headlines with her then new book: *It's Time for the World to Change in the Spirit of Dignity, Equity and Transparency: Divine Hand behind Avian Influenza*. One particular part of the book made the world's media sit up and take notice. It was the allegation

President Susilo Bambang Yudhoyono of Indonesia (shown here inspecting troops) believed his health minister's theory that the United States intended to turn bird flu into a biological weapon.

that a secret group within the U.S. government was covertly working to transform bird flu into a deadly, biological weapon. It was an allegation fully endorsed by Indonesia's president, Susilo Bambang Yudhoyono.

Supari became deeply worried by the fact that the World Health Organization shared samples with the United States' national laboratory in Los Alamos, New Mexico, where nuclear weapons are developed.

Supari additionally commented: "Whether they use it to make vaccine or develop chemical weapons, would depend on the need and interest of the U.S. government. It is indeed a very dangerous situation for the destiny of humanity. It is a matter of choice whether to use the material for vaccines or biological weapon development."

One year later, an Austrian journalist named Jane Bürgermeister filed criminal charges against a wealth of official bodies and agencies, including the FBI, the United Nations, the World Health Organization, and even President Barack Obama.

It was Bürgermeister's conclusion that a vast conspiracy was in the making, one that involved the development of a form of bird flu that (a) was designed to spread all across the planet, and (b) would kill billions in no time at all. In other words, Bürgermeister believed she had uncovered a plot to, in stark essence, cull the herd—chiefly, to keep populations low, and under manageable control by a martial-law obsessed New World Order.

In Bürgermeister's very own words: "There is evidence that an international corporate criminal syndicate, which has annexed high government office at Federal and State level, is intent on carrying out a mass genocide against the people of the United States by using an artificial (genetic) flu pandemic virus and forced vaccine program to cause mass death and injury and depopulate America in order to transfer control of the United States to the United Nations and affiliated security forces (UN troops from countries such as China, Canada, the U.K., and Mexico)."

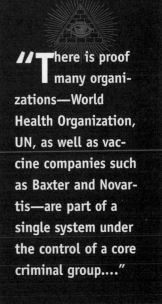

She added: "There is proof many organizations—World Health Organization, UN, as well as vaccine companies such as Baxter and Novartis—are part of a single system under the control of a core criminal group, who give the strategic leadership, and who have also funded the development, manufacturing and release of artificial viruses in order to justify mass vaccinations with a bioweapon substance in order to eliminate the people of the U.S.A, and so gain control of the assets, resources, etc. of North America.

"There is proof many organizations—World Health Organization, UN, as well as vaccine companies such as Baxter and Novartis—are part of a single system under the control of a core criminal group...."

"The motivation for the crime is classical robbery followed by murder although the scale and method are new in history. The core group sets its strategic goals and operative priorities in secret using committees such as the Trilateral Commission, and in person to person contact in the annual Bilderberg meeting."

Although Bürgermeister's suit proved unsuccessful in terms of bringing to justice what she perceived to be the guilty parties, she continues her work to expose what she believes is a malignant, worldwide plot to drastically change the face of human civilization.

Black-Eyed Children

Later in the pages of this book you will learn a great deal about the notorious Men in Black who—contrary to the Hollywood imagery presented in the very successful *Men in Black* movies starring Will Smith and Tommy Lee Jones—are not "government agents" but may be a secret cult intent on extinguishing interest and research into the world of all things paranormal. Inextricably linked to the MIB are an equally strange and secret band known as the Black-Eyed Children (BEC).

There can be very few people within the field of paranormal research who have not heard of the BEC, but the Men in Black parallels might be new to some. In the same way that the Men in Black wear black suits and black fedoras, the BEC almost exclusively wear black hoodies. So, we have a black outfit and black headgear present in both phenomena. Both the MIB and the BEC very often surface late at night. Trying to convince people to let them into their homes is one of the most chilling aspects of the activities of both the MIB and the BEC, and they are very good—almost too good—at making their escape. But, certainly, no one has done more to highlight the MIB–BEC connections and parallels than David Weatherly, whose 2012 book, *The Black-Eyed Children*, is essential reading.

Weatherly's research makes it very clear that there are far more BEC–MIB links than many might imagine. Weatherly says: "On the surface, there may seem to be few connections between the UFO connected MIB and creepy little kids with black eyes showing up on doorsteps. But, when we delve into the actual accounts, we find numerous similarities. Consider the appearance of both beings."

He makes a good point on this matter: "The BEKs [Black-Eyed Kids, which is a variation of BECs] are usually described as having pale or pasty skin. Some witnesses report that the skin looks 'artificial.' Still other accounts claim that the children have olive toned skin that implies they are of Mediterranean origin. Both of these descriptions are heard in classic MIB encounters. Oddly, no one who has ever encountered the BEKs report a blemish of any kind. Bear in mind, these are children usually in their pre-teen years. One would expect acne, pimples, freckles, something, but it's never the case."

Weatherly continues: "Next is the manner of speech. The black eyed children are reported to speak in a very monotone manner. Their use of language is often awkward and unusual. They will use phrases that simply aren't natural such as 'Is it food time?' Perhaps even more trou-

Mysterious, creepy black-eyed children seem to have some connection with UFOs and the Men in Black.

bling, many people who encounter the BEKs believe that the children are attempting to exert some type of mind control through the use of repeated phrases and their cold, monotone speech patterns. Typical MIB encounters certainly contain elements of attempted coercion by the strange gentlemen as witnesses to UFO sightings are encouraged to ignore what they saw. Are the attempts by the children another form of this same control dynamic?"

Then there is something that is reported very often in MIB-based situations: electronic interference and, particularly so, problems with phones. Weatherly makes it abundantly clear this is related to the Black-Eyed Children, too: "While I received a few minor reports of such things when doing research, it was only after the publication of my book, *The Black-Eyed Children*, that things got really interesting. The first indications came in the aftermath of the book's release. Appearing on various radio shows and podcasts to discuss the topic, some odd things began to occur. I found that I could talk about a wide range of paranormal topics, but, when the discussion turned to the black eyed children, things changed. Electronic issues would suddenly plague the program. Strange sounds and static would interrupt the show. Calls would be dropped and weird clicking noises would come from nowhere.

"Appearing on *Dreamland* with Whitley Strieber, technical issues started right from the beginning. Twice we were disconnected after strange sounds on the line. This could be easily dismissed but the problems didn't end there. The volume levels of the show were all over the place as Whitley recorded. 'I've never seen this happen before' Whitley reported as he attempted to correct the issues in his studio. I'll note here that Whitley and I discussed both the MIB and the BEK. In fact, on this particular show, Whitley revealed for the first time that he himself had encountered a black eyed child."

Weatherly concludes: "Whatever they are, the black eyed children don't appear to be going anywhere and they are leaving as many questions in their wake as the MIB before them. Whether the two are connected or not, it looks like we're in for more bizarre manifestations ahead. So pay attention. The next time there's a knock at your door, there's no telling what kind of strange figure is calling."

Black Helicopter Group

There can be very few people—if, indeed, any—with an interest in UFOs, conspiracies, cover-ups, and strange and sinister goings-on of a distinctly weird nature who have not heard of the so-called "black helicopters" or "phantom helicopters" that seem to play an integral—albeit admittedly

An unmarked black helicopter was seen in Colorado near where cattle mutilations had occurred.

unclear—role in perceived UFO-connected events, and one of the biggest misconceptions about this deeply weird phenomenon is that those same mysterious helicopters are lacking in official documentation. Actually not so at all. In fact, exactly the opposite if you know where to go looking.

The FBI's now-declassified files on cattle mutilations in 1970s U.S.A. make for fascinating reading and demonstrate the Bureau had a deep awareness of the presence of the enigmatic helicopters in affairs of the mute kind. On August 29, 1975, Floyd K. Haskell, a U.S. senator from Colorado, wrote an impassioned letter to Theodore P. Rosack, Special Agent in Charge of the FBI at Denver, Colorado, imploring the FBI to make a full investigation into the cattle mutilations, in an attempt to resolve the matter once and for all.

Haskell said: "For several months my office has been receiving reports of cattle mutilations throughout Colorado and other western states. At least 130 cases in Colorado alone have been reported to local officials and the Colorado Bureau of Investigation (CBI); the CBI has verified that the incidents have occurred for the last two years in nine states. The ranchers and rural residents of Colorado are concerned and frightened by these incidents. The bizarre mutilations are frightening in themselves: in virtually all the cases, the left ear, rectum, and sex organ of each animal has been cut away and the blood drained from the carcass, but with no traces of blood left on the ground and no footprints."

And there was an unmarked helicopter out in Colorado, as Senator Haskell was only too well aware: "In Colorado's Morgan County area there has [sic] also been reports that a helicopter was used by those who mutilated the carcasses of the cattle, and several persons have reported being chased by a similar helicopter. Because I am gravely concerned by this situation, I am asking that the Federal Bureau of Investigation enter the case. Although the CBI has been investigating the incidents, and local officials also have been involved, the lack of a central unified direction has frustrated the investigation."

He continued: "It seems to have progressed little, except for the recognition at long last that the incidents must be taken seriously. Now it appears that ranchers are arming themselves to protect their livestock, as well as their families and themselves, because they are frustrated by the unsuccessful investigation. Clearly something must be done before someone gets hurt."

The loss of livestock, in at least twenty-one states, under similar circumstances, suggested that an interstate operation was being coordinated. Senator Haskell closed his letter by urging the FBI to begin its investigation as soon as possible. Senator Haskell forced the issue by issuing a press release, informing the media that he had asked the FBI to investigate the mutilations. This caused the *Denver Post* newspaper to take up the senator's plea on September 3: "If the Bureau will not enter the investigation of the mysterious livestock deaths in Colorado and some adjacent states then Senator Floyd Haskell should take the matter to Congress for resolution."

Aware of previous FBI statements that the killings were not within the Bureau's jurisdiction, the *Denver Post* stated firmly: "The incidents are too widespread—and potentially too dangerous to public order—to ignore. Narrow interpretations of what the FBI's role is vis-à-vis state authority are not adequate to the need."

The issue of possible disregard for the law should the Bureau not wish to become involved was also high on the *Post*'s agenda: "There is already federal involvement. Consider this: Because of the gun-happy frame of mind developing in eastern Colorado (where most of the incidents have been occurring), the U.S. Bureau of Land Management (BLM) has had to cancel a helicopter inventory of its lands in six counties. BLM officials are simply afraid their helicopters might be shot down by ranchers and others frightened by cattle deaths."

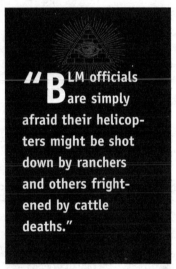

"**B**LM officials are simply afraid their helicopters might be shot down by ranchers and others frightened by cattle deaths."

On the day after publication, Special Agents Theodore Rosack and Donald Sebesta of the Colorado FBI made a visit to the offices of the *Denver Post*, where, in a meeting with three *Post* representatives, Charles R. Buxton, Lee Olson, and Robert Partridge, they spelled out the FBI's position with respect to mutilations: "… unless the FBI has investigative jurisdiction under Federal statute, we cannot enter any investigation."

One week later, on September 11, 1975, Senator Haskell telephoned Clarence M. Kelley at the FBI to discuss the issue of cattle and animal mutilation and the possibility of the FBI becoming involved in determining who, exactly, was responsible. Again, the FBI asserted that this was a matter outside of its jurisdiction. The Bureau noted: "Senator Haskell [said that] he understood our statutory limitations but he wished there was something we could do," reported an FBI official, R. J. Gallagher. Haskell had additional reasons for wanting the mutilation issue resolved swiftly, as Gallagher recorded in an internal memorandum of September 12, 1975: "Senator Haskell recontacted me this afternoon and said that he had received a call from Dane Edwards, editor of the paper in Brush, Colorado, who furnished information that U.S. Army helicopters had been seen in the vicinity of where some of the cattle were mutilated and that he, Edwards, had been threatened but Senator Haskell did not know what sort of threats Edwards had received or by whom. He was advised that this information would be furnished to our Denver Office and that Denver would closely follow the situation."

The FBI ultimately determined that the unidentified helicopter issue was also outside of its jurisdiction. Curiously, however, during this same time frame, numerous reports of both UFOs and unidentified helicopters surfaced in the immediate vicinity of strategic military installations around the U.S.A., and there is evidence that someone within the FBI was fully aware of this, and was taking more than a cursory interest in these sightings.

Proof comes via a number of Air Force reports forwarded to the FBI only weeks after its contact with Senator Haskell. One report from December 1975 states: "On 7 Nov 75 an off duty missile launch officer reported that unidentified aircraft resembling a helicopter had approached and hovered near a U.S.A.F missile launch control facility, near Lewistown. Source explained that at about 0020, 7 Nov 75, source and his deputy officer had just retired from crew rest in the Soft Support Building (SSB) at the LCF, when both heard the sound of a helicopter rotor above the SSB. The Deputy observed two red-and-white lights on the front of the aircraft, a white light on the bottom, and a white light on the rear.

"**L**ocal authorities denied the use of their helicopters during the period 6–7 Nov 75."

"On 7 Nov 75, Roscoe E. III, Captain, 341 Strategic Missile Wing, advised that during the hours of 6–7 Nov 75, two adjacent LCFs, approximately 50 miles south of aforementioned LCF, reported moving lights as unidentified flying objects (UFO). During this period there were no reports of helicopter noises from personnel at these LCFs.

"This office was recently notified of a message received by security police MAFB, MT., detailing a similar nocturnal approach by a helicopter at a U.S.A.F weapons storage area located at another U.S.A.F base in the Northern Tier states. Local authorities denied the use of their helicopters during the period 6–7 Nov 75."

It's curious that these reports should have been of interest to the FBI, given the statements made to Senator Haskell that the unidentified helicopter sightings reported in Colorado were outside of the FBI's jurisdiction.

It is also notable that an unauthenticated document made available to researcher William Moore (co-author with Charles Berlitz of a 1980 book, *The Roswell Incident*) refers to the Northern Tier helicopter and UFO sightings of 1975, and expresses concern that, in view of the fact that the media had picked up on the stories, there was a need on the part of some authority to develop an effective disinformation plan to counter the developing interest that was surrounding the sightings.

Today, the controversy surrounding who, precisely, is flying the black helicopters remains. A privately funded militia-type group? A secret arm of the U.S. military? No one knows. Except, of course, those who fly the mysterious craft.

Bohemian Club

Created in the nineteenth century—in April 1872, to be precise—the Bohemian Club began as an organization in which likeminded figures in the world of the arts could get together, and specifically so in San Francisco, California, where it was created. Indeed, San Francisco remains its home to this very day. Its bases of operations are San Francisco's Union Square and Bohemian Grove, which can be found in Sonoma County. Although the Bohemian Club initially invited the likes of poets, writers, playwrights, and

The Bohemian Club is located at the corner of Post and Taylor Streets in San Francisco.

painters into the fold, it wasn't long at all before powerful figures in the fields of politics, business, and the military became members. Eventually, as circumstances and history have shown, they would come to dominate it.

In 1862, the *Westminster Review* described Bohemianism as follows: "The term *Bohemian* has come to be very commonly accepted in our day as the description of a certain kind of literary gypsy, no matter in what language he speaks, or what city he inhabits. A Bohemian is simply an artist or 'littérateur' who, consciously or unconsciously, secedes from conventionality in life and in art."

As for the specific origins of the Bohemian Club, a concise explanation of its beginnings came from Michael Henry de Young, the owner of the *San Francisco Chronicle* newspaper. In 1915, de Young said: "The Bohemian Club was organized in the *Chronicle* office by Tommy Newcombe, Sutherland, Dan O'Connell, Harry Dam and others who were members of the staff. The boys wanted a place where they could get together after work, and they took a room on Sacramento Street below Kearny. That was the start of the Bohemian Club, and it was not an unmixed blessing for the *Chronicle* because the boys would go there sometimes when they should have reported at the office. Very often when Dan O'Connell sat down to a good dinner there he would forget that he had a pocketful of notes for an important story."

It's interesting to note that the de Young family had its very own ties to powerful and famous figures: Michael Henry de Young's grandfather, Benjamin Morange, was the minister from France to Spain under none other than Napoleon Bonaparte.

It is deeply ironic that the group became known as the Bohemian Club: over time the number of members who could rightly call themselves Bohemians fell, and to the point where they were eventually in the minority. The majority soon became those aforementioned politicians, businessmen, and military figures. U.S. presidents—and more than a few of them—would enter the fold, too. We're talking about the likes of President George H. W. Bush, publisher William Randolph Hearst, former National Security Agency director Bobby Ray Inman, Henry Kissinger, and President Ronald Reagan.

The Bohemian Club is most well-known—arguably, infamously well-known—for its annual, two-weeks-long get-together at Bohemian Grove, located in Monte Rio, California. While the club's public image is that of a group of likeminded figures getting together and hanging out at Bohemian Grove, that's far from the case. Indeed, behind the closed doors of Bohemian Grove, the club quickly transforms into a definitive secret society, replete with bizarre rituals and initiation rites—as we shall now see.

Bohemian Grove

A search on the Internet reveals that there is often confusion surrounding the Bohemian Club and Bohemian Grove. It's actually quite simple: the former is the name of the group, whereas Bohemian Grove is the location at which the members meet. Bohemian Grove is a huge compound, running close to three thousand acres in size and is located on the Russian River in Sonoma County, California, and just about everything that goes on there is shrouded in secrecy. It's also shrouded in Douglas firs and redwoods, all of which help keep prying eyes at bay. Bohemian Grove is also a place dominated by controversy, as author Brad Steiger notes: "Conspiracy theorists state that the principal theme of the annual meeting is celebration of patriarchy, racism, and class privilege."

The *Washington Post* reveals some notable facts about Bohemian Grove: "The club is so hush-hush that little can be definitively said about it, but much of what we know today is from those who have infiltrated the camp, including Texas-based filmmaker Alex Jones. In 2000, Jones and his cameraman entered the camp with a hidden camera and were able to film a Bohemian Grove ceremony, Cremation of the Care. During the ceremony, members wear costumes and cremate a coffin effigy called 'Care' before a 40-foot-owl, in deference to the surrounding Redwood trees."

Then, we have this from *Bohemian Grove Exposed*: "They secretly meet for seventeen days each July in a remote 'sacred grove' of ancient redwood trees in the deep forests surrounding San Francisco. Some 1,500 in number, their membership roll is kept secret, but includes the super-rich, blood dynasty member families of the Illuminati; heavy-hitting corporate chieftains and high government officials. Mingling among them are a number of Hollywood movie stars, Broadway producers, famous entertainers, musicians, authors, painters and poets. Great statesmen and—so we're told—gentlemen.

"Stories have come out of the Grove about wild homosexual orgies, male and female prostitutes being engaged in what can only be described as extreme sexual games, young chil-

A metal bas relief of an owl on the side of the Bohemian Club building in San Francisco is a nod to the sacred grove. It could also be seen as a symbol of the Egyptian goddess Sirius, or perhaps the goddess of wisdom, Sophia.

dren being exploited in unspeakable ways, up to and including cold-blooded ritual murder. There are stories involving actual human sacrifice on the 'altar' of the owl God statue. Understandably, it's all very hard to believe."

Mike Clelland is someone who made a careful study of Bohemian Grove and its history and activities. He says: "The club emblem is an owl with the motto 'Weaving Spiders Come Not Here.' This seems to trace back to Greek mythology. Arachne was a mortal woman who boasted that her weaving skill was greater than that of Athena. A contest took place, and Arachne's weaving was filled with imagery depicting ways that the gods had misled and abused mortals. Athena, goddess of wisdom and crafts, saw that Arachne's creation was not only mocking the gods, but it was far more beautiful than her own. Enraged, Athena turned Arachne into a spider. The scientific term for spiders, arachnids, goes back to the myth of Arachne.

"Starting in 1887, there has been an annual play performed by Bohemian members, often at the foot of the sinister looking giant stone owl. Roles for women are played by men, since women are not allowed as club members. The 1906 performance of *The Owl and Care, A Spectacle*, seems to be the only play with the word owl in its title. Curiously, it was performed the same year as the great San Francisco earthquake.

"This giant stone owl (although some reports describe it made of cement) is commonly known as Moloch, named after a god of the Canaanites, an evil deity that required the sacrifice of human children. But the ancient literature presents Moloch as a bull, and not an owl. No easy answers, but since the Bohemian Club is shrouded under so many layers of secrecy, it is easy to assume the worst. Given the state of the world today, many of these assumptions might be true."

The final words go to President Richard M. Nixon: "Anybody can be president of the United States, but very few can ever have any hope of becoming president of the Bohemian Club."

Brookings Institution

In late December 1960, a feature appeared in the pages of a flying saucer-themed publication, the *NICAP UFO Investigator* (NICAP being the National Investigations Committee on Aerial Phenomena). The title was "Space-Life Report Could be Shock." Readers were told: "The discovery of intelligent space beings could have a severe effect on the public, according to a research report released by the National Aeronautics and Space Administration. The report warned that America should prepare to meet the psychological impact of such a revelation. The 190-page report was the result of a $96,000 one-year study conducted by the Brookings Institution for NASA's long-range study committee.

"Public realization that intelligent beings live on other planets could bring about profound changes, or even the collapse of our civilization, the research report stated. 'Societies sure of their own place have disintegrated when confronted by a superior society,' said the NASA report. 'Others have survived even though changed. Clearly, the better we can come to understand the factors involved in responding to such crises the better prepared we may be.' Although the research group did not expect any immediate contact with other planet beings, it said that the discovery of intelligent space races 'could nevertheless happen at any time.'"

The report in question was titled "Proposed Studies on the Implications of Peaceful Space Activities for Human Affairs," and it was the work of the Brookings Institution. The group says of itself: "The Brookings Institution is a nonprofit public policy organization based in Washington, D.C. Our mission is to conduct in-depth research that leads to new ideas for solving problems facing a society at the local, national and global level."

And there are these words, of Lord Jonathan Hill, of the European Commission: "The Brookings Institution [is] a think tank as respected as it is long-lived. Over the last century, empires have come and gone, the world order has changed but Brookings has sailed on, not just commenting on events but shaping them."

As for the "Proposed Studies on the Implications of Peaceful Space Activities for Human Affairs" document, the fact that it spelled out a great deal on the possible nature of alien life and the outcome of contact with extraterrestrials has given rise to the theory that the Brookings Institution—which is an elite body that is contracted by numerous arms of government and the military—may have possessed secret, inside information on such issues. Let's take a look at what its author—one Donald N. Michael—said back in 1960.

Commissioned by NASA's Committee on Long Range Studies, Michael's document says: "While face-to-face meetings with it will not occur within the next twenty years (unless its

The Brookings Institution is a Washington, D.C., think tank that does research in such areas as foreign policy and government. One of its publications addresses the possibility of encountering alien species in space.

technology is more advanced than ours, qualifying it to visit earth), artifacts left at some point in time by these life forms might possibly be discovered through our space activities on the Moon, Mars, or Venus."

Michael's words about ancient artifacts on Mars has given rise to the theory that the Brookings Institution knew something of the infamous and so-called "Face on Mars" which has so intrigued the UFO research community for years. That the "Face" was not discovered (officially, at least) until 1976 makes Michael's words of 1976 all the more intriguing.

And then there's this: "Anthropological files contain many examples of societies, sure of their place in the universe, which have disintegrated when they have had to associate with previously unfamiliar societies espousing different ideas and different life ways; others that survived such an experience usually did so by paying the price of changes in values and attitudes and behavior. Since intelligent life might be discovered at any time via the radio telescope research presently under way, and since the consequences of such a discovery are presently unpredictable because of our limited knowledge of behavior under even an approximation of such dramatic circumstances, two research areas can be recommended: Continuing studies to determine emotional and intellectual understanding and attitudes—and successive alterations of them if any—regarding the possibility and consequences of discovering intelligent extraterrestrial life."

> **M**ichael's words about ancient artifacts on Mars has given rise to the theory that the Brookings Institution knew something of the infamous and so-called "Face on Mars"….

Michael also had this to say: "Historical and empirical studies of the behavior of peoples and their leaders when confronted with dramatic and unfamiliar events or social pressures … might help to provide programs for meeting and adjusting to the implications of such a discovery. Questions one might wish to answer by such studies would include: How might such information, under what circumstances, be presented to or withheld from the public for what ends? What might be the role of the discovering scientists and other decision makers regarding release of the fact of discovery?"

There was also this from the Brookings Institution: "The discovery would certainly be front-page news everywhere; the degree of political or social repercussion would probably depend on leadership's interpretation of (1) its own role, (2) threats to that role, and (3) national and personal opportunities to take advantage of the disruption or reinforcement of the attitudes and values of others. Since leadership itself might have great need to gauge the direction and intensity of public attitudes, to strengthen its own morale and for decision making purposes, it would be most advantageous to have more to go on than personal opinions about the opinions of the public and other leadership groups."

As for what a meeting with extraterrestrials might mean for us, as a species, Brookings informed NASA: "The knowledge that life existed in other parts of the universe might lead to a greater unity of men on earth, based on the 'oneness' of man or on the age-old assumption that any stranger is threatening. Much would depend on what, if anything, was communicated between man and the other beings. The positions of the major American religious denominations, the Christian sects, and the Eastern religions on the matter of extraterrestrial life need elucidation. Consider the following: 'The Fundamentalist (and anti-science) sects are growing apace around the world. For them, the discovery of other life—rather than any other space product—would be electrifying. Some scattered studies need to be made both in their home centers and churches and their missions, in relation to attitudes about space activities and extraterrestrial life.

"'If plant life or some subhuman intelligence were found on Mars or Venus, for example, there is on the face of it no good reason to suppose these discoveries, after the original novelty had been exploited to the fullest and worn off, would result in substantial changes in perspectives or philosophy in large parts of the American public, at least any more than, let us say, did the discovery of the coelacanth or the panda.'"

Was Donald N. Michael's report purely theoretical? Or, did the Brookings Institution—a powerful group with tentacles that extend far, wide and deep—know something, back in the early 1960s, that the rest of us still don't know?

Camorra

One of the most notorious of all Italian secret societies was the Camorra—a group ultimately absorbed into the much feared and powerful Mafia. The Camorra was one of many bands of criminals that operated out of Naples, Italy, during the 1800s. The majority of those bands were loose-knit in nature and—due to their lack of organizational skills—were largely ineffective. In terms of their activities, however, that was most certainly not the case when it came to the Camorra.

Although not entirely proven, there are indications that the origins of the Camorra may actually date back as far as the 1400s—albeit in Spain and before it eventually made its stealthy way to Italy. What began as a small and secret society of criminals soon mutated into something very different. It provoked terror and fear among the people of Naples, and particularly so when members began to engage in large-scale, widespread crimes, such as blackmail, robberies, burglaries, extortion, and even ruthless assassination.

The incredible power and influence that the Camorra ultimately wielded led it to infiltrate local law enforcement, the corrupt Bourbon monarchy, and the military. Dirty and deadly deeds that the Royals, the Army, and politicians may not have wished to have gotten involved in were handled by the Camorra—for substantial fees and with not even a single question asked. Or else. Nevertheless, by the early 1860s things began to change. It was specifically due to what became known as Italian Unification. On this matter, the

U.S. Department of State notes: "The northern Italian states held elections in 1859 and 1860 and voted to join the Kingdom of Piedmont-Sardinia, a major step towards unification, while Piedmont-Sardinia ceded Savoy and Nice to France. Giuseppi Garibaldi, a native of Piedmont-Sardinia, was instrumental in bringing the southern Italian states into the unification process. In 1860, Garibaldi cobbled together an army (referred to as the 'Thousand') to march into the southern part of the peninsula. Landing first in Sicily and then moving onwards into Naples, Garibaldi and his men overthrew the Bourbon monarchy and turned over the southern territories to Victor Emmanuel II, King of Piedmont-Sardinia. In early 1861 a national parliament convened and proclaimed the Kingdom of Italy, with Victor Emmanuel II as its king. At this point, there were only two major territories outside of the parameters of the new Kingdom of Italy: Rome and Venetia."

> **N**evertheless, the Camorra was not done yet: many of the members—realizing they were fighting a losing battle—secretly made their way to the United States where ... they were absorbed into the Mafia.

One of the results of unification—and of the overthrowing of the Bourbon monarchy—was that steps were finally taken to reel in the Camorra and bring its reign of crime, intimidation, and murder to an end. For decades, the military—following just about every conceivable lead available—hunted down the Camorra—and mercilessly so, too. In addition, its attempts to come to power in the 1901 Neapolitan election were thwarted. Nevertheless, the Camorra was not done yet: many of the members—realizing they were fighting a losing battle—secretly made their way to the United States where, after more than a few turf-wars, they were absorbed into the Mafia.

And it has made a remarkable comeback, as the FBI notes: "The word 'Camorra' means gang. The Camorra first appeared in the mid-1800s in Naples, Italy, as a prison gang. Once released, members formed clans in the cities and continued to grow in power. The Camorra has more than a hundred clans and approximately seven thousand members, making it the largest of the Italian organized crime groups. In the 1970s, the Sicilian Mafia convinced the Camorra to convert its cigarette smuggling routes into drug smuggling routes with the Sicilian Mafia's assistance. Not all Camorra leaders agreed, leading to the Camorra Wars that cost 400 lives. Opponents of drug trafficking lost the war. The Camorra made a fortune in reconstruction after an earthquake ravaged the Campania region in 1980. Now it specializes in cigarette smuggling and receives payoffs from other criminal groups for any cigarette traffic through Italy. The Camorra is also involved in money laundering, extortion, alien smuggling, robbery, blackmail, kidnapping, political corruption, and counterfeiting. It is believed that nearly two hundred Camorra affiliates reside in this country, many of whom arrived during the Camorra Wars."

Cannibal Cult

Bideford is an ancient town situated in the English county of Devon, the county in which Sir Arthur Conan Doyle set his classic Sherlock Holmes novel of 1902, *The Hound of the Baskervilles*. Devon is a place filled with bleak and ominous moorland, old stone circles, foggy landscapes, and picturesque sleepy villages that have remained relatively unchanged for centuries. Devon is also said to have played host to nothing less than savage, terrifying, and inbred people, a secret and deranged society that practiced nothing less than cannibalism.

The dark and turbulent story of the Gregg family of the Devon village of Clovelly can be found within the pages of an old manuscript. It's housed in a collection of centuries-old books in the aforementioned Bideford. From the

The village of Clovelly in Devon, England, was the home of the Gregg family, who terrorized the residents for over twenty-five years.

heart of a huge, dark cave on the coastal part of the moors, the Greggs held terrifying sway over the area for more than a quarter of a century, robbing, murdering, and eating just about anyone and everyone who had the misfortune to cross their path. Indeed, they appear to have become distinctly zombified as time, locale, and circumstances all took their toll.

According to the ancient papers held at Bideford, in excess of one thousand unfortunate souls became breakfast, lunch, and dinner for the hideous Gregg clan. Eventually, however, enough was seen as being well and truly enough: a posse of four hundred local men stormed the huge and labyrinthine cave to finally put an end to the reign of fear. When the men arrived, however, they got far more than even they had bargained for. The old records state that deep in the cave were found, "such a multitude of arms, legs, thighs, hands, and feet of men, women, and children hung up in rows, like dried beef and a great many lying in pickle."

Outraged and horrified by the shocking scene before them, the men hauled the entire Gregg family out of the cave—which amounted to around fifty people, most of whom were the result of endless incest, which had ensured they were physically deformed and mentally subnormal—and brought them before magistrates in the Devon city of Exeter. On the following day, and without benefit of a trial, they were all hung by the neck until they breathed no more. They did not reanimate, for those who may be wondering.

> **D**efoe suggested that the story of the Gregg family had its origins not in Devon, but hundreds of miles north, in Galloway, Scotland.

It must be noted that A. D. Hippisley-Coxe, who, in 1981, penned a book titled *The Cannibals of Clovelly: Fact or Fiction?*, offered that the story of the diabolical Gregg family had its roots in folklore, rather than reality—a piece of folklore deliberately spread by local smugglers and designed to keep terrified locals away from the areas where the smugglers operated. In this scenario, then, the flesh-eating sub-humans were merely a myth brought to life. Nevertheless, not everyone is quite so sure that is all there is to the mystery.

A near-identical story to that of the Greggs of Devon can be found in *The Legend of Sawney Bean*, which was the work of Daniel Defoe, the acclaimed genius behind *Gulliver's Travels*.

Defoe suggested that the story of the Gregg family had its origins not in Devon, but hundreds of miles north, in Galloway, Scotland. And, said Defoe, John Gregg was not the leader of the infernal pack, after all. It was one Sawney Bean who ruled the roost.

Whatever the real truth of the matter, it has failed to put to rest rumors that in some of the wilder parts of Devon, even more devolved, cannibalistic descendants of the Gregg family still lurk in the old caves that pepper mysterious Dartmoor, and who just may be responsible for the hundreds of people that go missing in the United Kingdom every year.

Carbonari Society

Global Security says that this particular group was: "… a secret political society, which became notorious in Italy and France about 1818, though it had existed for a number of years before."

Global Security also notes that there are "evident" parallels between Carbonari and the domain of Freemasonry. "Freemasons could enter the Carbonari as masters at once. The openly avowed aim of the Carbonari was political: they sought to bring about a constitutional monarchy or a republic, and to defend the rights of the people against all forms of absolutism. They did not hesitate to compass their ends by assassination and armed revolt. As early as the first years of the nineteenth century the society was widespread in Neapolitan territory, especially in the Abruzzi and Calabria. Not only men of low birth, but also government officials of high rank, officers, and even members of the clergy belonged to it."

Writer Juri Lina, a noted expert on the Carbonari and its history and activities, reveals: "The headquarters of the Carbonari was located in Rome. In the 1820s the movement had 700,000 armed members. They claimed that they could enlighten the world with the holy fire (illuminism!). The symbol of their message of truth was charcoal, the source of light. An upside-down tree symbolized the murdered king. They advocated removal of the wolves (tyrants) in the forest (society). The members of the same hut called themselves *boni cugini* (good cousins). Non-Carbonari were called *pagani* (heathens). The Carbonari were divided into two classes: apprentices and masters. No apprentice could rise to the degree of master until the end of six months. The Carbonari colours were blue (hope), red (love), and black (faith). At their gatherings they displayed five glowing triangles symbolizing the Illuminati five-point program."

Tom Frascella, who has carefully studied the Carbonari Society, says: "The Carbonari society had many secret rituals and members were required to take certain oaths of mutual support. Upon acceptance members would learn code words by which fellow members could recognize each other. Members would refer to each other as *buoni cugini* or good cousins. Their secret lodges were called *vendita*, or *sales*. Many of their rituals and ceremonies contained a mixture of both Christian and pagan references and symbols."

"**M**any of their rituals and ceremonies contained a mixture of both Christian and pagan references and symbols."

Their goals and ideology were, in their own words, as follows: "Crush the enemy whoever he may be; crush the powerful by means of lies and calumnies; but especially crush him in the egg. It is to the youth we must go. It is that which we must seduce; it is that which we must bring under the banner of the secret societies. In order to advance by steps, calculated but sure, in that perilous way, two things are of the first necessity. You ought to have the air of being simple as doves, but you must be prudent as the serpent. Your fathers, your children, your wives themselves, ought always to be ignorant of the secret, which you carry in your bosoms. If it pleases you, in order the better to deceive the inquisitorial eye, to go often to confession, you are, as by right authorized, to preserve the most absolute silence regarding these things. You know that the least revelation, that the slightest indication escaped from you in the tribunal of penance, or elsewhere, can bring on great calamities and that the sentence of death is already pronounced upon the revealers, whether voluntary or involuntary."

The final word goes to Tom Frascella: "After 1834 the Carbonari Movement slowly stops being center stage and the Giovane Italia Society comes to the forefront as a political movement. However the two movements are probably better regarded as an evolutionary development of practical political thought."

Cattle Mutilation Group

Is a clandestine group secretly monitoring the United States' cattle herd for evidence of emerging viruses, ones that are far worse than so-called "Mad Cow Disease?" This is an issue that was addressed deeply by author Chris O'Brien. He is the author of a number of books of a definitively Fortean nature, including *Enter the Valley*, *The Mysterious Valley*, *Stalking the Tricksters*, and *Secrets of the Mysterious Valley*. There can be very few people who are interested in the many and varied mysteries of our world who aren't aware of the phenomenon of "cattle mutilations," as well as the wider phenomenon of animal-mutes. Typically, cattle are found with organs removed from their bodies, with precise cuts to the skin that strongly suggest the presence and use of very sharp instruments, and with their eyeballs, ears, and tongues utterly gone.

But who is responsible? The skeptics claim it's all the work of wild animals, such as wolves, coyotes, and even birds. Of course, some cases of animal mutilation are indeed due to misidentification. But, mistaken identity is only a small part of the overall puzzle.

Moving on, there's the "satanic cult" theory, which may have some occasional relevancy to the puzzle—and particularly so in the United Kingdom, where more than a few such cases have been reported over the past few years. And, of course, there's the angle of the mutilations being the work of nefarious extraterrestrials engaged in sinister and diabolical experimentation of the genetic kind. Certainly, within the field of UFO research, the alien theory is one that is widely championed—and has been for decades.

But, despite the fact that many believe the UFO theory to have merit (and who, deep down, probably want it to be the answer), there is another possibility, one that brings us to the work of Chris O'Brien. His research suggests that the mutilations revolve around such issues as so-called "Mad Cow Disease," its human equivalent of Creutzfeldt-Jacob Disease, the disturbing and massive increase in Alzheimer's (or *presumed* Alzheimer's) in the United States in the last couple of decades, and deadly viruses.

In other words, O'Brien's work suggests the real mutilators are not extraterrestrials or devotees of the Devil. Rather, they are definitively human in nature. The actions of the mutilators seem to suggest that, somewhere—probably deeply buried within the official infrastructure—there is a clandestine group whose staff are deeply worried that America is becoming more and more infected with CJD, with Variant CJD, and/or with something even worse—possibly even a mutated form of the original strain.

Might that explain why there has been an enormous rise in what is assumed to be dementia-driven conditions all across the United States? Yes, it may well. Such a theory may also explain the presence of black, unmarked helicopters in the vicinity of the mutilations. After all, what's more likely: (a) that the crews of the infamous black helicopters are secretly observing the actions of extraterrestrial butchers; or (b) that the crews are the mutilators?

It's important to note that, while a theory is simply that—a theory—Chris O'Brien has undertaken a huge amount of research into this particular area and has uncovered a great deal of highly notable data and documentation that (a) connects mutilation sites to outbreaks of disease in animals; (b) reveals evidence of secret, decades-long, and large-scale monitoring of the cattle herd; and (c) concerns the carnage and chaos that could result (and perhaps

One theory about cattle mutilations is that the bovines are victims of satanic cult ceremonies.

which is now resulting) if and when something worse than CJD jumps from species to species. That's to say from cattle to us.

While the cattle mutilation puzzle is a very real one, it has nothing to do with aliens—hostile, friendly, or indifferent. It's far, far worse.

Chemtrail Group

Is a secret group working to lower the human population level by releasing deadly substances into the Earth's atmosphere? Welcome to the world of chemtrails. The controversy of chemtrails has attracted the attention of conspiracy theorists, the mainstream media, the U.S. Air Force, and the governments of both the United Kingdom and Canada. On the one hand, there are those who suggest it's all a matter of conspiratorial nonsense and fear-mongering. On the other hand, it's perceived by many as something dark and deadly; something that may even threaten our very existence as a species.

The official line is that chemtrails—in essence, trails in the sky, left by large aircraft—are simply regular contrails of the kind that can be seen in the skies anytime and everywhere. They are created when a high-flying aircraft reaches an altitude cold enough to cause exhaust vapor to transform into crystals of ice, which allows them to be seen as long trails of cloud-like vapor.

The unofficial view, however, is very different. It suggests that chemtrails are nothing less than prime evidence that someone is pumping into the atmosphere massive amounts of potentially deadly chemicals. The theories as to why such actions might be taking place are just about as many as they are varied: (a) to provoke widespread illness and death, as a means to lower the planet's ever-growing population levels; (b) to reduce the effects of global warming; (c) to alter the Earth's weather (for good or bad, is a matter of dispute amongst theorists); and (d) to adversely affect the human brain, and turn us into subservient, morose cat-

Those chemtrails you see in the sky that are left behind by airplanes might not be as innocent as you might think. Some theorize that they contain chemicals meant to poison humanity.

tle. Somewhere in this mass of tangled theories and claims lies the answer. But whose answer is the real one? That's the big question.

The U.S. Air Force says: "The Air Force's policy is to observe and forecast the weather. The Air Force is focused on observing and forecasting the weather so the information can be used to support military operations. The Air Force is not conducting any weather modification experiments or programs and has no plans to do so in the future. The 'Chemtrail' hoax has been investigated and refuted by many established and accredited universities, scientific organizations, and major media publications."

In 1999, the New Mexico attorney general's office contacted New Mexicans for Science and Reason (NMSR) member Kim Johnson to help answer questions from constituents regarding the alleged dangers of "chemtrails." After his investigation, Johnson told the attorney general: "I have viewed a number of photos purporting to be of aircraft spraying the chemical or biological material into the atmosphere. I have also discussed these letters with another scientist familiar with upper atmospheric phenomena from Sandia National Laboratory and a retired general and fighter pilot who is an Air Force Hall of Fame Member. In summary, there is no evidence that these 'chemtrails' are other than expected, normal contrails from jet aircraft that vary in their shapes, duration, and general presentation based on prevailing weather conditions.

"That is not to say that there could not be an occasional, purposeful experimental release of, say, high altitude barium for standard wind tracking experiments. There could also be other related experiments that occur from time-to-time which release agents into the atmosphere. However, not one single picture that was presented as evidence indicates other than normal contrail formation."

Mark Pilkington, an observer of, and commentator on, conspiracy theories, was doubtful of the idea that chemtrails were part of some terrible plot to kill whole swathes of the population or to manipulate the weather. Nevertheless, he did note the following: "The contrail threat isn't entirely imagined, however. NASA has been carrying out genuine research into the possible effects of contrails and increased air activity on the environment. An average contrail can last for hours before evolving into cirrus clouds—the largest measured covered 2,000 square miles (5,180 sq km) of west America. Scientists have long been concerned that, with an expected six-fold increase in plane flights, such cirrus spreads might trap heat in the Earth's atmosphere, so contributing to global warning. According to NASA research, cirrus cloud cover

"The contrail threat isn't entirely imagined, however. NASA has been carrying out genuine research into the possible effects of contrails and increased air activity on the environment."

over America has increased five per cent since 1971, with the figure higher in the north-east."

At the height of the controversy, chemtrails researcher Ken Adachi said: "Chemtrail spraying seems to be heaviest and most constant over North America and most countries of eastern Europe. Some countries in Asia are being sprayed (Japan and Korea), but the greatest exception to any chemtrail activity whatsoever is China. The Chinese are being spared completely because China is being groomed by the NWO to replace the United States as the leading nation of the world, both economically and militarily."

Adachi also noted something that suggested it wasn't the entire human race that was under assault, but possibly just specific portions of it: "It is being reported that people with average or below average immunity are experiencing pneumonia-like respiratory symptoms, while people with stronger immunity are only experiencing slight discomfort for a day or two or no symptoms at all. Some people have gotten very ill and the symptoms seem to keep returning after a short period of improvement. It's possible that some of these sprayings might contain special bioengineered pathogens designed to affect only certain racial groups."

Church of Light

It was in November 1932 that the Coral Street, Los Angeles, California-based Church of Light was established. The trio that created it was Benjamin Parker Williams (the president of the group, who went by the pseudonym of C. C. Zain and who also used the name of Elbert Benjamine), Elizabeth D. Benjamine, and Fred Skinner. Its goal: "to teach, practice, and disseminate the Religion of the Stars, a way of life for the Aquarian Age, as set forth in the writings of C. C. Zain."

Zain was an interesting figure who, in 1909, was invited into the fold of the Hermetic Brotherhood of Luxor, chiefly as a result of Zain's extensive knowledge of astrology. The brotherhood's previous astrologer was Minnie Higgin, who died in the same year. The Church of Light is an outgrowth of an earlier body, the Brotherhood of Light. It was created in 1915 and also operated out of Los Angeles. It became somewhat less of a secret society in 1918 when it invited members of the public to join the fold. For years, Zain wrote extensively on what were termed the lessons of the Brotherhood of Light, right up until the Church of Light came to full fruition in 1932. It still exists today, and as its members note:

"You will find that what makes us different from other orders and religions is our realization that, while there is much wisdom that comes to us from our ancient brothers and sisters, we of the present also have a contribution to make to expanding the Science of the Soul. The 21-volume *Brotherhood of Light Lessons* by C. C. Zain will get you started on the right path for making your contribution. They contain 210 serial lessons that are dedicated to helping each individual find his or her place in the universe and fill it. Through study and application of these lessons, you will find what you need to know about inner-plane physics, the hermetic cosmology and a science of the soul. In doing so, you will markedly increase your Happiness, Usefulness and Spirituality."

Church of Satan

According to the website of the Church of Satan: "We are the first above-ground organization in history openly dedicated to the acceptance of Man's true nature—that of a carnal beast, living in a cosmos that is indifferent to our existence. To us, Satan is the symbol that best suits the nature of we who are carnal by birth—people who feel no battles raging between our thoughts and feelings, we who do not embrace the concept of a soul imprisoned in a body. He represents pride, liberty, and individualism—qualities often defined as Evil by those who worship external deities, who feel there is a war between their minds and emotions."

The church continues: "As Anton LaVey explained in his classic work *The Satanic Bible*, Man—using his brain—invented all the Gods, doing so because many of our species cannot accept or control their personal egos, feeling compelled to conjure up one or a multiplicity of characters who can act without hindrance or guilt upon whims and desires. All Gods are thus externalized forms, magnified projections of the true nature of their creators, personifying aspects of the universe or personal temperaments which many of their followers find to be troubling. Worshipping any God is thus worshipping by proxy those who invented that God. Since the Satanist understands that all Gods are fiction, instead of bending a knee in worship to—or seeking friendship or unity with—such mythical entities, he places himself at the center of his own subjective universe as his own highest value. We Satanists are thus our own 'Gods,' and as beneficent 'deities' we can offer love to those who deserve it and deliver our wrath (within reasonable limits) upon those who seek to cause us—or that which we cherish—harm."

Author Brad Steiger says of the history of the Church of Satan: "On April 30, 1966 (Walpurgisnacht, a night legendarily favored by the disciples of darkness), Anton Szandor LaVey (1930–1997) shaved his head, donned black clerical clothing, complete with white collar, and proclaimed himself Satan's

The Sigil of Baphomet is a symbol of the Church of Satan and LaVeyan Satanism.

high priest. This was the dawn of the Age of Satan, LaVey boldly announced. It was the morning of magic and undefiled wisdom, and he thereby established the First Church of Satan in San Francisco."

Steiger also notes that, "There was nothing new about a belief in magical powers or in worshiping Satan. What was new was LaVey's use of the term 'church' as part of his organization's title. In addition to ceremonies and rituals devoted to the Prince of Darkness, there were weddings, funerals, and children baptized in the name of Satan."

Much of the work of the Church of Satan is shrouded in secrecy. For example, the church refuses to reveal how many people it has in its ranks: "Our founder established as policy that we should never give out a precise count of our members as that would allow people to quantify us. He always said that the Church of Satan should be like a custard which can't be nailed to the wall. He felt that if our numbers were judged to be too large, people might find us threatening. If too small, that might be used as a reason to dismiss our philosophy. All that we will say is that we have members in just about every nation on the planet, and the membership has always grown as the years pass."

In 1969, LaVey wrote *The Satanic Bible*, a book that became steeped in controversy as soon it was published. Such was the rapidly growing interest in LaVey and the Church of Satan, the book became a huge seller. Indeed, today, the book has sold well over one million copies, worldwide. As LaVey noted in *The Satanic Bible* there were certain criteria for those wishing to join the church, or to follow its practices: "Satanism advocates practicing a modified form of the Golden Rule. Our interpretation of this rule is: 'Do unto others as they do unto you,' because if you 'Do unto others as you would have them do unto you,' and they, in turn, treat you badly, it goes against human nature to continue to treat them with consideration. You should do unto others as you would have them do unto you, but if your courtesy is not returned, they should be treated with the wrath they deserve."

Then we have this from LaVey, which demonstrates how and why he had little love for the world of organized religion: "Some religions actually go so far as to label anyone who belongs to a religious sect other than their own a heretic, even though the overall doctrines and impressions of godliness are nearly the same. For example: The Catholics believe the Protestants are doomed to Hell simply because they do not belong to the Catholic Church. In the same way, many splinter groups of the Christian faith, such as the evangelical or revivalist churches, believe the Catholics worship graven images. (Christ is depicted in the image that is most physiologically akin to the individual worshipping him, and yet the Christians criticize 'heathens' for the worship of graven images) and the Jews have always been given the Devil's name."

And, we have this from LaVey's infamous book: "When a Satanist commits a wrong, he realizes that it is natural to make a mistake—and if he is truly sorry about what he has done, he will learn from it and take care not to do the same thing again. If he is not honestly sorry about what he has done, and knows he will do the same thing over and over, he has no business confessing and asking forgiveness in the first place."

LaVey died on October 29, 1997, of pulmonary edema. On November 7 of that same year, Larry D. Hatfield of the *San Francisco Chronicle* wrote: "A secret 'Satanic funeral' for Anton Szandor LaVey has been held in Colma and the remains of the self-promoting and self-proclaimed founder and high priest of the International Church of Satan have been cremated."

Nevertheless, the Church continues to both survive and thrive.

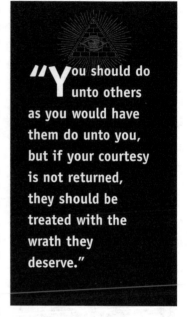

"You should do unto others as you would have them do unto you, but if your courtesy is not returned, they should be treated with the wrath they deserve."

Cicada 3301

Beyond any shadow of doubt, one of the most mysterious of all secret groups is that which has become known as Cicada 3301. In essence, the story behind the group goes like this: between 2012 and 2016 its still unknown members have posted online a series of highly complicated puzzles—with a challenge for people to try and crack those very same puzzles. As for Cicada 3301's motivations, speculation has long been rife that they are either a growing body of definitively secret society proportions, or—and rather intriguingly—that they are an ingenious front for an agency of government, possibly even the National Security Agency, the former employer of the world's most infamous whistleblower, Edward Snowden. As the theory goes, anyone who can crack the puzzle wide open is worthy of being secretly recruited into the mysterious world of codebreaking and ciphers.

Between 2012 and 2016 its still unknown members have posted online a series of highly complicated puzzles—with a challenge for people to try and crack those very same puzzles.

The controversy began in January 2012. That was when the first Cicada 3301 challenge was posted to the Internet. It began with a decidedly cryptic challenge: "Hello. We are looking for highly intelligent individuals. To find them, we have devised a test. There is a message hidden in this image. Find it, and it will lead you on the road to finding us. We look forward to meeting the few that will make it all the way through. Good luck."

Cue countless numbers of budding cipher-crackers who took up the enigma-filled challenge. While many have concluded this is nothing more than a highly sophisticated game, one intended purely as a form of entertainment, not everyone is quite so sure that's the case. Indeed, there are those who suggest Cicada 3301 is a downright sinister group, as the U.K.'s *Daily Telegraph* newspaper—which has taken a particular interest in the affair—has noted: "Nobody knows for sure the identity of the group behind the puzzles but speculation about who may be behind it includes the Freemasons, the Illuminati, the hacker group Anonymous, the U.S. Government or just a troll having some fun."

In November 2013, the *Daily Telegraph* noted: "One long, cautionary diatribe, left anonymously on the website Pastebin, claimed to be from an ex-Cicada member—a non-English military officer recruited to the organization 'by a superior.' Cicada, he said, 'was a Left-Hand Path religion disguised as a progressive scientific organization'—comprising … 'military officers, diplomats, and academics who were dissatisfied with the direction of the world.' Their plan, the writer claimed, was to transform humanity into the Nietzschen Übermensch. 'This is a dangerous organization,' he concluded, 'their ways are nefarious.' With no other clues, it was also assumed by many to be a recruitment drive by the CIA, MI6, or America's National Security Agency (NSA), as part of a search for highly talented cryptologists. It wouldn't have been the first time such tactics had been used."

Rolling Stone magazine stated that the 2013 version provided a wealth of "extremely complicated riddles," adding that there was "a cipher based on a book by occultist Aleister Crowley. There was another riddle embedded in a song, an amplified guitar instrumental that, upon spectral analysis, revealed a humming sound at a frequency of 15.4 to 16.1 kilohertz, and an analysis of the mp3 file uncovered a hidden message: 'Like the instar, tunneling to the surface, we must shed our own circumferences; find the divinity within and emerge.'"

In January 2016, yet another challenge from Cicada 3301 surfaced. It read as follows: "Hello. The path lies empty; epiphany seeks the devoted. Liber

Primus is the way. Its words are the map, their meaning is the road, and their numbers are the direction. Seek and you will be found. Good luck. 3301."

Kenny Paterson, a "crypto-professor" based at Britain's Royal Holloway University, is not of the opinion that Cicada 3301 is merely a publicity stunt, or the work of what are known as Internet trolls. Paterson explains why: "There's been several such competitions in the past. Google used to post puzzles on billboards beside the highways in Silicon Valley to attract people to come and work for them. A few years ago, our own GCHQ [Government Communications Headquarters, which is the U.K.'s equivalent of the National Security Agency] had a set of puzzles for people to solve as a way to recruit people with bright minds. It's unlikely to be a spoof due to the length they have gone to. They are really sophisticated; they have all kinds of amazing, esoteric references in there to the work of Aleister Crowley, for example, paintings by William Blake, and Mayan numerals. It takes a long, long time to set up puzzles like this. It's not something you can do in your spare time."

The mystery of Cicada 3301 is perhaps best summed up by the *Washington Post*: "Who's behind the puzzle is unclear, although many enthusiasts believe it's a large, well-funded and shadowy organization trying to recruit its membership. At this rate, we may never know."

Club of Rome

The official website of the Club of Rome provides the following information about this organization, a powerful body that has been targeted by New World Order researchers as a direct threat to the future of the human race.

"The Club of Rome was founded in 1968 as an informal association of independent leading personalities from politics, business and science, men and women who are long-term thinkers interested in contributing in a systemic interdisciplinary and holistic manner to a better world. The Club of Rome members share a common concern for the future of humanity and the planet.

"The aims of the Club of Rome are: to identify the most crucial problems which will

The logo of the Club of Rome.

> **"One of the major goals of the Club of Rome is to reduce the world's population by 2 billion people through war, famine, disease, and any other means necessary."**

determine the future of humanity through integrated and forward-looking analysis; to evaluate alternative scenarios for the future and to assess risks, choices and opportunities; to develop and propose practical solutions to the challenges identified; to communicate the new insights and knowledge derived from this analysis to decision-makers in the public and private sectors and also to the general public, and to stimulate public debate and effective action to improve the prospects for the future.

Not everyone, however, is quite so sure that the Club of Rome is as benevolent as it appears to be. Indeed, some students of conspiracy theories and secret societies believe the group to be downright dangerous, and a key player in the creation of a looming New World Order. The *Jeremiah Project* provides thought-provoking words: "To facilitate the management of the New World Order agenda calls for the elimination of most of the world's population through war, disease, abortion, and famine. According to the Club of Rome's publications, the common enemy of humanity is man. One of the major goals of the Club of Rome is to reduce the world's population by 2 billion people through war, famine, disease, and any other means necessary."

As controversial as this may sound, the Club of Rome makes no bones about the fact that it views man as man's own enemy. Consider the following, stated by the Club of Rome in 1991: "In searching for a new enemy to unite us, we came up with the idea that pollution, the threat of global warming, water shortages, famine, and the like would fit the bill.... But in designating them as the enemy, we fall into the trap of mistaking symptoms for causes. All these dangers are caused by human intervention, and it is only through changed attitudes and behavior that they can be overcome. The real enemy, then, is humanity itself."

Collins Elite

The idea that the U.S. government has a highly classified, secret group that believes that the UFO phenomenon is one of demonic—rather than extraterrestrial—origins may sound outlandish and unlikely. It is, however, absolute fact. It goes by the name of the Collins Elite, although don't expect the world of officialdom to confirm its existence. At least, not anytime soon. We know, however, that the group exists—and largely thanks to a man named Ray

Boeche. He is both a UFO investigator (and a former state director for the Mutual UFO Network, MUFON) and a priest.

It was as a result of his almost unique connections to two issues that most might assume are wholly unconnected that led Boeche to be exposed to the clandestine world of the Collins Elite. And, it all began in late 1991, when Boeche was contacted by two scientists who were undertaking work for the Pentagon: they had been secretly contracted to come on board with the Collins Elite. The purpose of their work was to research the UFO phenomenon and to try and make contact with the entities behind the same phenomenon via psychic, mind-to-mind means. As their work progressed, however, it became more and more clear to the pair—and to the rest of their colleagues— that the large-headed, black-eyed aliens the Collins Elite assumed they were in contact with were nothing of the sort. They were, the group concluded, nothing less than deceptive demons. And, as a result, they quickly sought out Boeche, due to his knowledge of both the UFO phenomenon and demonology. A meeting was set for November 25, 1991, in Lincoln, Nebraska's Cornhusker Hotel—Nebraska being Boeche's home state.

Boeche was definitely the ideal person for the two physicists to speak with, as he had long ago discarded the idea that UFOs were extraterrestrial in origin and was firmly in the demonic camp. As Boeche was told by his sources, the Collins Elite did not refer to the creatures as aliens or demons, but as "Non-Human Entities," or NHEs. And, in no time at all, it became very clear to them that by trying to psychically contact the NHEs they had "opened" a "doorway" to menacing creatures from a hellish realm that masqueraded as extraterrestrials to get their grips into the heart of the U.S. government—a kind of supernatural Trojan Horse, one might be justified in saying.

As Boeche listened, he was told that there had been a number of deaths in the program, bizarre runs of bad luck occurred, and unexplained illnesses blighted those on the program—all of which collectively led the Collins Elite to believe they were under demonic attack and had been, essentially, "cursed."

With their scientific background, they wanted guidance from someone well-versed in matters relative to the concept of Hell, the devil, and demonic hierarchies. Boeche was shocked but willing to help. Indeed, he was

The founding theory behind the Collins Elite is that UFOs are vehicles used by demons from another dimension, not aliens from another planet.

consulted by the group on a couple of occasions, something that made it very clear to him that the Collins Elite—as well as cleared people in the Pentagon—were deeply concerned about the "door" they had opened and which was showing no signs of closing anytime soon.

Additional revelations demonstrated that, by 1991, the Collins Elite had already existed for several decades. However, there was concern on its part that something dark and deadly was on the horizon, hence why the secret group opened its doors to Boeche—to a degree, at least. Further research into the strange and unsettling world of the Collins Elite has shown that the late President Ronald Reagan was briefed on the work of the Collins Elite, as were senior personnel in the National Security Agency, the CIA, and Naval Intelligence. Ancient manuscripts—such as Reginald C. Thompson's *Devils and Evil Spirits of Babylonia*, Edward Langton's *Essentials of Demonology*, and John Deacon and John Walker's 1601 publication *Dialogical Discourses of Spirits and Devils*—were carefully studied and scrutinized, to allow the Collins Elite to have a better understanding of what it was they were dealing with.

> **F**urther research into the strange and unsettling world of the Collins Elite has shown that the late President Ronald Reagan was briefed on the work of the Collins Elite....

As time progressed, however, the Collins Elite became less of a government think tank and more and more of a secret society. For example, the members of the group cultivated links with senior and influential figures in the clergy, specifically those that had links to the very heart of the Vatican itself. Archaeologists—particularly those who were deeply conversant with ancient Middle Eastern history, legend, folklore, and mythology—were secretly contracted and consulted to gain further knowledge on the nature and intent of the demonic threat.

The Collins Elite made approaches—apparently, successful approaches—to a number of U.S. presidents, including Reagan, a man who had a deep interest in both UFOs and "End Times" scenarios, both of which were (and still are) integral portions of the belief systems of the Collins Elite. Shadowy meetings with some of the world's most powerful people in the business world were arranged—chiefly to ensure massive, "under the table" funding for the group and in a fashion that would ensure budgetary data would not reach the likes of Congress, something that could have potentially blown the whole thing wide open.

Today, the Collins Elite still exists—despite the widespread denials of the U.S. government that it has ever existed. And, in the twenty-first century, the group is a definitive secret society. Entrance to the group is strictly limited to those who move effortlessly between the domains of the Pentagon and the Trilateral Commission, the Department of Defense and fringe archaeologists, the Pope, and those well-versed in the black arts.

As the Collins Elite sees it, the group is at the forefront of a worldwide, secret war to prevent a full-scale demonic invasion, worldwide martial law, Armageddon, the rise of the Anti-Christ, and a planet and its people plunged into a literal, hellish nightmare. Time may tell if the theories of this secret network are valid or not. For Ray Boeche, his views on the demonic theory for the UFO phenomenon are held as strongly today as they were when he had that near-unique meeting with two Department of Defense scientists back in November 1991.

Committee of 300

A powerful, worldwide network with an alleged sinister goal for humanity, the Committee of 300 was inspired—in terms of its make-up, ideology, and approach to manipulating key events—by the British East India Company's Council of 300, which was created in the early part of the eighteenth century, and which was largely funded by opium trading in the Far East. As for the British East India Company, its origins date back to the 1600s, thanks to the influence of the British royal family, which got things moving. Essentially, the Committee of 300 is at the forefront of a secret program designed to ultimately control the worlds of banking, politics, and the economy, and even the size of the Earth's human population. The number 300 comes from a statement made by General Electric's Walter Rathenau. In 1909, he said: "Three hundred men, all of whom know one another, direct the economic destiny of Europe and choose their successors from among themselves."

It's not just Europe, however, that the Committee of 300 has its sights set on controlling—and controlling completely. No, we're talking about the entire planet. The No Cancer Foundation notes of the Committee of 300

Walter Rathenau was a German politician during that country's Weimar Republic era in the 1920s. He famously asserted that the economy of Europe was controlled by just three hundred men.

that: "The Committee of 300 uses a network of roundtable groups, think tanks and secret societies which control the world's largest financial institutions and governments. The most prominent of these groups include Chatham House, Bilderberg Group, Trilateral Commission, Council on Foreign Relations, Ditchley Foundation, Club of Rome, RAND Corporation, PNAC and of course Freemasonry. The power behind the Committee of 300 is the Anglo-Jewish cousinhood that dominate the financial and political systems of the world. This cousinhood includes the Rothschild, Rockefeller, Oppenheimer, Goldsmid, Mocatta, Montefiore, Sassoon, Warburg, Samuel, Kadoorie, Franklin, Worms, Stern and Cohen families."

Dr. John Coleman, an expert on the Committee of 300, says that "the Committee of 300 long ago decreed that there shall be a smaller—much smaller—and better world, that is, their idea of what constitutes a better world. The myriads of useless eaters consuming scarce natural resources were to be culled. Industrial progress supports population growth. Therefore the command to

Members of the Committee of 300 supposedly include British royalty (Queen Elizabeth II and the Duke of Edinburgh pictured), captains of industry such as J. P. Morgan and David Rockefeller, and even philosophers and writers such as Bertrand Russell and H. G. Wells.

multiply and subdue the earth found in Genesis had to be subverted. This called for an attack upon Christianity; the slow but sure disintegration of industrial nation states; the destruction of hundreds of millions of people, referred to by the Committee of 300 as 'surplus population,' and the removal of any leader who dared to stand in the way of the Committee's global planning to reach the foregoing objectives. Not that the U.S. government didn't know, but as it was part of the conspiracy, it helped to keep the lid on information rather than let the truth be known. Queen Elizabeth II is the head of the Committee of 300."

As to how Coleman was exposed to the dark world of the Committee of 300, he reveals: "In my career as a professional intelligence officer, I had many occasions to access highly classified documents, but during service as a political science officer in the field in Angola, West Africa, I had the opportunity to view a series of top secret classified documents which were unusually explicit. What I saw filled me with anger and resentment and launched me on a course from which I have not deviated, namely to uncover what power it is that controls and manages the British and United States governments."

Of the membership of the Committee of 300, The Atlantean Conspiracy offers the following (as you'll see, those who have allied themselves to the group are powerful, indeed): "Some notable members of the Committee of 300 include: The British royal family, Dutch royal family, House of Hapsburg, House of Orange, Duke of Alba, Prince Philip Duke of Edinburgh, Lord Carrington, Lord Halifax, Lord Alfred Milner, John Jacob and Waldorf of the Astor Illuminati bloodline, Winston Churchill, Cecil Rhodes, Queen Elizabeth II, Queen Juliana, Queen Beatrix, Queen Magreta, King Haakon of Norway, Colonel Mandel House, Aldous Huxley, John Forbes, Averell Harriman, William and McGeorge Bundy, George Bush, Prescott Bush, Henry Kissinger, J. P. Morgan, Maurice Strong, David Rockefeller, David and Evelyn Rothschild, Paul, Max and Felix Warburg, Ormsby and Al Gore, Bertrand Russell, Sir Earnest and Harry of the Oppenheimer Illuminati bloodline, Warren Buffett, Giuseppe Mazzini, Sir William Hesse, George Schultz, H. G. Wells, and Ted Turner."

Communist Contactees

Today, when people think of extraterrestrials, they generally think of dwarfish creatures with large heads and huge, black eyes. Certainly, that's the way that numerous so-called "alien abductees" describe them, as did *The X-Files*. In the aftermath of World War II, however, many people asserted they had met with aliens of a very different kind. Namely, ones that looked just like us—to the point of being practically indistinguishable from us. Aside from one thing: their long blond hair, which was definitely not in fashion for men in the 1940s and 1950s. Such people were soon termed "Contactees," while the hippy-like aliens were known as the "Space Brothers."

What made the Contactee movement of the 1950s so controversial was that those who claimed alien encounters maintained that their cosmic friends had communist-style governments.

What made the Contactee movement of the 1950s so controversial was that those who claimed alien encounters maintained that their cosmic friends had communist-style governments. Or did they? A particularly thought-provoking theory suggests that the encounters between the Space Brothers and the Contactees were staged events. But, by whom? Nothing less than agents of the former Soviet Union's KGB. The purpose: to affect American morale and have the nation's people believe that communism was not just the way of the world, but of the entire universe too. Such a theory sounds outlandish; however, when one goes looking one finds more than a bit of data in support of the scenario.

On August 5, 1954, a resident of Yucca Valley, California, wrote to the FBI suggesting that one of the most famous of all the Contactees, George Van Tassel, be investigated to determine if he was working as a Soviet spy. No evidence to support such a scenario was ever found, but that the FBI dug into the theory at a deep level is notable in itself.

Then there is the FBI's dossier on the most famous of all the Contactees, a Polish-American named George Adamski. A 1953 document on Adamski, prepared by personnel from the FBI's office in Los Angeles, provides the following: "Adamski made the prediction that Russia will dominate the world and we will then have an era of peace for 1,000 years. He stated that Russia already has the atom bomb and the hydrogen bomb and that the great earthquake, which was reported behind the Iron Curtain recently, was actually a hydrogen bomb explosion being tried out by the Russians. Adamski states this 'earthquake' broke seismograph machines and he added that no normal earthquake can do that."

J. Edgar Hoover's finest were far from done with Adamski, noting that he "stated that within the next twelve months, San Diego will be bombed. Adamski stated that it does not make any difference if the United States has more atom bombs than Russia inasmuch as Russia needs only ten atom bombs to cripple the United States by placing these simultaneously on such spots as Chicago and other vital centers of this country. The United States today is in the same state of deterioration as was the Roman Empire prior to its collapse and it will fall just as the Roman Empire did. The Government in this country is a corrupt form of government and capitalists are enslaving the poor."

Moving on from George Adamski, there's the controversial account of a Californian named Truman Bethurum, a man who claimed repeated, face-to-face encounters with human-like aliens in both California and Nevada in the early 1950s. And, as with Adamski, the matter of communism reared its head, as Bethurum noted: "Two or three fellows who had sons in Korea and who read a lot in the newspapers about the Communist underground in this country, were convinced in their own minds that I was, if making contact with anyone at all, making it with enemy agents. They even went so far as to tell me belligerently that they intended to get guns and follow me nights, and if they caught up to me having intercourse with any people from planes, airships of any kind, they'd blast me and those people, too."

On a related matter, FBI records demonstrate that in December 1954, the Palm Springs Republican Club contacted the FBI to inquire if Bethurum might be guilty of "trying to put over any propaganda."

Then there are the recollections of the late Jim Moseley, who was the editor of *Saucer Smear* magazine. In his book coauthored with Karl Pflock, *Shockingly Close to the Truth*, Moseley noted that in the early to mid-1950s, "I had fallen under the influence of Charles Samwick, a retired army intelligence officer.... Quite sincere and most convincing, he told me ... 'the Communist Party has planted an agent in every civilian saucer club in the United States.'"

Similarly, in his earlier *Saucer News* publication of June-July 1955, Moseley commented thus: "Let us give some very serious consideration to the many alleged space men being called to the public's attention—all of whom invariably tell us of the dangers of war and the exploitation of atomic energy. No one desires peace any more sincerely than we do, but let us remember too that it is part of the Communist 'peace line' to frighten the American people into ceasing our atomic experiments. It is quite possible that some of these 'space men' are unwittingly playing into the hands of the Communists."

Moseley makes a very important point with respect to the Contactee movement in the United States, and which may help to explain why a significant degree of concern was shown at an official level about the politics of the players on the scene. He told me in 2009: "Adamski and the Contactees represented an early hippie philosophy of the time—a 1950s version of what came later in the Sixties with

An illustration of a UFO based on that reported by George Adamski.

flower-power and protests. A lot of what they were saying merged into the mainstream of liberal thinking at that time. So, in that way, it was a very significant movement."

Evidence that an element of the British Police Force called Special Branch took an interest in the Contactees because of communist-related concerns is now in the public domain, thanks to the persistent research of UFO investigators Andy Roberts and Dr. David Clarke, who have uncovered once-secret Special Branch files on George King of the Aetherius Society. As the files demonstrate, in the latter part of the 1950s, King became a well-known character to Special Branch, but for reasons that had little to do with flying saucers—directly, at least.

Roberts and Clarke cite one particularly important Special Branch document that states the Aetherius Society was "still active in its campaign against nuclear weapon tests, and in this respect its policy is closely allied with that of the Communist Party."

As this demonstrates, Special Branch was most certainly taking notice of King and Co., but not for reasons that had any direct bearing on the Contactee controversy. Rather, it was for other, more down-to-earth reasons and concerns relative to politics.

A strange Soviet group trying to convince people that aliens are communists? It certainly looks that way.

Conspiracy of the Equals

About the French Revolution (1789 to 1799), the website *Liberty, Equality, Fraternity* says: "Throughout 1794 and 1795, urban and rural radicals alike demanded 'bread and the constitution of 1793,' meaning that the government should feed the people and grant universal male suffrage. One such radical, who took the name Gracchus Babeuf, supposedly organized the 'Conspiracy of Equals,' a secret group that he hoped to lead in a surprise insurrection to take power and use it to distribute land equally among all citizens. When the 'conspiracy' was betrayed, Babeuf was arrested and tried. Before being sentenced and executed, Babeuf offered a statement of his principles and a defense of his action. His attack on private property scandalized many at the time, but others later called him the first socialist. In short, to those who would look back to the Revolution as the unsuccessful birth of socialist movements, Babeuf would remain an inspiration. To his contemporary critics, who were influenced in part by the Directory's successful propaganda, Babeuf's conspiracy demonstrated the instability of the Republic and the need for forceful government repression of popular political activity. In their view, such an approach would ensure stability and prevent a return to the chaos of the Terror."

As for the manifesto of the Conspiracy of Equals, in part it went as follows: "People of France! For fifteen centuries you lived as slaves and, consequently, unhappily. For the last six years you barely breathe, waiting for independence, freedom and equality. EQUALITY! The first wish of nature, the first need of man, the first bond of all legitimate association! People of France! You were not more blessed than the other nations that vegetate on this unfortunate globe! Everywhere and at all times the poor human race, delivered over to more or less deft cannibals, served as a plaything for all ambitions, as prey for all tyrannies.

"Everywhere and at all times men were lulled with beautiful words; at no time and in no place was the thing itself ever obtained along with the word. From time immemorial they hypocritically repeat to us: all men are equal; and from time immemorial the most degrading and monstrous inequality insolently weighs upon the human race.

François-Noël Babeuf (Gracchus Babeuf) was a journalist who wrote for *The People's Tribune* in France during the Revolutionary period. He was executed for participating in the Conspiracy of Equals.

As long as there have been human societies the most beautiful of humanity's privileges has been recognized without contradiction, but was only once put in practice: equality was nothing but a beautiful and sterile legal fiction, and now that it is called for with an even stronger voice the answer is: be quiet, you wretches! Real equality is nothing but a chimera; be satisfied with conditional equality; you're all equal before the law. What more do you want, filthy rabble? Legislators, rulers, rich landowners, it is now your turn to listen.

"Are we not all equal? This principle remains uncontested, because unless touched by insanity, one can't seriously say it is night when it is day. Well then! We aspire to live and die equal, the way we were born: we want real equality or death; this is what we need, and we'll have this real equality, at whatever the cost. Woe on those who stand between it and us! Woe on those who resist a wish so firmly expressed. The French Revolution is nothing but the precursor of another revolution, one that will be greater, more solemn, and which will be the last. The people marched over the bodies of kings and priests who were in league against it: it will do the same to the new tyrants, the new political Tartuffes seated in the place of the old.

"What do we need besides equality of rights? We need not only that equality of rights written into the Declaration of the Rights of Man and Citizen; we want it in our midst, under the roofs of our houses. We consent to everything for it, to make a clean slate so that we hold to it alone. Let all the arts perish, if need be, as long as real equality remains!

"Legislators and politicians, you have no more genius than you do good faith; gutless and rich landowners, in vain do you attempt to neutralize our holy enterprise by saying: They do nothing but reproduce that agrarian law asked for more than once in the past. Slanderers, be silent: and in the silence of your confusion listen to our demands, dictated by nature and based on justice. The Agrarian law, or the partitioning of land, was the spontaneous demand of some unprincipled soldiers, of some towns moved more by their instinct than by reason. We lean towards something more sublime and more just: the common good or the community of property! No more individual property in land: the land belongs to no one. We demand, we want, the common enjoyment of the fruits of the land: the fruits belong to all.

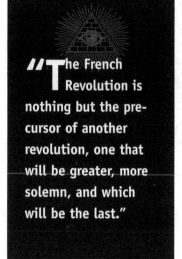

"The French Revolution is nothing but the precursor of another revolution, one that will be greater, more solemn, and which will be the last."

"They say to us: You are disorganizers and seditious; you want nothing but massacres and loot. We won't waste our time responding to them. We tell you: the holy enterprise that we are organizing has no other goal than that of putting an end to civil dissension and public poverty. Never before has more vast a plan been conceived of or carried out. Here and there a few men of genius, a few wise men, have spoken in a low and trembling voice. None have had the courage to tell the whole truth.

"The moment for great measures has arrived. Evil has reached its height: it covers the face of the earth. Under the name of politics, chaos has reigned for too many centuries. Let everything be set in order and take its proper place once again. Let the supporters of justice and happiness organize in the voice of equality. The moment has come to found the REPUBLIC OF EQUALS, the great home open to all men."

Council for National Policy

▮▮ The Council for National Policy (CNP) brings together the country's most influential conservative leaders in business, government, politics, religion, and academia to hear and learn from policy experts on a wide range of issues. In addition, we provide a forum that allows an open exchange between participants, presenting numerous opportunities to cultivate ideas to help solve America's growing problems."

Those are the words of the Council for National Policy, which U.S. president Ronald Reagan described as a "handful of men and women, individuals of character [who] had a vision. A vision to see the return of righteousness, justice, and truth to our great nation."

Alternet reveals some intriguing and illuminating material about the council: "CNP was founded in 1981 by Tim LaHaye, the right-wing, evangelical political motivator and author of the *Left Behind* serial, which chronicles a fictional Armageddon and second coming (in which the non-believers are left behind while believers are carried off in a rapturous moment without their clothes. It gives an eerie ring to the No Child Left Behind Act). LaHaye's empire includes his fingerprints on a number of evangelically oriented, right-wing political action groups, his wife Beverly's Concerned Women for America, along with the twelve *Left Behind* novels, which, according to the author's own web site, have sold 55 million copies worldwide since their introduction in 1995."

Then, we have these words from *Source-Watch*, which offers even more thought-provoking information: "The Council for National Policy (CNP) is a shadowy, secretive group dubbed 'Sith Lords of the Ultra-Right' by the liberal blog *DailyKos*. Mark Crispin Miller called CNP a 'highly secretive ... theocratic organization—what they want is basically religious rule.'"

Public Eye goes a step further, and adds more than a bit of controversial data to the story: "Clothed in secrecy since its founding in 1981, the Council for National Policy is a virtual who's who of the Hard Right. Its membership comprises the Right's Washington operatives and politicians, its financiers, and its hard-core religious arm. The Hard Right utilizes the CNP's three-times-a-year secret meetings to plan its strategy for implementing the radical right agenda. It is here that the organizers and activists meet with the financial backers who put up the money to carry out their agenda.

The late President Ronald Reagan praised the Council for National Policy, an umbrella organization for conservative activists, as a group dedicated to bringing truth and justice to the United States.

"Because CNP rules state that 'meetings are closed to the media and the general public' and 'our membership list is strictly confidential and should not be shared outside the Council,' the mainstream press knows very little about the CNP. Through this site, and the *Freedom Writer*, the Institute for First Amendment Studies is, for the first time, revealing the activities and current membership of the Council for National Policy."

Council on Foreign Relations

In concise terms, the Council on Foreign Relations describes itself as follows: "The Council on Foreign Relations (CFR) is an independent, nonpartisan membership organization, think tank and publisher. Each of these functions makes CFR an indispensable resource in a complex world."

There is, however, far more to the CFR than that. Founded in 1921, the group has close to five thousand members, many of whom are prominent politicians, federal judges, members of the intelligence community (and particularly so the CIA), and high-ranking officials from NATO. Then, there's the matter of U.S. presidents. The list of presidents attached to the CFR has included George H. W. Bush, Bill Clinton, Jimmy Carter, Gerald Ford, Richard Nixon, John F. Kennedy, Dwight Eisenhower, and Herbert Hoover. And, as the *Conspiracy Archive* notes: "If one group is effectively in control of national governments and multinational corporations; promotes world government through control of media, foundation grants, and education; and controls and guides the issues of the day; then they control most options available. The Council on Foreign Relations (CFR), and the financial powers behind it, have done all these things, and promote the 'New World Order,' as they have for over seventy years.

The Harold Pratt House in New York City serves as the headquarters for the Council on Foreign Relations.

"The CFR is the promotional arm of the Ruling Elite in the United States of America. Most influential politicians, academics and media personalities are members, and it uses its influence to infiltrate the New World Order into American life. Its 'experts' write scholarly pieces to be used in decision making, the academics expound on the wisdom of a united world, and the media members disseminate the message."

The *Jeremiah Project* provides the following: "Many of its own members admit the CFR goal is to subvert the democratic process. CFR member and Judge Advocate General of the U.S. Navy Admiral Chester Ward writes 'The main purpose of the (CFR) is promoting the disarmament of U.S. sovereignty and national dependence and submergence into an all powerful, one world government.' This high ranking military officer went on to explain their procedures for influencing policy, claiming: 'Once the ruling members of the CFR shadow government have decided that the U.S. government should adopt a particular policy, the very substantial research facilities of the CFR are put to work to develop arguments, intellectual and emotional, to support the new policy and to confound and discredit, intellectually and politically, any opposition.'"

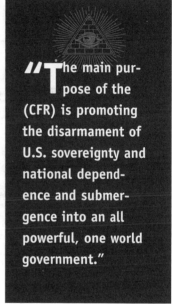

Gary Allen—of *None Dare Call It Conspiracy*—says of the CFR that it is a subsidiary of the Round Table Group. He continues: "This is the group which designed the United Nations—the first major successful step on the road to a World Superstate. At least forty-seven C.F.R. members were among the American delegates to the founding of the United Nations in San Francisco in 1945.… Today the C.F.R. remains active in working toward its final goal of a government over all the world—a government which the Insiders and their allies will control. The goal of the C.F.R. is simply to abolish the United States with its Constitutional guarantees of liberty, and they don't even try to hide it. Study No. 7, published by the C.F.R. on November 25, 1959, openly advocates building a new international order [which] must be responsive to world aspirations for peace, for social and economic change.…"

Cult of the Head

In December 1904, a weird story appeared in the U.K.'s *Hexham Courant* newspaper. The article was titled "Wolf at Large in Allendale." It told a remarkable story: "Local farmers from the village of Allendale, very near to Hexham, had reported the loss of their livestock, so serious that many sheep were being stabled at night to protect them. A shepherd found two of his flock slaughtered, one with its entrails hanging out, and all that remained of the other was its head and horns. Many of the sheep had been bitten about the

The attacks on livestock in Hexham, England, had all the signs of wolf predation, but how could that be when wolves had gone extinct there by the sixteenth century?

neck and the legs—common with an attack made by a wolf. Hysteria soon set in. During the night, lanterns were kept burning to scare away the wolf, and women and children were ordered to keep to the busy roads and be home before dusk. The 'Hexham Wolf Committee' was soon set up to organize search parties and hunts to bring down the beast using specialized hunting dogs, the 'Haydon Hounds', but even they could not find the wolf. The Wolf Committee took the next step and hired Mr. W. Briddick, a trained tracker. But he was also unsuccessful, despite searching the woods."

One month later, in early January 1905, the story took a new turn: the *Hexham Courant*, which was still following the story—given that wolves allegedly became extinct in the U.K. centuries earlier—reported that the body of a wolf had been found dead on a railway track at Cumwinton, Cumbria—which was approximately thirty miles from where the majority of the attacks had been occurring. However, it was the newspaper's firm opinion that this was not the same creature, but another one. In other words, the mystery beast of Hexham was still out there.

According to some theorists, there was a whole pack of such animals wildly roaming the countryside of northern England by night, and although the searches for the animal, or animals, continued for some time, they were finally brought to a halt when the attacks abruptly stopped. Hexham's mysterious and wolfish visitor was gone.

In 1972, however, it may well have returned—albeit in a slightly different guise, and as evidence of this, we have to turn our attention to the bizarre story of the Hexham Heads. The strange saga all began in February 1972. An eleven-year-old boy, Colin Robson, and his younger brother, Leslie, were digging up weeds in their parents' backyard in the town of Hexham, when they unearthed two carved, stone heads, slightly smaller than a tennis ball and very heavy in weight.

Crudely fashioned and weathered-looking, one resembled a skull-like masculine head crowned by a Celtic hairstyle, while the other was a slightly smaller female head that possessed what were said to be witch-like qualities, including the classic beaked nose. Shortly after the boys took the heads into their house, a number of peculiar incidents occurred in the family home. The heads would move by themselves. Household objects were found inexplicably broken, and at one point the boys' sister found her bed showered with glass. It was, however, the next-door neighbors who would go on to experience the most bizarre phenomena of all.

A few nights after the discovery of the heads, a mother living in the neighboring house, Ellen Dodd, was sitting up late with her daughter, who was suffering from a toothache, when both saw what they described as a hellish, "half-man, half-beast" enter the room. Naturally, both screamed for their lives and the woman's husband came running from another room to see what all the commotion was about. By this stage, however, the hairy creature had fled the room and could be heard "padding down the stairs as if on its hind legs." The front door was later found wide open and it was presumed that the creature had left the house in haste.

Crudely fashioned and weathered-looking, one resembled a skull-like masculine head crowned by a Celtic hairstyle, while the other was a slightly smaller female head that possessed what were said to be witch-like qualities....

Soon after that incident, one Anne Ross—a doctor who had studied the Celtic culture and who was the author of several books on the subject, including *Pagan Celtic Britain* and *The Folklore of the Scottish Highlands*—took possession of the stone heads to study them herself. She already had in her possession a number of similar heads and, as a result, she was certain that the Hexham Heads were Celtic in origin, and probably nearly two thousand years old. The *Urban Historian* notes: "It was not surprising that Anne Ross showed an interest in these strange little objects. She had long had a research interest in 'the cult of the head' across Celtic Europe, writing in 1967 that 'the human head was regarded by the Celts as being symbolic of divinity and otherworld powers.'"

The doctor, who lived in the English city of Southampton and about 150 miles from Hexham, had heard nothing at that time of the strange goings-on encountered by the previous owners of the heads. Having put the two stone heads with the rest of her collection, however, Dr. Ross, too, encountered the mysterious werewolf-like creature a few nights later. She awoke from her sleep feeling cold and frightened and, on looking up, found herself confronted by a horrific man-beast identical to that seen at Hexham.

Of the terrible creature, Dr. Ross said: "It was about six feet high, slightly stooping, and it was black, against the white door, and it was half animal and half man. The upper part, I would have said, was a wolf, and the lower part was human and, I would have again said, that it was covered with a kind of black, very dark fur. It went out and I just saw it clearly, and then it disappeared, and something made me run after it, a thing I wouldn't normally have done, but I felt compelled to run after it. I got out of bed and I ran, and I could hear it going down the stairs; then it disappeared toward the back of the house."

The fear-filled affair was not yet over, however: the man-monster manifested in the family home on several more occasions, usually on the staircase and making heavy, "padding" noises as it roamed around under cover of darkness. It wasn't just Dr. Ross who saw the beast: her daughter, Berenice, did too. It soon became clear to Dr. Ross that not only was her family being plagued by a monster, but the house itself appeared to be cloaked by an "evil presence." So, she did the only thing she could to rid the family of the turmoil: she got rid of the stone heads.

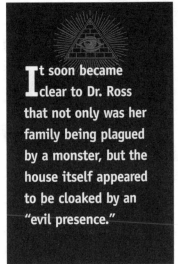

It soon became clear to Dr. Ross that not only was her family being plagued by a monster, but the house itself appeared to be cloaked by an "evil presence."

For a while they were actually on display at the British Museum, later falling into the hands of a man named Don Robins, the author of a book titled *Circles of Silence*, on the subject of ancient, sacred sites. Robins, apparently concerned by the air of negativity that descended upon him when he came into possession of the heads, passed them onto a dowser by the name of Frank Hyde. He decided to try and lessen the malevolent powers of the stones by coating them in a mesh made of copper, which he believed would prevent any supernatural phenomena from being released. Hyde, however, had no wish to hold onto the heads for too long and, as a result, they made their way around more than a few researchers of ancient anomalies. It's most revealing that no one kept them for long. Today, the location, and ownership, of the Hexham Heads is a mystery.

Cult of the Moon Beast

The summer of 1989 was a period when something dark and disturbing descended upon the town of Newport, England: farm animals were found dead under mysterious circumstances. They were not the victims of attack by wild animals, however. Rather, they gave every indication of having been ritually slaughtered; sacrificed, even. One of those who was determined to get to the bottom of the grisly matter was a man named Rob Lea, on whose farm some of the killings occurred.

According to Lea, in August 1989 his father woke to a shocking sight: nothing fewer than five sheep lying dead in a field and placed in circular fashion. Their throats had been cut open, too. Not by savage teeth, however, but by what appeared to have been a very sharp knife. Even worse, the bodily organs of the poor animals had been removed from the bodies and laid out in triangular patterns. Clearly, those responsible were human. But, what kind of human would stealthily kill someone's sheep in the dead of night? And why? Those were the questions swirling around the minds of both Rob Lea and his father. In view of all the above, it's very easy to see why the Lea family concluded that a secret band of "devil worshippers" were the culprits. As it transpires, they were not far from the truth.

Rob Lea's father quickly telephoned the local police, who were soon on the scene and who took the matter very seriously, suggesting that the family should not discuss it with anyone else, lest doing so might provoke deep concern—and maybe hysteria—across Newport and its immediate surroundings. The family, it transpires, was fine with that, as the last thing they wanted was the local media descending on the farm. Despite an intense investigation, the police found themselves with not even a single lead to go on. The outcome was that the matter was eventually dropped, amid apologies to the Lea family that—despite putting more than a few officers on the case—the authorities were at a loss to find the culprit. Or culprits.

> **The Lea family concluded that a secret band of "devil worshippers" were the culprits. As it transpires, they were not far from the truth.**

That wasn't the end of the story, though: Rob Lea decided to briefly become what we might call an amateur detective. He was determined to find the guilty parties, and he may well have done exactly that. I was able to meet personally with Lea in 2000 and listened carefully to his controversial story. Within minutes of us meeting, and from within the confines of a large, padded envelope, Lea extracted seven, 6×4, 35mm, color photographs that clearly and graphically showed the scene of complete carnage at his family's farm eleven years earlier. In other words, and if nothing else, that part of the story could at least be firmly validated. But this was merely the beginning of things—as I had suspected it almost certainly would be after Lea began to divulge the facts.

He continued, with a slightly detectable degree of nerves in his voice, and admitted to me that when he first began digging into the animal mutilation mystery he was, for a short while at least, a firm adherent of the theory that deadly extraterrestrials just might possibly have been behind the predatory attacks. As time progressed, however, and as he delved ever deeper into the heart of the puzzle, he found that, in many ways, something much more disturbing than alien visitations was firmly afoot.

By the late 1990s, said Lea, he had quietly and carefully traveled the length and breadth of the British Isles in hot and diligent pursuit of the answers to the conundrum, and had inadvertently stumbled upon a sinister, and possibly deadly, group of people based near the English city of Bristol—that Lea had grandly dubbed the Cult of the Moon Beast—that, he asserted to me, were using slaughtered farm animals, and even household pets, in ancient rites and archaic rituals of a sacrificial nature.

The purpose of the rites and rituals, said Lea, continuing, was to use the sacrificed unfortunates as a means of conjuring up monstrous entities from some vile netherworld that would then be dispatched to commit who-knew-what atrocities on behalf of their masters in the Cult of the Moon Beast.

It transpired that Lea had been stealthily watching the activities of the Cult of the Moon Beast—which, he stressed several times to me, was merely a term that he, himself, had applied to this closely knit group of individuals that numbered around fifteen—for approximately seven years by the time we met. He admitted he had no firm idea of the group's real name, or even if it actually had a designated moniker.

Although the cult was firmly based in the city of Bristol, England, said Lea, its members were spread both far and wide, with at least four hailing from the east coast town of Ipswich, two from the Staffordshire town of Cannock, two from the city of Exeter, one from Tavistock, Devonshire, and five from Bromley, in the county of Kent.

Lea related to me how he had clandestinely and doggedly tracked the movements of the group and had personally—albeit stealthily—viewed no fewer than three of their dark practices, one of which, he said, had occurred in early 2000 near the Ingrestre Park Golf Club, deep in the heart of the Cannock Chase woods in Staffordshire, which had been the site of numerous encounters

Rob Lea hunted for answers until he discovered what he called the Cult of the Moon Beast, which participated in animal sacrifices.

with a veritable menagerie of mysterious beasts, including werewolves, Bigfoot-type entities, ghostly black dogs, and huge marauding cats.

According to Lea, the Cult of the Moon Beast was engaged in occult-driven rites designed to summon unholy beasts that originated within a realm or dimension that coexisted with ours. He added that certain locales around the country—and, indeed, across the globe—allowed for a doorway or portal to be opened to order, if one followed the correct ancient rites, rituals, and rules of animal sacrifice, of which the Cult of the Moon Beast seemingly had a deep and profound knowledge and awareness. Numerous such portals existed in Devon, Cornwall, and Staffordshire, Lea assured me in an earnest fashion.

Lea told me that the beasts in question were not physical, flesh-and-blood-style beings—at least, not in the way that we, mere mortals, understand things. Rather, they were a form of nonphysical intelligence that could take on the appearance of whatever was in the mind's eye of the beholder—and, more often than not, that of a large black cat.

But why? According to Lea: "Mind-power: fright, suggestion. They'll stop your heart in a beat with fear. You want someone dead, you kill them through fear; fear of the unknown, fear of anything. That's much better than risking taking someone out with a gun or a knife; there's less of a chance of getting caught."

Lea continued further that the Cult of the Moon Beast was linked with some very influential people and that, when needed, the cult was hired for its services—and paid very handsomely, indeed—by the highest echelons of private industry, and even by the intelligence services of the British government. As he explained it to me: "You want someone dead, then you give them a heart-attack by having a monster appearing in their bedroom at night. Or you drive them to suicide by making them think they are going mad if they are seeing werewolves."

An ancient cult, working and killing in stealth? Death by conjured-up, monstrous entities? A conspiracy that reached the heart of the British government? Yes, so Rob Lea claimed.

> **A**ccording to Lea, the Cult of the Moon Beast was engaged in occult-driven rites designed to summon unholy beasts that originated within a realm or dimension that coexisted with ours.

Cult of the Peacock

In the summer of 2006, a large crop circle appeared in a field practically right next door to Chartley Castle, a centuries-old construction in the English county of Staffordshire. Not only that, strewn around the fringes of the crop circle was a not inconsiderable pile of large and colorful peacock feathers.

While the presence of the peacock feathers at the site of the circle was interesting and odd, it wasn't necessarily connected. Or, maybe it was; according to one person, at least. *The Dictionary of Phrase and Fable* recorded that:

"The peacock's tail is the emblem of an Evil Eye, or an ever-vigilant traitor. The tale is this: Argus was the chief Minister of Osiris, King of Egypt. When the king started on his Indian expedition, he left his queen, Isis, regent, and Argus was to be her chief adviser. Argus, with one hundred spies (called eyes), soon made himself so powerful and formidable that he shut up the

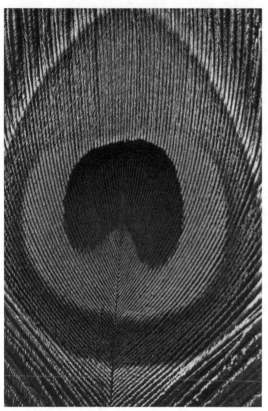

There is an old tradition that the markings on a peacock feather represent the "Evil Eye."

queen-regent in a strong castle, and proclaimed himself king. Mercury marched against him, took him prisoner, and cut off his head; whereupon Juno metamorphosed Argus into a peacock, and set his eyes in its tale."

And with that information now digested, I will acquaint you with the next player in the odd saga of the Chartley Castle apeman. Jane Adams is a devotee of Wicca who I first met in a Wiltshire crop circle back in August 1997. She has an intriguing theory to account for the presence of those out-of-place feathers.

She is of the opinion that the presence of the feathers at Chartley Castle is evidence that the people she believes are guilty of making the formations in the crops use the peacock's "Evil Eye" in what she describes as "black ceremonies."

Adams further claims that these very same ceremonies have been conducted—under the camouflage of the hours of darkness and on a whole variety of occasions—within British-based crop circles, and within ancient stone circles too. And, she adds that those responsible were endeavoring to create negativity and invoke bizarre, life-threatening creatures from darkened realms that coexist with ours, including some that would fit the image of a Bigfoot-type beast seen at Chartley Castle by a man named Mick Dodds and his wife in September 1986. As for the reason why, Adams claims the goal is to harness the beasts and then make use of them in, as she describe it, "psychic assassinations" of people who might be opposed to the activities of the group.

And there was more to come; much more, in fact. Adams also revealed to me that she possessed "personal knowledge"—as she specifically described it—that these same people had engaged in sacrificing animals "near a stone circle in Devon some time ago." The purpose? To try to conjure up, from some ethereal netherworld, both "a black cat" and a creature that would most certainly fit the description of a British Bigfoot and that would then duly perform the group's dark bidding. Adams's comments on this particular matter were of profound significance for one, prime reason: I knew very well that such attacks did occur in just such a fashion that she described, and in the precise locations to which she referred, too.

Dead Sea Scrolls

Longstanding rumors suggest that deeply buried within the heart of the Central Intelligence Agency (CIA) there exists a powerful, elite secret society that takes a deep interest in ancient and religious artifacts. Precisely why such a society should exist is as big a mystery as the legendary artifacts it has sought since 1947, the year in which the CIA was created. Nevertheless, we do have evidence of the existence of this elite and secret organization.

Miles Copeland was someone who spent most of his career working in the shadowy world of international espionage. Prior to joining the CIA in 1947, Copeland learned his spy craft with both the Office of Strategic Services and the Central Intelligence Group. In the post-World War II era, Copeland spent a great deal of time in Damascus, Syria—to the extent that he soon became the CIA's station officer in Damascus, working out of the American Embassy.

On one particular morning in the latter part of 1947, Copeland had a visitor he never forgot: it was a middle-aged man dressed in Bedouin clothing with something under his arm—wrapped in towels—that he dearly wanted to share with Copeland. Intrigued, Copeland invited the man into his office, at which point the man bent down on the floor, and proceeded to open the towels, as Copeland looked on. Contained within them was what Copeland could clearly see was an ancient and decaying parchment. He could also see that they closely resembled the famous Dead Sea Scrolls, which were found at

Qumran, on the northern side of the Dead Sea, in late 1946, and which made major, international news.

The mysterious visitor told Copeland he wanted someone to decipher the text of the parchment—after which he suddenly said his goodbyes and left the building. He was never seen again—at least, not by Copeland or any of his colleagues. Recognizing that this was a matter of deep significance, Copeland contacted a friend of his: Kermit Roosevelt, a man who was a director of the Institute of Arab Affairs and who had close ties to the CIA. Roosevelt was also someone well-versed in translating old Middle Eastern languages. In addition, Copeland took an entire reel of photographs of the extensive scroll—and then something very intriguing happened. Quite out of the blue, Copeland got a phone call from CIA headquarters, ordering him to have all the material—the parchment, the photos, and even the negatives—boxed up and sent by courier to HQ, and to discuss the matter with no one. History has shown that Copeland stayed silent on the matter for decades, finally coming clean in the 1990s, when he wrote his memoirs.

For the rest of his life, Copeland remained puzzled by the extreme secrecy surrounding this particular scroll: what was so special about it that it was

The Dead Sea Scrolls are a collection of ancient texts discovered between 1946 and 1956 in Qumram that date back 1,900 to 2,300 years.

considered a matter of deep concern on the part of the CIA? Why was it seen as being far more profound than the far more famous (but almost identical) Dead Sea Scrolls? The only reply that Copeland got from colleagues was that a "special group" within the CIA was working to understand "the human race's early origins and how religion tied in with it." In addition, Copeland heard rumors that the parchment was an early version of the biblical Book of Daniel, much of which was focused on prophetic material that the "secret group" was interested in determining whether it could be validated—or not. Notably, when Copeland pressed various colleagues on the nature of the group, he was told it would be "wise not to ask."

Decided Ones of Jupiter the Thunderer

An obscure cult that existed in the early part of the nineteenth century, the Decided Ones of Jupiter the Thunderer were brought into existence by Ciro Annunchiarico, who entered this world in Grottaglie, Italy, in December 1775. Initially, all looked good for Annunchiarico: he was born into a family that not only had money, but lots of it. And, he was determined to become a priest, which had been his calling from an early age. As his teens progressed, however, youthful rebellion set in and Annunchiarico became a changed person. While still forging ahead with his planned life in the priesthood, he was caught having sex with the girlfriend of one Giovanni Montolesi, who just happened to be the son of a powerful, local businessman. That's when things really began to change for Annunchiarico—and dangerously so, too.

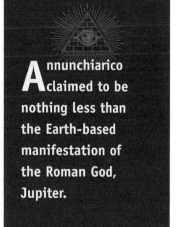

Annunchiarico claimed to be nothing less than the Earth-based manifestation of the Roman God, Jupiter.

In no time at all Montolesi discovered that not only had Annunchiarico seduced his girlfriend, but that the pair had had more than a few clandestine liaisons. Quite understandably, Montolesi verbally lashed out at Annunchiarico for stealing his girl, and also for shaming the Church. Annunchiarico's response was to violently stab Montolesi in the chest. The blade pierced his heart, killing him almost instantly. Annunchiarico was not done with the Montolesis, however. Across a period of around ten weeks, he killed more than a dozen members of the Montolesi family. He had no choice but to flee to nearby mountains—along with a number of friends.

Annunchiarico spent most of his life on the run, avoiding law enforcement officials who were determined to bring Annunchiarico to justice because of his widespread slaughter of the Montolesis. While on the run—and specifically in 1816—he established a violent and murderous cult, the aforementioned Decided Ones of Jupiter the Thunderer. The name was an apt but odd one: Annunchiarico claimed to be nothing less than the Earth-based manifestation of the Roman God, Jupiter. At its peak the group had about 20,000 members—all of whom engaged in robbery, murder, and mayhem. Annunchiarico himself was alleged to have murdered around six dozen people who dared to cross his path.

Inevitably, time ran out for Annunchiarico: in early 1817 he was ambushed by a force of men under the control of an English general named Church. In no time at all, Annunchiarico became a victim of a firing squad and the Decided Ones of Jupiter the Thunderer were no more.

Deros

The editor of the now-acclaimed, and near-legendary, *Amazing Stories* magazine from 1938 to 1949, Ray Palmer, who was born in 1910, had a hell of a hard time as a kid: at the age of only seven, he was involved in a violent accident that shattered his spine, something that significantly stunted his growth and provoked endless health-related issues throughout his entire life.

None of us, unless we have personally undergone such a traumatic event, can even begin to imagine how we might react in the aftermath of such a situation in the formative years of our childhood. Maybe we would do precisely what the young Ray Palmer did: he became somewhat reclusive—as a result of cruel taunts from local kids and ignorant adults. And, from the solitary atmosphere of his bedroom, Palmer buried his head deeply within the imaginative pages of the science-fiction-themed magazines of the 1920s and 1930s.

If the real world was just too much for the deformed and damaged Palmer to deal with, then the realm of futuristic fantasy would have to take its place, and it most certainly did. In the final year of his teens Palmer started coediting his very own fanzine titled *The Comet*, which was enthusiastically and eagerly welcomed by the burgeoning science fiction community of the day. But the biggest event in Palmer's life came in 1938. In fact, it was a veritable dream come true.

Ziff-Davis, the publisher of *Amazing Stories* magazine, had just moved its base of operations from the Big Apple to the Windy City, and, in the process, dumped its editor, one T. O'Connor-Sloane. As Palmer didn't live too far away—in the heart of Milwaukee—and Ziff-Davis knew of *The Comet*, an offer was made to Palmer that he could not, and most certainly did not, refuse: a full-time gig as the editor of *Amazing Stories*.

Today, Palmer's position as head honcho of *Amazing Stories* is remembered, chiefly, for two specific reasons: (a) he bought and published Isaac Asimov's very first science fiction story, titled "Marooned off Vesta," and (b) he became the leading light in a decidedly odd affair that became known as the Shaver Mystery. But, whether the Shaver saga was science fiction or science fact is a matter that still has people guessing and musing to the present day. It's a strange and controversial saga of a secret society of entities living deep below the surface of the Earth.

The Shaver Mystery had its origins at the height of World War II. It was a relatively normal day in 1943 when Palmer was opening the daily delivery of mail that regularly poured into the offices of *Amazing Stories* and came across one particular missive penned by a certain Richard Shaver, and weird barely begins to describe it. Shaver wrote that he, personally, had uncovered a sensational and terrifying secret: in our distant past a race of ancient,

A sketch of Ray Palmer made when he was twenty years old. He would go on to become editor of *Amazing Stories* and *Fate*.

highly evolved entities lived right under our very feet. Massive caverns, huge caves, and near-endless tunnels were the dark, damp places they called home.

At least, that is, before they decided to exit the Earth and headed away to a whole new, light-years away world on the other side of the galaxy. But, when these particular entities said their final goodbyes to our planet, they left behind them something truly sinister and abominable: their diseased offspring, which were said to be called the Deros.

And mentally deranged, sick puppies they were, too. Taunting the human race, finding more and more ways to screw up our lives and plague our minds, and even worse, using us as food were just some of their bad habits. Yes, according to Shaver, human beings were being systematically kidnapped and, equally systematically, devoured by cave-dwelling monsters.

If you were one of the poor souls destined to end up on a Deros dinner plate, it can't have been much fun. But, for Palmer, this is exactly what it was. Not only was Palmer the editor of *Amazing Stories*, but he was a highly astute editor, too. He quickly grasped the significance and potential enormity of the story that had fallen into his lap. He knew it was one that would likely highly entertain the readers of the magazine to an infinite degree, and he realized

Shaver's ranting probably wouldn't hurt sales figures of the magazine, either. History has proven Palmer correct on each and every one of those counts.

Certainly, before he could proceed any further, Palmer realized that he needed much more from Shaver. Important questions needing answering: had Shaver been to this terrifying underworld? Might he even have personally encountered the deadly, psychotic Deros? But, if not, then from where was Shaver getting his information? This is where things get even more warped. Shaver eagerly wrote back to Palmer with the answers, although one is strongly inclined to suspect the answers that came Palmer's way were not the ones he was expecting.

Shaver wrote that, in 1932, he was employed as a welder in a car factory. Most days were routine. One most certainly was not. On the occasion in question, wrote a deadpanning Shaver, his welding gun began talking to him. No, that's not a typo. It did so, said Shaver, in classic, scientific gobbledygook tones, "by some freak of its coil's field attunements." Of course, what else? Telepathically delivered tales of a horrific nature were beamed into what amounted to Shaver's mind, all relative to the Deros, their penchant for human meat, and their underground cities.

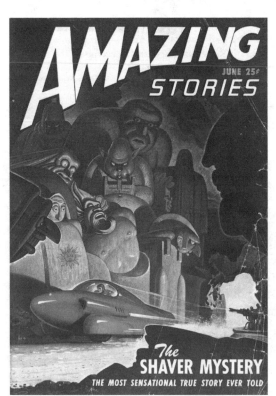

The June 1947 issue of *Amazing Story* in which Richard Shaver relates the tale of the Shaver Mystery.

In fact, so pleased was Shaver by Palmer's quick reply to his original missive that he penned a ten-thousand-plus-word brainstorming story that detailed the salient points of the affair, including the outrageous claim that he, Shaver, had been the captive of the Deros for a number of years, prior to making good his escape, and before ending up in the inevitable cooking pot.

This was absolutely great, thought Palmer, who duly burned the midnight oil, tidying up and editing Shaver's story, which finally appeared in *Amazing Stories*, in March 1945, in a feature titled "I Remember Lemuria." Never mind through the roof: sales of the particular issue went through the stratosphere, and both Palmer and the publisher were delighted. Neither, however, was quite prepared for the thousands of letters that poured into the offices of *Amazing Stories* from a multitude of readers who had become fascinated by the tales of Richard Shaver.

We want more: those were the words coming from the huge readership, and Palmer did not disappoint in the slightest. The Shaver controversy continued for decades, constantly being added to by other characters who claimed knowledge of the Deros and their evil underworld. Today, the entire issue is viewed by the majority of UFO researchers as nothing more than a practical joke, one initiated by Shaver—for whom the expression "nutty as a fruitcake" might very well have been invented—and then expanded upon by Palmer, ever ready to increase the audience size of his cherished magazine, no matter how tall the tale.

That said, Shaver still has a huge following today. And, after all, who really knows what sort of monstrous entities might be lurking and living deep below us?

Devil's Breath Group

On October 23, 1971, a very strange and ominous incident was reported by the U.S. media: "A part-time housekeeper at President Nixon's Key Biscayne retreat has testified she was put in a hypnotic daze by a stranger who told her to shoplift four dresses. Shirley Cromartie, 32, and a mother of three, pleaded no contest Thursday and was given a suspended sentence after law enforcement officers and a psychiatrist testified they believed she was telling the truth. Mrs. Cromartie holds a security clearance to work in the Florida White House, according to testimony. She said a woman met her in a parking lot and asked the time, then ordered her to take the items and bring them to her.

"Mrs. Cromartie testified she fell into a daze when the young woman released a jasmine-like scent from her left hand. 'I just sort of lost my will … it was a terrifying experience,' she testified. Mrs. Cromartie joined the Key Biscayne White House housekeeping staff about a year ago, according to FBI agent Leo McClairen. He testified her background was impeccable.

"Dr. Albert Jaslow, a psychiatrist, said he examined her and found she could be hypnotized 'quickly and easily' and believed she was telling the truth. 'But it wasn't the same when he hypnotized me,' Mrs. Cromartie said. 'I couldn't remember anything afterwards. Whatever that young woman did to me, it was like being in a sleep-walk, only awake.'"

As the media continued to dig into the story, things got even stranger. The mysterious woman with the mind-altering, "jasmine-like scent" was described as being attractive, young, dressed completely in black, and wearing a wig. Metro Court judge Frederick Barad said of this surreal saga: "This is all so bizarre that I'm frightened what could happen to the president."

Almost certainly, "the jasmine-like scent" was a substance that is known officially as scopolamine, but which has a far more ominous slang name: The Devil's Breath. It is synthesized from the borrachero tree, which grows widely in Colombia. Aside from its jasmine-like odor, scopolamine is a powerful drug, exposure to which can almost instantaneously take away a person's free will, self-preservation, and self-control. To demonstrate its power, there are accounts—from Colombia—of people exposed to scopolamine emptying their bank account, and handing over their precious savings to criminals using the drug against unwitting souls. It's no wonder, then, that Mrs. Cromartie acted in such a strange, detached, and atypical fashion. But that's not all.

The CIA made great use of scopolamine at the height of the Cold War, using it on captured Soviet spies and defecting agents. Britain's intelligence agency, MI6, has even been rumored to have used scopolamine to provoke troublesome characters—those having a bearing on national security issues—into committing suicide. That Mrs. Cromartie worked for the U.S. government—and for no less a source than the president of the United States—makes one wonder if there was some sort of presently unclear connection between her experience, the Nixon administration, and the secret CIA world of scopolamine use and manipulation of the human mind.

Indeed, that may well have been the case, as heavily redacted FBI files—declassified under Freedom of Information legislation—point in the direction of a secret Devil's Breath Group operating in the United States in the 1970s, and specifically using scopolamine as a means to secure state secrets from those targeted by the group and its mind-altering weaponry.

Diana, Princess of Wales, Death

When Diana, Princess of Wales, was killed in a car crash in Paris, France, on August 31, 1997, the world was shocked. But, was Diana's death nothing stranger than a tragic accident? Not everyone is quite so sure. Indeed, there is a wealth of material linking Diana's death to the secret activities of certain, clandestine, powerful groups. *Vigilant Citizen* provides the following:

"Similarly to the Virgin Mary, Diana had (and still has) legions of followers, worshiping her giving nature and her maternal energy. In other words, she seems to fulfill the almost inherent need in human beings to worship a female goddess, giver of life and filled with compassion. The media has been a key actor in the creation of this icon by documenting every detail of her fairytale wedding, her troubled marriage, her humanitarian activities and, finally, her untimely death. Was Diana picked and groomed to become a sort of a 'modern day Goddess' to ultimately be sacrificed, in accordance with ancient pagan practices? This might sound preposterous to the average *National Inquirer* reader, but not to the connoisseur of the occult practices of the world elite. Furthermore, numerous clues and symbols have been placed by this group to subtly commemorate the occult nature of Lady Di's death."

Vigilant Citizen continues: "The city of Paris was built by the Merovingians, a medieval dynasty which ruled France for numerous generations. Before converting to Christianity, the Merovingian religion was a mysterious brand of paganism. The Pont D'Alma Tunnel was a sacred site dedicated to the Moon Goddess Diana, where they used to practice ritual sacrifices. During those ceremonies, it was of an utmost importance that the sacrificed victim died inside the underground temple. The assassination of Diana was a reenactment of this ancient pagan tradition."

As for who, exactly, the Merovingians were, James Wiener provides this: "Mythologized and circumscribed for over 1,500 years, the

Diana, Princess of Wales, died in 1997, when her limousine crashed while trying to escape a hoard of paparazzi.

Merovingians were a powerful Frankish dynasty, which exercised control over much of modern-day France, Germany, Switzerland, Austria, and the Low Countries. During the Early Middle Ages, the Merovingian kingdoms were arguably the most powerful and most important polities to emerge after the collapse of the Western Roman Empire, blending Gallo-Roman institutions with Germanic Frankish customs."

IlluminatiWatcher expands on this issue: "The Merovingian dynasty worshiped the goddess Diana, and the murder of Princess Diana is a ritual sacrifice to the goddess Diana. To believe this, we must believe that the Merovingian dynasty secretly retained power up to present day, which isn't too far of a stretch. If the British Royal Family can continue to hold a position of power over the citizens simply because they have a 'superior' blood, perhaps France has Merovingian bloodlines in positions of power unknown to the citizens."

Intriguing words, to say the very least.

Dianic Cult

In 1921, Margaret Alice Murray wrote an acclaimed book titled *The Witch-Cult in Western Europe*. A renowned expert in her field, Murray spent much of her

Francisco Goya's painting "Witches' Sabbath," c. 1797, depicts witches worshipping an animal god.

time studying ritual witchcraft, or as she termed it, the Dianic Cult. She said that it "embraces the religious beliefs and ritual of the people, known in late mediaeval times as 'Witches.' The evidence proves that underlying the Christian religion was a cult practiced by many classes of the community, chiefly, however, by the more ignorant or those in the less thickly inhabited parts of the country. It can be traced back to pre-Christian times, and appears to be the ancient religion of Western Europe. The god, anthropomorphic or theriomorphic, was worshiped in well-defined rites; the organization was highly developed; and the ritual is analogous to many other ancient rituals. The dates of the chief festivals suggest that the religion belonged to a race which had not reached the agricultural stage; and the evidence shows that various modifications were introduced, probably by invading peoples who brought in their own beliefs. I have not attempted to disentangle the various cults; I am content merely to point out that it was a definite religion with beliefs, ritual, and organization as highly developed as that of any other cult in the world.

"The deity of this cult was incarnate in a man, a woman, or an animal; the animal form being apparently earlier than the human, for the god was often spoken of as wearing the skin or attributes of an animal. At the same time, however, there was another form of the god in the shape of a man with two faces. Such a god is found in Italy (where he was called Janus or Dianus), in Southern France, and in the English Midlands. The feminine form of the name, Diana, is found throughout Western Europe as the name of the female deity or leader of the so-called Witches, and it is for this reason that I have called this ancient religion the Dianic cult."

Dick, Philip K.

One of the foremost figures in the field of science fiction writing, Philip K. Dick was the author of many novels, including *Do Androids Dream of Electric Sheep?* In 1982, it was made into a blockbuster Hollywood movie, *Blade*

Runner. Then, in 2011, Dick's short story of 1954, *Adjustment Team*, was made into a hit movie starring Matt Damon, *The Adjustment Bureau*. It's to Dick's relationship to the FBI that we have to turn our attention, however. According to what Dick told the Bureau, in 1972 he had uncovered details of a highly secret Nazi cabal in the United States that was trying to infiltrate the world of science fiction to further its aims and goals. In other words, science fiction authors were being threatened and bullied by this secret group into promoting Nazi ideologies in their stories.

On October 28, 1972, Dick wrote the following to the FBI: "I am a well-known author of science fiction novels, one of which dealt with Nazi Germany (called *Man in the High Castle*, it described an 'alternate world' in which the Germans and the Japanese won World War Two and jointly occupied the United States). This novel, published in 1962 by Putnam & Co., won the Hugo Award for Best Novel of the Year and hence was widely read both here and abroad; for example, a Japanese edition printed in Tokyo ran into several editions."

Dick continued and got to the point of his letter: "I bring this to your attention because several months ago I was approached by an individual who I have reason to believe belonged to a covert organization involved in politics, illegal weapons, etc., who put great pressure on me to place coded information in future novels 'to be read by the right people here and there,' as he phrased it. I refused to do this."

The FBI was further told by the famous writer: "The reason why I am contacting you about this now is that it now appears that other science fiction writers may have been so approached by other members of this obviously Anti-American organization and may have yielded to the threats and deceitful statements such as were used on me. Therefore I would like to give you any and all information and help I can regarding this, and I ask that your nearest office contact me as soon as possible."

Dick added: "I heard only one code identification by this individual: Solarcon-6."

In further correspondence, Dick revealed that on November 17, 1971, his house—on Hacienda Way, Santa Venetia—was broken into and "extensively robbed." A follow-up break-in occurred in March 1972. Dick said that, "My realtor, Mrs. Annie Reagan had stored my things and at least one room of stuff is missing; the bedroom in which the control system of the burglar alarm was located, the one room not covered by the scanner. Obviously it was robbed by someone who intimately knew the layout of the alarm system and how to bypass it."

Dick had a few ideas as to who was responsible: "Only two or three persons that I can recall knew the layout of the burglar alarm system. One was Harold Kinchen, who was under investigation by Air Force Intelligence at

Hamilton Field…. It had to do with an attempt on the arsenal of the Air Force Intelligence people at Hamilton on I recall January first of this year."

The story got even more complicated, as Dick revealed: "I have come to know something about the rightwing paramilitary Minutemen illegal people here—they tell me confidentially that from my description of events surrounding that November robbery of my house, the methods used, the activities of Harry Kinchen in particular, it sounds to them like their counterparts up there, and possibly even a neo-Nazi group….

"Kinchen is an ardent Nazi trained in such skills as weapons-use, explosives, wire-tapping, chemistry, psychology, toxins and poisons, electronics, auto repair, sabotage, the manufacture of narcotics."

Over the course of several more months, Dick detailed for the FBI yet further information he believed supported the notion that a highly secret, well-funded, cabal of Nazis—a secret society, determined to revive Adolf Hitler's Third Reich—existed in the United States. We may never know to what extent Philip K. Dick was onto something, as many of the pages contained within the FBI's files on the man are, to this day, classified under national security legislation, which in itself is highly intriguing for someone who was, chiefly, a writer of sci-fi.

Dowsers

One of the strangest skills and talents allegedly possessed by humans is water divining, or dowsing as it is more popularly known. While there is not, specifically, a secret society of dowsers, those who practice this ancient tradition are very careful to protect the secrets behind their uncanny skills. Although the ability of the dowser to locate water by unconventional means is looked on with suspicion and skepticism in some quarters, for many it is an age-old tradition that remains as absolutely relevant and vital today as it was centuries ago.

Not only that: the skill has attracted the secret attention of some quite unlikely parties, including the U.S. intelligence community, the government of the former Soviet Union, Adolf Hitler, the British Police Force, and a department of the British government that played a key role in the battle against the Nazis during World War II.

The CIA, for example, has in its archives nothing less than a file on dowsing that is, quite literally, of biblical proportions, and it all revolves around a certain Mount Horeb, where, according to the book of Deuteronomy in the Hebrew Bible, Moses received the Ten Commandments from God. And although some biblical students perceive Mount Horeb and Mount Sinai to be one and the same, a significant number of scholars most certainly do not. Thus, we may never know for sure precisely where Moses allegedly received the legendary commandments.

One of the tales attached to the story of Mount Horeb is that when the Israelites were in the wilderness and perilously short of fresh drinking water, Moses supposedly climbed the mountain and struck a particular piece of rock, which cracked open and—lo and behold—water came pouring out, thus saving the Israelites from otherwise certain death by dehydration. An early example of dowsing, perhaps?

Certainly, the CIA considered it to be just such a possibility. While it may sound strange to suggest the CIA has taken an interest in dowsing—and chiefly from the era of Moses, no less—this is, incredibly, most certainly the case, and the CIA is not the only official agency to have displayed such interest in matters relative to water divining.

Moving on, in 1978, staff at the Foreign Technology Division (FTD) at Wright-Patterson Air Force Base, in Dayton, Ohio, prepared an extensive paper titled *Paraphysics R&D—Warsaw Pact* [R&D referring to Research and Development]. Page twenty-three of the document details positive results of both American and Soviet research in the field of dowsing. Notably, a copy of the entire FTD document was sent to the CIA's Office of Science and Technology (OSI) shortly after its publication.

And, on more than several occasions, as additional Air Force files reveal, Adolf Hitler consulted German dowsers as a means to try and determine the most profitable locales where he could get deep, restful sleep in between waging war on the Allies. And speaking of the Allies, during World War II, England's Warwickshire Police Force secretly used one of its own officers skilled in the art of dowsing to try and locate the bodies of two local men—James Hiatt and Harry Marston—who had been buried under the rubble caused by the bombs of Nazi Germany. We assume that dowsing is something specifically employed to locating underground bodies of water, and certainly not secret searches for dead bodies. Our assumption is wrong, very wrong in fact.

A once-classified report of July 1941 that was prepared by a Sergeant J. Hall of Warwickshire Police states: "I was at the scene when I noticed P.C. 319 Terry coming from a nearby

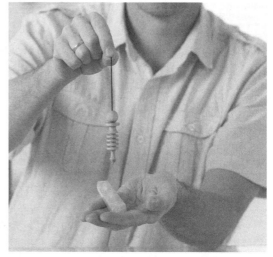

Although sticks are usually used, a pendant also suffices to practice dowsing.

thicket fashioning a forked stick with a pen-knife. P.C. Terry commenced to walk over the bomb craters. About 30 seconds later he came to a standstill and I noticed that the forked stick which he was holding had commenced to wriggle very violently and he had great difficulty in holding it. He pointed to a particular portion of heaped soil near to one of the craters and said: 'They are under there.'"

Sergeant Hall added: "A quarter of an hour later the bodies of both men were recovered." As the files also reveal, Police Constable Terry had a solid—and growing—reputation in the field of dowsing, and his skills were used on several occasions in matters of a similar, secret nature. For a while, at least, they were. It wasn't long, however, before that situation changed drastically.

Notably, official files on this particular matter reveal that the British government's Ministry of Home Security expressed deep skepticism and concern over the whole affair and concluded that the Warwickshire Police Force's use of "spiritualism" and "the mysterious" in such a fashion during wartime was "particularly dangerous." Clearly, there were those at an official level in the U.K. who did not wish to see the world of the unknown playing a role in warfare.

From the CIA to Soviet Russia, and from Adolf Hitler to the British Police Force, dowsing is a matter that has attracted profound and secret interest. And maybe that profound and secret interest still continues.

Druids

In 1861, W. Winwood Reade—a well-regarded authority on not just the history of the Druids, but also of their teachings and beliefs, said: "This priesthood flourished in Gaul and in Britain, and in the islands which encircled them. In whichever country they may first have struck root we at least know that the British Druids were the most famous, and that it was a custom in the time of Julius Caesar for the Gallic students to cross the British channel to study in the seminaries of the sister island. But by that time, Druidism had begun to wane in Gaul, and to be deprived of many of its privileges by the growing intelligence of the secular power."

But, let's not get too ahead of ourselves. The Druidic religion—to give it its most accurate title—takes its inspiration from ancient cults that worshipped the world of fertility. That worship included sacrificial offerings to gods of the Earth and of the sky, and they weren't just animal sacrifices, but human offerings, too. So far as can be determined, the world of the Druids reached a period of organized solidity around 350 B.C.E. That solidity also ensured that many of the previously warring, Celtic tribes in what is now the United Kingdom had something that finally unified them—rather than something that caused the Celts to splinter and engage in violent turf wars, as had been their previous activities. Toyne Newton, who has made a careful appraisal of the history of the Druids, says that under their management, "the beginnings of a fighting army and warrior class of Celt emerged."

And they looked impressive, mysterious, and imposing, as W. Winwood Reade made abundantly clear: "In all things, therefore, they endeavored to draw a line between themselves and the mass. In their habits, in their demeanor, in their very dress. They wore long robes which descended to the heel, while that of others came only to the knee; their hair was short and their beards long, while the Britons wore but moustaches on their upper lips, and their hair generally long. Instead of sandals they wore wooden shoes of a pentagonal shape, and carried in their hands a white wand called *slatan drui' eachd*, or magic wand, and certain mystical ornaments around their necks and upon their breasts."

As evidence of the way in which the world and landscape dominated the beliefs of the Druids, the late anomalies researcher and author John Michell offered the following, which gets into highly alternative skills, and even near-paranormal activity: "It is certain that underground caverns, both natural and artificial, were the scenes of prehistoric magical rites. In several cases their entrances have been found directed onto leys [ley lines] or towards significant astronomical declinations. The druids, in common with the shamans of Asia and North America are said to have accomplished magical flights, often from those very mounds and hill-tops where the great heroes of mythology achieved their apotheosis. There may be something about such places which attracts those forces capable of modifying the normal influence of gravity, or which, alternatively, reacts upon an intensified field of human magnetism to produce circumstances conducive to levitation."

The Druids are known to have spread far and wide, as Reade revealed back in the nineteenth century: "Some centuries ago in a

The Druids were largely conquered by the Romans and Julius Caesar in the first century, after which their religion was suppressed or banned in the empire.

monastery upon the borders of Vaitland, in Germany, were found six old statues which being exposed to view, Conradus Celtes, who was present, was of opinion that they were figures of ancient Druids. They were seven feet in height, bare-footed, their heads covered with a Greek hood, a scrip by their sides and a beard descending from their nostrils plaited out in two divisions to the middle; in their hands a book and a Diogenes staff five feet in length; their features stern and morose; their eyes lowered to the ground. Such evidence is mere food for conjecture. Of the ancient German priests we only know that they resembled the Druids, and the medicine-men of the American aborigines in being doctors as well as priests."

The Druids, Reade expanded, possessed remarkable powers and immunities. Like the Levites, the Hebrews, and the Egyptian priests, they were exempt from paying taxes and from serving in the military. They also annually elected the magistrates of cities: they educated all children of whatever station, not permitting their parents to receive them till they were fourteen years of age. Thus the Druids were regarded as the real fathers of the people.

On top of that, and demonstrating the incredible power the Druids yielded, they held sway over not just the folk of the land, but over kings and queens, too. This is an area that Reade was particularly learned on: "The Persian Magi were entrusted with the education of their sovereign; but in Britain the kings were not only brought up by the Druids, but also relieved by them of all but the odium and ceremonies of sovereignty. These terrible priests formed the councils of the state, and declared peace or war as they pleased. The poor slave whom they seated on a throne, and whom they permitted to wear robes more gorgeous even than their own, was surrounded, not by his noblemen, but by Druids. He was a prisoner in his court, and his jailors were inexorable, for they were priests."

And, finally, we have this from Reade, whose words from 1871 are as valuable and insightful today as they were when he wrote them: "It may naturally excite surprise that a nation should remain so barbarous and illiterate as the Britons undoubtedly were, when ruled by an order of men so polished and so learned. But these wise men of the West were no less learned in human hearts than in the triplet verses, and oral of their fathers. They imbibed with eagerness the heathen rites of the Phúnician Cabiri, and studied to involve their doctrines and their ceremonies in the deepest mystery. They knew that it is almost impossible to bring women and the vulgar herd of mankind to piety and virtue by the unadorned dictates of reason. They knew the admiration which uneducated minds have always for those things which they cannot understand. They knew that to retain their own sway they must preserve these barren minds in their abject ignorance and superstition. These Druids were despots; and yea they must have exercised their power wisely and temperately to have retained so long their dominion over a rude and warlike race."

Dulce Secret Base

Longstanding rumors suggest that a vast underground alien base exists within, and below, a massive mesa at Dulce, New Mexico. Interestingly, we can prove there has been a wealth of weird activity in the area. For example, the FBI has officially declassified a large file on cattle mutilations in and around Dulce, spanning the mid to late 1970s. And, on December 10, 1967, the Atomic Energy Commission (AEC) detonated a twenty-nine kiloton nuclear device 4,240 feet below ground level, in an attempt to provoke the release and, as a direct consequence, production of natural gas. Thus was born Gasbuggy: a program of an overall project known as Operation Plowshare, which, ostensibly, was designed to explore the peaceful uses of atomic energy. Notably, the location of the Gasbuggy test—that covered an area of 640 acres—was New Mexico's Carson National Forest, which just happens to be situated only twelve miles from the town of Dulce. Today, people are forbidden from digging underground in that very area—which is interesting in view of the underground base allegations.

Longstanding rumors suggest that a vast underground alien base exists within, and below, a massive mesa at Dulce, New Mexico.

Within conspiracy-based research circles, it has been suggested that the nuclear detonation had a very different goal; namely, to destroy the aforementioned alien base and wipe out the deadly, hostile ETs. Certainly, it's a strange and foreboding story, and there are no shortages of accounts suggesting that such a base existed (and may still exist), and in which freakish monsters were being created by the alien entities. As one example of many, we have the following, from someone we might justifiably call a ufological whistleblower: "Sir, first off, if you want the full story let me know. But this will explain how Mothman came about. U.S. Energy Secretary John Herrington named the Lawrence Berkeley Laboratory and New Mexico's Los Alamos National Laboratory to house advanced genetic research centers as part of a project to decipher the human genome. The genome holds the genetically coded instructions that guide the transformation of a single cell, a fertilized egg, into a biological organism.

"'The Human Genome Project may well have the greatest direct impact on humanity of any scientific initiative before us today,' said David Shirley, Director of the Berkeley Laboratory. Covertly, this research has been going on for years at the Dulce bio-genetics labs. Level 6 is hauntingly known by employees as 'Nightmare Hall.' It holds the genetic labs at Dulce. Reports from workers who have seen bizarre experimentation, are as follows: "I have seen multi-legged 'humans' that look like half-human/half-octopus. Also reptilian-humans, and furry creatures that have hands like humans and [cry] like a baby, [they mimic] human words. Also, huge mixtures of lizard-humans in cages. There are fish, seals, birds and mice that can barely be considered those species. There are several cages (and vats) of winged-humanoids, grotesque bat-like creatures, but 3 1/2 to 7 feet tall. Gargoyle-like beings and Draco-Reptoids.

"Level 7 is worse, row after row of thousands of humans and human mixtures in cold storage. Here too are embryo storage vats of humanoids in various stages of development. I frequently encountered humans in cages, usually dazed or drugged, but sometimes they cried and begged for help. We were told they were hopelessly insane, and involved in high risk drug tests to cure insanity. We were told to never try to speak to them at all."

Egyptian Magicians

A study of the history, lore, and beliefs of the ancient Egyptians has revealed that they were highly reliant on the teachings and secret activities of those learned in the fields of mysticism, and the worlds of the supernatural and the paranormal. We're talking about Egyptian magicians. One of the most knowledgeable figures in the field of such issues was E. A. Wallis Budge. The British Museum says of Budge: "Born 27 July 1857 in Bodmin, Cornwall; taught himself Hebrew and Syriac, and copied cuneiform inscriptions at The British Museum, before going to study Semitic languages at Christ's College Cambridge from October 1878, and where he became Tyrwhitt Hebrew scholar. He joined the British Museum as an assistant in 1883 and where he eventually became Keeper of Egyptian and Assyrian Antiquities from 1894–1924. As early as 1886 he visited Egypt under instructions to supply antiquities to the BM. Died 23 November 1934. He was a Fellow of the Society of Antiquaries and was knighted in 1920. He married Dora Helen Emerson on 24 March 1883. Budge energetically acquired a large number of antiquities and manuscripts during the course of his work in Egypt and Mesopotamia. His three trips to these countries in 1887, 1888 and 1890 are described rather colorfully in his book 'By Nile and Tigris' (London, 1920). He gained the Arabic nicknames of 'Father of Skulls' and 'Father of Antiquities' as a direct result of his collecting activities in Egypt and Sudan. He was a prolific writer on Assyriological and Egyptological matters, and edited Syriac and Ethiopian manuscripts."

In 1901, Budge said of his studies in the field of Egyptians magicians: "Many writers on the Egyptian religion have somewhat blinked the fact that it had two sides; on the one it closely resembles in many respects the Christian religion of to-day, and on the other the religion of many of the sects which flourished in the first three or four centuries of our era, and which may be said to have held beliefs which were part Christian and part non-Christian. In its non-Christian aspect it represents a collection of ideas and superstitions which belong to a savage or semi-savage state of existence, and which maintained their hold in a degree upon the minds of the Egyptians long after they had advanced to a high state of civilization."

He continued that while we may think that such ideas and beliefs are both childish and foolish, there is no possible reason for doubting that they were very real things to those who held them, and whether they are childish or foolish or both they certainly passed into the religion of the people of Egypt, wherein they grew and flourished, and were, at least many of them, adopted by the Egyptian converts to Christianity, or Copts.

"Reference is made to them," he added, "in the best classical works of the ancient Egyptians, and it is more than probable that from them they found their way into the literatures of the other great nations of antiquity, and through the Greeks, Romans, Arabs, and others into the countries of Europe. In the following pages an attempt will be made to place in the reader's hands the evidence as to the magical side of the Egyptian religion, which would have been out of place in the former work, the object of which was to describe beliefs of a more spiritual nature. But, as in the book on the Egyptian Ideas of the Future Life, the facts here given are drawn from papyri and other native documents, and the extracts are quoted from compositions which were actually employed by the Egyptians to produce magical effects."

Budge said that there are two distinct kinds of Egyptian magic: "(1) that which was employed for legitimate purposes and with the idea of benefiting either the living or the dead, and (2) that which was made use of in the furtherance of nefarious plots and schemes and was intended to bring calamities upon those against whom it was directed."

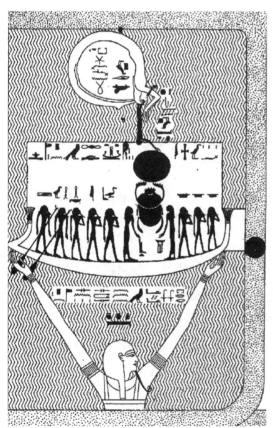

A drawing by E. A. Wallis Budge showing the god Nu lifting the boat of the Sun god, Ra.

He expanded: "In the religious texts and works we see how magic is made to be the handmaiden of religion, and how it appears in certain passages side by side with the most exalted spiritual conceptions; and there can be no doubt that the chief object of magical books and ceremonies was to benefit those who had by some means attained sufficient knowledge to make use of them. But the Egyptians were unfortunate enough not to be understood by many of the strangers who found their way into their country, and as a result wrong and exaggerated ideas of their religion were circulated among the surrounding nations, and the magical ceremonies which were performed at their funerals were represented by the ignorant either as silly acts of superstition or as tricks of the 'black' art.

"But whereas the magic of every other nation of the ancient East was directed entirely against the powers of darkness, and was invented in order to frustrate their fell designs by invoking a class of benevolent beings to their aid, the Egyptians aimed being able to command their gods to work for them, and to compel them to appear at their desire. These great results were to be obtained by the use of certain words which, to be efficacious, must be uttered in a proper tone of voice by a duly qualified man; such words might be written upon some substance, papyrus, precious stones, and the like, and worn on the person, when their effect could be transmitted to any distance. As almost every man, woman, and child in Egypt who could afford it wore some such charm or talisman, it is not to be wondered at that the Egyptians were at a very early period regarded as a nation of magicians and sorcerers. Hebrew, and Greek, and Roman writers referred to them as experts in the occult sciences, and as the possessors of powers which could, according to circumstances, be employed to do either good or harm to man."

Fabian Society

According to its members, "The Fabian Society is Britain's oldest political think tank. Founded in 1884, the Society is at the forefront of developing political ideas and public policy on the left. We aim to promote: greater equality of power, wealth and opportunity; the value of collective action and public service; an accountable, tolerant and active democracy; citizenship, liberty and human rights; sustainable development; multilateral international cooperation.

"The society is alone among think tanks in being a democratically constituted membership organization, with almost 7,000 members. The Fabian Society is governed by the democratically elected Executive Committee while the day-to-day operation of the society is overseen by the General Secretary.

"The society was one of the original founders of the Labor Party and is constitutionally affiliated to the party as a Socialist Society. These are membership

This plaque identifies the original location of the Fabian Society in London, England.

organizations in sympathy with the party, which sit alongside trade unions as organizational members. The society is however editorially, organizationally and financially independent of the Labor Party and works with a wide range of partners of all political persuasions and none.

"We are not a doctrinal organization but the Fabian tradition informs how we think and what we do. No other think tank has an adjective of its own. Our commitment to Fabianism means we believe in the fight against inequality, the power of collective action and an internationalist outlook. We believe in social progress, evidence, expertise, rationality and long-termism. We advocate gradualist, reformist and democratic means in a journey towards radical ends. We are a pluralist movement and create space for open debate."

All well and good, except for one thing: not everyone is quite so sure the Fabian Society is as open, innocent, and benevolent as it suggests. The Fabian Society website (which is actually an anti-Fabians website and should not, therefore, be confused with the official website of the Fabian Society) states: "The Fabian Society has … been close to the Rockefellers who are covert Fabian Socialists. David Rockefeller wrote a sympathetic senior thesis on Fabian Socialism at Harvard and studied left-wing economics at the Fabian Society's London School of Economics. Not surprisingly, the Rockefellers have funded countless Fabian projects (including the LSE) from the early 1920s.

"The Fabian Society continues to be funded by subversive entities like the European Commission and the Foundation for European Progressive Studies (FEPS), an EU-wide operation co-funded by the European Parliament, which works for a Socialist Europe, and it operates in partnership with global companies like Pearson, a long-time Lazard and Rothschild associate (Pearson has been a major stockholder in the Milner Group's bank Lazard from the early 1900s and co-owns The Economist Group with the Rothschilds)."

Federal Emergency Management Agency

Established in 1978 and fully functional by 1979, FEMA—the Federal Emergency Management Agency—has the role of providing relief and support in the event that large scale disasters occur in the United States. There is, however, one key and important stipulation: a state of emergency has to be officially declared before FEMA can officially act, something that a state governor or the president has the power to declare. When formally created, FEMA took on the responsibility of running the nation's entire civil defense programs, which were previously overseen by the Department of Defense. In the wake of the terrible events of September 11, 2001, however, FEMA was radically reorganized and integrated into the newly created Department of Homeland Security (DHS), which came into being in November 2002.

Since becoming an integral part of the DHS, FEMA, which has an annual budget of $10 billion, has played leading roles in managing many high profile disasters, including Hurricane Katrina, which, in 2005, pummeled New Orleans; the Buffalo, New York, snowstorm of 2006; and the raging fires that devastated much of southern California in 2007. There is, however, a reported darker side to FEMA.

In the wake of the terrible events of September 11, 2001, however, FEMA was radically reorganized and integrated into the newly created Department of Homeland Security....

Within the field of conspiracy theories and cover-ups, much attention has been given to the subject of what have become known as "FEMA camps." Supposedly, according to the theorists that hold such beliefs, the camps are being secretly created for the day when the people of the United States will be placed under martial law, and any and all individuals the government considers to be undesirables will be rounded up and placed in such detention camps for indefinite periods—perhaps even for the rest of their lives.

At the extreme end of this particularly controversial area of conspiracy research, there are those who suspect that Nazi-style concentration camps are also being built in stealth, where thousands upon thousands of people who the government views as troublesome and a threat to national security—such as agitators, activists, and demonstrators—will be put to death at a time of a nationwide crisis.

While those of a skeptical nature might dismiss such controversial issues, consider the following words of author Brad Steiger: "Among the concerns of many serious-minded guardians of America's freedoms and liberties is an executive order signed into existence by President George H. W. Bush in 1989. This document authorized FEMA to build forty-three primary camps, each of which would have the capacity of housing 35,000 to 45,000 people, and hundreds of secondary facilities, some of which could accommodate 100,000 individuals."

Food for thought, indeed.

Fountain of the World

It was in the 1940s that one Francis Herman Penovic—who went by the very different name of Krishna Venta—created what was popularly known as the Fountain of the World. Its official title, however, was WKFL Fountain of the World; the WKFL meaning "Wisdom, Knowledge, Faith, and Love." It was a pretty harmless group, albeit one that had its moments of violence and even death. The Fountain of the World had its base of operations in Simi Valley, California, and it thrived very nicely—which is hardly surprising, given that those who chose to join the cult were required to hand over their entire belongings and life savings. Members were also made to wear what became the *de rigeur* Fountain of the World uniform—namely, robes and sandals.

The group was very much a benevolent one, working to improve conditions for the homeless who lived on the streets in Simi Valley—usually by

Krishna Venta (seated at center) holds a meeting in Worcester, England, in this 1949 photo. He considered himself to be the new incarnation of Christ.

offering beds and food at the Fountain of the World headquarters. Without doubt, the most visible example of the Fountain of the World's determination to help whenever and wherever it could surfaced on July 12, 1949. That was the date on which a Standard Airlines aircraft slammed into the Simi Hills, killing around three-quarters of those on board. Members of the Fountain of the World were quickly on the scene to try and lend whatever help they could.

Like so many cult leaders, Venta had delusions of grandeur. Just one year before the tragic crash of Flight 897R into the Simi Hills, he proclaimed: "I may as well say it: I am Christ. I am the new messiah." UFOs even came into the story: Venta/Jesus maintained he had spent time on a planet called Neophrates and had commanded a veritable armada of spacecraft from Neophrates to the Earth, and as is the case with so many cult leaders, it all ended violently.

On December 10, 1958, two men—Ralph Muller and Peter Duma Kamenoff, both of whom were ex-members of the Fountain of the World, and who believed Venta had been engaged in affairs with their wives—planned to go on a suicide-driven bombing mission to kill Venta. They succeeded. The heyday of the Fountain of the World was abruptly at an end. After years of languishing in obscurity, it finally closed its doors in 1975.

Freemasons

The Masonic Service Association of North America says of the world's most famous secret society: "No one knows with certainty how or when the Masonic Fraternity was formed. A widely accepted theory among Masonic scholars is that it arose from the stonemasons' guilds during the Middle Ages. The language and symbols used in the fraternity's rituals come from this era. The oldest document that makes reference to Masons is the Regius Poem, printed about 1390, which was a copy of an earlier work. In 1717, four lodges in London formed the first Grand Lodge of England, and records from that point on are more complete."

As for that 1390 document, the Masonic Dictionary states: "The manuscript is in the King's Library of the British Museum. It was published in 1840 by James O. Halliwell, and again in 1844, under the title of *The Early History of Freemasonry in England*. The Masonic character of the poem remained unknown until its discovery by Halliwell, who was not a Freemason, because it was catalogued as *A Poem of Moral Duties*. It is now more commonly known as the *Regius Manuscript* because it formed part of the Royal Library commenced by Henry VII and presented to the British Museum by George II."

By 1750, the world of the Masons had come to dominate practically all of Europe and was destined to become a powerful force within the growing America, as the Texas State Historical Association demonstrates: "The Masonic fraternity, brought to the American colonies in the mid-eighteenth century, was well established in all of the United States by 1820. Among the first Americans to migrate to Texas in the 1820s were a number of Masons, including Stephen F. Austin. Austin attempted to organize a Masonic lodge in 1828, when he and six other Masons met at San Felipe and petitioned the Grand York Lodge of Mexico for a charter dispensation. The petition evidently reached Mexico at the height of a quarrel between the 'Yorkinos' and 'Escoceses' (adherents of the Scottish Rite) and disappeared. A more successful effort occurred in the spring of 1835 when Dr. Anson Jones and five others, fearing Mexican reprisals, met secretly under the Masonic Oak near Brazoria and petitioned the Grand Lodge of Louisiana for a charter. The grand master of that state, John Henry Holland, issued the dispensation, and Holland Lodge No. 36 met for the first time on December 27, 1835, with Jones presiding as worshipful master."

Indeed, stateside the Masons soon made major footholds. For example, both Benjamin Franklin and George Washington were Masons. That the fraternity had members holding the highest office in the United States, and in quick time, demonstrates the power and influence the Masons wielded. On top of that, Chief Justice John Marshall—the one man, more than any other, who molded the Supreme Court into what it is today—was also a member.

The compass and square symbol of the Freemasons is indicative of their origin as a fraternity of stonemasons.

In terms of the modern era, author Brad Steiger notes that after the American Revolution, "Freemasonry became extremely powerful in the United States. Lodges sprang up in the smallest of villages, and it became an undeniable sign of prestige in any community to be a member. For businessmen who wished to succeed, it was almost a requirement to join the Masons."

In the wake of the still-unsolved murder in 1826 of a Mason named William Morgan—of Batavia, New York—there was an uprising against the Masons in the United States, chiefly out of fear of the power they wielded, both as a secret society and in terms of being able to stonewall the investigation into the Morgan death. The result, as Brad Steiger says, was that Freemasonry in the United States "never again achieved the social status it had once enjoyed."

And as Steiger also states: "Depending upon the prejudices of the beholder, the Freemasons remain a fraternal group that donates generously to charities—or an insidious secret society bent on world conquest."

Friends of Hecate

Martin J. Clemens says, "Located in West Sussex, England, Clapham Wood stands to the north of the small village of Clapham. Historically, Clapham has been an archetypal English village, one that's been around, likely, since Saxon times. Over the last 300 years, it has remained largely hidden from the outside world, except, that is, for the last four decades."

The "four decades" comment is a very apt one. Since the early 1970s, Clapham Woods has been associated with murder, mystery, and a secret society called the Friends of Hecate. It was in 1972 that the mystery began. In June of that year, a police constable named Peter Goldsmith disappeared while walking through the woods. His body was not found for around six months, specifically on December 13. What makes this even more intriguing is the fact that two months before P. C. Goldsmith vanished, he had investigated the death of a woman who had been murdered in the very same woods. Two victims were inextricably linked to one another.

And, as Clemens reveals, "In July 1975, pensioner Leon Foster disappeared and was subsequently found three weeks later, by a couple who were searching for a horse in the wood, a horse that had also gone missing under mysterious circumstances. Next, on Halloween of 1978, the vicar of Clapham, the retired Reverend Harry Snelling went missing. His body was found three years later, by a Canadian tourist. Again, no cause of death could be identified."

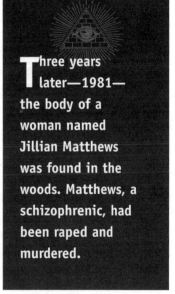

Three years later—1981—the body of a woman named Jillian Matthews was found in the woods. Matthews, a schizophrenic, had been raped and murdered.

Things were far from over. Three years later—1981—the body of a woman named Jillian Matthews was found in the woods. Matthews, a schizophrenic, had been raped and murdered. Moving away from the human casualties of Clapham Woods, there's the matter of the disappearance of a number of dogs. On this matter, Clemens says: "Three cases in particular—which were covered widely by the press—told of two dogs that went missing without a trace and a third that suffered a mysterious paralysation. The son of Peter Love, while walking their family chow in the wood, watched as his dog ran amongst thicket of trees in the forest and disappeared, never to be seen again. The following week, farmer John Cornford's collie disappeared in the same place. A third dog, a golden retriever owned by Mr. E. F. Rawlins was found partially paralyzed after running into the woods, the cause of which was never determined and which eventually led to its being euthanized."

It's hardly surprising that Clapham Woods gained a reputation as a place filled with menace and mystery. In 1987, information surfaced suggesting that Clapham Woods was filled with something else too: a powerful and dangerous group—whose membership included elements of the British government—called the Friends of Hecate.

Of Hecate, Aaron J. Atsma says: "HEKATE (or Hecate) was the goddess of magic, witchcraft, the night, moon, ghosts and necromancy. She was the only child of the Titanes Perses and Asteria from whom she received her power over heaven, earth, and sea. Hekate assisted Demeter in her search for Persephone, guiding her through the night with flaming torches. After the mother-daughter reunion she became Persephone's minister and companion in Haides.

"Two metamorphosis myths describe the origins of her animal familiars: the black she-dog and the polecat (a mustelid house pet kept to hunt vermin). The bitch was originally the Trojan Queen Hekabe, who leapt into the sea after the fall of Troy and was transformed by the goddess into her familiar. The polecat was originally the witch Gale who was transformed into the beast to punish her for her incontinence. Others say it was Galinthias, the nurse of Alkmene, transformed by the angry Eileithyia, but received by Hekate as her animal."

The story of the Friends of Hecate first surfaced publicly in the pages of *The Demonic Connection*, a 1987 book written by Toyne Newton, Charles Walker, and Alan Brown. According to Walker, he met with one of the members of the secret group, who confirmed that the deaths of the various people—and the disappearances of the dogs—were the work of the Friends of Hecate, which has been described as "a quasi-pagan British occult order."

While the existence of the Friends of Hecate has yet to be fully confirmed, the unsettling story of dark and mysterious deaths in the heart of Clapham Woods has ensured the legend of the group survives and thrives.

Garduña

The saga of the secret society of the Garduña is highly controversial, and for one specific reason: historians cannot agree on whether or not it really existed. The story goes that the group had its origins in Spain, and at some unspecified period in the Middle Ages, but probably at some point in the early 1400s in, or around, Toledo. The tale continues that the Garduña was composed of prisoners—both former and escapees—who engaged in just about any and all unlawful acts in exchange for money. Assassinations, burglaries, and the destruction of property were always high on the list. Reportedly, the Garduña existed for more than four centuries—with the bulk of its activities undertaken during the Spanish Inquisition, which was established in 1478 and lasted until 1834.

On the other hand, there is the research of a pair of Spanish historians, Hipólito Sanchiz and León Arsenal. They dug very deeply into the story of the Garduña and found that references to the Garduña did not date back any further than the 1800s, and specifically to the pages of a book titled *Misterios de la inquisición española y otras sociedades secretas de España*. It was written by Víctor de Féréal and Manuel de Cuendías, and was published in 1850. As a result of their research, Sanchiz and Arsenal concluded that, in all likelihood, the stories surrounding the Garduña were far more suited to fiction than to fact.

It has been suggested that the stories of the Garduña inspired—or even joined forces with, at times—the Camorra, an early Mafia-like organization that operated out of southern Italy and is believed to have come to prominence in the 1600s. Although, it may have existed much earlier—possibly as many as two centuries earlier. As with many secret societies, the truth (or lack thereof) behind the story of the Garduña remains a mystery.

Germanenorden

Just two years before World War I erupted in 1914, a secret body was created and given the title of Germanenorden, which translates as the Germanic Order (some prefer the Teutonic Order). Germanenorden had its origins in Berlin, Germany, and was the work of one Theodor Fritsch. *Metapedia* says of Fritsch: "In 1893, Fritsch published his most famous work, *The Handbook of the Jewish Question*, also known as the *Anti-Semitic Catechism*, which criticized the Jews and called upon Germans to refrain from intermingling with them. Vastly popular, the book was read by millions and was in its 49th edition by 1944 (330,000 copies). The ideas espoused by the work greatly influenced Hitler and his party during their rise to power after World War I. Fritsch also founded a journal—the *Hammer* (in 1902) and this became the basis of a movement, the Reichshammerbund, in 1912."

Other influential players in the Germanenorden were Phillip Stauff (a reporter-publisher) and Hermann Pohl, a man who came to lead the Germanenorden. Both men were heavily influenced by the world of the occult and ancient rite and ritual, as they sought to achieve their goal of seeing Germanenorden rise to power. Very controversially, most of the visible symbolic imagery of Germanenorden revolved around the Swastika, which was elevated to notorious levels when Adolf Hitler came to power and plunged the planet into World War II. In addition, much of the design and structure of the group was based upon tried and tested methods employed by Freemasons and similar secret societies. Not surprisingly, the group was deeply anti-Semitic and taught that the "Nordics" were the superior race, above all others. But, Germanenorden went a step further: it insisted that all members and

Author Theodor Fritsch wrote *Anti-Semitic Catechism* and founded the Germanenorden.

prospective members prove that they were pure Aryan in nature. For the racist extremists in Germanenorden, nothing but absolute purity was good enough.

It's hardly surprising that amid the chaos of World War I, which lasted from 1914 to 1918, the Germanenorden splintered and fragmented. By 1916, there were two incarnations: the original version and the Germanenorden Walvater of the Holy Grail. One of those who joined the latter was Rudolf von Sebottendorff, an Indiana Jones-type character who was well-traveled and steeped in occult lore and teachings—and a Freemason, too.

Perhaps the most significant part of the history of the Germanenorden—although, certainly not from a positive perspective—is that its Munich, Germany-based office was designated the Thule Society—the very body that helped bring the Deutsche Arbeiterpartei (DAP) to fruition. It was the DAP that later gave rise to Hitler and the National Socialist German Workers' Party (Nazis).

Goff, Kenneth

Kenneth Goff is described in now-declassified FBI files of May 6, 1955, as "a self-styled freelance Evangelist who for the past number of years has been speaking around the United States regarding the threat of communism to the United States." Lectures that Goff routinely delivered to interested parties included: *Treason in our State Department*; *Should we use the Atom Bomb?*; *Red Secret Plot for Seizure of Denver*; and *Do the Reds Plan to Come by Alaska?*

As the FBI additionally noted: "Also, some of the titles of Goff's books, which he publishes voluminously are: *Will Russia Invade America?*, *One World, A Red World*, and *Confessions of Stalin's Agent*." But, the FBI had other concerns about Goff. He had once been a rabid commie himself, and there were certain figures in the Bureau who believed Goff was not quite the now-anticommunist that he professed to be. Rather, there was a suspicion that Goff had gone deep-cover and his red-hating ravings were merely a collective, ingenious ruse to camouflage his real intent: establishing networks of communist sympathizers across the United States.

The FBI certainly had a fine stash of material on Goff, who, it was recorded, "is a self-admitted former member of the Communist Party," and who "was found guilty by jury trial on February 25, 1948, in United States District Court, District of

> He had once been a rabid commie himself, and there were certain figures in the Bureau who believed Goff was not quite the now-anticommunist that he professed to be.

Columbia, and was fined $100 as a result of the subject's placing anti-communist signs before the Soviet Embassy in Washington, D.C."

FBI files on Goff also noted, "The *Rocky Mountain News* on October 25, 1951, contained an article stating that three Englewood persons were ordered to appear in Denver Municipal Court as an aftermath of the ripping of the Soviet flag yesterday at Civic Center. Mr. and Mrs. Kenneth Goff were two of these three individuals."

Patriots might say that protesting outside the Soviet Embassy and tearing up the Soviet flag were very laudable actions for a U.S. citizen to undertake on home turf at the height of the fraught and dicey Cold War. The FBI wasn't quite so sure, however: "It has been our concern that Goff always ensures he is seen while displaying anti-Soviet tendencies. [Deleted] has remarked that if Goff is still privately 'of a party mind' this might explain his public displays."

Goff was certainly an interesting character and had made comments in the 1950s about communist-based plans to covertly introduce fluoride into the U.S. water supply, to create a "spirit of lethargy" in the nation. And guess what? Goff had a deep interest in flying saucers. Indeed, one of Goff's regular lectures was titled: *Traitors in the Pulpit, or What's Behind the Flying Saucers—Are They from Russia, Another Planet, or God?* But it was not so much from the perspective of UFOs being alien or even Russian, however, that interested Goff. His concern was how the UFO subject could be utilized as a tool of manipulation and control by government.

Orson Welles (shown here in 1937) created the famous radio broadcast of H. G. Wells's *War of the Worlds* in 1938. Goff believed it to be a rehearsal for a Communist Revolution.

In his 1959 publication, *Red Shadows*, Goff offered the following to his readers—which, of course, secretly included the FBI: "During the past few years, the flying saucer scare has rapidly become one of the main issues, used by organizations working for a one-world government, to frighten people into the belief that we will need a super world government to cope with an invasion from another planet. Many means are being used to create a vast amount of imagination in the minds of the general public, concerning the possibilities of an invasion by strange creatures from Mars or Venus."

He continued: "This drive began early in the '40s, with a radio drama, put on by Orson Welles, which caused panic in many of the larger cities of the East, and resulted in the death of several people. The Orson Welles program of invasion from Mars was used by the Communist Party as a test to find out how the people would react on instructions given out over the radio. It was an important part of the Communist rehearsal for the Revolution."

The now-infamous Welles broadcast was, of course, based upon H. G. Wells's acclaimed novel *War of the Worlds*, and while today it is fashionable and almost *de rigueur* within ufological circles to suggest the Welles broadcast and deep conspiracy go together hand-in-glove, it was far less so in the 1950s. Goff, then, was quite the prophet—and particularly so when one takes into consideration the fact that he had been mouthing off about *War of the Worlds*, a "one-world government," and a secret program to manipulate the public with staged UFO encounters as far back as 1951.

And of relevance to this book, Goff made brief yet further tantalizing comments concerning what he referred to as that "super world government." According to Goff, that same, worldwide, iron-fisted body was comprised primarily of "the most powerful Masons."

Green Man

Elizabeth Randall says of the Green Man—a wild, pagan character linked with places perceived as magical, such as woods, glades, and streams, and whose very image provokes thoughts of ancient proto-humans roaming the land—that: "Usually these figures are male, although there are a very few Green Women, together with green cats, green demons, and green lions. The Green Man can appear in different forms, although there are three types that are normally represented. These are the Disgorging Head, which emits foliage from the mouth; the Foliate Head, which is entirely covered in green leaves; [and] the Blood-sucker Head, which has foliage emerging from all the facial outlets."

As for the point of origin for the phenomenon, Randall suggests that the Green Man quite possibly surfaced out of the mythology of fantastic deities and mighty gods in very early times. Perhaps, in the British Isles, she muses, the Green Man arose from the Celtic god of light, Lud (also referred to as Lug or Lyg). On a similar track, in 1942, at West Row, Suffolk, a silver salver which dated from the fourth century, was found and, today, comprises an integral and important part of what has become known as the Mildenhall Treasure.

The salver in question, which was uncovered at the site of an old Roman villa and is now on display at the British Museum, contains an intriguing image. It resembles a partly leafy mask thought to represent Neptune—the

Roman god of the sea and the water—with the foliage being seaweed. But, pretty much for all intents and purposes, it is definitively Green Man-like in its appearance.

Randall has far more to say, too, of a nature that provides us with a solid body of data and history on the mysterious figure. She notes that carved depictions of the Green Man can be found not only in churches but also in secular buildings. Plus, it is a common name for a public house, where it would appear on inn signs that, occasionally, show a full figure instead of simply a head. The motif can be found right across the world and is, more often than not, related to natural vegetative divinities from throughout the ages. It is first and foremost a symbol of rebirth that represents the spring cycle of growth. From Asia to Europe there are representations of the image. From the second century to the modern day, the Green Man can be associated with similar beliefs.

Randall suggests that the Green Man quite possibly surfaced out of the mythology of fantastic deities and mighty gods in very early times.

It may surprise some to learn that while the Green Man—as a specific entity of traditional British folklore, at least—certainly has ancient origins, the usage of those two combined words ("Green" and "Man," in the particular context they appear in this book to explain the nature of the phenomenon), is most certainly not old in the slightest.

The first person to use the term "Green Man" was Lady Raglan, wife of Major FitzRoy Richard Somerset, 4th Baron Raglan. At one time he was the president of the Folklore Society. And, in 1939 his wife, Lady Raglan, created the phrase "Green Man" in her one and only article that appeared in the *Folklore* journal. She invented the term to define the leaf-decorated heads seen in English churches, and to this day her theory concerning where they come from is still discussed.

So, yes, the *name* most certainly is recent. But the *motif* is far, far less so. Kithra shows that, the name issue aside, its origins are just about as long as they are winding and open to question and debate: "On the surface it seems these images are pagan, but they can often be found in ecclesiastical buildings from the 11th century onwards. Many look either unsettling or mystical, which is sometimes thought to show the vitality of the Green Man in that it was capable of enduring as a character from pre-Christian traditions. This was probably due to the fact that in early Christianity old symbols were often incorporated into the newer religion. And, from around the 14th century on they were also included simply as decoration in things such as manuscripts, stained glass, and other items."

Randall also notes that in Britain, at least, the Green Man icon became very fashionable again during the nineteenth century, when it was used in architecture and arts and crafts. Moreover, to this day, the image is still used as decoration in many parts of the world by artists using many different types of media, including literature.

There is another aspect to the mystery, too. The expression shown on the faces of many Green Men found in churches seems to suggest some form of torture. It may be that such expressions were to remind people of sin and that their souls would burn in hell if they committed such transgressions. As the image also represents renewal and rebirth, in a church the image might be a sign of resurrection where it appears, especially when found on tombs. It might also be a sign of creation. Or, it may just be a sign of nature and fertility.

It is thought that the Celts adorned their victim's head with leaves, which might lead us to speculate that the Green Man has Celtic origins; however the first depictions of Green Men come from classical Roman times. But, if it is Celtic, then—where it is shown next to, or above, doors—it might be to protect the building from evil spirits.

Representations of the Green Man are often seen as architectural decorations, such as this example found on Norwich Cathedral, East Anglia, England.

The problem, however, remains that—as Randall notes—"in the very early years of the Church, and when it took over in Britain, all pagan images were destroyed and banned. So it's hard to see how the Green Man should then have been included in church architecture, and yet, there are no accounts from Mediaeval Times that tell us how the image of the Green Man came to be included in churches. Regardless of what the Green Man was intended to represent in church architecture current congregants see him as the archetype of our oneness with the earth. And, for Wiccans and Neo-pagans he portrays an earth-centred idea of male divinity."

She adds: "Today, the symbolism of the Green Man has come to mean the relationship between man and nature. It reveals an essential basic pattern deep in the human mind. It has become an archetype that is common to all and represents a profoundly sympathetic feeling for, and with, nature. This has probably arisen from our current concerns about the ecology, and environment, of Planet Earth."

Luke Mastin notes: "Many modern Neo-Pagan, New Age and Wiccan organizations and practitioners have incorporated the Green Man into their artwork and symbology, and he is sometimes used as a representation of the Horned God (which is itself a syncretic deity inclusive of several ancient pagan gods such as the Celtic Cernunnos and the Greek Pan)."

Guild of St. Bernulphus

Agroup that operated in a distinctly shadowy fashion, the Guild of St. Bernulphus was created in December 1869 in Holland. It was formed in the Dutch city of Utrecht by Father Gerard van Heukelum, a collector of mediaeval artwork and, at the time, the chaplain of Utrecht's St. Catherine's Cathedral. The guild took its name from a bishop of Utrecht, named Bernold, who oversaw the city in the eleventh century. It was van Heukelum's passion for rare, old art that prompted him to establish the Guild of St. Bernulphus—essentially, as a body that could secretly protect priceless and rare items of art. In that sense, the secrecy surrounding the group was not so much provoked by its activities, but by its decision to ensure that the storage locations for such priceless items remained largely unknown outside of the guild itself.

An 1881 edition of the *Guild Book of St. Bernulphus,* the official publication of the guild that included information about meetings and trade news.

Father Heukelum was very strict with regard to who, exactly, was permitted to join the guild: it was open to those who were employed by the church and no one else. At least, that was the case for a while. Father Heukelum soon realized that it would very much benefit the Guild of St. Bernulphus to have on board both painters and architects who specialized in the field of religious artwork, and for two reasons: such people would likely have contacts who could help the guild to acquire otherwise hard-to-find examples of religious art, and they would likely be able to determine the age and value of such items, too. Among those who came aboard were Friedrich Wilhelm Mengelberg, a German-Dutch sculptor very much in the Gothic vein, and Alfred Tepe, an architect whose work paralleled that of Mengelberg.

It wasn't long before the guild spread its wings: although it began in the province of Utrecht, it didn't take long before a network of members and associates began to spread all across Holland, and even to the extent of not just collecting religious artwork and architecture, but also offering advice on the construction and design of new churches and places of worship. It was the guild's reasoning that by ensuring a significant role in both design and construction, they would be able to ensure an adherence to the medieval, Gothic designs that Fatrher Heukelum so admired.

A perfect example is the Utrecht-based Willibrord Church—named after a seventh century missionary and saint. The Netherlands tourist board notes: "The St. Willibrord Church is one of the most beautiful neo-Gothic churches in the Netherlands and certainly one of the churches to visit when in Utrecht. You can find it in the historic city center. The church is a richly decorated church. Admire the colorful stained-glass windows, beautiful wood carvings and ironwork and exuberantly painted walls and ceilings. A unique opportunity to sample a medieval church before the iconoclasm."

It should be noted, however, that the first such church created according to the vision of the Guild of St. Bernulphus was St. Nicolas at Jutphaas, constructed in 1874.

Such was the interest in the ever-growing collection of the guild that it prompted the establishment of a museum—very much inspired by Father Heukelum's work. Known as the Archbishop's Museum, it later became the Museum Catharijneconven, which continues to stand to this day.

Halloween

Today, it is, beyond any shadow of doubt, the spookiest and most chillingly atmospheric night of the year. It is Halloween. It's the one night of the year when kids, all across the world, dress up as ghosts, skeletons, witches, and zombies, and knock on the doors of their neighbors in search of plentiful amounts of candy, and it's all done in good fun and humor. In centuries past, however, Halloween was far from being a night on which to hit the streets and have a good time. In fact, the exact opposite was the case. Long before Halloween existed, as we know it today, there was All Hallows' Eve, which was inextricably linked to the surfacing of the dead. It was hardly a time for laughs and jokes of the supernatural variety. As for candy, there was none in sight, none at all. Indeed, what we term, today, Halloween, actually had its origins in secret, pagan rituals and rites.

In 1919, Ruth Edna Kelley said: "Pomona, the Roman goddess of fruit, lends us the harvest element of Hallowe'en; the Celtic day of 'summer's end' was a time when spirits, mostly evil, were abroad; the gods whom Christ dethroned joined the ill-omened throng; the Church festivals of All Saints' and All Souls' coming at the same time of year—the first of November—contributed the idea of the return of the dead; and the Teutonic May Eve assemblage of witches brought its hags and their attendant beasts to help celebrate the night of October 31st."

All Hallows' Eve was terminology first employed in the early part of the sixteenth century. Its direct association with All Saints Day (celebrated on

November 1, the day after Halloween) has led to an understandable assumption that Halloween has its roots firmly in the domain of Christianity and its teachings. It is an assumption that is wrong, however. Christianity most certainly did help to model Halloween and make it what it is today. The reality, however, is that the origins of the event date back to much earlier times. They were times when paganism ruled on high. While some aspects of the earliest years of Halloween are lost to the inevitable fog of time, there is very little doubt that the Gaelic festival of Samhain played a large role in its development. As far back as at least the tenth century, Samhain was celebrated by the people of Wales, Ireland, Scotland, and Brittany.

Commencing on October 31 and lasting for twenty-four hours, Samhain marked the beginning of the darker months ahead and the looming, ice-cold winter. Samhain was also perceived as the one night of the year when the dead walked the landscape. The concept of the dead rising from the grave as Samhain struck was somewhat different to that portrayed in the average zom-

Faithful Catholics honoring All Saints' Day by lighting candles in a graveyard and remembering departed loved ones. In recent years, however, the American version, Halloween, has been gaining popularity in Europe.

bie movie, however. For the Gaels, Samhain was actually a time to invite the souls of the dead to join them for a hearty feast. This was done as much out of fear as it was a desire to see deceased loved ones again. Of course, in spirit form, there was little—if anything at all—upon which the dead could literally dine.

The invite, therefore, was more of a welcoming symbol than anything else. There is, however, another matter that bears mention. While the Samhain invite was open to friendly spirits, Gaelic teachings and folklore made it very clear that some of those souls of the dead were hardly what one might term friendly in nature.

To make sure that one or more of the malignant dead would not recognize a living person when they saw one, many Gaels elected to wear costumes as a cunning means of disguise on October 31. Camouflaging themselves as the very ghouls, ghosts, and strange creatures that were hunting them down helped the Gaels to avoid detection by the predatory souls of the departed. Interestingly, taking on the guise of the dead (or the undead) to ensure that one can move amongst them—at least, for a while, if nothing else—is something that was put to good use, on several occasions, in *The Walking Dead*, in *Shaun of the Dead*, and in the movie version of Max Brooks's *World War Z*, too.

In *The Walking Dead*, Rick Grimes and his band of survivors smeared the blood of the dead on their clothes to mask their human odor. In *Shaun of the Dead*, matters were played strictly for laughs: Shaun and his own group of survivors staggered drunkenly around the streets, hoping they wouldn't get recognized by the dead. Their hopes were decisively dashed; they were recognized by the astute zombies in mere seconds. And, in *World War Z*, the zombie onslaught is finally contained when a viral cocktail is created that effectively camouflages the living and the healthy from detection by the dead. Thus, we see uncanny similarities when it comes to Halloween, the ancient beliefs of Samhain, the rise of the dead in centuries long gone, and the world of today's zombie.

Hamatsa

The *Canadian Encyclopedia* says: "The Kwakwaka'wakw peoples are traditional inhabitants of the coastal areas of northeastern Vancouver Island and mainland British Columbia. Originally made up of about 28 communities speaking dialects of Kwak'wala, some groups died out or joined others, cutting

A Hamatsa shaman performs a ritual for the Kwakwaka'wakw people.

the number of communities approximately in half. After sustained contact beginning in the late 18th century, Europeans applied the name of one band, the Kwakiutl, to the whole group, a tradition that persists. The name Kwakwaka'wakw means those who speak Kwak'wala, which itself includes five dialects."

Within the Kwakwaka'wakw people there exists a secret society known as Hamatsa. It's a very controversial society too, and there's a very good reason for that: Hamatsa is tied to the world of cannibalism. Indeed, to insiders its most important aspect is known as the "Cannibal Ritual." As controversial as it may sound, even those who have carefully and deeply studied the world of Hamatsa are unsure if the cannibalistic aspects of the group's rites are symbolic in nature, or if literal cannibalism is part and parcel of their activities—such is the blanket of secrecy that surrounds Hamatsa.

This particularly mysterious society brings new members—males only—into the fold when they reach the age of twenty-five. They are taken to a secret, remote area of forestland where they are exposed to the clandestine history and rituals of Hamatsa. The life-force of a huge, Goliath-like giant—one who plays a large role in Kwakwaka'wakw legend, lore, and history—is conjured up. On top of that, the new member is expected to display animalistic tendencies, to the point that growling, snarling, and even the biting of other Kwakwaka'wakw people in attendance are routine—and hence the cannibalism rumors. Wild and frantic dancing follows.

The Hamatsa ritual comes to an end with the ceasing of the dancing and the return of the beast-like initiate to a normal state of mind. Things aren't quite over, however: the new member of the secret society is ordered to dine on human flesh. Franz Uri Boas, a German-American anthropologist—and the author of an 1897 book, *The Social Organization and the Secret Societies of the Kwakiutl Indians*—claimed to have witnessed such flesh-feasting in the late-nineteenth century. When the flesh has been devoured, the person is then required to swallow significant amounts of seawater—something intended to promote vomiting and ensuring a "cleansing" of mind and body. As for those "lucky" enough to have been bitten, they have numerous gifts bestowed on them.

Heaven's Gate

L ife is something that we experience until we no longer do so. Depending on your personal beliefs, death is either a state of never-ending lights out or the start of a new and endless adventure. But, what about reanimation and resurrection? Someone who was convinced that dying and coming back—in some form, at least—would be a wholly positive experience was a controversial character named Marshall Herff Applewhite Jr.

A native of Texas, Applewhite gained infamy in 1997 when he convinced thirty-eight of his followers in the so-called Heaven's Gate cult to take their own lives—chiefly because doing so would see them return in reanimated, immortal form. But before we get to death, reanimation, and immortality, let's see what it was that led to that terrible tragedy.

From a very young age Applewhite's life was dominated by religious teachings: his father was a minister who lectured to, and thundered at, his meek followers. It was made clear to Applewhite that he was expected to do likewise. Exhibiting a high degree of youthful rebellion, however, Applewhite did not.

Instead, he joined the U.S. Army. After leaving the military (which involved him spending a lot of time at the White Sands Proving Ground, New Mexico), Applewhite's life went in a very different direction: he became a music teacher. He could not, however, shake off altogether that religious programming he received as a child and took a job with Houston, Texas's St. Mark's Episcopal Church. But, demonstrating that he was not quite so saintly after all, in 1974, he was arrested for credit card fraud. It was also in the 1970s that Applewhite met the love of his life: Bonnie Nettles.

> **T**hree weeks into the month, Applewhite started brainwashing his duped clan into believing that if they killed themselves they would all reanimate....

From then on, the devoted pair began to more and more delve into the world of cultish, crackpot activity: they established the Total Overcomers Anonymous group, which assured its followers benevolent aliens were out there, ready and willing to help all those who pledged allegiance to the TOA, and many did exactly that. It was a group that eventually mutated into the infamous Heaven's Gate cult. All of which brings us up to March 1997.

Three weeks into the month, Applewhite started brainwashing his duped clan into believing that if they killed themselves they would all reanimate—in some angelic dimension far different to, and far away from, our own earthly realm. Since the comet Hale-Bopp was just around the corner, so to speak, Applewhite even weaved that into his story. There was, he said, a huge UFO flying right behind the comet, and when death came for the group it would transfer them to that same UFO and new and undead lives elsewhere.

His loyal followers eagerly swallowed every word. To their eternal cost, they eagerly swallowed something else, too: highly potent amounts of phenobarbital and vodka. In no time at all, almost forty people were dead, all thanks to the words of Applewhite. Aliens did not call upon the members of the Heaven's Gate group. No UFO was ever detected behind Hale-Bopp, and the dead did not rise from the floor of the Heaven's Gate abode, which was situated at Rancho Santa Fe, California, and where one and all took their lives. Their bodies stayed exactly where they were until the authorities took them to the morgue for autopsy.

There is a major lesson to be learned here: don't base your life around the claims of a man who tells you that knocking back large amounts of phenobarbital and vodka will ensure your reanimation and immortality. It won't.

Hellfire Club

It was in the 1700s that a like-minded number of figures in England—all having a deep interest in demonology—banded together and created a group whose activities were as notorious as their name: the Hellfire Club. For the most part, they were powerful, influential figures in English society, people who had tentacles that spread to the worlds of politics, royalty, and the media. The Hellfire Club was overseen by one Sir Francis Dashwood, who held a lease over Medmenham Abbey, in the English county of Buckinghamshire. It was within the confines of the old abbey—which Dashwood termed his "palace of delights"—that the Hellfire Club had its dark and wild meetings.

Members were expected to dress in monk-like outfits, including cowls. The meetings occurred almost exclusively in the dead of night, and paying homage to—and worshipping—the Devil was the order of the day. Or, rather, of the night. While the members of the Hellfire Club certainly took their devotion to the Devil very seriously, the meetings were also noted for their "food, drink, gaming and sex."

Toyne Newton, the author of *The Demonic Connection: An Investigation into Satanism in England and the International Black Magic Conspiracy*, says: "As their basic activities were partially rooted in the heretic practices of the London Hellfire clubs of an earlier period—though the Medmenham Monks were far more dedicated to Luciferian worship than these earlier blasphemers who frequented London's old taverns and they should not be confused with them—

they were more commonly known as 'The Hellfire Club,' and the most notorious Satanists of their day."

As for the membership of the Hellfire Club, it included figures from the British government's House of Commons, as well as the Marquis of Bute, Lord Sandwich (who was the son of the Archbishop of Canterbury), and politician John Wilkes. Other members included Thomas Potter, whose participation in the wild sex, drugs, and alcohol-fueled events, Toyne Newton notes, "reduced him to a gouty and palsied wreck."

In terms of the structure of the Hellfire Club, it was composed of what were termed the Superior Order of 12 and the Inferior Order of 12. As the titles suggest, the former was composed of the most powerful, rich, and well-connected figures in the group, while the latter was for those perceived as being very much further down the ladder. Certainly, the Superior Order of 12 was the only part of the Hellfire Club that was allowed to partake in the satanic rites and rituals held specifically in the chapel of Medmenham Abbey.

A 1764 portrait of Hellfire Club founder Sir Francis Dashwood by William Hogarth parodies an earlier work portraying St. Francis of Assisi.

By the turn of the 1760s, and rather astonishingly and controversially, the vast majority of the Superior Order of 12 held major, significant positions in the British government—and right to the very top. The Marquis of Bute, for example, was nothing less than the nation's prime minister (the U.K.'s equivalent of the United States' president), and Dashwood himself was the chancellor of the exchequer. It was, however, the actions of another politician linked to the Hellfire Club—John Wilkes—that led to the ultimate downfall of this particular secret society. Back to Toyne Newton, who says of Wilkes, who became highly disillusioned by the Hellfire Club's antics and activities and who was determined to bring down the club and Dashwood: "[Wilkes] engineered this most humorously by concealing an ape equipped with artificial horns and dressed in a long black cloak in a box, and releasing it during one of 'St. Francis's' Satanic ceremonies. The sudden appearance of this devil bounding about their midst can best be imagined, but in the melee that followed, Lord Sandwich apparently fell to the floor screaming for mercy when the 'devil' fastened itself upon him, and it was some time before he could be rescued from the attentions of the amorous ape."

The story soon got out widely across England—which led to the exposure of the Hellfire Club—and Dashwood was forced to cease the satanic activity at Medmenham Abbey. Worse, too, for Dashwood: the populace and the press of the day were not outraged by the Hellfire Club's rituals and rites. Rather, the group became the subject of endless jokes, jibes, and ridicule. The Hellfire Club was over. As for Dashwood, he died in 1781, having largely descended into obscurity more than a decade earlier.

Hemingway, Ernest

Of the many and varied official files that the FBI has declassified into the public domain, certainly one of the most intriguing is the dossier on Ernest Hemingway—without doubt one of the finest novelists of the twentieth century and the author of such classics as *A Farewell to Arms* (1929), *For Whom the Bell Tolls* (1940), and *The Old Man and the Sea* (1951).

Under the provisions of the Freedom of Information Act, the FBI has declassified a file 122 pages long on Hemingway, which makes for notable reading, and which demonstrates that the legendary writer undertook classified work for a number of secret groups and agencies. The collection makes it clear that Hemingway was perceived by at least some in the FBI as a person who could offer assistance to the cause of intelligence-gathering. His time spent in Spain during the Spanish Civil War, and his time living on the island of Cuba, both caught the attention of J. Edgar Hoover.

On the other hand, Hoover was not at all comfortable. A 1942 document from the FBI tells us the following: "While in Spain during the Spanish Revolution, Hemingway was said to have associated with Jay Allen, of the North American Newspaper Alliance. It has been alleged by a number of sources that Allen was a Communist and he is known to have been affiliated with alleged Communist Front organizations. In the fall of 1940 Hemingway's name was included in a group of names of individuals who were said to be engaged in Communist activities. These individuals were reported to occupy positions on the 'intellectual front' and were said to be engaged in Communist activities."

None of this went down well with Hoover. However, in early October 1942—when he was living in Cuba—Hemingway made an approach to the FBI to offer his services as, in effect, an undercover agent. The FBI noted that Hemingway had become friends with Consul Kenneth Potter and the Second Secretary of Embassy, Robert P. Joyce. In a memo to Hoover, R. G. Leddy—the FBI's legal attaché at Havana—wrote that "at several conferences with the

Ambassador and officers of the Embassy late in August 1942, the topic of using Hemingway's services in intelligence activities was discussed."

Hoover continued to have his doubts, but he did see the logic in bringing Hemingway on-board. Files reveal that, although Hemingway wished to get further involved with the FBI, at least a month prior to the events of October 1942, he was already spying for the American Embassy. FBI files make that very clear: "Early in September 1942, Ernest Hemingway began to engage directly in intelligence activities on behalf of the American Embassy in Havana. He is operating through Spanish Republicans whose identities have not been furnished by which we are assured are obtainable when desired."

The document continues: "[Hemingway] advised that he now has four men operating on a full-time basis, and 14 more whose positions are barmen, waiters, and the like, operating on a part-time basis.... [Hemingway] ... wishes to suggest that his interest thus far has not been limited to the Spanish Falange and Spanish activities, but that he has included numerous German suspects."

Because of his time spent in Spain and Cuba, Ernest Hemingway was of interest to the FBI as someone who might be useful in intelligence-gathering.

Again, matters became fraught: yes, apparently, Hemingway was in a position to do good work. Or, so it seemed. However, shortly after his espionage work began, Hemingway introduced the aforementioned R. G. Leddy to a friend as "a member of the Gestapo" and that did not go down well! Hoover's blood pressure was ready to go through the roof. He wrote of the "complete undesirability" of having Hemingway on board, noting that "Hemingway is the last man, in my estimation, to be used in any such capacity," and adding that his "sobriety" was "certainly questionable."

On top of that, as the files demonstrate, Hemingway proved to be no James Bond. FBI assistant director Quinn Tamm called him a "phony." Records show that Hemingway incorrectly put Prince Camillo Ruspoli—an Italian fascist interned by the Cubans—as being present at a lunch at the Hotel Nacional in honor of the new Spanish Charges d'affaires, Pelayo Garcia Olay. Also, a "tightly wrapped box" left at the Bar Basque and acquired by one of Hemingway's operatives was believed by Hemingway to contain "espionage information." It did not: when it reached Robert P. Joyce, it was found to contain "only

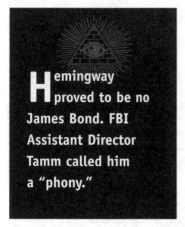

Hemingway proved to be no James Bond. FBI Assistant Director Tamm called him a "phony."

a cheap edition of the 'Life of St. Teresa.'" No one was impressed. Hemingway was "irritated."

The FBI was soon done with the acclaimed writer. Back to Assistant Director Tamm: "The Bureau has by careful and impartial investigation, from time to time disproved practically all of the so-called Hemingway information." The FBI washed its hands of him. There are, however, indications that Hemingway's work in the field of espionage for other secret groups did not end there. Consider the following from 1943 FBI documents on Hemingway: "At the present time [Hemingway] is alleged to be performing a highly secret naval operation for the Navy Department. In this connection, the Navy Department is said to be paying the expenses for the operation of Hemingway's boat, furnishing him with arms and charting courses in the Cuban area." On this same matter of the Navy, the FBI recorded the following on June 23, 1943: "[Hemingway] is on a special confidential assignment for the Naval Attaché chasing submarines along the Cuban coast and keeping a careful observance on the movements of the Spanish steamers which occasionally come to Cuba."

In view of these latter revelations, perhaps, one day, we'll see even more classified files on Ernest Hemingway finally become unclassified.

Hermetic Brotherhood of Luxor

While it was not until 1884 that the existence of the Hermetic Brotherhood of Luxor became public, it's acknowledged by students of the world of secret societies that its origins date back to around 1870. Samuel Scarborough notes of the H. B. of L.—as it is usually referred to—that "the order was very similar to the later Golden Dawn in that it had both an Outer Order or Circle and an Inner Circle. The function of this 'Outer Circle' of the H. B. of L. was to offer a correspondence course on practical occultism, which set it apart from the Theosophical Society. Its curriculum included a number of selections from the writings of Hargrave Jennings and Paschal Beverly Randolph. Hargrave Jennings was a prominent Rosicrucian in Europe who wrote *The Rosicrucians, Their Rites and Mysteries*, in 1870, one of the most influential books on the Rosicrucians to have been written at that time."

It was the creation of a man named Max Théon, whose real name was Louis-Maximilian Bimstein, and about whom Kheper.net states: "Théon was in many ways a latter-day Gnostic, an enigmatic occultist whose evolutionary and occult teachings were indirectly taken up by the Indian philosopher-sage Sri Aurobindo, and may have also had some influence on the metaphysics of H. P. Blavatsky. A Polish Jew, he travelled to London, France, Egypt, and finally Algeria, founding several esoteric groups along the way. He was known under several names, but we can refer to him as 'Max Théon,' the pseudonym he adopted while in Algeria."

It should be noted that although Théon was the driving force behind the Hermetic Brotherhood of Luxor, publicly (at least) it was seen to be run by Thomas Burgoyne and Peter Davidson. The group offered teachings in the domain of the occult and established a successful, monthly publication, *The Occult Magazine*. All was going well until information surfaced showing that Burgoyne had spent time in prison as a result of engaging in postal fraud. In no time at all it spelled the end of this obscure, yet fascinating, body.

Jewish occultist Max Théon founded the Hermetic Brotherhood of Luxor.

Hermetic Order of the Golden Dawn

On the matter of the Hermetic Order of the Golden Dawn, we have this from *The Mystica*, which states that it is "an organization exerting one of three most significant influences on Western occultism in the 19th and 20th centuries. The second and third influences were the Theosophical Society and G. I. Gurdjieff.

"As a secret society the organization's membership included some of the most distinguished and talented personalities of the times such as W. B. Yeats, Annie Horniman (who sponsored the Abbey Theatre, Dublin), Florence Farr (mistress of G. B. Shaw), S. L. MacGregor Mathers, Aleister Crowley, Israel Regardie, A. E. Waite, Algernon Blackwood, Arthue Machen, and many others."

The Mystica continues: "Some claim the society's basis is dubious. Its key founder was Dr. William Wynn Westcott, a London coroner and a Rosicrucian, who in 1887 obtained part of a manuscript that was written in brown-ink cipher from a Reverend A. F. A. Woodford, a Mason. The manuscript appeared to be old although probably it was not. However, with his Hermetic knowledge Westcott deciphered the manuscript and discovered it contained fragments of mystical rituals of the 'Golden Dawn' an unknown organization which admitted both men and women.

"Westcott approached his occultist friend Samuel Liddell MacGregor Mathers who he asked to transform the ritual fragments into expanded and systematized rituals. Among the papers contained within the manuscript was a slip of paper bearing the name of Fraulein Anna Sprengel, a Rosicrucian adept living in Germany.

"Through correspondence with this woman Westcott obtained her permission to organize the English branch of the occult society Die Goldene Dammerung (The Golden Dawn). However, the authenticity of this establishment of the English order has been suspect. It has been suggested the character of Fraulein Sprengel might have been mythologized by Westcott in order to fabricate the correspondence which established the new secret society."

S. L. MacGregor Mathers in a circa 1918 photo, wearing Egyptian-style costume. Egyptian culture, as well as Greek and Jewish, imbued the Hermetic Order's ideology.

"The Hermetic Order of the Golden Dawn," says The Golden Dawn, of the group's ideologies and initiations, "is an initiatory society devoted to spiritual, philosophical, and magical development. The ideas studied by Golden Dawn initiates are a unique combination of Jewish Kabbalah, ancient Egyptian and Greek mysteries, several strands of Christianity, and many other Western esoteric traditions. To quote its 'history lecture,' (from Israel Regardie's book, *The Golden Dawn*), 'The Order of the G.D. is an Hermetic Society whose members are taught the principles of Occult Science and the Magic of Hermes.'"

It continues: "The Golden Dawn was founded in 1887 by three British Freemasons … and it admitted hundreds of men and women over the next several decades. The original Golden Dawn generated a body of esoteric knowledge about Hermetic magic, divination, alchemy, and philosophy that is unparalleled to this day. Traditions as seemingly different as Chaos Magic and Gardnerian Wicca have roots in the Golden Dawn, and it has been of profound influence in the lives of artists (e.g., the poet W. B. Yeats, the author Arthur Machen) and scholars (e.g., A. E. Waite). The fascinating spiritual mysteries taught by the Golden Dawn continue to have a profound impact on people from all walks of life.

"The Golden Dawn 'system of magic' is a tool designed to educate the student of the esoteric in both practical matters of ritual and divination, and in abstract metaphysical ideas. The focus of the Golden Dawn material is primarily Western—i.e., Judeo-Christian, Greek, and Egyptian—but some Eastern ideas have crept in over the years."

Hitler, Adolf

It's a little-known fact that the FBI, in the post-World War II era, began to quietly compile what ultimately turned out to be a large dossier of material on claims that Adolf Hitler had survived World War II and—due to the actions of a secret, elite group of Nazis—secretly fled to South America. It's a dossier that has now been declassified and can be accessed at the FBI's website, *The Vault*.

As one might expect to be the case, many of the claims are scant in data, secondhand or thirdhand in nature, or written by individuals with more time on their hands than sense in their heads. That said, however, one section of the file is particularly intriguing and noteworthy. Incredibly, it suggests that none other than Allan Dulles—who, in World War II, made his mark in the Office of Strategic Services, and served as director of the CIA from 1953 to 1961—was complicit in a certain, top secret program of highly controversial proportions. It was a program reportedly run by a well-connected group of powerful figures in government who wished to see Hitler secretly shipped out to South America, when the Nazis were defeated.

The files in question refer to stories coming out of Los Angeles, California, which reached the eyes and ears of the L.A. office of the FBI. According to what the FBI was told, two Nazi-controlled submarines made their stealthy way to the Argentinean coastline, where they covertly deposited high-ranking Nazis who had escaped the wrath of the United States, the United Kingdom, and the former Soviet Union. One of the most astounding rumors concerning this story was that it was not just high-rankers who were making new lives for themselves on the other side of the world. It was *the* most high-ranking Nazi, too: Adolf Hitler, who, allegedly, was by now hunkered down, somewhere, in the heart of the Andes.

Adolf Hitler in 1934.

The big question is: who was the FBI's informant? Unfortunately, we don't know, since his name is excised from the relevant, released documents. Nevertheless, he had a great deal of data to impart, something that definitely made the FBI sit up and take careful notice. It must be noted that the Bureau's source, himself a former Nazi, offered the information—with a promise of more to come—in return for safe haven in the United States. As to how the person claimed to know that Hitler had survived the war, it was, if true, sensational. The man said he had been personally present when the submarines in question reached the coastline of Argentina. Aboard one of them were Adolf Hitler and Eva Braun—neither displaying *any* evidence of bullet wounds or the effects of cyanide. Quite the opposite: they were vibrant, healthy, and very much alive.

If the story was simply that—a tall tale told to try and secure asylum in the United States—the man had certainly crafted an elaborate story. The FBI's source provided details of the specific villages that Hitler, and the rest of the straggling remnants of "The Master Race," passed through on their way to safe haven, somewhere in Argentina.

Adding further credence to this, additional files—also declassified under Freedom of Information legislation—revealed that amongst staff of the U.S. Naval Attaché in Buenos Aires rumors were circulating that Hitler did not die in Berlin, but was now hiding out in Argentina.

In 2014, there was a dramatic, new development in the saga of whether or not Adolf Hitler died in Berlin, Germany, in 1945, or secretly made a new life for himself in South America—first in Paraguay and then in Brazil. The new data came from Simoni Renee Guerreiro Dias, the author of a book entitled *Hitler in Brazil—His Life and His Death*. Dias's research suggests that Hitler changed his name to Adolf Leipzig, living out his life in Nossa Senhora do Livramento, a small village not far from the Brazilian town of Cuiabá. Supposedly, to the villagers, Hitler was known as the "Old German."

As to how Dias found out this information, the story is a thought-provoking one: during the course of her research, Dias found an old, fading photograph of Adolf Leipzig and then compared it to photos of Hitler. The suggestion is they were one and the same. Additional confirmation came from a nun who had seen Hitler, when he was in his eighties, hospitalized in Cuiabá. Attempts to have Hitler removed from the hospital were denied, amid rumors that Vatican officials had the last word on the matter—and the last word, apparently, was that Hitler should remain where he was: out of sight and protected.

At the time of writing, the story is progressing in dramatic fashion: the body of Leipzig has been secured and permission has been given for DNA to be extracted from it. And, to ensure there is comparative material, a relative of Hitler, now living in Israel, has offered to provide a sample of DNA to determine if the two match.

The story is not as unlikely as many might assume. As *Liberty Voice* noted, when the Leipzig-Hitler story surfaced in early 2014: "Thousands of Nazis escaped Germany after the war, including Adolf Eichmann and Josef Mengele. Eichmann and Mengele, two of Hitler's most trusted henchman, both lived in Argentina in the 1940s. The Argentine President, Juan Domingo Peron, did everything that could be done to get the Nazis to South America's second largest country. Argentine agents were sent to Europe to make passage easy by providing falsified travel documents and, in many instances, travel expenses were covered. Even Nazis accused of the most horrific crimes, such as Mengele and Eichmann, were welcomed."

Horsa Tradition

A secret group dedicated to the subject of witchcraft, the Horsa tradition had its origins in England's vast New Forest in the early twentieth century, having taken its inspiration from earlier, pagan beliefs. It's also a group that has ties to the New Forest Coven, which Gerald Gardner—the father of modern day paganism—worked with in the early 1940s to prevent Adolf Hitler's hordes from invading the U.K. According to the teachings of the Horsa Tradition: "In Horsa, we view life as the arena whereby spirit seeks to attain 'absolute good.' 'Absolute good' is viewed as Spirit fully evolved. This evolution takes place, during each incarnation, according to our state of spiritual development. We seek to attain this 'absolute good' by living our lives according to the Immutable universal laws. We come to realize these laws, instinctively, through successive incarnation, and through the application of the faculty of reason and the mind."

The Horsa Tradition continues that the individual "spirit" that exists within all of us "retains elements of personality and experiences from each

The Horsa Tradition continues that the individual "spirit" that exists within all of us "retains elements of personality and experiences from each incarnation."

incarnation." This is perceived by the members as "the faculty of 'conscience,' or as the "'residue' of personality and experience of our previous incarnations."

The group explains that "we use this faculty as a standard against which we weigh our thoughts and actions, and act accordingly. We perfect this faculty by looking within ourselves, and seeking to bring into harmony the areas in our own life, which fall under our power to change. Our thoughts are the seeds, out of which our actions grow, creating vibrations, which blossom as effects, bearing good or ill fruit, thus one must act in accordance with 'conscience.'"

As for the issues of good and evil, for the Horsa Tradition, they are, as with all opposites, "purely subjective." They perceive evil as "an unharmonious state which arises from the misapplication of will and reason, as an excess towards one 'node' of polarity. We do not view evil as a natural state. We hold that good lies in the active aspect of a person, in the will of a person not the person themselves, Evil can only manifest by one consciously and willfully seeking it."

According to the Horsa Tradition, anything that has a detrimental effect upon spiritual evolution, is viewed as negative and evil. Their position is as follows: "Events and experiences that we may subjectively judge as 'evil' or bad, if these experiences add to our spiritual evolution, are, when objectively viewed, essentially good. Actions which subjectively appear good, can, when objectively viewed, be a hindrance to spiritual growth, hence essentially evil. We hold that the essential part of one's self cannot be affected by any action, over which one's self is not capable of controlling through one's will."

I AM

Back in the 1950s, numerous people claimed contact with eerily human-looking extraterrestrials. The aliens in question—who were typically tall and sported long blond hair—became known as the Space Brothers, while those who had the experiences became known as Contactees. Among the most famous of all the Contactees were George Adamski (co-author with Desmond Leslie of the 1952 book *Flying Saucers Have Landed*) and George Hunt Williamson, who, from the early 1950s to the late 1970s held a yearly Contactee convention in the desert near Landers, California. At its height, the event attracted audiences in excess of ten thousand. Then, there was George Hunt Williamson.

A controversial figure with a checkered past, Williamson—in the 1940s—spent time working with William Pelley, who headed a fascist organization popularly known as the Silver Shirts, but which was actually titled the Silver Legion of America. Williamson helped to produce the group's monthly publication, *Valor*. Occult lore had fascinated Williamson since he was a teenager, and under Pelley's influence he began to take an interest in flying saucers as well, eventually trying to contact extraterrestrial intelligence through occult methods like automatic writing. Williamson later teamed with the better known Contactee George Adamski and helped pioneer the modern flying saucer channeling movement, a direct descendant of Frederick Oliver's work. Williamson was also deeply fascinated by the work of a man named Guy Ballard.

John Gordon Melton says of Guy Ballard: "Writing under the name Godfrey Ray King, Ballard compiled his experiences in a book, *Unveiled Mysteries*, published in 1934, and he afterward claimed to receive regular messages, termed 'discourses,' from St. Germain and other Masters. Because one of the Masters from whom Ballard received dictations was Jesus, members of the I AM movement consider themselves Christian. The Ballards claimed to have received more than 3,000 messages, which formed the body of the movement's teachings.

"The Ballards incorporated the I AM movement in 1932. Following Guy Ballard's death, Edna Ballard became the movement's leader and revealed the messages she had received from St. Germain. With her death in 1971, the Board of Directors, which had been established at the movement's incorporation in 1932, took control of the movement. Since then, no further dictations from the Masters have been received, because no new messenger has been appointed to succeed the Ballards."

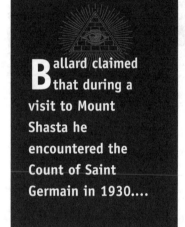

Ballard claimed that during a visit to Mount Shasta he encountered the Count of Saint Germain in 1930....

Ballard claimed that during a visit to Mount Shasta he encountered the Count of Saint Germain in 1930, an eighteenth-century alchemist often credited with finding the secret of immortality, which enables him to turn up repeatedly in our own time and create still another New Age legend.

During this experience on Mount Shasta, the Count told Ballard many things regarding America's future role in ushering in a new era for the people of Earth, as well as his personal knowledge of the so-called Ascended Masters, who included the living Christ. By the 1940s, Ballard's followers in the I AM movement exceeded the one million mark; people who apparently believed Ballard had been chosen to impart words of deep wisdom sent to him by the Ascended Masters. Unfortunately, Ballard also had ties to the fascistic Silver Shirts, led by the racist and anti-Semitic William Pelley. It was as a result of Ballard's links to Pelley's organization that George Hunt Williamson gravitated towards the world of the Silver Shirts.

After Ballard's death in 1942, his widow and son were charged with eighteen counts of mail fraud on the grounds that the claims made in their literature relative to the Ascended Masters and Mount Shasta, in books and pamphlets sold through the mail, could not be proven. They were convicted on all eighteen counts, but the convictions were later overturned in what turned out to be a landmark case concerning what claims could and could not be made in the name of religion.

Today, decades after Ballard's passing, devotees of his movement continue to hold an annual event on Mount Shasta called the "I AM Come!" pageant, which gives praise to Jesus Christ.

Illuminati

Although what is known officially as the Order of the Illuminati did not come into being until the 1700s, the word "Illuminati" has origins that date back to at least the 1400s. In Spain, at that time, those who immersed themselves in the world of the black arts identified occultists, alchemists, and witches as having been given "the light." We're talking about nothing less than a supernatural form of illumination that gave them extraordinary powers. Hence, the term "Illuminati." As for the Order of the Illuminati, it was created in 1776—specifically on May 1. The man behind the mysterious group was Adam Weishaupt. The location: Ingolstadt, Bavaria. At the time, Weishaupt was approaching his thirties and worked as a professor of religious law. As author Brad Steiger notes, Weishaupt "blended mysticism into the workings of the brotherhood in order to make his agenda of republicanism appear to be more mysterious than those of a political reform group."

The group had decidedly small-scale origins: it began with just five members, one being Weishaupt himself. The Illuminati was not destined to stay that way, however. Bit by bit, the group began to grow, to the point where, by 1780, the membership was around five dozen and extended to six cities. Certainly, many were attracted to Weishaupt's group as a result of the fact that it paralleled the Masons—specifically in relation to levels and orders of hierarchy that could be achieved. Indeed, Weishaupt was careful to point out to his followers that the further they immersed themselves in the domain of the Illuminati, the greater level of illuminated, supernatural knowledge they would achieve.

History has shown that Weishaupt was not alone in ensuring the Illuminati prospered. He was aided to a very significant degree by one Adolf Francis, better known as Baron von Knigge. A renowned and influential figure with an expert knowledge of all things of an occult nature, von Knigge was a powerful individual who had risen through the ranks of the

German philosopher Adam Weishaupt founded the Illuminati in 1776.

Masons. And, he shared Weishaupt's desire for political revolution. In no time, and as a result of von Knigge's contacts and ability to entice others to the cause, the Illuminati grew to a group of several hundred. The Illuminati was not a group open to everyone, however. In fact, quite the opposite: the powerful, the rich, and the well-connected were those who Weishaupt and von Knigge worked hard to bring on board. Rituals and rites for those who wished to be a part of Weishaupt's vision were established, as was the wearing of specific clothes—or as Brad Steiger described them, "bizarre costumes." And, the membership expanded ever further.

By the mid-1780s, the Illuminati was no longer a group with hundreds of followers, but thousands. In 1784, however, there was dissent in the ranks. It was in April of that year when von Knigge and Weishaupt had a major falling out, which led to von Knigge walking away from the group. There was another problem, too: the occult illumination that Weishaupt had promised his followers failed to appear. Many of them became disillusioned, suspecting that Weishaupt actually had very little interest in the domain of the occult, but had really sought out the rich and powerful as a means to help his plans for revolution. The outcome was that many walked away from the Illuminati, fearful that it was becoming a manipulative, sinister body with hidden agendas. It wasn't at all long before the Illuminati was no more. On this issue, let's turn again to Brad Steiger: "In June 1784 Karl Theodor [the Duke of Bavaria] issued an edict outlawing all secret societies in his province. In March 1785 another edict specifically condemned the Illuminati. Weishaupt had already fled to a neighboring province, where he hoped to inspire the loyal members of the Illuminati to continue as a society. In 1787 the duke issued a final edict against the Order of the Illuminati, and Weishaupt apparently faded into obscurity."

Immortality Group

On more than a few occasions, I have been the recipient of fantastic accounts of a mind-blowing nature. The problem, however, is that no matter how deeply I pursued the relevant story, I reached nothing but an endless brick wall. So, I figured I would share with you one of those cases—right here, right now. Of course, I can't say for sure that it isn't the work of nothing but a fantasist or a hoaxer, one with an agenda of the very obscure kind. But, by at least putting the data out there, I also figure it may well provoke debate.

It's a story that was told to me in 2012 and which focuses on the not insignificant matter of immortality. We all want to live forever, right? Well, yes, we do. Providing, of course, we can remain at the age of our choosing, and not spend our days forever locked into extremely elderly, decrepit mode. As for the story, it was all focused on a hush-hush program that was run out of a particular facility in Utah.

It was a program that allegedly began in 2003 and was prompted by the discovery of certain, unspecified, ancient "things" in Baghdad, after the invasion of Iraq began. The project had at its heart something both amazing and controversial. It all revolved around nothing less than attempts to bring the human aging process to a halt—and maybe, even … to reverse it. This was, however, a very unusual program, in the sense that it didn't just rely on modern day technology and medicine. That may sound odd, but bear with me and I'll explain what I mean by that.

Yes, the program had a number of brilliant scientists attached to it, but it was also populated by theologians, historians, and archaeologists—who were quietly contracted and hired and subjected to grim non-disclosure agreements. The quest for the truth of immortality was, to a very significant degree, not based around the present or the future, but on the distant past. Much time was spent digging into accounts of none other than Manna from Heaven and the controversies surrounding what has become known as White Powder Gold, the Bread of Presence, and Amrita.

All of these have several things in common: (a) they have ancient origins; (b) they have to be ingested; (c) they have the potential to offer perfect health; and (d) they promise never-ending life. Of course, it must be stressed that this is what legend, mythology, and ancient religious texts tell us. Actually proving that these mysterious "things" exist and also proving they can do what we are told they can do, is a very different matter. So, I did what I always do in these situations, which is to listen very carefully to what the relevant person has to say. True or not, the story was pretty incredible.

Deep underground, scientists who had spent much of their working lives striving to understand why, exactly, the aging process occurs as it does, were sat next to biblical experts who were deciphering and interpreting ancient texts on the aforementioned life-extending, digestible substances. Military personnel, who were dutifully ensuring the program ran under the strictest levels of security and safety, rubbed shoulders with modern-day alchemists, who were striving to crack the White Powder Gold conundrum, and learned souls in the fields of none other than ancient astronauts, and the Bible's legendary "men of renown," crossed paths with demonologists.

The story continued that, at least as late as 2010, absolutely no progress had been made beyond adding to the lore and legend that surround tales of immortality and massive lifespans in times long gone. Rather ironically, the fact that I was told the project was a hundred percent failure added credibility to the story—for me, at least, it did. You may think otherwise.

To me, it sounds exactly like the kind of off-the-wall program that a significant amount of money might be provided to, in the event that it just might, one day, offer something sensational and literally life-changing. That the source of the story specifically didn't spin some controversial and conspiratorial tale of a secret, ruling elite living forever, was one of the things that makes me think there just might have been something to all this—and perhaps there still is.

Improved Order of Red Men

The Improved Order of Red Men state: "The fraternity traces its origins back to 1765 and is descended from the Sons of Liberty. These patriots concealed their identities and worked 'underground' to help establish freedom and liberty in the early Colonies. They patterned themselves after the great Iroquois Confederacy and its democratic governing body. Their system, with elected representatives to govern tribal councils, had been in existence for several centuries. After the War of 1812 the name was changed to the Society of Red Men and in 1834 to the Improved Order of Red Men. They kept the customs and terminology of Native Americans as a basic part of the fraternity. Some of the words and terms may sound strange, but they soon become a familiar part of the language for every member. The Improved Order of Red Men (IORM) is similar in many ways to other major fraternal organizations in the United States."

Additional background on the fraternity comes from the Williamsport Red Men, who offer the following: "With the formation of a national organization, the Improved Order of Red Men soon spread, and within thirty years there were State Great Councils in 21 states with a membership of over 150,000. The Order continued to grow, and by the mid-1920s there were tribes in forty-six states and territories with a membership totaling over one-half million. Today, The Improved Order of Red Men continues to offer all patriotic Americans an organization that is pledged to the high ideals of Freedom, Friendship, and Charity. These are the same ideals of which the American nation was founded. By belonging to this proud and historic organization you can demonstrate your desire to continue the battle started at Lexington and Concord to promote Freedom and protect the American Way of Life."

StichingArgus provides us with an insight into the world of the Red Men: "Rather astonishingly, the Improved Order of Red Men uses alongside the Gregorian calendar its own system of reckoning, based on the 'discovery' of the

Americas by Columbus in 1492; 1992 was, therefore, the year 500 of the I.O.R.M calendar. The rituals are based on white perceptions of some northeastern Native American tribes, especially those of the Algonquian linguistic group. There are three degrees, Adoptive, Warrior, and Chief. There is also a non-initiatory Beneficiary Degree for insurance. The Adoption and Warrior degrees illustrate the order's line of thought. For the Adoption degree, a hunting expedition (made up of Wigwam members) has stopped for the night, when a lost paleface comes upon their camp. He is captured, taken back to the main encampment, and tied to a stake to be killed. At the instigation of the Prophet, the tribe changes its mind and adopts him into the tribe, giving him a new tribal name based on an animal or bird, or on some trait of character."

As for the oath of the Red Men, it goes like this: "I, [Name], being desirous of becoming acquainted with the mysteries of the Improved Order of Red Men, do hereby solemnly promise and declare, that I will keep secret from all persons, except such as I shall prove to be Improved Red Men, all signs, passwords, and other matters that are to be kept secret.

An 1889 membership certificate issued by the Improved Order of Red Men. The fraternity descended from the Sons of Liberty.

And I do further promise, that I will never attempt to kindle a council fire unless I am duly and regularly authorized to do so, or assist or participate in any council the fire of which has been kindled by a suspended or expelled brother, or any other person not authorized by the Great Council of the United States to kindle the same. To all this I promise and pledge my sacred honor, without intending any evasion whatever. So help me, the Great Spirit."

Jack the Ripper

In the latter part of 1888, a deadly figure roamed the shadowy and foggy back-streets of Whitechapel, London, England, by night, violently slaughtering prostitutes and provoking terror throughout the entire capital. He quickly became—and still remains to this very day—the world's most notorious serial killer. He was, in case you haven't guessed, Jack the Ripper. But, what makes the Ripper so infamous, more than a century after his terrible crimes were committed, is that his identity still remains a mystery, and everyone loves a mystery.

So, who might Jack have been? The theories are almost endless. Indeed, no fewer than thirty potential suspects have been identified. They include a powerful Freemason, a surgeon, a doctor, a poet, and even a member of the British Royal Family. What follows is a list of those individuals who have had more fingers pointed at them than any others.

Without doubt, the most controversial theory for whom, exactly, Jack the Ripper might have been, is that he was a member of the British Royal Family, specifically Prince Albert Victor, the Duke of Clarence. It was a theory that first surfaced in the early 1960s, specifically in the pages of a book by French author Philippe Julian. In the 1967 English language version, Julian wrote:

"Before he died, poor Clarence was a great anxiety to his family. He was quite characterless and would soon have fallen a prey to some intriguer or group of roués, of which his regiment was full. They indulged in every form of debauchery, and on one occasion the police discovered the Duke in a *maison de recontre* of a particularly equivocal nature during a raid. The young man's evil reputation soon spread. The rumor gained ground that he was Jack the Ripper."

Additional rumors suggested that Albert had caught syphilis from a London prostitute and, in a deranged state of mind caused by the increasing effects of his condition, roamed the Whitechapel district of London in search of prostitutes, upon whom he could take out his rage and revenge. Nothing concrete, however, has surfaced—so far, at least—to suggest the prince was Jack. That hasn't stopped the theory from thriving, however.

A variation on the theory that the Duke of Clarence was Jack the Ripper is that he was not the killer but was connected to him in a roundabout fashion. The Duke, theorists suggest, secretly married a woman who was a Catholic. This was too much for Queen Victoria, and so a dark plan was put into place. Sir William Withey Gull, the 1st Baronet of Brook Street, and a

One of the more startling Jack the Ripper theories is that the murderer might have been Prince Albert Victor, the Duke of Clarence.

noted physician and Freemason, took on the grim task of killing the friends of the young woman in question who knew of the secret marriage. Gull, then, trying to protect the Royals from scandal, was the man behind the Ripper legend, and to ensure that the killings were not traceable back to the highest levels of the British Royal Family, the legend of the serial killer, Jack the Ripper, was created as a convenient cover and diversion. Maybe.

As early as the 1890s, American newspapers were reporting on the rumor that Jack was actually a prominent figure in London medicine, one who, according to the man's wife, had displayed violent characteristics at the height of the killings. Supposedly, the story got back to the man's coworkers. They quickly visited the family home and found a number of undisclosed items that strongly suggested the man was indeed Jack the Ripper. He was reportedly hospitalized for his own good and died soon after. Perhaps of some significance, Gull—who famously coined the term anorexia nervosa—died in 1890, just two years after the Ripper murders took place.

In 1970, the late English physician Thomas Edmund Alexander Stowell stated that Gull was not the Ripper but was the killer's doctor. Although Stowell did not come straight to the point and name Jack, his words and description of the man make it clear that he was talking about the Duke of Clarence.

Six years later, in 1976, the Gull theory was advanced at length in the pages of Stephen Knight's book, *Jack the Ripper: The Final Solution.* Knight's book was lauded at the time, but the story he told—of Gull, of a huge Masonic conspiracy, and of terrible murders that were linked to the British monarchy—has since been very convincingly denounced, even by leading figures in the Jack the Ripper research community.

John Hamill, of the Freemasons' United Grand Lodge of England, said: "The Stephen Knight thesis is based upon the claim that the main protagonists, the Prime Minister Lord Salisbury, Sir Charles Warren, Sir James Anderson and Sir William Gull were all high-ranking Freemasons. Knight knew his claim to be false for, in 1973, I received a phone call from him in the Library, in which he asked for confirmation of their membership. After a lengthy search I informed him that only Sir Charles Warren had been a Freemason. Regrettably, he chose to ignore this answer as it ruined his story."

Jacobin Club

It was in the eighteenth century that the France-based Society of the Friends of the Constitution was created. In the early 1790s, however, it took on a new title: the Society of the Jacobins, Friends of Freedom and Equality. It was, however, most often referred to as the Jacobin Club. At the height of the French Revolution—which ran from 1789 to 1799—the Jacobin Club was, beyond any shadow of a doubt, the one group that held more political sway than any other. Although, initially, a small body that operated out of Brittany, it rapidly became a countrywide organization that swelled in size to the point where its followers were numbered at around half a million.

Jonah Walter says that the Jacobin Club "embodied the most radical response to the revolutionary crisis; to defeat the forces of reaction, they found themselves compelled to take radical measures—including price controls, food seizures, and the period of tactical violence that would come to be known as the 'Reign of Terror.' While in early periods the Jacobin Club had included more moderate actors, the radical wing that cohered around Robespierre— known as the Montagnards—ultimately became the dominant tendency within the Jacobins' ranks."

The *Columbia Encyclopedia* notes: "In the National Convention, which proclaimed the French republic, the Jacobins and other opponents of the Girondists sat in the raised seats and were called the Mountain. Their leaders—Maximilien Robespierre and Louis de Saint-Just, among others—relied mainly on the strength of the Paris commune and the Parisian sans-culottes. After the fall of the Girondists (June, 1793), for which the Jacobins were largely responsible, the Jacobin leaders instituted the Reign of Terror. Under Robespierre, who came to dominate the government, the Terror was used not only against counterrevolutionaries, but also against former allies of the Jacobins, such as the Cordeliers and the Dantonists (followers of Georges Danton). The fall of Robespierre on 9 Thermidor (July 27, 1794) meant the fall of the Jacobins, but their spirit lived on in revolutionary doctrine."

Jet Propulsion Laboratory

Of its Jet Propulsion Laboratory—based in Pasadena, California—the National Aeronautics and Space Administration (NASA), says: "JPL grew up with the Space Age and helped bring it into being. It is a place where science, technology, and engineering intermix in unique ways: to produce iconic robotic space explorers sent to every corner of the solar system, to peer deep into the Milky Way galaxy and beyond, and to keep a watchful eye on our home planet. Analyzing the data pouring back from these machine emissaries, scientists around the world continue to discover how the universe, the solar system, and life formed and evolved.

"JPL's beginnings can be traced to the mid-1930s, when a few Caltech students and amateur rocket enthusiasts started tinkering with rockets. After an unintended explosion occurred on campus, the group and its experiments relocated to an isolated area next to the San Gabriel Mountains, the present-day site of JPL. In the following decade, as an anxious country sought to respond to the menacing challenge of German V-2 rockets, the fledgling Jet Propulsion Laboratory (officially named in 1944, some 14 years before NASA was formed) was sponsored by the U.S. Army to develop rocket technology and the Corporal and Sergeant missile-systems."

What is left out of this statement from the JPL is that among those "students and amateur rocket enthusiasts" who "started tinkering with rockets," one of them was Marvel Whiteside Parsons—better known as Jack Parsons, a brilliant pioneer in the field of rocketry who ran Aleister Crowley's Agape Lodge of the Thelemic Ordo Templi Orientis (O.T.O.) in California. It's notable that Parsons's company, the Aerojet Corporation, made the solid-fuel rocket boosters that ensured NASA's Space Shuttle fleet took to the heavens. Parsons even has a crater named after him on the surface of the Moon. But, that's not all.

The Jet Propulsion Laboratory is located outside of Los Angeles, California, in La Cañada Flintridge.

On every Halloween, the staff of the Jet Propulsion Laboratory perform an intriguing ritual—in Parsons's honor. Halloween takes its name from All Hallows' Eve, a term first used in the 1500s. That Halloween is tied to All Saints Day (which is celebrated on November 1, one day after Halloween) had led to an understandable assumption that Halloween has Christian-based origins. It does not. There's no doubt that the ancient, Gaelic festival of Samhain played a significant role in the development of Halloween. Pagan rites and Druidic rituals were part and parcel of the way in which Halloween came to be, too. It is, therefore, very intriguing that the staff of the Jet Propulsion Laboratory embraces the world's creepiest night—and its attendant ties to paganism and the world of the Druids—by paying homage to Jack Parsons. They do so in a very strange fashion.

Mannequins—dressed in white lab-style coats and designed to represent Parsons and his colleagues in the early years of rocketry—are wheeled into the JPL. The staff holds nothing less than a memorial to the man and his groundbreaking work. Within the world of the JPL, the joke is that those three letters actually stand for "Jack Parsons Lives."

While the JPL is not itself a secret society, the fact that once a year its personnel embraces a ceremony born out of paganism and secret, Druidic teachings—and also embraces Parsons, who was a disciple of Aleister Crowley, a man who had fingers in numerous secret pies—is intriguing. More correctly, it's beyond intriguing.

John Birch Society

The website of the John Birch Society provides the following on this particular group: "Formed by Robert Welch in December 1958, The John Birch Society takes its name from World War II Army Captain John Birch, an unsung hero. The organization's overall goal is to educate the American people about their country and its enemies, in order to protect our freedom and the nation's independence."

The JBS continues that, since the late 1950s, it has remained "an education and action organization. With organized chapters in all 50 states, the JBS stands firm in its defense of freedom, morality, and the U.S. Constitution. John Birch, our namesake, worked hard to serve God, family, and country. As a solo missionary in China, he brought God's Word to remote villages.

"During WWII, John risked his life to rescue American prisoners and pilots, volunteered for spy missions, and transmitted enemy locations to Allied Forces.

As a guiding strength to others, he never lost faith. Tragically, he was murdered by Chinese Communists 10 days after the war ended. John was only 27.

"Robert Welch, a child prodigy, graduated high school at the age of 12 and college at 16. He attended the U.S. Naval Academy and Harvard Law School. Highly educated, Welch became a successful candy manufacturer, retiring in 1956. Robert Welch recognized that the U.S. Constitution and our God-given rights were under attack. As a result, in 1958, he created The John Birch Society, uniting citizens to effectively battle those who threaten our freedoms. Today, The John Birch Society is known as the defender of freedom, as inspired by the selfless John Birch and established by the determined Robert Welch."

Author Brad Steiger has noted that the influence on U.S. politics by the John Birch Society really came into being in 1964, when there was a major push to have Republican senator Barry Goldwater elected president of the United States. JBS personnel, says Steiger, "published several widely distributed books that simultaneously promoted conspiracy theories and support for Goldwater. *None Dare Call It Treason*, by John A. Stormer, warned about decay in the public schools and the advance of Communism throughout the world; it sold over 7 million copies."

> The influence on U.S. politics by the John Birch Society really came into being in 1964, when there was a major push to have Republican senator Barry Goldwater elected president of the United States.

Steiger also notes: "*A Choice, Not an Echo*, by Phylis Schafly, worried about the Republican Party's being controlled by elitists and Bilderbergers. *The Gravediggers*, coauthored by Schafly and retired rear admiral Chester Ward, revealed that U.S. military strategy had paved the way for Communist conquest of the world."

John Michael Greer, an expert on the domain of secret societies observes that the John Birch Society "remains a small but vocal presence on the extreme right, while the ideas it launched into popular culture have become central elements of the worldviews of tens of millions of Americans."

The final word goes to the John Birch Society: "By definition, a conspiracy is when two or more people work in secret for evil purposes. The John Birch Society believes this definition fits a number of groups working against the independence of the United States. Extensive study has shown us that history is rarely accidental."

Kabbalistic Order of the Rose and Cross

"From the 18th century to our modern era," says the Ordre Kabbalistique de la Rose-Croix, "South-Western France has played an important role in the world of Hermetism." They note that it was the birthplace of "the modern religious currents," those specifically inspired by "Gnosticism, Occult Freemasonry side-degrees (degrees above the 3rd degree in Freemasonry) and several Rosicrucian and Kabbalistic schools."

The Ordre adds: "This area remained the incontrovertible place of origin of the Western Initiatic societies and continues to have a special stature in the collective history which has grown larger than its French origins. We may remind the reader of the mystery of 'Rennes le Château' and the 'Priory of Sion' which took place in the region call 'Razes.' The hermetic and teachings were, and continue to be, a given in this part of France. Consequently, it was in this region that an essential initiatic tradition appeared. We know this tradition today as the Rose-Cross."

Gnostique says of the order that it was largely based upon "the classical occult disciplines such as QBL, Tarot, Astrology, Alchemy, Theurgy, Numerology, Divination and Rituals."

It offers the following, too: "The initiations consisted of 3 degrees, and one secret fourth degree. OKRC was closely attached to the Martinist Order and the Gnostic Church. The first exam resulted in a Bachelor's in Kabbalah and consisted of the study of the western tradition, particularly that of the Rose-Croix and the knowledge of the letters of the Hebrew Aleph-Bet, their form, their name and their symbolism; the second conferred a Licentiate in Kabbalah focusing on the general history of religious traditions throughout history and how they reflect a more universal Truth as well as the study of certain Hebrew words. This part of the exam was oral. A second written part consisted of a philosophical, moral or mystical question whose answer ought to have been made evident to the candidate by this point; the third consisted of the defense of a thesis with discussions on all the points of the Tradition and conferred the degree of Doctorate of Kabbalah."

King Arthur Secrets

Colin Perks—an Englishman who died prematurely from a heart attack while walking around the fence line of Stonehenge in 2009—was, for years, possessed by a definitive obsession. As a child, Perks became fascinated by the legends pertaining to one of the most well-known and cherished figures of British folklore: King Arthur. For Perks, however, Arthur was far more than mere myth. Perks, like so many other students of Arthurian lore, came to believe that the stories of King Arthur were based upon the exploits and battles of a very real ruler of that name. This Arthur held sway over significant portions of ancient Britain from the latter part of the fifth century to the early part of the sixth. He, and his fearless soldiers, bravely fought off invading hordes of Germanic Saxons and, as a result, left major marks upon British history and mythology.

By the time Perks reached his thirties, he was the proud possessor of a huge library on all things of a King Arthur-themed nature. His research, by now, was not just focused on the past, however. Rather, Perks, following clues that he believed were hidden in a series of complex codes and ciphers that had been provided to him by a fellow Arthur enthusiast in 1978, was a man on a mission to find the final resting place of King Arthur. The location, Perks concluded, was somewhere in the vicinity of the old English town of Glastonbury.

Late one evening in September 2000, and after a day and evening spent digging in the woods, Perks received a very weird, and somewhat disturbing, phone call. It was from a woman who made it very clear that she wanted to discuss with Perks his studies of an Arthurian nature. She also made it clear she would not take no for an answer.

Several nights later, and at the arranged time of 7:00 P.M., there was a knock at the door. Perks took a deep breath and opened it. He was confronted by what can only be described as a Woman in Black. Standing before him was a beautiful woman, thirty-five to forty years of age. She was dressed in a smart and expensive-looking outfit, had a long and full-bodied head of black hair, and the palest and smoothest skin. For a moment there was silence. Perks simply stared, feeling various parts captivated, intimidated, and downright frightened. Although the woman's face appeared utterly emotionless, Perks detected a hard-to-define air of hostility, and perhaps even hatred, of him. This was hardly a good start to the evening, and it proceeded to get even worse.

Wasting no time, Sarah Key got straight to the point and informed Perks that she, and what she described as her "colleagues," had been carefully watching him for years. She added, in no uncertain terms, that the purpose of her visit was to request that Perks cease his research. A suddenly defensive Perks loudly responded that there was no way he would ever stop his work to find King Arthur's burial site. On top of that he scoffed at the very idea that shadowy figures were watching his every move, both in Glastonbury and in the heart of the old woods. Or, it's more correct to say he scoffed until Sarah Key reeled off fact upon fact about where Perks was on specific days and nights, even down to which local pubs he visited for dinner and a pint of Guinness after his nightly work in the woods was over. That's when the scoffing came to a shuddering halt.

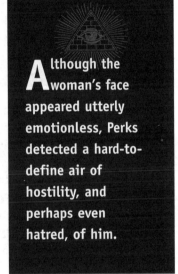

Although the woman's face appeared utterly emotionless, Perks detected a hard-to-define air of hostility, and perhaps even hatred, of him.

As Colin Perks sat silently, Sarah Key continued that Arthur's grave—or his "chamber," as she specifically described it—was no ordinary resting place. Rather, it was built atop a paranormal gateway, a portal, to other dimensions where there dwelled hideous and terrible beasts of the kind that H. P. Lovecraft would have been forever proud. The chamber had been constructed as a means to prevent the foul things of this strange realm from entering our world. Perks's dabbling and digging, Key told him, might have been innocent and earnest, but he was playing with definitive fire that could result in catastrophe and carnage if the magical gateway was opened.

Sarah Key's tone then became downright menacing and her face became grim in the extreme. She explained that if Perks did not give up his quest, he would receive yet another visit. From whom, or what, was not made entirely clear, but Perks knew it was destined to be nothing positive or friendly.

It was roughly two months later, and late at night, when Perks had a truly terrifying encounter. He was driving back to Glastonbury from the city of Bath—which, like Glastonbury, is also located in the English county of Somerset. On one piece of road that lacked illumination and which was curiously free of any other traffic, a bizarre figure suddenly materialized in the road ahead.

One week later, and not long after the witching hour, Perks was awakened from his sleep by the horrific sight of the gargoyle looming menacingly over his bed.

Luckily, as the road was a small and winding one, Perks's speed was barely twenty-five miles per hour, which gave him time to quickly apply the brakes. In front of him was what can only be described as the closest thing one could imagine to a gargoyle. That's to say a tall, man-like figure sporting nothing less than a large pair of bat-style wings. A pair of blazing red eyes penetrated Perks's very soul. Hysterical with fear, Perks hit the accelerator pedal and the creature vanished before his eyes before impact could occur. Matters weren't quite over, however.

One week later, and not long after the witching hour, Perks was awakened from his sleep by the horrific sight of the gargoyle looming menacingly over his bed. Paralyzed with fear, and with the creature gripping his wrists tightly, Perks could only stare in utter shock as the beast delivered a telepathic-style message to stay away from the woods, and to cease looking for the chamber of King Arthur. An instant later, the monstrous form was gone. Perks wondered for a few seconds if it had all been a horrific nightmare. In his heart of hearts, however, he knew it wasn't. In fact, Perks ultimately came to believe that Sarah Key—Perks's very own Woman in Black—and the gargoyle were not just interconnected. Rather, he concluded that Key was a hideous and supernatural shapeshifter, one that could take on any form it desired, including that of something akin to a gargoyle.

Colin Perks did not—despite the traumatic nature of the encounters with the gargoyle—give up his research. Nevertheless, he remained a shell of his former self for the rest of his days, living on his nerves and fearing that the gargoyle lurked around every darkened corner.

Knights Templar

In his 1842 book, *The History of the Knights Templar*, Charles G. Addison wrote: "The extraordinary and romantic career of the Knights Templars, their exploits and their misfortunes, render their history a subject of peculiar interest. Born during the first fervor of the Crusades, they were flattered and aggrandized as long as their great military power and religious fanaticism could be made available for the support of the Eastern church and the retention of the Holy Land, but when the crescent had ultimately triumphed over the cross, and the religion-military enthusiasm of Christendom had died away, they encountered the basest ingratitude in return for the services they had rendered to the Christian faith, and were plundered, persecuted, and condemned to a cruel death, by those who ought in justice to have been their defenders and supporters. The memory of these holy warriors is embalmed in all our recollections of the wars of the cross; they were the bulwarks of the Latin kingdom of Jerusalem during the short period of its existence, and were the last band of Europe's host that contended for the possession of Palestine."

There was, however, far more than that to the group. The Knights Templar website says: "Once the Crusade was finished, most of the surviving crusaders, having fulfilled their vows, returned home. The Knights Templar would provide the solution by becoming the first international standing army. The opportunity came in 1118–19, when an idealistic band of knights led by Hugues de Payens offered their services to protect pilgrims en route to the Holy Places. Organizing themselves into a religious community, vows were made to the Latin Patriarch of Jerusalem. Baldwin II, king of Jerusalem, provided them with quarters in what had been the al-Aqsa Mosque, thought to be part of Solomon's Temple. They became known as the Poor Knights of

The Convent of Christ Castle, located in Tomar, Portugal, was a stronghold of the Knights Templar in the twelfth century.

Christ of the Temple of Solomon, or simply the Knights of the Temple. Perhaps it was the King, who saw in these Poor Knights of Christ, the opportunity to create a fighting force. This was reinforced when the counts of Anjou and Champagne joined the Order."

Christopher Check expands our knowledge: "By the middle of the 12th century, the Templars had an extensive network of agricultural estates, or preceptors, throughout France, Italy, Spain, and England. These funded the high cost of the Templars' defense of Christianity's tenuous hold on the Holy Land. Secular knights would come and go, but it was the military religious orders—the Templars, the Hospitallers, and the Teutonic Knights—who constituted the standing army of the Crusades."

The Knights Templar was an imposing powerful force, as a twelfth century pilgrim noted: "Their black and white standard, which is called the baucent, goes before them into battle. They go into battle without making a noise. They are the first to desire engagement and more vigorous than the others. When the trumpet sounds for advance, they piously sing this psalm of David: 'Not to us Lord, not to us but to your name give the glory.' They couch their lances and charge into the enemy. As one body they ravage the ranks of the enemy, they never yield. They either destroy the foe completely or they die. In returning from battle they are the last to go behind the rest of the crowd looking after all the rest and protecting them."

The Library of Halexandria reveals what turned out to be the downfall of the Knights Templar: "In 1306, Philippe IV of France, was acutely anxious to rid his territory of the Templars, who were, at their best, arrogant and unruly. But for Philippe, the Templars were also efficient and highly trained, a professional military force much stronger and better organized than anything Philippe IV could muster. Philippe had no control over them, as their allegiance was only to the Pope, and even the latter was only a nominal allegiance. On top of all of this, Philippe owed the Templars money. A great deal of money! But worse yet, Philippe had also been humiliated by the Templars on more than one occasion, including the indignity of having been haughtily rejected when he applied to join the order as a postulant. All of this prompted Philippe to act against the Templars, using heresy as a convenient excuse.

"In 1312, the bullied Pope officially dissolved the Knights Templar—despite the lack of a conclusive verdict of guilt or innocence ever being pronounced—and despite Philippe's attempts for another two years to extract information. In March 1314, Jacques de Molay, the grand master of the Templars, and Geoffroi de Charnay, preceptor of Normandy, were roasted to death over a slow fire. With their execution the Templars supposedly vanished from the stage of history. Nevertheless, the order did not cease to exist, and given the number of knights who escaped, who remained at large, or who were acquitted, it would be surprising if it had."

Know-Nothing Party

*O*hio History Central says of the Know-Nothing Party: "The Know-Nothing Party, also known as the American Party, was a prominent United States political party during the late 1840s and the early 1850s. The American Party originated in 1849. Its members strongly opposed immigrants and followers of the Catholic Church. The majority of white Americans followed Protestant faiths. Many of these people feared Catholics because members of this faith followed the teachings of the Pope. The Know-Nothings feared that the Catholics were more loyal to the Pope than to the United States."

Some of the members of the Know-Nothing Party went much further than that: they came to suspect that the Catholic Church had nothing less than a secret agenda to essentially seize control of the United States, from the heart of the government and right down to the populace itself. From there, those same believers concluded, the United States would be placed under the control of the pope, and the United States would be effectively ruled by the Vatican. With these beliefs in place, the Know-Nothing Party came up with a plan: if members of the party were elected, it was their intent to ban anyone and everyone of a Catholic persuasion—and all immigrants—from running for the presidential office. They intended to go further still, to the point of trying to ensure both Catholics and immigrants would be barred from taking employment with powerful, American businesses.

Back to *Ohio History Central:* "The majority of Know-Nothings came from middle and working-class backgrounds. These people feared competition for jobs from immigrants coming to the United States. Critics of this party named it the Know-Nothing Party because it was a secret organization. Its members would not reveal the party's doctrines to non-members. Know-Nothings were to respond to questions about their beliefs with, 'I know nothing.' The Know-Nothing Party adopted the American Party as its official name in 1854. The Know-Nothing Party quickly grew in popularity in the North, where most recent immigrants to the United States resided. In 1854, Know-Nothing candidates even won control of the Massachusetts legislature."

President Abraham Lincoln was someone who was highly disturbed by the actions and ideas of the Know-Nothing Party. He made his views very clear to one and all: "Our progress in degeneracy appears to me to be pretty

rapid. As a nation, we begin by declaring that 'all men are created equal.' We now practically read it 'all men are created equal, except negroes.' When the Know-Nothings get control, it will read 'all men are created equal, except negroes, and foreigners, and Catholics.' When it comes to this I should prefer emigrating to some country where they make no pretense of loving liberty—to Russia, for instance, where despotism can be taken pure, and without the base alloy of hypocrisy."

Britannica offers this: "By 1852 the Know-Nothing party was achieving phenomenal growth. It did very well that year in state and local elections, and with passage of the Kansas-Nebraska Act in 1854 it won additional adherents from the ranks of conservatives who could support neither the proslavery Democrats nor antislavery Republicans. When Congress assembled on Dec. 3, 1855, 43 representatives were avowed members of the Know-Nothing party."

Things failed to stay like that, however. By the following year, the Know-Nothing Party was very much on a near-irreversible downward trend. Disagreements on policy—chiefly those relative to slavery—caused the group to split. The result was chaos and a loss of any and all strength and influence. Those from the party who elected to continue working in the field of politics primarily joined the Republican Party, while those members who were still pro-slavery gravitated to the Democratic Party. By 1856, the Know-Nothing Party was no more.

Ku Klux Klan

The Know-Nothing Party fronted several candidates during its heyday, including Millard Fillmore, who ran under its ticket in 1856, unsuccessfully, after serving as U.S. president from 1850 to 1853.

Few people know more about the controversial activities of the KKK than the FBI. Since its creation—now close to a century ago—the Bureau has been at the forefront of combating

KKK-driven hate crimes. From the files of the FBI we learn the following: "In February 1915 the D. W. Griffith movie later titled *The Birth of a Nation* premiered in a Los Angeles theater. Though considered progressive in its technique and style, the film had a decidedly backwards plot that glorified a short-lived, post-Civil War white supremacist group called the Ku Klux Klan. The movie's broad release in March provoked riots and even bloodshed nationwide.

"It also revived interest in the KKK, leading to the birth of several new local groups that summer and fall. Many more followed, mostly in southern states at first. Some of these groups focused on supporting the U.S. effort in World War I, but most wallowed in a toxic mix of secrecy, racism, and violence.

"As the Klan grew, it attracted the attention of the young Bureau. Created just a few years earlier—in July 1908—the Bureau of Investigation (as the organization was known then) had few federal laws to combat the KKK in these formative days. Cross burnings and lynchings, for example, were local issues. But under its general domestic security responsibilities, the Bureau was able to start gathering information and intelligence on the Klan and its activities, and wherever possible, we looked for federal violations and shared information with state and local law enforcement for its cases....

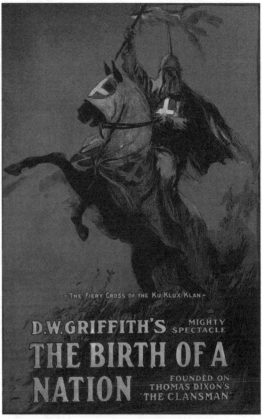

The 1915 D. W. Griffith film *The Birth of a Nation* glamorized the Ku Klux Klan, making its members heroes of the movie.

"In the early 1920s, membership in the KKK quickly escalated to six figures under the leadership of 'Colonel' William Simmons and advertising guru Edward Young Clarke. By the middle of the decade, the group boasted several million members. The crimes committed in the name of its bigoted beliefs were despicable—hangings, floggings, mutilations, tarring and featherings, kidnappings, brandings by acid, along with a new intimidation tactic, cross burnings. The Klan had become a clear threat to public safety and order.

"As the civil rights movement began to take shape in the 1950s, its important work was often met with opposition—and more significantly, with violence—by the increasingly resurgent white supremacist groups of the KKK. FBI agents in our southern field offices were on the front lines of this battle, working to see that the guilty were brought to justice and to undermine the efforts of the Klan in states like Mississippi. That was often difficult given the reluctance of witnesses to come forward and testify in court and the unwillingness of juries to convict Klansmen even in the face of clear evidence."

The FBI adds: "Over that time, the Klan has continued to morph and change. Today, it's a shadow of its brazen, lawless self in the 1950s and 1960s—thanks in large part to the dogged work of the FBI and its partners during that era—but ... the threat remains."

La Cosa Nostra

One of the most feared groups of all, La Cosa Nostra is, as the FBI notes, "the foremost organized criminal threat to American society. Literally translated into English it means 'this thing of ours.' It is a nationwide alliance of criminals—linked by blood ties or through conspiracy—dedicated to pursuing crime and protecting its members."

The FBI has made available detailed documentation that describes the origins and activities of La Cosa Nostra, as well as its fight against the group. The FBI says that La Cosa Nostra, or the LCN as it is known by the FBI, consists of different families or groups that are generally arranged geographically and engaged in significant and organized racketeering activity. It is also known as the Mafia, a term used to describe other organized crime groups. The LCN is most active in the New York metropolitan area, parts of New Jersey, Philadelphia, Detroit, Chicago, and New England. It has members in other major cities and is involved in international crimes.

Although La Cosa Nostra has its roots in Italian organized crime, it has been a separate organization for many years. Today, La Cosa Nostra cooperates in various criminal activities with different criminal groups that are headquartered in Italy. Giuseppe Esposito was the first known Sicilian Mafia member to immigrate to the United States. He and six other Sicilians fled to New York after murdering the chancellor and a vice chancellor of a Sicilian province and eleven wealthy landowners. He was arrested in New Orleans in 1881 and extradited to Italy.

New Orleans was also the site of the first major Mafia incident in this country. On October 15, 1890, New Orleans Police Superintendent David Hennessey was murdered execution-style. Hundreds of Sicilians were arrested, and nineteen were eventually indicted for the murder. An acquittal generated rumors of widespread bribery and intimidated witnesses. Outraged citizens of New Orleans organized a lynch mob and killed eleven of the nineteen defendants. Two were hanged, nine were shot, and the remaining eight escaped.

The American Mafia has evolved over the years as various gangs assumed—and lost—dominance over the years: the Black Hand gangs around 1900; the Five Points Gang in the 1910s and 1920s in New York City; Al Capone's Syndicate in Chicago in the 1920s. By the end of the 1920s, two primary factions had emerged, leading to a war for control of organized crime in New York City. The murder of faction leader Joseph Masseria brought an end to the gang warfare, and the two groups united to form the organization now dubbed La Cosa Nostra. It was not a peaceful beginning: Salvatore Maranzano, the first leader of La Cosa Nostra, was murdered within six months.

> The murder of faction leader Joseph Masseria brought an end to the gang warfare, and the two groups united to form the organization now dubbed La Cosa Nostra.

Charles "Lucky" Luciano became the new leader. Maranzano had established the La Cosa Nostra code of conduct, set up the family divisions and structure, and established procedures for resolving disputes. Luciano set up the Commission to rule all La Cosa Nostra activities. The Commission included bosses from six or seven families. Luciano was deported back to Italy in 1946 based on his conviction for operating a prostitution ring. There, he became a liaison between the Sicilian Mafia and La Cosa Nostra. Today, La Cosa Nostra is involved in a broad spectrum of illegal activities: murder, extortion, drug trafficking, corruption of public officials, gambling, infiltration of legitimate businesses, labor racketeering, loan sharking, prostitution, pornography, tax fraud schemes, and stock manipulation schemes."

League of the Just

In 1983, William Josiah Sutton (the author of *The Illuminati 666*) wrote that, "In 1785, the Bavarian Government exposed Adam Weishaupt's plan to destroy Christianity and control governments. However, this was not the end of the Illuminati, as most historians have written. Weishaupt's plans were only interrupted and dealt with as a dangerous revolutionary force in Germany. The other nations that the Illuminati were operating in did not heed the warning from the Bavarian Government."

Sutton continued: "Just a couple of years later, the plan to destroy Christianity and World Governments was first seen in the French Revolution. This same revolutionary force reappeared again in Germany, called 'The League of the Just,' with branches in London, Brussels, Paris, and Switzerland.

"Napoleon, when he came into power, would not tolerate the activities of the Jacobin Clubs with their independent opposition, so he completely suppressed it. However, the Illuminati just operated under other names. It was under the name of 'The League of the Just' that Karl Marx became a member. He was hired to update the writings of Adam Weishaupt, written seventy years earlier. Weishaupt died in 1830, but his revolutionary plans were carried on by a list of his successors."

As for the League of the Just, its origins can be traced back to 1836. That was the year in which a group of Germans—who had migrated to France specifically for political reasons—established what would soon become a powerful and secret body: the League of the Just, of course. Its teachings were very much in accord with those of François-Noël Babeuf, a French journalist and anarchist who was a major figure in the French Revolution of 1789 to 1799. The group's manifesto taught that "all men are brothers" and "the establishment of the Kingdom of God on Earth, based on the ideals of love of one's neighbor, equality and justice."

It's important to note that although the League of the Just came into being in 1836, there was a precursor to it, as Global Security notes: "The League of the Just was a splinter group from the League of Outlaws (Bund der Geaechteten) created in Paris in 1834 by Theodore Schuster, Wilhelm Weitling and other German emigres. Schuster was inspired by the works of Philippe Buonarroti. The League of Outlaws had a pyramidal structure inspired by the secret society of the Republican

Famous communist philosopher Karl Marx was a member of the League of the Just and helped update the original writings of Adam Weishaupt for the organization.

Carbonari, and shared ideas with Saint-Simon and Charles Fourier's utopic socialism. Their aim was to establish a 'Social Republic' in the German states which would respect 'freedom,' 'equality' and 'civic virtue.'

"In 1836 the most extreme, chiefly proletarian elements of the secret democratic-republican Outlaws' League, which was founded by German refugees in Paris in 1834, split off and formed the new secret League of the Just. The parent League, in which only sleepy-headed elements à la Jakobus Venedey were left, soon fell asleep altogether; when in 1840 the police scented out a few sections in Germany, it was hardly even a shadow of its former self."

The League of the Just continued to flex its muscles in the political arena. For example, its members played a significant role in the May 1839 Blanquist uprising, which attempted to overthrow France's King Louis Philippe. Amid all of the chaos that occurred during the uprising, several members of the group fled to London, England, where they established, in 1840, the Educational Society for German Working-Men. Then, seven years later, the League of the Just combined with figures from the Communist Corresponding Committee—overseen by Karl Marx and Friedrich Engels—and became the Communist League. It closed its doors in 1852.

Leek, Sybil

A prestigious author of books on numerous aspects of the world of magic and sorcery—including *How to be Your Own Astrologer*, *Diary of a Witch*, and *Cast Your Own Spell*—Sybil Leek was a woman who moved almost effortlessly in the worlds of secret, occult-driven groups, and those of influential and famous figures with whom such groups have become associated. She was born in Normacot, England, in 1917 and has been referred to as "Britain's most famous witch."

Leek was someone who became exposed to the old ways by her father, and while she was still a child. The magical properties of herbs, the ability of some animals to shapeshift, and matters relative to curses, invocations, and magical rites were all part of young Sybil's life. They stayed with her until the day she died. It wasn't just her father who inspired Sybil; it was also her grandmother. She, too, was well-acquainted with the world of the witch and matters of a sorcery-based nature. Her grandmother was also an expert in the field of astrology, something else that rubbed off on Sybil to a significant degree. She also had an alternative education. Her family preferred to homeschool her, albeit not in regular subjects, but chiefly in matters relative to all things of a psychic and divination nature.

A regular visitor to the Leek home was someone who surfaces on more than a few occasions in the pages of this book: Aleister Crowley. It was the "Great Beast" himself who pressed Leek to get involved in the field of writing. As history has shown, she did exactly that. A short-lived marriage began for Leek at the age of just sixteen (her husband died only two years later), after which she spent time in a French coven before finally returning to England. On doing so, she moved to the New Forest area of southern England—home to the New Forest Coven, which played an instrumental role in the development of modern day Wicca.

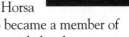

It was the "Great Beast" himself who pressed Leek to get involved in the field of writing.

Leek didn't just move to the New Forest—she lived in the woods, literally. Her friends were the local Romany Gypsy people, who took her in like one of their own, and with whom she stayed for around a year. It was in this specific period that Leek attended, and took part in, the rituals of the New Forest-based Horsa Coven—attaining the position of High Priestess—and also became a member of the Nine Covens Council, and all this before she left her teens behind.

At the age of twenty, Leek moved back in with her family and did nothing stranger than open a trio of antique shops—an ambitious plan, to be sure, for someone of such a young age. Unfortunately, although the shops were a success, Leek's reputation as a witch provoked a number of problems—and particularly so thanks to the media, which was constantly bombarding her for interviews and provoking what Leek considered to be unwelcome attention. It all came to a head when Leek's landlord—tired of his infamous renter—asked her to leave. But, as one door closed, another one opened, as it often does.

It's not at all out of the question that Leek—having lived in the New Forest—played a direct role in the matter of how the New Forest Coven, along with Gerald Gardner, allegedly thwarted Adolf Hitler's plans to invade the U.K. While we cannot be entirely sure, the fact that she lived in the area, and spent time with Gardner, strongly suggests that was the case. In addition, there is the fact that at the height of World War II, British Intelligence quietly hired her to create bogus horoscopes for the astrology-obsessed Nazis—horoscopes designed to adversely affect the Nazi morale by suggesting that Hitler's hordes were destined to lose the war, which, history has shown, they thankfully did.

In early 1964, Leek was invited to speak in the United States, chiefly on her work in the antiques trade, but which was quickly—and probably inevitably—eclipsed by her links to the world of secret societies, witchcraft, and the occult. She was very soon in high demand, and television, radio, and the lecture circuit all soon beckoned. She decided to remain in the United States, pleased at the way her career was growing, and spending much time with parapsychologist Hans Holzer. Leek soon moved to Los Angeles, where she met

Dr. Israel Regardie, a noted expert on Kabbalah and someone who shared her deep interest in Aleister Crowley's Hermetic Order of the Golden Dawn.

Sybil Leek died—in Melbourne Beach, Florida—in October 1982. She continued her work in the field of witchcraft until the very end.

Lemurians

Situated on the southern tip of the vast and mountainous Cascade Range—which encompasses parts of British Columbia, California, Washington state, and Oregon—Mount Shasta is a huge, all-dominating peak that, at nearly 15,000 feet, is the fifth tallest mountain in the Golden State, and one that has been home to human civilization, in varying degrees, since around 5000 B.C.E. It's also a mountain steeped in matters mysterious, unearthly, and deeply ancient.

Indeed, the interior of Mount Shasta is said to house the last vestiges of a mighty, renowned race of legendary people that dominated the planet in the fog-shrouded past. They were known as the Lemurians and were said to have inhabited a now sunken land, possibly situated somewhere in either the Pacific or Indian Ocean.

Although the people of Lemuria reportedly attained their peak millennia upon millennia ago, it was not until the late nineteenth century, and through the middle years of the twentieth century, that they caught the public's attention on a large scale—and particularly so in relation to a certain connection with Mount Shasta. Truly, the story is a swirling cauldron of deep strangeness and controversy.

Back in the 1800s, Helena Blavatsky, the cofounder with William Quan Judge and Colonel Henry S. Olcott of the Theosophical Society—the original mandate of which was the study of occultism—claimed to have been exposed to an ancient text of mysterious proportions that was said to have predated the times and people of Atlantis. Its title was the *Book of Dzyan* and was guarded with near paranoid zeal by a brotherhood of powerful and ancient proportions.

As a result of her alleged exposure to the old and mighty tome, and while in Tibet studying esoteric lore, Blavatsky developed a remarkable framework concerning, and a belief in, the Lemurians that ultimately led to the very heart of Mount Shasta itself.

According to Blavatsky's findings, the Lemurians were the type of people for whom the phrase "once seen, never forgotten" might justifiably have been created. Around seven feet in height, they were egg-laying hermaphrodites who, while not overly mentally developed, were, spiritually speaking, far more advanced than those who came before them.

As Blavatsky described it, the Lemurians were the Third Root Race of a total of seven who were ultimately destroyed by appalled and angered gods after they, the people of Lemuria, turned to bestiality, and in doing so sealed their doom, around 12,500 B.C.E. But, the gods were not done with life on Earth: they soon embarked on the creation of a Fourth Root Race, the equally legendary Atlanteans.

Little did the gods realize that when they set about the creation of a new race, some of the Lemurians escaped the destruction and made their secret way to—as you may by now have guessed—a certain mountain in the Cascades.

The revelations of Helena Blavatsky were elaborated on to a considerable degree by a British theosophist named William Scott-Elliot. He, in turn, had acquired his data from yet another theosophist, Charles Webster Leadbeater, who claimed clairvoyant communication with spiritually advanced, supernatural masters that imparted a wealth of data on both Lemuria and Atlantis.

Also hot on the heels of Blavatsky, and only six years before the dawning of the twentieth century, a teenager named Frederick Spencer Oliver completed the writing of his book *A Dweller on Two Planets*. Published in 1905, six years after Oliver's untimely and very early death, the book caused a firestorm of controversy with its claims that the Lemurians shared a lineage with the Atlanteans, and that those Lemurians who escaped the pummeling wrath of the gods made their secret and collective way to Mount Shasta, just as Blavatsky had asserted.

And they weren't just living on the mountain, but deep within it, too, in certain, secret, cavernous depths that Oliver asserted could be accessed if one only knew the specific and secret entrance points of old. If one should ever encounter a tall, white-robed figure on Mount Shasta, said Oliver, it was all but certain to be a Lemurian.

How, exactly, did Oliver know all this? Well, he claimed to have been in contact with a being that called itself Phylos the Tibetan.

Helen Blavatsky of Russia cofounded the Theosophical Society in 1875. She became convinced that there was a civilization called Lemuria, and evidence for this lay in Mount Shasta.

Phylos, whose controversial data was imparted to Oliver by a mind-to-mind process known as channeling, was said to have lived a number of lives or incarnations—one as a Lemurian and another as an Atlantean.

Leopard Society

❝In the spiritual beliefs of many African tribes," says author Brad Steiger, "the leopard is a totem animal that guides the spirits of the dead to rest. For many centuries there has existed a leopard cult in West Africa, particularly in Nigeria and Sierra Leone, whose members kill as does the leopard, by slashing, gashing, and mauling their human prey with steel claws and knives. Once a victim has been chosen and the date and time of the killing agreed upon, the executioner, known as the Bati Yeli, is selected. The Bati Yeli wears the ritual leopard mask and a leopardskin robe. Preferably, the human sacrifice is performed at one of the leopard cult's jungle shrines. After the cult has killed their victim, they drink the blood and eat the flesh. The cultists believe that a magical elixir known as borfima, which they brew from their victim's intestines, grants them superhuman powers and enables them to transform into leopards."

A man named Pat O'Dwyer stumbled upon such a secret cult—in the 1930s—in Makeni, Sierra Leone. O'Dwyer, the assistant district commissioner at Port Loko, said: "I had not been alone in charge of the station for long before a dead body was brought in from the country very much disintegrating. You can imagine that a dead body would not last long in the tropics. The chief's messenger, who brought it, said that the chief's view was that the man had been the victim of a secret society and that it was murder. The body had obviously been clawed about and the first thing for me to find out was what the doctor thought about the body's injuries.

"The corpse was taken, therefore, to the doctor who said that it was so decomposed that he could not really tell. However, the claw marks could be those of a leopard, or they could be imposed by metal claws and inflicted by man. I held an enquiry and the most feasible thing seemed to me to return a verdict of accidental death. I concluded that the man, who was a farmer living far out in the bush in a hut on the edge of the forest, had been the victim of a real leopard's attack and had thus met his death.

"After the verdict I heard murmurings by the Court Messengers to the effect that really he had been murdered by a secret society. Well, this is where the African's mind becomes very confused. There is no doubt that secret societies did exist, which were really murder societies: the Leopard Society, the Alligator Society and the Baboon Society. The allegations were that members of each of these societies took very secret and binding vows and associating themselves with these animals, simulated their methods of killing their selected victims.

"Thus, the Leopard Society would dress themselves in leopard skins and attach to their hands and feet metal claws. They would then lay in wait for their victim and pounce on him, clawing him to death. The Alligator Society would similarly attire themselves and wait by the water side and drown their victims and the Baboon Society would batter their victims to death. It was well known that these animals would also attack human beings and kill them, particularly children, out in the bush.

"A further possibility which the Africans believed in was that a member of these societies had the power to direct his soul into the body of a leopard, alligator or baboon and conduct that animal to attack the victim of his choice. A little while after this time there was trouble in the Kenema district where members of the baboon society were put on trial for murder. The evidence against them was very strong, and the accused themselves added evidence to prove their own guilt. They were found guilty and sentenced to death for murder and the sentence was carried out."

A particularly harrowing story came from Dr. Werner Junge, a German who, in 1930, traveled to Liberia and ended up staying for approximately ten years. He said of his discovery of someone who had fallen victim to the Leopard Society: "There, on a mat in a house, I found the horribly mutilated body of a fifteen-year-old girl. The neck was torn to ribbons by the teeth and claws of the animal, the intestines were torn out, the pelvis shattered, and one thigh was missing. A part of the thigh, gnawed to the bone, and a piece of the shin-bone lay near the body. It seemed at first glance that only a beast of prey could have treated the girl's body in this way, but closer investigation brought certain particularities to light which did not fit in with the picture. I observed, for example, that the skin at the edge of the undamaged part of the chest was torn by strangely regular gashes about an inch long. Also the liver had been removed from the body with a clean cut no beast could make. I was struck, too, by a piece of intestine the ends of which appeared to have been smoothly cut off, and, lastly, there was the fracture of the thigh—a classic example of fracture by bending."

Liberty Lobby

Created just a few years before the dawning of the 1960s, Liberty Lobby was a body of individuals that had patriotism at its heart. It was singlehandedly put together by a man named Willis Allison Carto, a right-wing extremist denied the Holocaust and was openly anti-Semitic. In the group's very own words, Liberty Lobby was, "a pressure group for patriotism; the only lobby in Washington, D.C., registered with Congress which is wholly dedicated to the advancement of government policies based on our Constitution and conservative principles."

Carto was heavily influenced by the controversial beliefs and ideologies of Francis Parker Yockey, an American attorney who was enamored by Adolf Hitler's National Socialism. Like Carto, Yockey had no time for the Jewish people. Such was the influence that Yockey's beliefs had over Carto, the latter modelled Liberty Lobby on the words of Yockey as presented in his book, *Imperium: The Philosophy of History and Politics.*

Proof that Carto was deeply anti-Semitic surfaced early on. As one example, take note of the following words of Carto: "How could the West [have] been so blind. It was the Jews and their lies that blinded the West as to what Germany was doing. Hitler's defeat was the defeat of Europe and America."

On top of all that, Carto had ties to the Ku Klux Klan. It's hardly surprising, then, that when Liberty Lobby surfaced, it attracted the attention of the mainstream media. Among the journalists who took note of the controversial group were Jack Anderson and Drew Pearson. In the mid-to-late 1960s, and in a number of widely read articles, the pair cited the words of a former member of Liberty Lobby, one Jeremy Horne. The data provided to Anderson and Pearson was, to say the very least, inflammatory. Horne had uncovered letters that demonstrated links between Carto and certain people in government that led to the creation of the Joint Council of Repatriation—a poisonous group that was intent on repatriating African Americans to Africa.

When the 1970s dawned, Liberty Lobby attempted to change its public image, by claiming to be a "politically populist organization," and not the far-right, Hitler-loving, Jew-hating body that it really was. The group also published its own magazine, *The Spotlight.* Disturbingly, the magazine sold extremely well: by the 1980s it had a readership of close to a quarter of a million.

Liberty Lobby finally came to an end in 2001: as a result of a civil lawsuit, the group was bankrupted. It never recovered. It was the end of the line for Willis Allison Carto, who died in October 2015.

Lincoln, President Abraham

Any mention of presidential assassinations that changed the face of the United States will, probably first and foremost, conjure up imagery relative to the November 22, 1963, assassination of President John F. Kennedy, at Dealey Plaza, Dallas, Texas. Long before JFK was killed, however (whether by Lee Harvey Oswald, the Cubans, the Mafia, or the KGB), there was the murder of President Abraham Lincoln, on April 15, 1865.

Unlike so many presidents of the twentieth century, President Abraham Lincoln was not born into a rich, powerful family. It was exactly the opposite: Lincoln was very much a self-made man, one who was brought up in near poverty in Hardin County, Kentucky. Lincoln was determined to make a significant life for himself, however, and he achieved exactly that—and much more, besides. Prior to his election to the position of president of the United States in November 1860, Lincoln had worked as both a state legislator and a lawyer, and, in 1846, was elected to the U.S. House of Representatives. From there, it was a case of the sky being the limit; until, that is, a man named John Wilkes Booth put an end to all of that, on April 15, 1865. There are, however, widely held beliefs that Booth did not act alone when he shot and killed Lincoln. It has been suggested that high-ranking Masons may have been in on the deadly act.

To understand the conventional theory that John Wilkes Booth was the only guilty party, we have to go back to the dawning of the 1860s. In the pres-

Conspiracy theorists believe that actor John Wilkes Booth's assassination of President Abraham Lincoln was about more than just one disgruntled, anti-black conspirator upset about blacks being freed.

idential election of 1860, Lincoln gained a great deal of support from those who demanded an end to slavery—as did Lincoln himself. There were, however, significant numbers who were vehemently against the abolition of slavery. They were the people of Georgia, Mississippi, Texas, South Carolina, Louisiana, Alabama, and Florida. So vehemently anti-abolition were they, they created what became known as the Confederate States of America. Tensions began to mount between north and south, to the point when, on April 12, 1861, civil war broke out. It continued until May 9, 1865, and saw the South soundly defeated. Slavery was no more, and the Confederate States of America was gone, too. It was a decisive victory for the United States and its people. Unfortunately, Lincoln would not live to see the final peace declared and the war formally ended. Someone was planning a quick demise for the nation's victorious leader.

It's ironic that John Wilkes Booth was so anti-Lincoln, and for this particular reason: despite his hatred of the president, Booth chose never to enlist with the Confederate military and do in-the-field battle with the North. That's not to say he was a coward, though. Rather, Booth forged deep and intriguing links to the world of espionage, acting for the Confederates in decidedly James Bond style. Demonstrating his loathing for the president, more than a year before Lincoln was killed, Booth had secretly devised an operation to have the president kidnapped but held off until such time that Lincoln authorized the release of a large number of southern soldiers. Things really reached their peak in early April 1865, however. That was when Booth, outraged by Lincoln's plans to allow black people to vote, decided that kidnapping wasn't enough for Lincoln: nothing less than the president's death would satisfy Booth.

The date on which America was changed was April 14, 1865. It was Good Friday. The location was the Washington, D.C.-based Ford's Theatre, where Lincoln and his wife, Mary, were due to watch Tom Taylor's play *Our American Cousin*. It was during an interval that disaster struck. Lincoln's main bodyguard was a man named John Parker. During the interval, Parker left the president and headed for a drink or two at the Star Saloon, which stood adjacent to the theater. It was the perfect moment for Booth to strike—and strike he did. It was shortly before 10:15 P.M. when Booth stealthily made his way to the balcony seats in which Lincoln and Mary were sitting and fired a bullet at the president's head.

Pandemonium broke out. Booth was almost apprehended, by one Major Henry Rathbone, but managed to escape by plunging a knife into the major. As for the president, his hours were numbered. It turns out that sitting hardly any distance from the president was a Dr. Charles Leale, who raced over to the rapidly fading Lincoln. Despite frantic attempts to save his life, and after plunging into a coma for more than eight hours, Lincoln died. As for Booth, he fled the theater, and outwitted and outmaneuvered his military pursuers for almost two weeks. A standoff occurred at a Virginia farm, where Booth was shot to death by a Sergeant Boston Corbett.

When it comes to the conspiracy theories concerning the death of President Abraham Lincoln, they differ significantly from the killing of President John F. Kennedy in November 1963. Whereas most conspiracy researchers of the JFK affair suggest Lee Harvey Oswald was nothing but a convenient patsy who never fired even a single bullet, when it comes to the killing of Lincoln, most investigators are convinced Booth was the gunman. A big question, however, exists: was Booth the brains behind the operation, or was someone else pulling the strings? To try and answer that question, let's start with the Masonic theory.

Researcher John Daniel lays the blame squarely on the tentacles of British-based Masonry. He suggests that the reason why powerful figures in the British establishment wanted President Lincoln gone were twofold. First, by having Lincoln assassinated it would splinter the United States into two less-than-powerful sections, both of which could be conquered more easily than could one unified nation. Daniel also argued that the Brits wished to create a central bank under their control.

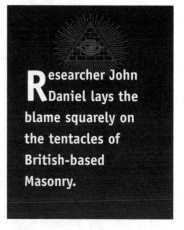

Researcher John Daniel lays the blame squarely on the tentacles of British-based Masonry.

Such a bank would likely have been established under the powerful Rothschilds, who, history has shown, did offer the Lincoln government a loan—one with an extremely high interest rate. The Rothschilds were convinced that Lincoln would have no choice but to accept the loan to help get the United States back on its feet. Lincoln chose not to, however. The Rothschilds were soundly rebuffed.

Daniel says: "Had it not been for Abraham Lincoln, English Freemasonry would have succeeded. When Lincoln restored the Union, the British Brotherhood, out of revenge, plotted his assassination. The Knights of the Golden Circle, bankrolled by British Masonic interests, selected John Wilkes Booth, a 33rd degree Mason and member of Mazzini's Young America, for the task."

As for how the crime was hidden, Daniel concludes that Edwin Stanton—both a Freemason and the Secretary of War during the Lincoln administration—coordinated the effort to bury the truth. He says that it was Stanton who ordered the blocking of all the roads out of Washington, D.C., aside from the one from which John Wilkes Booth was able to escape and make his way to Virginia. On top of that, Daniel does not believe that Booth died at the Virginia farm that the history books assure us he did: "Stanton then arranged for a drunk man to be found, similar in build and appearance to Booth. This man was to be murdered and his body burned in a barn adjacent to the only road not guarded by the military. Stanton just happened to be on that road when he 'found' the murdered man, certifying that the charred body was the remains of John Wilkes Booth. The real John Wilkes Booth escaped."

Loch Ness Dragon Cult

The summer of 1969 was a strange period in the quest for the truth behind the legend of the Loch Ness Monster. It was a decidedly alternative period, too, given that information surfaced on a secret dragon cult operating in the vicinity of the huge lake. In early June, three American students paid a visit to Loch Ness. The purpose of their visit was to see Boleskine House, an old hunting lodge (which burned down in 2015) that had once been owned by one of the key players in the world of secret societies. We're talking about none other than Aleister Crowley.

It was while walking around a centuries-old cemetery that stands close to where Boleskine House stood that they came across a strangely decorated piece of cloth—a tapestry, one might say. It was roughly four feet by five feet and was wrapped around a large sea snail shell. It was covered in artwork of snakes and words that were soon shown to have been written in Turkish. One of the words translated as "serpent," which was a most apt description for the beast of Loch Ness. Rather notably, Turkey has its very own lake monster, one that is said to dwell in the waters of Lake Van. But there was more to come: the tapestry found by the three students was adorned with images of lotus flowers. In ancient Chinese folklore, dragons had a particular taste for lotus flowers—to the extent that in lakes where dragons were said to reside, the people of China would leave such flowers on the shores, as a means to appease the violent beasts.

Loch Ness in Scotland has not only the legend of the monster that lives within its waters, but also a dragon cult that practices in the area.

Of the several other people who had the opportunity to see and examine the tapestry in June 1969—in fact, only mere hours after it was found—one was a near-full-time Nessie-seeker named Frederick "Ted" Holiday. He couldn't fail to make a connection between the Loch Ness Monster and the dragon- and serpent-based imagery. On top of that, the matter of the lotus flowers led Holiday to conclude that all of this was evidence of some kind of clandestine dragon cult operating in the area. That Holiday knew all too well that Aleister Crowley was linked to all manner of secret societies was yet another reason that led Holiday to suspect the presence of a dragon cult in the area. As he began to dig even further into the story, Holiday uncovered rumors of alleged human sacrifice in the wooded areas surrounding Loch Ness, as well as attempts by the secret group to try and invoke supernatural serpents from the dark waters of the loch.

The mysterious group in question, Holiday believed, was said to worship Tiamat, a terrifying Babylonian snake goddess, or sea dragon, who was revered as much as she was feared—and chiefly because of her murderous, homicidal ways. She mated with Abzu, the god of freshwater, to create a number of supernatural offspring, all of dragon- and serpent-like appearance. Then there were the dreaded Scorpion Men, equally hideous offspring of Tiamat that were, as their name suggests, a horrific combination of man and giant arachnids. So the legend goes, Abzu planned to secretly kill his children, but was thwarted from doing so when they rose up and slayed him instead. Likewise, Tiamat was ultimately slaughtered—by the god of storms, the four-eyed giant known as Marduk.

If, however, one knew the ways of the ancients, one could still call upon the power and essence of Tiamat—despite her death—as a means to achieve power, wealth, influence, and sex. Such rituals were definitively Faustian in nature, however (as they almost always are), and the conjurer had to take great heed when summoning the spirit form of Tiamat, lest violent, deadly forces be unleashed. It was highly possible, thought Holiday, that the monsters seen at Loch Ness were manifestations of Tiamat, in some latter-day incarnation, and specifically provoked to manifest by that aforementioned cult.

Nothing was ever conclusively proved, but the entire situation left a bad taste in Holiday's mouth, made him deeply worried for his own safety, and eventually convinced him that the legendary creature of Loch Ness was itself supernatural in nature.

London Underground Society

Over the years, I have collected a number of very weird stories on one particular subject that doesn't necessarily always get the coverage it deserves—regardless of whether the subject actually has any merit to it or not! It's the issue of strange, humanoid creatures living deep below the surface of the United Kingdom, whether in caverns, caves, huge tunnels, and/or old and disused mines, and we're talking about the modern era: the twentieth and twenty-first centuries.

It sounds like something straight out of H. P. Lovecraft. And, perhaps, that's all it is. The fact is, however, there are more than a few stories out there that suggest—just maybe—there is something to the controversy, and I stress the maybe. We only have to look at the phenomenal interest that the claims of Richard Shaver still provoke to this day to recognize that the human race has a fascination for secrets and tales of the underground kind.

It's almost as if each and every one of us possesses a kind of vague, inherited memory of times long gone when the under-dwellers were all-too-real, and not just perceived as the stuff of legend and folklore. That may also be the reason why Mac Tonnies's book, *The Cryptoterrestrials*, caught the attention of so many people when it was published back in 2010.

As for the stories I have personally come across, well, they are a strange bunch, to be sure. Here is just one of what amounts to around thirty stories or thereabouts.

Before his passing in 2007, Frank Wiley, who spent his entire working life in the British Police Force, told me a bizarre and unsettling tale of his personal memories and investigations of a number of very weird killings on the London Underground, always late at night, in a particular period of time that covered 1967 to 1969. The killings, Wiley said, occurred on at least three stations, and were hushed up by the police, under the guise of being the unfortunate results of particularly vicious, late night muggings.

In reality, Wiley explained, the muggings were nothing of the sort at all. They were far, far more horrific in nature. There were, he recalled, seven such deaths during the time period that he was assigned to the investigations. As for the particular cases of which Wiley did have personal awareness, he said the *modus operandi* was always exactly the same.

The bodies of the people—a couple of whom were commuters and the rest hobos simply looking for shelter on cold, windswept nights—were found, always after at least 10:00 P.M., a significant distance into the tunnels, with arms and/or legs viciously amputated—or possibly even gnawed off. Stomachs were ripped open, innards were torn out, and throats were violently slashed.

A definitive man-eater—or worse still, a whole group of man-eaters—was seemingly prowling around the most shadowy corners of London's dark underworld after sunset, and it, or they, had only one cold and lethal goal: to

> **W**e only have to look at the phenomenal interest that the claims of Richard Shaver still provoke to this day to recognize that the human race has a fascination for secrets and tales of the underground kind.

seek out fresh flesh with which to nourish their ever-hungry bellies. Wiley's theory was that the killers were nothing less than a secret society of devolved humans who dwelled in the lower levels of the old tunnels.

It was a great story, except for one thing: it paralleled (to a very suspicious degree) the plotline of a British horror movie made in 1972 called *Death Line*. It starred Donald Pleasence and was released in the United States as *Raw Meat*. The biggest problem of all is that Wiley didn't tell his tale until decades after *Death Line* was released. I often think about Wiley's claims and the possibility that something savage lurks deep under London. In a strange and kind of exciting way, I hope it's true. Without any kind of backup, however, it remains unresolved and extremely controversial.

Lone Gunmen

Did a secret group within the U.S. government leak classified material on 9/11—months before the terrible event occurred—to the creators of *The X-Files*? As fans of *The X-Files* will recall, although Mulder and Scully were the focus of just about every episode, from time to time they received significant help, in their efforts to uncover the truth of a number of cosmic conspiracies, from a trio of conspiracy theorists. They were John Byers, Melvin Frohike, and Richard Langly, who published the *Magic Bullet Newsletter*.

The three characters became better known as the Lone Gunmen. Such was the enthusiasm that the show's fans had for Langly, Frohike, and Byers, in early 2001 they were given their very own, short-lived series. The name of the series surprised no one: *The Lone Gunmen*. The first episode aired on March 4, 2001. Its title was "Pilot." In the show, a computer hacker takes control of a Boeing 727 passenger plane and flies it towards the World Trade Center, with the specific intention of crashing the plane into one of the Twin Towers. It's only at the very last moment that the Lone Gunmen are able to hack the hacker and avert disaster and death for those aboard the plane and those inside the World Trade Center.

The story gets even more intriguing: the hacker is not just some random, crazy guy. The plot is all the work of a powerful, rogue group buried deep within the world of officialdom. The secret plan, had it worked, was to put the blame for the World Trade Center attacks on one or more foreign dictators who are "begging to be smart-bombed."

Did the creators of *The Lone Gunmen* have advance knowledge of 9/11? It is worth noting, that there seemed to be a deep reluctance on the part of the

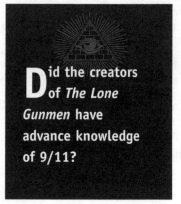

Did the creators of *The Lone Gunmen* have advance knowledge of 9/11?

mainstream media to address the storyline of "Pilot" and its parallels to 9/11—not to mention that the episode had its premiere broadcast in Australia just thirteen days before the events of September 11 occurred.

One of those who commented on this odd state of affairs was Christopher Bollyn. He said that "rather than being discussed in the media as a prescient warning of the possibility of such an attack, the pilot episode of *The Lone Gunmen* series seemed to have been quietly forgotten."

Frank Spotnitz was one of the executive producers of *The Lone Gunmen*. He said: "I woke up on September 11 and saw it on TV and the first thing I thought of was *The Lone Gunmen*. But then in the weeks and months that followed, almost no one noticed the connection. What's disturbing about it to me is, you think as a fiction writer that if you can imagine this scenario, then the people in power in the government who are there to imagine disaster scenarios can imagine it, too."

Robert McLachlan was the director of photography on *The Lone Gunmen*. He had words to say, too: "It was odd that nobody referenced it. In the ensuing press nobody mentioned that [9-11] echoed something that had been seen before."

Coincidence? Conspiracy? Or something else? Those are the questions that continue to perplex.

Macumba

Brad Steiger—an authority on the issue of secret societies—says: "In its outward appearances and in some of its practices, Macumba (also known as Spiritism, Candomble, and Umbanda) resembles Voodoo. Trance states among the practitioners are induced by dancing and drumming, and the ceremony climaxes with an animal sacrifice. The ancient role of the Shaman remains central to Macumba. He (it is most often a male) or she enters into a trance state and talks to the spirits in order to gain advice or aid for the supplicants. Before anyone can participate in a Macumba ceremony, he or she must undergo an initiation. The aspirants must enter a trance during the dancing and the drumming and allow a god to possess them. Once the possession has taken place, the shaman must determine which gods are in which initiate so that the correct rituals can be performed. The process is enhanced by the sacrifice of an animal and the smearing of its blood over the initiates. Once the initiates have been bloodied, they take an oath of loyalty to the cult. Later, when the trance state and the possessing spirit have left them, the aspirants, now members of the Macumba cult, usually have no memory of the ritual proceedings."

As for the history of Macumba, *African American Registry* provides this: "Macumba is the 'umbrella' term used for two principle forms of African spirit worship: Candomble and Umbanda. It is the Brazilian equivalent of Voudon and Santeria. Although macumba is connected with black magic, a more suitable term is Quimbanda. When the Portuguese began shipping Black slaves to

A chicken has been sacrificed and placed next to this cross as part of a Macumba ritual.

Brazil in the 16th century, the country already had a mixture of religions. Catholicism was desperately trying to rid the area of the native Indian beliefs.

"The slaves found their beliefs in spirits and magic synonymous with their native faiths. The two blended; while the slaves on the surface worshipped under the Catholic faith, they secretly carried on their religious beliefs until their liberation in 1888.... Publicly, Umbanda (Macumba) began in 1904. Black magic or Quimbanda came with the slave ships, and is still in use today. Much of the teachings are still oral. Negative sentiments are typically implied when the concepts 'cult' and 'sect' are used in popular conversation."

Mad Gasser of Mattoon

Back in the 1940s, the people of Mattoon, Illinois, were plagued by a sinister character that became known as the Mad Gasser of Mattoon. The name was a very apt one: the mysterious figure gassed his victims, as a means to gain entry to their property, and to take advantage of whatever caught his eye. His actions followed a similar wave of attacks—in the 1930s—in Botetourt County, Virginia. But, today at least, let's focus on the later events. On the night of August 31, 1944, a man named Urban Raef was overcome by a mysterious gas that provoked sickness, weakness, and vomiting. Despite Mr. Raef's fear that there was a gas leak in the house, such was not the case. Rafe's wife—to her horror—found herself briefly paralyzed.

Also among the Gasser's victims was Mrs. Bert Kearney, who also lived in Mattoon. On September 1, 1944, and approximately an hour before the witching hour struck, Mrs. Kearney was hit by what was described as a "sickening, sweet odor in the bedroom." As was the case with Mrs. Raef, the "gas" caused temporary paralysis in her legs. It also resulted in a burning sensation to her lips and a parched feeling in her mouth.

Mrs. Kearney cried out for her sister—whose name was Martha and who came running to see what was going on. She too was unable to avoid the powerful smell. In no time, the police were on the scene, but the Mad Gasser was nowhere to be seen. At least, not for a while. As Bert Kearney drove home—after his shift as a cabdriver was over—he caught sight of a darkly dressed man peering through the window of the Kearney's bedroom. It was a thin man wearing a tight, dark cap on his head. He quickly fled the scene.

In the wake of the curious affair, other reports of the Mad Gasser's infernal activities surfaced—to the extent that both the local police and the FBI got involved. The townsfolk were plunged into states of fear and paranoia. While some cases were put down to nothing more than hysteria, that was not the beginning and end of the story. For example, Thomas V. Wright, the Commissioner of Public Health, said: "There is no doubt that a gas maniac exists and has made a number of attacks. But many of the reported attacks are nothing more than hysteria. Fear of the gas man is entirely out of proportion to the menace of the relatively harmless gas he is spraying. The whole town is sick with hysteria."

One theory offers that the Mad Gasser of Mattoon was actually nothing stranger than a bunch of kids.

The mystery was never resolved to the satisfaction of everyone. One theory offers that the Mad Gasser of Mattoon was actually nothing stranger than a bunch of kids. Writer Scott Maruna suggests that the Gasser was a University of Illinois student, Farley Llewellyn, who had a deep knowledge of chemistry and who went to school with the initial victims. Other theories include burglars and even extraterrestrials. But, there's another possibility.

Perhaps the most intriguing explanation for the Mad Gasser of Mattoon appears in the now-declassified files of the U.S. government. Thanks to the provisions of the Freedom of Information Act, we now know that one particularly notable theory being secretly pursued by U.S. law enforcement officials was taken very seriously: namely, that the Gasser was not a solitary individual, but an entire group of Mad Gassers. A secret society, one might say. According to the now-released files, Illinois authorities had heard disturbing stories of a clandestine cult operating in northern Illinois that was inspired by the work of the "Great Beast" himself, Aleister Crowley—and specifically by Crowley's position on the matter of sacrifice, including human sacrifice.

Crowley himself said of this issue: "It is necessary for us to consider carefully the problems connected with the bloody sacrifice, for this question is indeed traditionally important in Magick. Nigh all ancient Magick revolves around this matter. In particular all the Osirian religions—the rites of the Dying God—refer to this. The slaying of Osiris and Adonis; the mutilation of Attis; the cults of Mexico and Peru; the story of Hercules or Melcarth; the leg-

Poet, magician, and Thelema religion founder Aleister Crowley was said to have possibly inspired the sacrificial activities of the Mad Gassers.

ends of Dionysus and of Mithra, are all connected with this one idea. In the Hebrew religion we find the same thing inculcated. The first ethical lesson in the Bible is that the only sacrifice pleasing to the Lord is the sacrifice of blood; Abel, who made this, finding favour with the Lord, while Cain, who offered cabbages, was rather naturally considered a cheap sport. The idea recurs again and again. We have the sacrifice of the Passover, following on the story of Abraham's being commanded to sacrifice his firstborn son, with the idea of the substitution of animal for human life. The annual ceremony of the two goats carries out this in perpetuity, and we see again the domination of this idea in the romance of Esther, where Haman and Mordecai are the two goats or gods; and ultimately in the presentation of the rite of Purim in Palestine, where Jesus and Barabbas happened to be the Goats in that particular year of which we hear so much, without agreement on the date."

Crowley continued: "Enough has now been said to show that the bloody sacrifice has from time immemorial been the most considered part of Magick…. It would be unwise to condemn as irrational the practice of those savages who tear the heart and liver from an adversary, and devour them while yet warm. In any case it was the theory of the ancient Magicians, that any living being is a storehouse of energy varying in quantity according to the size and health of the animal, and in quality according to its mental and moral character. At the death of the animal this energy is liberated suddenly.

"The animal should therefore be killed within the Circle, or the Triangle, as the case may be, so that its energy cannot escape. An animal should be selected whose nature accords with that of the ceremony—thus, by sacrificing a female lamb one would not obtain any appreciative quantity of the fierce energy useful to a Magician who was invoking Mars. In such a case a ram would be more suitable, and this ram should be virgin—the whole potential of its original total energy should not have been diminished in any way.

"For the highest spiritual working one must accordingly choose that victim which contains the greatest and purest force. A male child of perfect innocence and high intelligence is the most satisfactory and suitable victim. For evocations it would be more convenient to place the blood of the victim in the Triangle—the idea being that the spirit might obtain from the blood this subtle but physical substance which was the quintessence of its life in such a manner as to enable it to take on a visible and tangible shape."

It was Crowley's words that prompted the "Illinois sect," as the group is referenced in the files, to explore the issue of human sacrifice for personal gain. From a budding author in Decatur, Illinois (whose name is deleted from the declassified papers), there came a long and rambling letter in which he claimed personal knowledge of the group in question. Supposedly, its members had engaged in the ritualistic sacrifice of animals from 1942 to 1943 and were, by 1944, ready to do the unthinkable: namely, kill people according to ancient rite and ritual. Our unnamed author further claimed that the "gassing attempts" were undertaken by group members as a means to try and render unconscious, and kidnap, the largely female victims, and then end their lives according to infernal, occult beliefs.

Although the matter was taken seriously by the authorities, the odd and controversial saga fizzled out when suspicions rose that the author was lying and was simply trying to insert himself into the saga of the Mad Gasser of Mattoon, and for two particular reasons: to whip up the controversy and then write his very own book on the subject. On the other hand, perhaps there was some truth to the matter, after all, and the Mad Gasser was actually nothing less than a cult of Mad Gassers with human sacrifice on their dangerous minds.

Mafia

While a great deal has been written about the Mafia, few know more about its origins, history, and activities than the FBI. Under the terms of the Freedom of Information Act, the FBI has declassified thousands of Mafia-related documents into the public domain. One particularly notable document reveals the story of the Mafia and how the FBI waged war on it. The FBI states: "Since their appearance in the 1800s, the Italian criminal societies known as the Mafia have infiltrated the social and economic fabric of Italy and now impact the world. They are some of the most notorious and widespread of all criminal societies. There are several groups currently active in the United States: the Sicilian Mafia; the Camorra or Neapolitan Mafia; the 'Ndrangheta or Calabrian Mafia; and the Sacra Corona Unita or United Sacred Crown.

"We estimate the four groups have approximately 25,000 members total, with 250,000 affiliates worldwide. There are more than 3,000 members and affiliates in the United States, scattered mostly throughout the major cities in

Probably the secret crime organization most familiar to many people is the Mafia, which dates back to nineteenth-century Italy.

the Northeast, the Midwest, California, and the South. Their largest presence centers around New York, southern New Jersey, and Philadelphia."

The FBI continues that the Mafia's criminal activities are international with members and affiliates in Canada, South America, Australia, and parts of Europe. They are also known to collaborate with other international organized crime groups from all over the world, especially in drug trafficking. The major threats to American society posed by these groups are drug trafficking and money laundering. They have been involved in heroin trafficking for decades. Two major investigations that targeted Italian organized crime drug trafficking in the 1980s are known as the French Connection and the Pizza Connection.

These groups don't limit themselves to drug running, though. They're also involved in illegal gambling, political corruption, extortion, kidnapping, fraud, counterfeiting, infiltration of legitimate businesses, murders, bombings, and weapons trafficking. Industry experts in Italy estimate that their worldwide criminal activity is worth more than one hundred billion dollars annually.

These enterprises evolved over the course of three thousand years during numerous periods of invasion and exploitation by numerous conquering armies in Italy. Over the millennia, Sicilians became more clannish and began to rely on familial ties for safety, protection, justice, and survival. An underground secret society formed initially as resistance fighters against the invaders and to exact frontier vigilante justice against oppression. A member was known as a Man of Honor, respected and admired because he protected his family and friends and kept silent even unto death.

Sicilians weren't concerned if the group profited from its actions because it came at the expense of the oppressive authorities. These secret societies eventually grew into the Mafia. Since the 1900s, thousands of Italian organized crime figures—mostly Sicilian Mafiosi—have come illegally to this country. Many who fled here in the early 1920s helped establish what is known today as La Cosa Nostra or the American Mafia.

Charles "Lucky" Luciano, a Mafioso from Sicily, came to the United States during this era and is credited with making the American La Cosa Nostra what it is today. Luciano structured La Cosa Nostra after the Sicilian Mafia.

When Luciano was deported back to Italy in 1946 for operating a prostitution ring, he became a liaison between the Sicilian Mafia and La Cosa Nostra.

The Sicilian Mafia formed in the mid-1800s to unify the Sicilian peasants against their enemies. In Sicily, the word Mafia tends to mean "manly." The Sicilian Mafia changed from a group of honorable Sicilian men to an organized criminal group in the 1920s. In the 1950s, Sicily enjoyed a massive building boom. Taking advantage of the opportunity, the Sicilian Mafia gained control of the building contracts and made millions of dollars. Today, the Sicilian Mafia has evolved into an international organized crime group. Some experts estimate it is the second largest organization in Italy.

The Sicilian Mafia specializes in heroin trafficking, political corruption, and military arms trafficking—and is also known to engage in arson, fraud, counterfeiting, and other racketeering crimes. With an estimated 2,500 Sicilian Mafia affiliates, it is the most powerful and most active Italian organized crime group in the United States.

The Sicilian Mafia is infamous for its aggressive assaults on Italian law enforcement officials. In Sicily the term "Excellent Cadaver" is used to distinguish the assassination of prominent government officials from the common criminals and ordinary citizens killed by the Mafia. High-ranking victims include police commissioners, mayors, judges, police colonels and generals, and Parliament members.

On May 23, 1992, the Sicilian Mafia struck Italian law enforcement with a vengeance. At approximately 6 P.M., Italian magistrate Giovanni Falcone, his wife, and three police bodyguards were killed by a massive bomb. Falcone was the director of criminal affairs in Rome. The bomb made a crater thirty feet in diameter in the road. The murders became known as the Capaci Massacre. Less than two months later, on July 19, the Mafia struck Falcone's newly named replacement, Judge Paolo Borsellino in Palermo, Sicily. Borsellino and five bodyguards were killed outside the apartment of Borsellino's mother when a car packed with explosives was detonated by remote control. Under Judge Falcone's tenure the FBI and Italian law enforcement established a close working relationship aimed at dismantling Italian organized crime groups operating in both countries. That relationship has intensified since then.

Majestic 12

On July 8, 1947, the front page headline of the *Roswell Daily Record* announced a truly startling story, about which controversy continues to

The emblem of the 509th Bomb Wing, which was the group that reportedly captured a flying saucer at Roswell.

reverberate to this day: "RAAF Captures Flying Saucer on Ranch in Roswell Region." Most remarkably, the newspaper report was based upon an officially sanctioned press release issued by Walter Haut, the Press Information Officer at the nearby Roswell Army Air Field (AAF) and read thus: "The many rumors regarding the flying disc became a reality yesterday when the Intelligence office of the 509th Bomb Group of the Eighth Air Force, Roswell Army Air Field, was fortunate to gain possession of a disc through the cooperation of one of the local ranchers and the sheriff's office of Chaves County. The flying object landed on a ranch near Roswell sometime last week. Not having phone facilities, the rancher stored the disc until such time as he was able to contact the sheriff's office, who in turn notified Maj. Jesse A. Marcel of the 509th Bomb Group Intelligence Office. Action was immediately taken and the disc was picked up at the rancher's home. It was inspected at the Roswell Army Air Field and subsequently loaned by Major Marcel to higher headquarters."

UFO researchers have suggested that the Roswell wreckage—and the attendant alien bodies reportedly found at the crash site—fell under the control of a hastily created secret group called Majestic 12, or MJ12. The Majestic 12 affair involves tales of crashed UFOs, dead aliens in the possession of the U.S. government, the possible theft and unauthorized release of highly classified documents and a shadowy counterintelligence operation——at the heart of which, some believe, lies the undeniable evidence that humankind is not alone in the universe.

Following the publication of his coauthored 1980 book *The Roswell Incident*, William Moore was contacted by a number of military and intelligence insiders who claimed that they wished to reveal to Moore—and ultimately to the public, the media, and the world—classified data and documents on UFOs that would otherwise never see the light of day. It was as a result of this "Deep Throat"-style contact that Moore and his research partner Jaime Shandera obtained in 1984 a series of controversial and official-looking documents that detailed the existence and work of an allegedly top-secret group known as Majestic 12.

Supposedly established in 1947 by then-President Harry Truman, Majestic 12 was tasked with keeping the lid on the extraterrestrial secret while striving to understand and exploit the science and technology inherent in the material that had literally fallen into the hands of the U.S. government in the desert of New Mexico.

At the heart of these documents was a Top Secret memorandum titled "BRIEFING DOCUMENT: OPERATION MAJESTIC 12 / PREPARED FOR PRESIDENT-ELECT DWIGHT D. EISENHOWER: (EYES ONLY) / 18 November, 1952." (It was later stamped "TOP SECRET / MAJIC EYES ONLY.") The briefing described how, following public hysteria in 1947 over UFO sightings in Washington State and secret recovery of crashed objects in New Mexico, President Truman created "OPERATION MAJESTIC 12 [as] a TOP SECRET Research and Development/Intelligence operation responsible directly and only to the President of the United States."

The documents, first published in 1987 by the British author Timothy Good in his book *Above Top Secret,* revealed the membership of Majestic 12 to include high-ranking military personnel and senior sources within the intelligence community, as well as key scientific personnel in post-World War II America—several of whom were Masons. Understandably, the documents have been the subject of much controversy and comment, with some researchers believing them to be the real thing, while others cry hoax and/or disinformation.

Following the initial release to Moore and Shandera in 1984, literally thousands of additional pages of Majestic 12 documentation surfaced in the late 1990s from a California UFO researcher, Timothy Cooper. Asserting that this sensational body of information came to him from a number of retired, insider whistleblowers attached to the military and the murky world of American intelligence, Cooper shared his collection of documents with the father-and-son research team of Dr. Robert and Ryan Wood of www.majesticdocuments.com——now home to the most comprehensive online collection of data, supporting materials and research papers on the Majestic documents. The controversy surrounding the Majestic 12 saga continues.

Martian Face

In the same way there are claims that Jonathan Swift—the acclaimed author of *Gulliver's Travels*—may have acquired ancient knowledge on the planet Mars from his links to Freemasonry, similar rumors abound with regard to the late Jack Kirby, one of the leading figures in the field of superhero comic books. Kirby was a skilled artist and storyteller who—with Marvel Comics' Stan Lee—co-created such characters as the Incredible Hulk, the Avengers, and the

Fantastic Four. But, it's to a 1958 series that we have to turn our attentions. Its title was *Race for the Moon*, and it was solely the work of Jack Kirby.

Race for the Moon was a trilogy, with the second installment titled "The Face on Mars." It is focused upon the discovery on Mars—by U.S. astronauts—of a vast, carved human-like face on the surface of the so-called Red Planet. Kirby's story would likely have fallen into obscurity were it not for one significant fact: in 1976, what appeared to be a huge, human-like face—cast out of rock—was photographed in a region of Mars called Cydonia. The late Mac Tonnies—the author of *After the Martian Apocalypse*—spent years addressing, and studying, the matter of what became known as a real-life Face on Mars.

Tonnies told me: "The first two objects to attract attention were the Face and the 'D&M Pyramid,' both unearthed by digital imaging specialists Vincent DiPietro and Gregory Molenaar. Their research was published in 'Unusual Martian Surface Features'; shortly after, Richard Hoagland pointed out a collection of features near the Face which he termed the 'City.' NASA itself discovered the Face and even showed it at a press conference after it had been photographed by the Viking mission in the 1970s. Of course, it was written off as a curiosity. Scientific analysis would have to await independent researchers.

"When NASA dismissed the Face as a 'trick of light,' they cited a second, disconfirming photo allegedly taken at a different sun-angle. This photo

Comic book artist Jack Kirby wrote about a face on Mars years before one was apparently discovered.

never existed. DiPietro and Molenaar had to dig through NASA archives to find a second image of the Face—and, far from disputing the face-like appearance, it strengthened the argument that the Face remained face-like from multiple viewing angles. The prevailing alternative to NASA's geological explanation—that the Face and other formations are natural landforms—is that we're seeing extremely ancient artificial structures built by an unknown civilization.

"NASA chooses to ignore that there is a controversy, or at least a controversy in the scientific sense. Since making the Face public in the 1970s, NASA has made vague allusions to humans' ability to 'see faces' (e.g. the 'Man in the Moon') and has made lofty dismissals, but it has yet to launch any sort of methodical study of the objects under investigation. Collectively, NASA frowns on the whole endeavor. Mainstream SETI theorists are equally hostile.

"Basically, the Face—if artificial—doesn't fall into academically palatable models of how extraterrestrial intelligence will reveal itself, if it is in fact 'out there.' Searching for radio signals is well and good, but scanning the surface of a neighboring planet for signs of prior occupation is met with a very carefully cultivated institutionalized scorn, and of course it doesn't help that some of the proponents of the Face have indulged in more than a little baseless 'investigation.'

"I think some of the objects in the Cydonia region of Mars are probably artificial, and I think the only way this controversy will end is to send a manned mission. The features under investigation are extremely old and warrant on-site archaeological analysis. We've learned—painfully—that images from orbiting satellites won't answer the fundamental questions raised by the Artificiality Hypothesis. I suspect that we're seeing a fusion of natural geology and megascale engineering. For example, the Face is likely a modified natural mesa, not entirely unlike some rock sculptures on Earth but on a vastly larger and more technically challenging scale."

Given that the Face on Mars—regardless of what it is or isn't—was not found and photographed until 1976, how is it possible that Jack Kirby was able to seemingly anticipate all this back in the late 1950s? It's an enigma that eerily parallels the story of Jonathan Swift and the matter of the Martian moons, Phobos and Deimos. In the same way that Swift may have been provided ancient and archaic knowledge on Mars's moons from his colleagues in the field of Freemasonry, Kirby may have had insider sources, too.

So the theory goes that, back in the 1950s, a clandestine, secret group was created by the U.S. government to oversee something astonishing; namely, priceless, ancient manuscripts dating back thousands of years that were created by a long gone race of highly advanced people—possibly the fabled Atlanteans. Among those manuscripts was one that described the true history of Mars and its now long-extinct civilization—which met a terrible end in a planet-wide nuclear war. The group—which reportedly had the curious title of The Summit—operated out of a secure installation in New York State; an installation that, by all accounts, mirrored the final scenes in the 1981 movie *Raiders of the Lost Ark*, in which all manner of secret, ancient artifacts and priceless relics from millennia ago are secretly hidden, including knowledge of the Face on Mars.

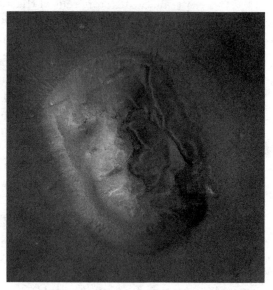

A close-up look at the "face on Mars" reveals it to be not very facelike, after all, according to critics.

But, why would such information be given to Jack Kirby, a comic book artist? The answer is simple: Kirby was not just a man with a flair for creating some of the world's most famous superheroes. Rumors suggest he had connections to the shadowy worlds of secret societies and the U.S. intelligence community—and to The Summit, too. If true, then perhaps Kirby was invited to write about the Face on Mars, possibly to determine how people might react when the real Face was unleashed upon the world in 1976.

Martian Moon Secrets

Was Jonathan Swift—the author of the widely acclaimed novel *Gulliver's Travels*—in possession of secret and astonishing data on the moons of Mars? And, did that same secret data come from nothing less than the remnants of a secret society that, thousands of years ago, possessed incredible knowledge of the universe? It sounds like the perfect plot for a movie rivalling the likes of *Raiders of the Lost Ark* and *The Da Vinci Code*. Except for one thing: the story of Jonathan Swift is not fiction. It's amazing fact.

It was in 1726 that the English publishing house of Benjamin Motte released *Gulliver's Travels*. It's a book that captivated its readers—and still does, to this very day—and which became a bestseller in practically no time at all. Swift's story tells of the adventures of Lemuel Gulliver, a seafaring character who is well traveled and who has a passion for adventure and exciting and mysterious places. He certainly gets both in Swift's novel.

One particular part of *Gulliver's Travels* really stands out. It's while Gulliver is on the island of Laputa that he learns something amazing from its residents. As Swift worded it, those same scientists had found "two lesser stars, or satellites, which revolve around Mars; whereof the innermost is distant from the center of the primary planet exactly three of its diameters, and the outermost five; the former revolves in the space of ten hours, and the latter in twenty one and a half; so that the squares of their periodical times are very near in the same proportion with the cubes of their distance from the center of Mars; which evidently shows them to be governed by the same law of gravitation that influences the other heavenly bodies."

As we know today, Mars certainly does have two moons. Their names are Phobos and Deimos. But, here's the important factor in all this: it wasn't until August 1877 that the two moons were discovered. The man who made the historic find was Asaph Hall, of the Washington, D.C.-based U.S. Naval Observatory. Of course, some might say that it was mere coincidence that Swift gave

Mars two moons in his novel and that there just happens to be two real moons that orbit the red planet. That theory—as reasonable as it might sound for many people—fails to explain something else.

Phobos is located around six thousand kilometers from Mars. It orbits Mars once every 7.7 hours. In *Gulliver's Travels*, the distance is 13,600 kilometers and the orbit is ten hours. In that sense, Swift was somewhat off, in terms of accuracy. However, when it comes to Mars's other moon, Deimos, the story is far more intriguing. Deimos orbits Mars once every 30.3 hours. In his novel, Swift gave a figure of 21.5 hours. Deimos is roughly 20,000 kilometers from Mars. In *Gulliver's Travels*, Mars's second moon is 27,200 kilometers away. In other words, Swift was not too far from the truth of the Martian moons.

Adding to the mystery of the Martian moons—and Jonathan Swift's apparent knowledge of their existence more than 150 years

British satirist Jonathan Swift wrote about Mars having two moons centuries before those moons were actually observed by astronomers.

before they were officially found—there's the matter of Voltaire's 1750 science fiction saga, *Micromegas*, which also tells of Mars having a pair of moons. Those of a skeptical nature might say that Voltaire was simply inspired by Swift. Or, perhaps, Voltaire too knew something of the Martian moons and also acquired his data from ancient, mysterious sources. As for who, exactly, those same mysterious sources may have been, leading the pack is an elite, secret society composed of the descendants of nothing less than the long-destroyed, legendary land of Atlantis. On top of that, both Swift and Voltaire were Freemasons, which has given rise to the theory that the pair may have uncovered ancient texts on the Martian moons as a result of their affiliations to Freemasonry.

On the matter of Freemasonry and ancient times, it's worth noting the words of Acharya S., a noted expert on this famous, secret society: "Although the brotherhood of Masonry appears to be relatively new, it is in reality the oldest continuous network on the planet, dating back many thousands of years, beginning when stones were first dressed. Masonry today has a generally sinister reputation, because the people suspect that this powerful brotherhood has been manipulating and exploiting them. However, the average Mason has never been 'in the know' and is, therefore, merely a member of a social club. Nevertheless, the higher-ups have indeed had their hand in creation on this planet on a large scale for a long time…. The Masons are there, perpetually hidden behind the scenes, leaving clues to their existence as a brotherhood, some of which are evident yet still not seen. For example, the biblical Nimrod, the king who built the tower of Babel, is considered the first Mason."

Were early Masons—those who surfaced in the biblical era—in possession of incredible data acquired from surviving Atlanteans who knew a great deal about not just our world, but also Mars, too? That we see a connection between the Masons and both Voltaire and Jonathan Swift is, at the very least, intriguing.

Mermaid Cult

The notion that the United Kingdom might actually be the home of living, breathing, flesh-and-blood mermaids will inevitably be greeted by many with the justified rolling of eyes and hoots of derision. It is, however, an undeniable and astonishing fact that such beliefs persisted for centuries. And, in those parts of the U.K. where the many and varied traditions and superstitions of times past can still be found lurking, that belief actually quietly continues—to a shocking and sinister degree. To the extent that there now exists what we might term a secret mermaid cult.

The word "mermaid" is derived from a combination of "mere," the Old English word for sea, and "maid," meaning, of course, woman. According to old seafaring legends, mermaids would often deliberately sing to sailors to try and enchant them, with the secret and malevolent intent of distracting them from their work and causing their ships to run disastrously aground.

Other ancient tales tell of mermaids inadvertently squeezing the last breaths out of drowning men while attempting to rescue them. They are also said to particularly enjoy taking humans to their underwater lairs. In Hans Christian Andersen's *The Little Mermaid*, for example, it is said that mermaids often forget that humans cannot breathe underwater, while other legends suggest the sinister she-creatures deliberately drown men—out of sheer, venomous spite, no less.

The fabled sirens of Greek mythology are sometimes portrayed in later folklore as being mermaid-like in nature and appearance; in fact, some languages use the same word for both bird and fish creatures, such as the Maltese word, "Sirena." Other related types of mythical or legendary creatures include water nymphs and selkies (animals that can allegedly transform themselves from seals into human beings and vice versa).

Mermaids were noted in British folklore as being distinctly unlucky omens—occasionally foretelling disaster and sometimes even maliciously provoking it. As evidence of this, versions of the ballad "Sir Patrick Spens" depict a mermaid speaking to the doomed ships. In some, she tells the crews they will never see land again, and in others, she claims they are near shore, which the men are wise and astute enough to know means that deep, malevolent deception is at work.

It's worth noting that the English county of Staffordshire and the bordering county of Shropshire are packed with tales of mermaids. One such account tells of a deadly mermaid inhabiting a small pool in the pleasant little village of Childs Ercall. In 1893, writer Robert Charles Hope described the story as follows: "[T]here was a mermaid seen there once. It was a good while ago, before my time. I dare say it might be a hundred years ago. There were two men going to work early one morning, and they had got as far as the side of the pond in [a] field, and they saw something on the top of the water which scared them not a little. They thought it was going to take them straight off to the Old Lad himself! I can't say exactly what it was like, I wasn't there, you know; but it was a mermaid, the same as you read of in the papers.

Today, the word "mermaid" elicits the charming image of a heroine from the Hans Christian Andersen tale, but in many folkloric traditions mermaids were bad omens.

"The fellows had almost run away at first, they were so frightened, but as soon as the mermaid had spoken to them, they thought no more of that. Her voice was so sweet and pleasant, that they fell in love with her there and then, both of them. Well, she told them there was a treasure hidden at the bottom of the pond—lumps of gold, and no one knows what, and she would give them as much as ever they liked if they would come to her in the water and take it out of her hands.

"So they went in, though it was almost up to their chins, and she dived into the water and brought up a lump of gold almost as big as a man's head, and the men were just going to take it, when one of them said: 'Eh!' he said (and swore, you know), 'if this isn't a bit of luck!' And, my word, if the mermaid didn't take it away from them again, and gave a scream, and dived down into the pond, and they saw no more of her, and got none of her gold, and nobody has ever seen her since then. No doubt the story once ran that the oath which scared the uncanny creature involved the mention of the Holy Name."

Moving on, situated barely a stone's throw from the Shropshire town of Newport and just over the border into rural Staffordshire, Aqualate Mere—at 1.5 kilometers long and 0.5 kilometers wide—is the largest natural lake in the Midlands; yet it is very shallow, extending down to little more than a uniform three feet.

Legend has it that one day many years ago, when the Mere was being cleaned, a mermaid violently rose out of the water—quite naturally scaring the living daylights out of the workmen—while simultaneously making shrieking, disturbing and damning threats to utterly destroy the town of Newport if any attempt was ever made to empty Aqualate Mere of its precious waters. Very wisely, perhaps, the Mere was not—and, to date, never has been—drained.

All of which brings us to a highly controversial story of a Shropshire- and Staffordshire-based mermaid cult (which is the best way I can describe it) that fully believes in the existence of such creatures, and that reportedly has engaged in sinister animal sacrifices to appease these ancient, deadly water maidens. Its membership is reputedly composed of powerful figures in local and national government, occultists, demonologists, and historians of U.K.-based folklore and mythology. As for those sacrifices, there's no doubt that they are a reality. For years reports have surfaced from both Staffordshire and Shropshire of sheep, chickens, and wild deer having been found dead in the rural countryside. We are not, however, talking about attacks by wild animals. Rather, we're talking about ritualistic killings—sometimes in darkened woods late at night—and sacrificial rites, and all in the name of the dangerous mermaid.

Microbiology Deaths

From the final months of 2001 to mid-2005, numerous people employed in the elite field of microbiology—which is defined as the study of organisms that are too small to be seen with the naked eye, such as bacteria and viruses—died under circumstances that some within the media and government came to view as highly suspicious and deeply disturbing in nature. It would be impossible to list all of the deaths in a single article. However, a summary of a number of cases will let you see what was afoot. The number of deaths involved points in the direction of a secret band of assassins being the culprits.

The controversy largely began in November 2001, when Dr. Benito Que, a cell biologist working on infectious diseases, including HIV, was found dead outside of his laboratory at the Miami Medical School, Florida. The *Miami Herald* stated that his death occurred as he headed for his car, a white Ford

Explorer, parked on Northwest 10th Avenue. Police said that he was possibly the victim of muggers.

Then, on November 21, Dr. Vladimir Pasechnik, a former microbiologist for Biopreparat, a bioweapons production facility that existed in Russia prior to the collapse of the Soviet Union, was found dead near his home in the county of Wiltshire, England. His defection to Britain in 1989 revealed to the West for the very first time the incredible scale of the Soviet Union's clandestine biological warfare program.

Pasechnik's revelations about the scale of the Soviet Union's production of biological agents, including anthrax, plague, tularemia, and smallpox, provided an inside account of one of the best kept secrets of the Cold War. According to British Intelligence, Pasechnik passed away from the effects of a massive stroke and nothing more.

Three days later, the FBI announced it was monitoring an investigation into the disappearance of a Harvard biologist because of "his research into potentially lethal viruses," including Ebola. Dr. Don C. Wiley, 57, had last been seen in Memphis, Tennessee, where he attended the annual meeting of the Scientific Advisory Board of the St. Jude Children's Research Hospital. His rented car was found on November 16 on a bridge over the Mississippi River, with a full fuel tank, and the key still in the ignition. His body was eventually discovered near a hydroelectric plant in the Mississippi River.

Pasechnik's revelations about the scale of the Soviet Union's production of biological agents ... provided an inside account of one of the best kept secrets of the Cold War.

Controversial deaths continued to occur, this time in Russia. On January 28, 2002, a microbiologist, and a member of the Russian Academy of Science, Alexi Brushlinski, died as the result of what was blamed on a bandit attack in the heart of Moscow. Then, just two weeks later, Victor Korshunov, 56, also a noted microbiologist, was hit over the head and killed at the entrance of his home—which also happened to be in Moscow. He was none other than the head of the microbiology sub faculty at the Russian State Medical University.

On July 18, 2003, it was reported in the British press that David Kelly, a British biological weapons expert, had slashed his own wrists while walking in woods near his home. Kelly was the British Ministry of Defense's chief scientific officer and the senior adviser to the Proliferation and Arms Control Secretariat and the Foreign Office's Non-Proliferation Department. The senior adviser on biological weapons to the UN biological weapons inspections teams (Unscom) from 1994 to 1999, Kelly was also, in the opinion of his peers, preeminent in his field—not only in the U.K., but in the world, too. The list, unfortunately, goes on and on, and just like the affair of the Marconi scientists, matters were relegated to the worlds of suicide, ill health, muggings, and accidents.

Mind Control Groups

Within the annals of research into conspiracy theories, there is perhaps no more emotive term than that of mind control. Indeed, mention those two words to anyone who is even remotely aware of the term and it will invariably and inevitably (and wholly justifiably, too!) provoke imagery and comments pertaining to political assassinations, dark and disturbing CIA chicanery, sexual slavery, secret government projects—and even alien abductions and subliminal advertising on the part of the world's media and advertising agencies.

Yes: the specter of mind control is one that has firmly worked its ominous way into numerous facets of modern-day society, and it has been doing so for years. Consider, for example, the following: "I can hypnotize a man, without his knowledge or consent, into committing treason against the United States," asserted Dr. George Estabrooks, Ph.D., and chairman of the Department of Psychology at Colgate University, way back in 1942, and before a select group of personnel attached to the United States' War Department. Estabrooks added: "Two hundred trained foreign operators, working in the United States, could develop a uniquely dangerous army of hypnotically controlled Sixth Columnists." Estabrooks's pièce de résistance, however, was to capitalize on an ingenious plan that had been postulated as far back as World War I.

As he explained: "During World War One, a leading psychologist made a startling proposal to the navy. He offered to take a submarine steered by a captured U-boat captain, placed under his hypnotic control, through enemy mine fields to attack the German fleet. Washington nixed the stratagem as too risky. First, because there was no disguised method by which the captain's mind could be outflanked. Second, because today's technique of day-by-day breaking down of ethical conflicts brainwashing was still unknown. The indirect approach to hypnotism would, I believe,

The prospect of having one's mind controlled by someone else is understandably terrifying.

change the navy's answer today. Personally, I am convinced that hypnosis is a bristling, dangerous armament which makes it doubly imperative to avoid the war of tomorrow."

A perfect example of the way in which the will of a person could be completely controlled and manipulated was amply and graphically spelled out in an article that Dr. George Estabrooks wrote in April 1971 for the now-defunct publication *Science Digest*. Titled "Hypnosis Comes of Age," it stated the following: "Communication in war is always a headache. Codes can be broken. A professional spy may or may not stay bought. Your own man may have unquestionable loyalty, but his judgment is always open to question. The 'hypnotic courier,' on the other hand, provides a unique solution. I was involved in preparing many subjects for this work during World War II. One successful case involved an Army Service Corps Captain whom we'll call George Smith.

"Captain Smith had undergone months of training. He was an excellent subject but did not realize it. I had removed from him, by post-hypnotic suggestion, all recollection of ever having been hypnotized. First I had the Service Corps call the captain to Washington and tell him they needed a report of the mechanical equipment of Division X headquartered in Tokyo. Smith was ordered to leave by jet next morning, pick up the report and return at once. Consciously, that was all he knew, and it was the story he gave to his wife and friends.

"Then I put him under deep hypnosis, and gave him—orally—a vital message to be delivered directly on his arrival in Japan to a certain colonel—let's say his name was Brown—of military intelligence.

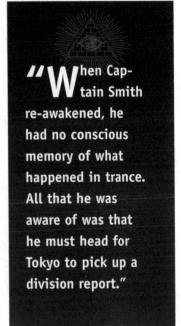

"**W**hen Captain Smith re-awakened, he had no conscious memory of what happened in trance. All that he was aware of was that he must head for Tokyo to pick up a division report."

"Outside of myself, Colonel Brown was the only person who could hypnotize Captain Smith. This is 'locking.'

"I performed it by saying to the hypnotized Captain: 'Until further orders from me, only Colonel Brown and I can hypnotize you. We will use a signal phrase *the moon is clear*. Whenever you hear this phrase from Brown or myself you will pass instantly into deep hypnosis.'

"When Captain Smith re-awakened, he had no conscious memory of what happened in trance. All that he was aware of was that he must head for Tokyo to pick up a division report.

"On arrival there, Smith reported to Brown, who hypnotized him with the signal phrase. Under hypnosis, Smith delivered my message and received one to bring back. Awakened, he was given the division report and returned home by jet. There I hypnotized him once more with the signal phrase, and he spieled off Brown's answer that had been dutifully tucked away in his unconscious mind."

Ministry of the Chalcedon Foundation

According to the official website of the Ministry of the Chalcedon Founda-tion—which was founded in 1965 by a theologian named Rousas Rush-doony—they are a body comprising people who "understand that Jesus Christ speaks to the mind as well as to the heart. We believe that the whole Word of God must be applied to all of life. It is not only our duty as individuals, fami-lies and churches to be Christian, but it is also the duty of the state, the school, the arts and sciences, law, economics, and every other sphere to be under Christ the King. Nothing is exempt from His dominion. We must live by His Word, not our own."

They continue: "The Chalcedon Foundation is premised on the belief that ideas have consequences. It takes seriously the words of Professor F. A. Hayek: 'It may well be that scholars tend to overestimate the influence which we can exer-cise on contemporary affairs. But I doubt whether it is possible to overestimate the influence which ideas have in the long run.' Our resources are being used to remind Christians of this basic truth: What men believe makes a difference."

That all sounds well and good; however, there is a darker side to the Min-istry. They also say: "Our activities include foundational and leadership roles in Christian reconstruction. Our emphasis on the Cultural or Dominion Mandate (Genesis 1:28) and the necessity of a return to Biblical Law has been a crucial fac-tor in the challenge to Humanism by Christians in this country and elsewhere."

And it's the matter of Biblical Law that has caused such a great deal of controversy. In 2005, the Ministry of the Chalcedon Foundation was identi-fied as a hate group by the Southern Poverty Law Center. The SPLC further added that the Ministry desires the "imposition of Old Testament law on America and the world," and "embraces the most draconian of religious views." On top of that, the SPLC loudly pronounced that Rushdoony believed that gay people should be put to death, that he frowned on interracial rela-tionships, and that he was a Holocaust denier.

Minutemen

In chronicling the history of the Minutemen, the U.S. government offers the following words: "According to Massachusetts colonial law, all able-bodied men between the ages of 16 and 60 were required to keep a serviceable firearm and serve in a part-time citizen army called the militia. Their duty was to defend the colony against her enemies; chiefly the Indians and the French. The colonial militia sometimes fought side by side with British soldiers, particularly during the last French and Indian War in the 1750s and early '60s. However, as a result of the mounting tensions between Great Britain and her American colonies, that would soon change.

"In October of 1774, following the lead of the Worchester County Convention, the Massachusetts Provincial Congress called upon all militia officers to resign their commissions under the old Royal Government and for new elections to be held. This effectively purged the officer corps of loyalists. They also called upon the towns (most of which supported one or more companies of militia) to set aside a portion of its militia and form them into new, special companies called Minute Men. Minute Men were different from the militia in the following ways: "While service in the militia was required by law, minute men were volunteers. The minute men trained far more frequently than the militia. Two or three times per week was common. Because of this serious commitment of time, they were paid. One shilling per drill was average. Militia only trained once every few months (on average) and were paid only if they were called out beyond their town, or formed part of an expedition. Minute Men were expected to keep their arms and equipment with them at all times, and in the event of an alarm, be ready to march at a minute's warning—hence they were called 'Minute Men.'"

It's important to note, however, that the Minutemen actually existed in an earlier form, as *USHistory* points out: "Although today Minutemen are thought of as connected to the Revolutionary War in America, their existence was conceived in Massachusetts during the mid-seventeenth century. As early as 1645, men were selected from the militia ranks to be dressed with matchlocks or pikes and accoutrements within half an hour of being warned. In 1689 another type of Minuteman company came into existence. Called Snowshoemen, each was to 'provide himself with a good pair of snowshoes, one pair of moggisons, and one hatchet' and to be ready to march on a moment's warning."

Mithraism

A religion steeped in deep secrecy and extensive rituals, Mithraism took its name from the Roman deity known as Mithras, who—so far as history currently tells us—first surfaced in the latter part of the first century C.E., and who vanished from Roman culture approximately three hundred years later. Devotion to Mithras in that three-centuries-long period, undertaken chiefly in the city of Rome itself, was actually born out of an earlier God. It was known as Mithra, who was a powerful deity in the history of the Persian Empire. Those secretly brought into the fold were known as Syndexioi, which means "united by the handshake," and which is a decidedly apt term for a secret society to utilize. Meetings were held in labyrinthine tunnels below Rome; tunnels were converted into temples to their deity of choice (Mithras, of course).

A great deal of data on Mithraism comes from the late Manly P. Hall, a mystic born in Canada in 1901 and whose written works included *The Secret Teachings of all Ages*, *The Secret Destiny of America*, and *The Lost Keys of Freemasonry*. Hall, who died in 1990, said back in 1928:

"Initiation into the rites of Mithras, like initiation into many other ancient schools of philosophy, apparently consisted of three important degrees. Preparation for these degrees consisted of self-purification, the building up of the intellectual powers, and the control of the animal nature. In the first degree the candidate was given a crown upon the point of a sword and instructed in the mysteries of Mithras' hidden power. Probably he was taught that the golden crown represented his own spiritual nature, which must be objectified and unfolded before he could truly glorify Mithras; for Mithras was his own soul, standing as mediator between Ormuzd, his spirit, and Ahriman, his animal nature."

The Roman god Mithras has his origins back in the first century C.E.

Hall continued: "In the second degree he was given the armor of intelligence and purity and sent into the darkness of subterranean pits to fight the beasts of lust, passion, and degeneracy. In the third degree he was given a cape, upon which were drawn or woven the signs of the zodiac and other astronomical symbols. After his initiations were over, he was hailed as one who had risen from the dead, was instructed in the secret teachings of the Persian mystics, and became a full-fledged member of the order. Candidates who successfully passed the Mithraic initiations were called Lions and were marked upon their foreheads with the Egyptian cross. Mithras himself is often pictured with the head of a lion and two pairs of wings. Throughout the entire ritual were repeated references to the birth of Mithras as the Sun God, his sacrifice for man, his death that men might have eternal life, and lastly, his resurrection and the saving of all humanity by his intercession before the throne of Ormuzd."

Hall also said: "While the cult of Mithras did not reach the philosophic heights attained by Zarathustra, its effect upon the civilization of the Western world was far-reaching, for at one time nearly all Europe was converted to its doctrines. Rome, in her intercourse with other nations, inoculated them with her religious principles; and many later institutions have exhibited Mithraic culture. The reference to the 'Lion' and the 'Grip of the Lion's Paw' in the Master Mason's degree have a strong Mithraic tinge and may easily have originated from this cult. A ladder of seven rungs appears in the Mithraic initiation. Faber is of the opinion that this ladder was originally a pyramid of seven steps. It is possible that the Masonic ladder with seven rungs had its origin in this Mithraic symbol.

"Women were never permitted to enter the Mithraic Order, but children of the male sex were initiates long before they reached maturity. The refusal to permit women to join the Masonic Order may be based on the esoteric reason given in the secret instructions of the Mithraics. This cult is another excellent example of those secret societies whose legends are largely symbolic representations of the sun and his journey through the houses of the heavens. Mithras, rising from a stone, is merely the sun rising over the horizon, or, as the ancients supposed, out of the horizon, at the vernal equinox."

MKNaomi

MKNaomi was a major CIA program in the field of mind control, but certainly not as infamous as the far more well-known MKUltra. In 1967, the CIA summarized the purposes of MKNaomi thus: "(a) To provide for a covert support base to meet clandestine operational requirements. (b) To stockpile severely incapacitating and lethal materials for the specific use of TSD [Technical Services Division]. (c) To maintain in operational readiness special and unique items for the dissemination of biological and chemical materials. (d) To provide for the required surveillance, testing, upgrading, and evaluation of materials and items in order to assure absence of defects and complete predictability of results to be expected under operational conditions."

Under an agreement reached with the Army in 1952, the Special Operations Division (SOD) at Fort Detrick was to assist the CIA in developing, testing, and maintaining biological agents and delivery systems—some of which were directly related to mind control experimentation. By this agreement, the CIA finally acquired the knowledge, skill, and facilities of the Army to develop biological weapons specifically suited for CIA use.

Under an agreement reached with the Army in 1952, the Special Operations Division (SOD) at Fort Detrick was to assist the CIA in developing, testing, and maintaining biological agents and delivery systems....

The Committee also noted: "SOD developed darts coated with biological agents and pills containing several different biological agents which could remain potent for weeks or months. SOD developed a special gun for firing darts coated with a chemical which could allow CIA agents to incapacitate a guard dog, enter an installation secretly, and return the dog to consciousness when leaving. SOD scientists were unable to develop a similar incapacitant [sic] for humans. SOD also physically transferred to CIA personnel biological agents in 'bulk' form, and delivery devices, including some containing biological agents."

In addition to the CIA's interest in using biological weapons and mind control against humans, it also asked SOD to study use of biological agents against crops and animals. In its 1967 memorandum, the CIA stated: "Three methods and systems for carrying out a covert attack against crops and causing severe crop loss have been developed and evaluated under field conditions. This was accomplished in anticipation of a requirement which was later developed but was subsequently scrubbed just prior to putting into action."

The Committee concluded with respect to MKNaomi that the project was "terminated in 1970. On November 25, 1969, President Nixon renounced the use of any form of biological weapons that kill or incapacitate and ordered the disposal of existing stocks of bacteriological weapons. On February 14, 1970, the President clarified the extent of his earlier order and indicated that toxins—chemicals that are not living organisms but are produced by living organisms—were considered biological weapons subject to his previous directive and were to be destroyed."

Persistent rumors, however, suggest the destruction was not quite as widespread as many on the Committee had hoped for. The result: the research still continues, under a blanket of secrecy and overseen by secret groups whose names are known only to an elite few.

MKUltra

Although the U.S. intelligence community, military, and government have undertaken countless official (and off-the-record) projects pertaining to both mind control and mind manipulation, without any doubt whatsoever, the most notorious of all was Project MKUltra: a clandestine group that operated out of the CIA's Office of Scientific Intelligence and that had its beginnings in the Cold War era of the early 1950s.

To demonstrate the level of secrecy that surrounded Project MKUltra, even though it had kicked off at the dawn of the 1950s, its existence was largely unknown outside of the intelligence world until 1975—when the Church Committee and the Rockefeller Commission began making their own investigations of the CIA's mind control-related activities—in part to determine if (A) the CIA had engaged in illegal activity, (B) the personal rights of citizens had been violated, and (C) if the projects at issue had resulted in fatalities—which they most assuredly and unfortunately did.

Rather conveniently, and highly suspiciously, too, it was asserted at the height of the inquires in 1975 that two years earlier, in 1973, CIA director Richard Helms had ordered the destruction of the Agency's MKUltra files. Fortunately, this did not stop the Church Committee or the Rockefeller Commission—both of whom had the courage and tenacity to forge ahead with their investigations, relying on sworn testimony from players in MKUltra, where documentation was no longer available for scrutiny, study, and evaluation.

The story that unfolded was both dark and disturbing in equal degrees. Indeed, the scope of the project—and allied operations, too—was spelled out in an August 1977 document titled *The Senate MKUltra Hearings*, which was prepared by the Senate Select Committee on Intelligence and the Committee on Human Resources, as a result of its probing into the secret world of the CIA.

As the document explained: "Research and development programs to find materials which could be used to alter human behavior were initiated in the late 1940s and early 1950s. These experimental programs originally included testing of drugs involving witting human subjects, and culminated in tests using unwitting, non-volunteer human subjects. These tests were designed to determine the potential effects of chemical or biological agents when used operationally against individuals unaware that they had received a drug."

The Committee then turned its attention to the overwhelming secrecy that surrounded these early 1940s/1950s projects: "The testing

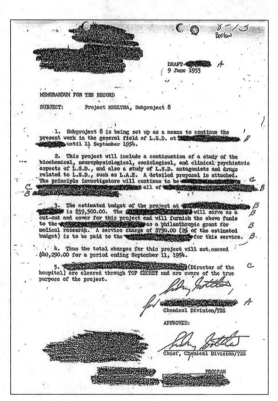

A censored 1953 letter approving an MKUltra project involving LSD.

The research and development programs, and particularly the covert testing programs, resulted in massive abridgments of the rights of American citizens, and sometimes with tragic consequences.

programs were considered highly sensitive by the intelligence agencies administering them. Few people, even within the agencies, knew of the programs and there is no evidence that either the Executive Branch or Congress were ever informed of them.

"The highly compartmented nature of these programs may be explained in part by an observation made by the CIA Inspector General that, 'the knowledge that the Agency is engaging in unethical and illicit activities would have serious repercussions in political and diplomatic circles and would be detrimental to the accomplishment of its missions.'"

The research and development programs, and particularly the covert testing programs, resulted in massive abridgments of the rights of American citizens, and sometimes with tragic consequences.

As prime evidence of this, the Committee uncovered details on the deaths of two Americans that were firmly attributed to the programs at issue, while other participants in the testing programs were said to still be suffering from the residual effects of the tests as late as the mid-1970s.

And as the Committee starkly noted: "While some controlled testing of these substances might be defended, the nature of the tests, their scale, and the fact that they were continued for years after the danger of surreptitious administration of LSD to unwitting individuals was known, demonstrate a fundamental disregard for the value of human life."

Montauk Project

Situated on Long Island is a facility that, within the field of conspiracy theorizing, has become infamous. It was in 1917 that the Naval Air Station Montauk, situated at the east end of the South Shore of Long Island, came into being. Then, in 1942, it became known as Fort Hero (after Major General Andrew Hero Jr.). Strategically, it was a highly important facility, one that kept a careful watch on the coastal waters for Nazi U-Boats. In the 1950s, when the Russians began to flex their muscles and the threat of atomic war became all too real, the base was upgraded with new and revolutionary radar-based equipment that would provide the U.S. military with advance warning of incoming Soviet bombers. The base was finally shut down in 1981. Or was it?

There are persistent and widespread rumors that Montauk was, for decades, the home of a highly secret group that engaged in a wide variety of research into all manner of bizarre topics, including invisibility, time travel, genetic manipulation, and more.

Joe Nickell is a senior research fellow of the Committee for Skeptical Inquiry (CSI) and 'Investigative Files' columnist for *Skeptical Inquirer*. A former stage magician, private investigator, and teacher, he is the author of numerous books, including *Inquest on the Shroud of Turin* (1998), *Pen, Ink and Evidence* (2003), *Unsolved History* (2005), and *Adventures in Paranormal Investigation* (2007).

He notes that: "In July 2008, the carcass of a creature soon dubbed the 'Montauk Monster' allegedly washed ashore near Montauk, Long Island, New York. It sparked much speculation and controversy, with some suggesting it was a shell-less sea turtle, a dog or other canid, a sheep, or a rodent—or even a latex fake or possible mutation experiment from the nearby Plum Island Animal Disease Center."

The strange saga of the admittedly very weird beast was one that caught the attention of not just national, but international, media. This was hardly

The Camp Hero radar in Montauk, New York, has never been torn down, but is used by local boaters as a landmark for navigation.

surprising, since the animal appeared to have a beak-like face, large claws, and a dog-like body. While the controversy rolled on for a long time—and provoked deep rumors about what "the government" was doing—an answer to the riddle finally came, as Dr. Darren Naish noted: "Is the carcass that of a dog? Dogs have an inflated frontal region that gives them a pronounced bony brow or forehead, and in contrast the Montauk monster's head seems smoothly convex. As many people have now noticed, there is a much better match: Raccoon *Procyon lotor*. It was the digits of the hands that gave this away for me: the Montauk carcass has very strange, elongated, almost human-like fingers with short claws. Given that we're clearly dealing with a North American carnivoran, raccoon is the obvious choice: raccoons are well known for having particularly dexterous fingers that lack the sort of interdigital webbing normally present in carnivorans. The match for a raccoon is perfect once we compare the dentition and proportions. The Montauk animal has lost its upper canines and incisors (you can even see the empty sockets), and if you're surprised by the length of the Montauk animal's limbs, note that—like a lot of mammals we ordinarily assume to be relatively short-legged—raccoons are actually surprisingly leggy (claims that the limb proportions of the Montauk carcass are unlike those of raccoons are not correct)."

Rumors of the military perfecting invisibility, traveling through time, encountering both friendly and hostile aliens as a result of its work, and much more abound.

Then, there's the matter of Bigfoot. The claim is that top-secret research is afoot deep below the old Montauk base to create Tulpa-style versions of Bigfoot. That's to say: monsters conjured up in the imagination that can then be projected outwardly and given some degree of quasi-independent life in the real world. *Weird U.S.* notes that on one occasion, one of those attached to the secret experiments—a man named Duncan Cameron—envisioned in his mind "a large, angry, powerful Sasquatch-like" entity that "materialized at Montauk and began destroying the base in a rage. It utterly decimated the place, tanking the project and disconnecting it from the past. As soon as the equipment harnessing people's psychic power was destroyed, the beast disappeared."

There's no doubt, however, that the one conspiracy—more than any other—attached to the Montauk saga is that of the so-called Philadelphia Experiment. So, the story goes, throughout 1943, at the Philadelphia Naval Yard, the U.S. Navy was secretly working hard to make its ships radar-invisible—a concept very similar to that in today's so-called stealth aircraft. According to legend, the Navy did far more than that: one fringe experiment resulted in one ship, the *USS Eldridge*, becoming literally invisible—which had a catastrophic effect on the crew, many of whom were allegedly driven mad or died during the experiment. The Navy, unsure of what had happened, hastily shut down the program. At least, for a while. The story continues that in the 1950s, the research was restarted, deep below Montauk, in a series of cavernous facilities. Rumors of the military perfecting invisibility, traveling through time, encountering both friendly and hostile aliens as a result of its work, and much more abound. All such claims are denied by the U.S. government—as one might expect if they have any validity to them.

Moon Secrets

A secret group interested in the mysteries of the Moon, including the possibility that it is home to a race of extraterrestrials that live deep below its surface, it sounds incredible. It is, however, amazing fact. The late Ingo Swann was considered to be one of the U.S. government's leading remote viewers, those near-unique individuals whose psychic powers and extrasensory perception (ESP) were harnessed, from the 1970s onwards, to spy on the former Soviet Union. Swann proved to be a highly skilled remote viewer, one whose talents were employed on a number of espionage-themed operations focusing on overseas targets that might have proven hostile to the United States. As a result, Swann came into contact with a variety of shadowy figures within the realm of government secrecy, and the world of intelligence gathering, including a truly Machiavellian character known, very mysteriously, only by the name of Mr. Axelrod—seemingly a leading figure in this hidden group.

It was in February 1975 that Swann was contacted out of the blue by what he personally described as a certain highly placed figure in Washington, D.C., who guardedly advised Swann that he, Swann, would soon be receiving a telephone call from the aforementioned Mr. Axelrod. Swann's source quietly advised him that while he could not offer much at that time by way of a meaningful explanation, Swann should be keenly aware that the call would concern a matter of great urgency and importance. A somewhat concerned Swann waited … and waited … and waited. Finally, around four weeks later, a call arrived, and Swann was asked to make a cloak-and-dagger rendezvous, only mere hours later, at the National Museum of Natural History within the Smithsonian.

Despite the somewhat fraught, last-minute nature of the conversation, Swann unhesitatingly agreed, and quickly—albeit with a degree of concern and trepidation—made his careful way to the meeting place, where he was greeted by a man who Swann said looked like a Marine. Although basic formalities were exchanged, Swann was hardly clear on what was afoot: he was driven by car to a second location, where nothing less than a helicopter was waiting to take him to a destination unknown. Such was the security and secrecy surrounding the journey that Swann was blindfolded for the approximately thirty-minute flight. In other words, the experience was rapidly becoming one of near-007-like proportions.

On landing, Swann was taken to an elevator that descended for a significant period of time—perhaps into the bowels of some secret, underground installation, Swann thought, and probably with a high degree of logical justification. With the blindfold finally removed, Swann gathered his bearings, and was then introduced to the enigmatic Mr. Axelrod, who admitted this was not his real name, but suggested to Swann it was an identity that served the particular purposes of the meeting.

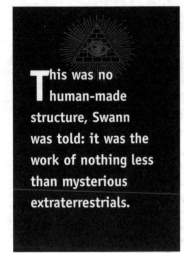

This was no human-made structure, Swann was told: it was the work of nothing less than mysterious extraterrestrials.

Axelrod wasted no time and got straight to the point, asking Swann many questions about the nature of remote viewing. Axelrod also made it clear that he wished to make use of Swann's skills—on what was clearly a secret operation—for a significant sum of money. It truly was one of those offers that one cannot refuse, and Swann, most assuredly, did not refuse it.

Axelrod asked Swann, pointedly, what he knew about our Moon. Now, finally, the purpose of the strange meeting was becoming much clearer. Someone within officialdom was secretly looking to have the Moon remote viewed—which is precisely what Swann went ahead and did. By Swann's own admission, he was utterly floored by what he found: during an initial targeting, his mind focused in on sensational imagery of what looked to be a huge tower, similar in size to the Secretariat Building at the United Nations, but one that soared upwards from the Moon's surface. This was no human-made structure, Swann was told: it was the work of nothing less than mysterious extraterrestrials.

In follow-up remote viewing sessions, Swann was able to perceive on the surface of the Moon a wealth of domed structures, advanced machinery, additional tall towers, large cross-like structures, curious tubular constructions across the landscape, and even evidence of what looked like extensive mining operations. Someone, or something, had secretly constructed nothing less than a Moon base.

Intriguingly, Swann was also able to focus his mind on what appeared to be a group of people—that appeared very human—housed in some sort of enclosure on the Moon, that were busily burrowing into the side of a cliff. The only oddity: they were all utterly naked. Rather ominously, and very quickly, at that point Axelrod terminated the experiment, amid dark and disturbing allusions to the possibility that the Moon-based entities were possibly acutely aware they were being spied upon via the means of astral travel. It was even implied that Swann's very actions might now place him in grave danger, if the beings decided to turn the tables and pay him a visit of a deadly, cosmic kind— which, very fortunately for Swann, they did not.

Notably, Axelrod also inquired of Swann if he knew of a man named George Leonard. Swann replied that, no, he was not familiar with the name. It transpired that during that very same timeframe that the shadowy Axelrod was employing Swann to seek out the mysteries of the Moon, Leonard, an author, was hard at work, toiling on a manuscript titled *Somebody Else Is on the Moon*. In 1977, Leonard's manuscript appeared in book form, and, to a significant degree, focused its attention upon the very matter about which Axelrod was so deeply troubled: namely, unusual, intelligently designed structures, or installations, on the Moon.

The strange meetings between Swann and Axelrod—on the nature of what was afoot on the Moon—continued until 1977, after which time they came to an abrupt end, with Swann, unsurprisingly, left scratching his head about the distinctly odd sequence of events. Had Swann really psychically accessed a fantastically advanced base on the Moon that had been constructed by spacefaring extraterrestrials? Or, does the fact Swann recalled that those working on the facility looked like everyday members of the human race— albeit naked ones!—mean that this was a secret installation of very terrestrial origins, one that Axelrod was trying to learn more about, due to being left out of a particular, highly classified governmental loop?

Nazis

Adolf Hitler's Nazi Germany held that the collective Germanic and Nordic populations were the closest thing that existed to a pure race. It was a much-disputed concept that caused wholly justified outrage in many quarters. It had its origins in a nineteenth-century scenario that placed African bushmen and Australian Aborigines at the foot of a ladder and (what a surprise) the Nordics at the very top. Aside from those racists who adhered to the theory (and who, in some cases, still adhere to it, to this very day), it was utterly lacking in any scientific merit at all. The Nazis were as fascinated with the occult as they were with the notion of creating the perfect superman.

As far as the Nazis themselves were concerned, they were firmly of the opinion that the people of both Southern and Eastern Europe were racially mixed with non-Europeans from across the Mediterranean Sea, while it was strictly the Northern Europeans who successfully remained pure. Adherents of this nutty belief maintained that not only had the Nordics remained pure, but that as a result of the cold, harsh climate in which they had mostly been raised, they also just happened to be the physically toughest and strongest of all peoples, and so, the ominous image of the blond and blue-eyed superman of Nazi Germany began to develop—in leaps and bounds.

Somewhat ironically, however, the Nazis did not discriminate against Germans who were not blond and/or blue-eyed, and who were considered Aryans (the term "Aryan" being derived from the ancient peoples who lived

Nazis parade in 1938. A driving force behind the movement was that "Aryans" were a superior race.

in Iran and the Indus Valley). The Nazi theorist Alfred Rosenberg argued that they were fierce, warrior-like people whose point of origin was actually well into the northern hemisphere, but who migrated south in times past and were the ancestors of early Germanic clans and tribes. Fortunately for all of us, the Master Race proved to be not quite so masterly, after all.

New Forest Coven

The website *iNewForest* says of witchcraft in England: "The New Forest is an important place in the history of Wicca. Gerald Gardner, the 'Father of Wicca,' was initiated into the New Forest Coven in 1939. However the 'old religion' has been practiced in the forest for a long time before then. 'Cunning folk' from Medieval times and all over Britain would practice their form of magic to help heal, cast spells and in fortune telling. These wise men and women would often be persecuted for witch craft. So, understandably these 'witches' would often keep a very low profile and their faith quiet."

Much of the witchcraft that *iNewForest* refers to operated out of the village of Bursley. The BBC notes that "Burley is one of the New Forest's most picturesque villages, but behind the postcard image, there lies a secret past … in the 1950s a woman called Sybil Leek lived in Burley with her pet Jackdaw. She became a TV reporter but primarily claimed to be a witch. Sybil had lived with gypsies and gained an excellent knowledge of the New Forest. She was recognized as an expert on forest ways and wrote several books on the subject. She also named a witchcraft shop, 'A Coven of Witches.'"

Then, there's the matter of the New Forest Coven, a secret society of witches who also operated out of broadly the same area. So far as can be determined, the presence of the coven in the New Forest first appeared around 1937 or 1938. That does not mean it didn't exist in some prior form elsewhere, however. Rather, it simply means we're unable to find evidence of its existence before the late 1930s. The primary source for information on the New Forest Coven was Gerald Gardner, a man who is acknowledged as spearheading the creation of today's Wicca movement. According to Gardner, he was invited to become one of the New Forest Coven in September 1939—the very month that World War II began. Gardner wasn't just invited, however: he was initiated.

According to what Gardner was told by the members of the New Forest Coven, its beliefs and practices dated back to pre-Christian eras, when early paganism dominated much of Europe. The group had its very own deity, a horned one, and was—to a degree, at least—inspired by the work of Dr. Margaret Murray, an Egyptologist who wrote and spoke widely on the matter of early European witch-cults. Indeed, in 1921 Murray wrote a book titled *The Witch-Cult in Europe*. It was a book that Gerald Gardner suspected may have had an influence on the New Forest Coven, even if it existed—in some form—much earlier.

This house in Dorset, England, was where Gerald Gardner was allegedly initiated into the New Forest Coven. He later founded the modern version of Wicca.

While a great deal of data relative to the origins of the New Forest Coven are inevitably lost to the fog of time, what we do know is that one of the prime movers in the cult was a woman named Rosamund Sabine—who, prior to becoming involved in the New Forest Coven, was heavily involved with the Hermetic Order of the Golden Dawn. Perhaps most controversial of all is the claim that in August 1940 the New Forest Coven engaged in a lengthy and complicated ritual to try and prevent Adolf Hitler's hordes from invading the United Kingdom—all, allegedly, with the secret consent of the British government and its then-burgeoning intelligence community. Supposedly, the ritual was known as the Cone of Power. True or not, it remains the pinnacle of the occult-based work of the New Forest Coven.

Octopus

August 9, 1991, was the date on which a man named Danny Casolaro was found dead in the shower of room 517 of the Martinsburg, West Virginia-based Sheraton Inn. It appeared that Casolaro had committed suicide: both of his wrists were slashed and there was a suicide note left for his family. But, was it really as tragically straightforward as it seemed? Not for the field of conspiracy theorizing, it wasn't. At the time of his death, Casolaro—an investigative journalist—was chasing down a powerful, secret society that he termed the Octopus—on account of the fact that it appeared to have powerful and influential tentacles that extended across just about the entire planet.

For Casolaro, it all began around one and a half years before his death. That was when he started digging into the saga of a man named William Hamilton, formerly of the National Security Agency, and an acknowledged leading figure in the world of computer software. Hamilton had come up with a highly sophisticated program for the Department of Justice, one that would significantly help the DoJ to track and locate wanted criminals. When the DoJ claimed that Hamilton was overcharging them, a long and complicated legal battle began—and Hamilton was the loser. But it wasn't the end for Hamilton's program—which was called PROMIS.

> **The further Caso-laro dug, the more complicated the story got: the Octopus was composed of numerous powerful people in the worlds of big business, politics, the military, and the intelligence community.**

Shadowy figures in the intelligence community were making their own versions of Hamilton's program, but with one big difference: the new versions contained a deeply buried backdoor that would allow U.S. intelligence to spy on just about anyone and everyone who used the program—which included Israel and Iran, and the operation could all be traced back to the mysterious Octopus.

The further Casolaro dug, the more complicated the story got: the Octopus was composed of numerous powerful people in the worlds of big business, politics, the military, and the intelligence community. They were somewhat loose knit and fluid, but they had the power and muscle to influence world events on a massive scale. As Casolaro headed ever deeper into the rabbit hole, he found that the Octopus had played key roles in the 1962 Cuban missile crisis (which brought the world to the brink of nuclear war), the Watergate scandal (which brought down President Richard M. Nixon), and the December 1988 destruction of a Boeing 747 aircraft over Lockerbie, Scotland. Then things got really weird.

The Octopus, Casolaro discovered, had a significant presence at the world's most famous secret base: Area 51, Nevada. The Octopus was reportedly funding research to create deadly viruses at both Area 51 and at an underground facility in northern New Mexico. Casolaro also made a connection between the Octopus and Majestic 12—the alleged secret group that oversees the secrecy surrounding what happened at Roswell, New Mexico, in early July 1947. Things then took a strange turn when Casolaro met with a man named Michael Riconosciuto, who had worked in the field of spies, espionage, and intelligence for years, and who advised Casolaro that many assumed UFOs were actually highly advanced, unusual aircraft of the military.

Casolaro's research continued at a phenomenal rate, to the point where he came to see the presence—and manipulative skills—of the Octopus in just about each and every major world event since the end of World War II. Of course, it all came crashing down for Casolaro when he was found dead in the tub. But, was it really just a suicide? Many within the field of conspiracy cried "No!" They pointed to the fact that less than a day before his death, Casolaro had a relaxing time hanging out with a man named William Turner, who was one of Casolaro's sources in the defense industry. Casolaro was apparently enthused and excited about where his research was taking him. Police investigators discovered that Casolaro had a chat with the man in the adjacent hotel room about his Octopus-based work—the man said Casolaro didn't appear depressed, down, or anxious. Quite the opposite. Nevertheless, the official verdict was suicide. There were, however, problems with the verdict: the main one being that both wrists were deeply cut. While it would have been easy for Casolaro to have inflicted the deep wounds to one wrist, doing so to the other—when the first was already viciously hacked into—would have been much more difficult, some said.

In 1996, authors Jim Keith and Kenn Thomas wrote a book on the affair and Casolaro's suspiciously timed death. Its title? What else? *The Octopus*. Keith soon found that his computer had been hacked and that someone was reading his every written word. Then, in 1999, Keith died in a Reno hospital—and under questionable circumstances—after falling off a stage and fracturing his tibia at the annual Burning Man festival in Nevada's Black Rock Desert. Then, in 2001, Ron Bonds—the publisher of *The Octopus*—died, under equally controversial circumstances. The Octopus, it seems, is determined to ensure that no one gets too close to the truth of its world-manipulating activities—no matter what the cost.

Operation Often

Earlier in the pages of this book you were introduced to the world of a secret order that calls itself the Collins Elite. It's a group composed of high-ranking figures in the Church, government, the military, the field of archaeology, and the domain of demonology. Whereas the Collins Elite was (and, apparently, still is) doing its utmost to stave off demonic assaults on the human race, another group, created in the late 1960s, was doing the exact opposite. Its name was Operation Often. Its goal? Nothing less than learning how to harness what might be termed supernatural and demonic powers of the weaponized kind.

It all began in the latter part of the 1960s with one Dr. Sydney Gottlieb. Having secured a Ph.D. in chemistry from the California Institute of Tech-

Richard Helms was director of the CIA when Dr. Sydney Gottlieb convinced him to back Operation Often.

nology in the 1940s, Gottlieb, in 1951, was offered the position of head of the Chemical Division of the CIA's Technical Services Staff. Mind control, hypnosis, the manipulation of the human mind, and the nurturing of Manchurian candidate-style figures were very much the order of the day. It was work that Gottlieb dedicated himself to for years. In 1968, however, life and work changed significantly for Gottlieb. Welcome to the world of Operation Often.

Without a doubt the brainchild of Gottlieb, Operation Often was kick-started thanks to the then-director of the CIA, Richard Helms. Gottlieb very quickly convinced Helms that the CIA should explore the fields of the paranormal, the demonic, and the occult, to determine if, and how, they could be used against the likes of the former Soviet Union and the Chinese. An initial grant of $150,000 was quickly provided. Investigative writer Gordon Thomas says: "Operation Often was intended … to explore the world of black magic and the supernatural." It did precisely that.

In no time at all, and mirroring the Collins Elite, Operation Often became something of a secret order, one that was dominated by disturbing phenomena, the study of ancient and priceless books on the occult, and a long list of notable characters. As evidence of this, the personnel on board with Operation Often were soon mixing with (among many others) fortune tellers, mediums, psychics, demonologists, astrologers, Satanists, clairvoyants, and even those who practiced sacrificial rituals—such as the followers of Santeria.

In essence, Gottlieb and his team were looking to hit and pummel the Russians and the Chinese with hexes, curses, bad luck, ill health, and even death—all by engaging in Faustian-like pacts with paranormal entities from dark and disturbing dimensions beyond ours. Volunteers of the program were placed into altered states of mind, in the hope that doing so might provoke out-of-body experiences that, then, would allow mind-to-mind contact with anything and everything that might be on the other side, such as demons, devils, and the like.

To what extent the program worked is open to debate. Not because the data is sketchy. Rather, the data and the results of the work of Operation Often remain classified—decades after the program was initiated in the late 1960s. This begs an important question: if Operation Often achieved nothing of significance, why not let us know? Where's the harm in that? That the CIA flatly refuses to release it files on the project strongly suggests that some success—maybe even a great deal of success—was achieved. Of course, when you deal with the Devil, there's always a price to pay. Perhaps the nature of that price remains classified, too.

Order of Nine Angles

*T*he *Satanic Wiki* says: "The Order of Nine Angles (ONA) is a purported secretive Satanist organization, initially formed in the United Kingdom, and which rose to public note during the 1980s and 1990s after having been mentioned in books detailing fascist Satanism. Presently, the ONA is organized around clandestine cells (which it calls 'traditional nexions') and around what it calls 'sinister tribes.'

"According to their own testimony, the Order of Nine Angles was originally formed in England in the 1960s, with the merger of three neopagan temples called Camlad, The Noctulians, and Temple of the Sun. Following the original leader's emigration to Australia, it has been alleged that David Myatt took over the order and began writing the now publicly available teachings of the ONA. The ONA now has associates, and groups, in the United States, Europe, Australia, New Zealand, Canada, Russia, and Iceland.

"Author Nick Ryan has asserted that Anton Long, the author of the ONA's public tracts, is a pseudonym of David Myatt, a person who was involved with the neo-Nazi movement in England. This assertion is repeated by Nicholas Goodrick-Clarke, who claims that David Myatt was the founder of the ONA and writer of most of the ONA documents, and had previously acted as bodyguard for 'British Nazi Colin Jordan.'"

Grand Magister Blackwood is far from impressed with the group: "After exhaustive research into the Illustrious Order of Nine Angles, I have found three things that seem to permeate the miserable and pathetic creation that is simply created and recreated in the minds of those who desire some resolve to Satanism, by claiming sinister and arcane knowledge, nothing short of convulsed and distorted information plagiarized from ancient tomes and remixed into a formula that proves this group nothing short of Pseudo."

This is a view also adhered to by Sinister Moon, who offers the following: "The belief that there is—or was—a real person, one person, behind the name 'Anton Long,' with that person being David Myatt, is false; a myth. For the real story is one of a deception intended to enhance the image, the credibility, of the Order of Nine Angles, a group which never existed as a real functioning Occult order let alone a Satanist one. The ONA itself was never more than a myth, a marketing device, a honeytrap, and—latterly—just an Internet phenomenon."

Ordo Aurum Solis

It was three years before the commencement of the twentieth century that the Societas Rotae Fulgentis—the Society of the Burning Wheel—changed its name to Aurum Solis. The origins of the society, however, date back much further. Indeed, its origins are traceable back to pre-Christian eras and to the heart of ancient Egypt.

"A lineage of initiates, the Masters of the gold chain, maintained this Ogdoadic heritage (tradition of the God Thoth) that lead to the Aurum Solis. Since its inception, the Order of the Aurum Solis has maintained a clear and unique lineage of Grand Masters. This is rare among contemporary initiatic Orders who seem to spend their time bickering and dividing. Since the Ogdoadic Tradition took the name Aurum Solis in 1897, there have been 10 Grand Masters, always appointed for life. (Note that some had to interrupt their duties for health issues). Vivian Godfrey, is the Grand Master who remained in office for the longest period of time until her death: 20 years. Jean-Louis de Biasi is the current Grand Master and received the full powers of the Tradition in 2003." Those are the words of the Ordo Aurum Solis, itself.

The seal of the Ordo Aurum Solis.

The Ordo Aurum Solis (Latin for "Gold of the Sun") came into being as a result of the work of two men: an Anglican bishop named George Henry Stanton and Charles Kingold, an occultist. Senior figures within, and linked to, Ordo Aurum Solis have notable backgrounds, as *Liquisearch* reveals: "Melita Denning and Osborne Phillips are the pen-names of Vivian Godfrey and Leon Barcynski, who together authored many books.... Chief among these was the formal presentation of the Order Aurum Solis' philosophy and praxis: *The Magical Philosophy*.

"Melita Denning, a Jungian scholar, was the first female Grand Master of the Order. She led the Order from 1976 to 1987, and from 1988 till her death on March 23, 1997. Earlier in her life, she had traveled throughout the Middle East and the Mediterranean in search of occult knowledge. It was after six years of research that she finally came upon Ordo Aurum Solis.

"Osborne Phillips was Grand Master of the Order from 1997 to 2003. He received magical training early in his life at the hands of Ernest Page, a London astrologer of some repute. In the early 1970s, he was in charge of psychic investigation as conducted by certain initiates of Ordo Aurum Solis. Phillips was also a student of U Maung Maung Ji, who specialized in Eastern philosophical systems and was a co-worker of the UN Secretary-General U Thant."

Ordo Templi Orientis

The Ordo Templi Orientis is also known as the Order of Oriental Templars and as the Order of the Temple of the East. It is far better known, however, as simply the O.T.O. The society's members note that they are dedicated to what is described as the "high purpose of securing the Liberty of the Individual and his or her advancement in Light, Wisdom, Understanding, Knowledge, and Power through Beauty, Courage, and Wit, on the Foundation of Universal Brotherhood."

Ordo Templi Orientis, its followers state, is the first of the great Old Æon orders to accept The Book of the Law, which was received by Aleister Crowley—the Great Beast—in 1904. It's a mighty tome that offers a "New Æon in human thought, culture and religion." The Æon arises from a single supreme injunction, says the O.T.O: "… the Law of Thelema, which is Do what thou wilt. U.S. Grand Lodge is the governing body of O.T.O. in the United States. It is the most populous and active branch of O.T.O., with many local bodies spread throughout the country."

Bill Heidrick, who is an acknowledged expert on the O.T.O, notes: "The immediate precursor organization was the Hermetic Brotherhood of Light, a mystical society founded in the mid-19th century, with branches in Europe and North America. Prior to the Hermetic Brotherhood of Light, O.T.O. 'traditional' history includes the Weishaupt Illuminati of the late 18th century and the Crusading Order of Knights Templar of the 11th century as precursors."

Heidrick stresses, however, that's it's very important to be aware of the fact that numerous other societies and orders of the secret kind have claimed derivation from the Illuminati and the Templars of the eleventh century—but

Ordo Templi Orientis, its followers state, is the first of the great Old Æon orders to accept The Book of the Law, which was received by Aleister Crowley—the Great Beast—in 1904.

all without any evidence to back up their claims. Heidrick expands on this: "'Traditional' history is a euphemism for 'mythology' in Masonic and mystical organizations; and, as such, 'traditional' history expresses precursor relationships which are incapable of documentation and may be inaccurate. It is documented that O.T.O. sprang from the Hermetic Brotherhood of Light as the creation of Karl Kellner, a member of that fraternity. The Hermetic Brotherhood of Light continued independently of O.T.O., in its own right, and was still in existence in Oakland, California as late as 1970."

Peter-Robert Koenig has this to say: "The O.T.O. is a pseudo-masonic organization. Neither the use of the letters nor of the full name is unique to any group. Since the founding of the O.T.O. in 1906 in Germany, many groups have appropriated the name, its abbreviations, and acronyms and imbued them with contents to their own taste and liking. There are several rival groups using the name Ordo Templi Orientis or O.T.O. Some of them derive from an 'original' that is, a 'first', O.T.O. but not all. Not all but a few of them can lay some claim to stem from the "original" i.e. first O.T.O. (of 1906). The structure of the O.T.O., like that of Freemasonry, is based on a staged series of initiations or degrees. The essence/secrets of the Ordo Templi Orientis—variations are in their higher degrees; strictly speaking only members of these degrees are considered to be members of the O.T.O. proper."

And then there is the "Manifesto of the O.T.O.," which offers the following for its devotees: "The privileges of members of the O.T.O. are very numerous. These are the principal:

They have not only access to, but instruction in, the whole body of hidden knowledge preserved in the Sanctuary from the beginning of its manifestation. In the lower grades the final secrets are hinted and conveyed in symbol, beneath veil, and through sacrament. In this way the intelligence of the initiate is called into play, so that he who well uses the knowledge of the lower grades may be selected for invitation to the higher, where all things are declared openly.

"They become partakers of the current of Universal Life in Liberty, Beauty, Harmony, and Love which flames within the heart of the O.T.O., and the Light of that august fraternity insensibly illuminates them ever more and more as they approach its central Sun. They meet those persons most complemental to their own natures, and find unexpected help and brotherhood in the whole world wherever they may travel.

"They obtain the right to sojourn in the secret houses of the O.T.O., permanently or for a greater or lesser period of the year according to their rank in the Order; or, in the case of those of the Fifth and lower degrees, are candidates for invitation to these houses. The Knowledge of the Preparation and Use of the Universal Medicine is restricted to members of the IX°; but it may be administered to members of the VIII° and VII° in special circumstances by favour of the National Grand Masters General, and even in particular emergency to members of lower degrees.

"In the V° all members are pledged to bring immediate and perfect relief to all distress of mind, body, or estate, in which they may find any of their fellows of that degree. In the higher degrees the Bonds of Fraternity are still further strengthened. The Order thus affords a perfect system of insurance against every misfortune or accident of life.

"Members of the IX° become part proprietors of the Estates and Goods of the Order, so that the attainment of this degree implies a return with interest of the fees and subscriptions paid.

"The Order gives practical assistance in life to worthy members of even its lower degrees, so that, even if originally poor, they become well able to afford the comparatively high fees of the VII°, VIII°, and IX°. On exaltation to the IV° each Companion may file an account of his circumstances, and state in what direction he requires help."

Parsons, Jack

In 1942 Aleister Crowley chose Jack Parsons (a.k.a. John Whiteside Parsons and Marvel Whiteside Parsons), a noted occultist and rocket scientist, to head the Agape Lodge of the Thelemic Ordo Templi Orientis in Pasadena, California. We can learn a great deal about Parsons by studying the FBI's now-declassified records on Parsons. On November 2, 1950, a California-based special agent of the FBI prepared a report on the actions of Jack Parsons that stated in part: "Subject, on September 15, 1950, removed certain documents pertaining to jet propulsion motors and rocket propellants without authority from Hughes Aircraft Company, Culver City, California; his place of employment [and which had been his place of employment since May 8, 1949]."

On September 25, after the documents in question had been retrieved by the authorities, they were duly handed over to an Air Force Major, E. J. Krenz, after which, the FBI recorded: "[Parsons] voluntarily came to the Los Angeles office, September 27, 1950, and in [a] signed statement admitted removing documents without authority stating he desired to extract certain information from them as aid in computing [the] cost proposal on jet propulsion motors. He planned to submit this with [an] employment application through American Technion Society for employment in the country of Israel."

Twenty-four hours later, an FBI agent, whose name has been excised from the available papers, "displayed the document and papers to John T. Berdner, Air Provost Marshal, U.S. Army, who advised that it would be necessary for

A chemist and rocket engineer by trade, Jack Parsons was a follower of Aleister Crowley's Thelemite beliefs.

him to forward copies of them to the Chief of the Security and Policy Division, Intelligence Department, Headquarters, Air Materiel Command, Wright Field, Dayton, Ohio, where the documents would be examined for the purpose of determining whether or not they contained classified or non-classified information."

As a result of the brewing trouble surrounding Parsons, he was fired from Hughes Aircraft on that very day. Hughes's security personnel hastily advised the military that, at the very least, the documents should be classified Confidential. Then the next morning Parsons prepared a written statement for the FBI, the Army, and Air Materiel Command in which he conceded: "I now realize that I was wrong in taking this material from the Hughes Aircraft Plant."

Whether his apology was genuine or simply a groveling attempt to try and avoid serious problems with the authorities and charges that he was secretly engaged in espionage operations for Israel, Parsons certainly obfuscated the facts and played down his ongoing involvement in matters of an occult nature. When interviewed by the FBI on September 28, he said that he had "severed all relations" with the dark world that had so dominated his earlier years, and "described himself as being an 'individualist,'" according to the interviewing special agent in his report.

Significantly, files pertaining to Parsons's theft of the papers from Hughes Aircraft reveal that, several years earlier, he had worked with some notable bodies, including the government's Office of Scientific Research and Development, the National Defense Research Council, and the Northrop Aircraft Company. Meanwhile, several FBI offices across the state of California tried to determine—with help from the military—if Parsons was acting as an Israeli spy or if his actions were just plain reckless and stupid. The Cincinnati FBI office entered into a period of liaison with the Air Force's Office of Special Investigations to "ascertain the facts" concerning Air Force knowledge of Parsons's activities.

A Major Sam Bruno of the U.S.A.F. advised the FBI that the Air Force did have files on Parsons, including some that related to his relationship with Aleister Crowley, one of which, dated May 17, 1948, stated: "A religious cult, believed to advocate sexual perversion, was organized at subject's home at

1003 South Orange Grove Avenue, Pasadena, California, which has been reported subversive...."

The same documentation referred to U.S.A.F. and FBI knowledge of the Church of Thelema, explaining that "this cult broadly hinted at free love," that there had been "several complaints of 'strange goings on at this home,'" and that an unnamed source had described the church as "a gathering place of perverts." The military's records also noted that in 1943, Parsons was interviewed by the FBI and "stated that the Church of Thelema was a lodge and fraternity as well as a church, and that they studied philosophy as well as religion and attempted to inform themselves concerning all types and kinds of religion."

Parsons admitted that the church was based on the teachings of Crowley (who, rather amusingly, was described in the files merely as "an internationally known poet!") and added that "the organization was sometimes referred to as Crowleyism or Crowleyites."

A less-than-impressed Air Force advised the equally unimpressed FBI that "women of loose morals were involved and ... the story of Parsons' activities had become fairly common knowledge among scientists in the Pasadena area."

Then, on November 14, 1950, Major Frank J. Austin Jr. of the Ordnance Liaison Office at the Redstone Arsenal, determined that most of the documents from Hughes Aircraft should be classified as Confidential—with four remaining unclassified. It's eye-opening that on the very same day, Major Donald Detwiler, of AFOSI, admitted in a letter to the FBI that on March 7, 1949, the Industrial Employment Review Board had authorized Parsons "access to [top secret] military information."

That Parsons had been granted a Top Secret clearance, which covered the work of the Army, Navy, and Air Force in relation to rocketry, was seen as being utterly beyond the pale.

That Parsons had been highly cavalier with confidential files and papers was a serious matter in itself. But that Parsons had been granted a Top Secret clearance, which covered the work of the Army, Navy, and Air Force in relation to rocketry, was seen as being utterly beyond the pale. As a result, on January 9, 1952, Parsons was informed by one J. Mason, the chairman of the Industrial Employment Review Board, that: "The board has decided as of 7 January 1952 to revoke the clearance granted you through top secret of 7 March 1949, and to withdraw access by you to Department of Defense classified information and/or material. The foregoing and all the evidence in the case file, when considered with the duties and responsibilities of any position in which you may be engaged with Department of Defense classified contract work, indicate that you might voluntarily or involuntarily act against the security interest of the United States and constitute a danger to the national security."

It scarcely mattered. Months later—specifically on June 17, 1952—Parsons was dead as a result of an explosion in his lab. Some say it was the result of an accident. Others suspect suicide. Then there's the murder theory. Jack Parsons was an enigma right up until the very end.

Pasadena Wolves

Much of Jack Parsons's initial rocket research in the 1930s was undertaken at the appropriately named Devil's Gate Dam in Pasadena, California. Interestingly, NASA's Jet Propulsion Laboratory was, itself, established at this very locale in 1930 by the California Institute of Technology. The dam had been constructed a decade earlier by engineers from the Los Angeles County Flood Control District and took its title from Devil's Gate Gorge, a rocky outcropping that eerily resembles a demonic face and which is located in a narrow canyon of the Arroyo Seco, which is a riverbed that extends from the San Gabriel Mountains into the Los Angeles basin.

Some say that the face is merely a classic case of pareidolia—the process by which the human brain can interpret random imagery as having some meaning or significance behind it. A classic example being the way in which, at one time or another, most of us have seen faces in clouds. But is that really all that is behind the satanic face of the old dam? Maybe not.

Certainly, the most disturbing thing about Devil's Gate Dam and Devil's Gate Gorge were the tragic deaths and disappearances of a number of children in the area back in the 1950s. In August of 1956, Donald Lee Baker (thirteen) and Brenda Jo Howell (eleven) vanished while riding their bikes on land directly behind the dam. Both bikes and Brenda's jacket were subsequently found nearby. The children, unfortunately, were not.

Then, in March 1957, an eight-year-old boy—Tommy Bowman—seemingly vanished into the middle of nowhere while hiking around the gorge with his family. One minute, little Tommy was there, the next he was utterly and forever gone. Three years later, in 1960, a young boy named Bruce Kremen vanished under mysterious circumstances in the same area.

As for Donald and Brenda, their disappearances were finally solved when a deranged serial killer named Mack Ray Edwards confessed to having killed them; he later committed suicide while doing time in San Quentin. The other two cases remain unsolved, and additional tragedy and death dominate the bleak area, too. Pasadena is also home to the Colorado Street Bridge, which just happens to cross over the Arroyo Seco bed. Locally, the large construction has a very different name: Suicide Bridge. Its name is very apt: the number of people who have now thrown themselves off the bridge—to their deaths—since its construction in 1912 is now into three figures.

Studies of the world of the occult undertaken by the CIA in the late 1960s and early to-mid-1970s—as a means to try and determine if paranormal phenomena could be used as weaponry against the former Soviet Union—reveal something notable. A January 1972, in-house document titled *A History of the Occult in California*—which was heavily censored before its release under Freedom of Information legislation—refers to a previously hitherto unknown, secret group said to have engaged in ancient and occult rituals at Devil's Gate Dam as a means to secure wealth and power. Interestingly, the file makes a brief reference to staff of the Jet Propulsion Laboratory having heard of the activities of the group—which, apparently, always occurred in the early hours of the morning. It was said to be known as the Pasadena Wolves.

> **C**IA personnel reportedly met with two ex-members of the group ...who alluded to the group having performed human sacrifices in the area, as well as rape and mutilation....

CIA personnel reportedly met with two ex-members of the group—at the time, both men were incarcerated in Californian prisons—who alluded to the group having performed human sacrifices in the area, as well as rape and mutilation—all to appease supernatural entities that the Wolves believed could provide them the influence and wealth they so craved. Notably, less than two paragraphs of the three pages of official documentation on the Pasadena Wolves have been declassified.

Patriot Act

Eight days after the attacks on the World Trade Center and the Pentagon, new legislation was presented to Congress by the Department of Justice. It was a bill entitled the Anti-Terrorism Act. It was also a bill that introduced Congress to the Patriot Act. It's an act whose very title has meaning. "Patriot" stands for "Provide Appropriate Tools Required to Intercept and Obstruct Terrorism." In one sense, that was all well and good, since the act would clearly help in the fight against those who wish to do us harm. It was, however, the negative impact that the tools used in the fight could have on American society that concerned so many. Indeed, the Anti-Terrorism Act swept aside pre-existing acts designed to protect the rights of each and every U.S. citizen, including the Bank Secrecy

Act, the Electronic Communications Privacy Act, the Money Laundering Control Act, and the Foreign Intelligence Surveillance Act.

One of the most outrageous aspects of the story of the Patriot Act is how it came to be so easily passed, and why there was only one dissenter, Senator Russell Feingold, of Wisconsin. Put simply, and astonishingly, the overwhelming majority who voted to enact the new legislation did not read it prior to agreeing to its creation. Worse still, there are solid indications that it was deliberately made difficult for senators to see the bill before passing it.

Alex Jones wrote: "Congressman Ron Paul (R-Tex) told the *Washington Times* that no member of Congress was allowed to read the first Patriot Act that was passed by the House on October 27, 2001. The first Patriot Act was universally decried by civil libertarians and Constitutional scholars from across the political spectrum." Jones also noted that William Safire, writing for the *New York Times*, detailed the first Patriot Act's powers by saying that "President Bush was seizing dictatorial control."

Jones continued: "The secretive tactics being used by the White House and Speaker [Dennis] Hastert to keep even the existence of this legislation secret would be more at home in Communist China than in the United States. The fact that Dick Cheney publicly managed the steamroller passage of the first Patriot Act, insuring that no one was allowed to read it and publicly threatening members of Congress that if they didn't vote in favor of it that they would

be blamed for the next terrorist attack, is by the White House's own definition terrorism. The move to clandestinely craft and then bully passage of any legislation by the Executive Branch is clearly an impeachable offense."

This scenario was further noted by Michael Moore in his 2004 documentary, *Fahrenheit 9/11*. Congressman John Conyers makes an incredible statement in the movie, on the matter of those who did or did not read the act before passing it. In Conyers' very own words: "We don't read most of the bills: do you really know what that would entail if we read every bill that we passed?"

Faced with such an extraordinary and mind-numbing statement—that major, congressional figures do not read the bills they may be asked to pass, bills that can have significant bearing on the entire American population—it's hardly surprising that the Patriot Act made an

Dick Cheney was vice president under President George W. Bush and was instrumental in pushing the Patriot Act through Congress while preventing members the time to actually read what it said.

almost effortless transition from concept to reality. The passing of the law did not, however, stop numerous attempts to have the act modified and curtailed. At the same time that critics of the act were trying to reign in its abilities, however, government personnel were trying to make it even more powerful.

The Benjamin Franklin True Patriot Act and the Protecting the Rights of Individuals Act were among the bills that sought to cap the capability of the Patriot Act to intrude into, and limit, the rights of U.S. citizens and residents. It's a sign of the power that those who wanted the act passed yielded, since neither bill had any bearing on the power of the Patriot Act—they both failed. The government responded by, in 2003, creating what was known as the Domestic Security Enhancement Act, which, in essence, was an outgrowth of, and an amendment to, the original Patriot Act. When copies were leaked to the media, it caused a sensation, despite assertions from officialdom that it was nothing more than a concept for change, rather than a literal, soon-to-be-in-place plan.

It was specifically thanks to the Center for Public Integrity that the document (draft or otherwise) surfaced. The CPI notes: "The Center for Public Integrity was founded in 1989 by Charles Lewis. We are one of the country's oldest and largest nonpartisan, nonprofit investigative news organizations. Our mission: To serve democracy by revealing abuses of power, corruption and betrayal of public trust by powerful public and private institutions, using the tools of investigative journalism."

> **W**ithout doubt the creepiest part of the Patriot Act was that alluded to earlier—namely, the government's legal and wide-reaching ability to monitor the reading habits of every single American citizen.

In the first week of February 2003 the CPI acquired the document, which contained two key amendments: the government planned to (a) increase its ability to intrude into the lives of American citizens, and (b) make it more and more difficult for courts to deny the instigation of the amendments. It is, almost certainly, due to the actions of the CPI—who quickly posted the document to its website—that the draft was pulled.

Had it gone through, in its original form, it would have allowed for (a) the collection of DNA from people suspected of having terrorist links—even if wholly unproven, (b) the legal ability to undertake so-called search-and-surveillance overseas, and without any kind of court order needed, and (c) extensions and modifications to the death penalty.

Without doubt the creepiest part of the Patriot Act was that alluded to earlier—namely, the government's legal and wide-reaching ability to monitor the reading habits of every single American citizen. This relates to what are termed National Security Letters, or NSLs. They are, essentially, subpoenas that are used "to protect against international terrorism or clandestine intelligence activities."

Such NSLs can permit agencies to demand access to—and with potential imprisonment for those who do not comply—bank account data, email history and address books, telephone numbers (both called and received), and books bought, borrowed, and read. All of this falls under Section 215 of the Patriot Act. In a decidedly hazy fashion—that conveniently allows for widespread interpretation on the part of those who employ it—the act notes that certain "tangible things" may be accessed, such as "books, records, papers, documents, and other items."

Four years after the Patriot Act was passed, Library Connection—a Connecticut-based body—joined forces with the ACLU to highlight and curtail the government's ability to monitor the reading matter of the average American: "Librarians need to understand their country's legal balance between the protection of freedom of expression and the protection of national security. Many librarians believe that the interests of national security, important as they are, have become an excuse for chilling the freedom to read."

Peoples Temple

While much has been written about Jim Jones and his ultimately, and tragically, doomed followers in the Peoples Temple, few know more about the affair than the FBI, which has compiled numerous files on the shocking ending of the group in 1978. From the FBI's very own records, we have the following: "California Congressman Leo Ryan was concerned. He'd been hearing that there was trouble in 'Jonestown,' the makeshift settlement carved out of the jungle of Guyana by the charismatic Jim Jones and his cult-like following called the Peoples Temple. The allegations were serious: Jonestown sounded more like a slave camp than a religious center. There was talk of beatings, forced labor and imprisonments, the use of drugs to control behavior, suspicious deaths, and even rehearsals for a mass suicide."

In the fall of 1978, the FBI notes, Ryan decided to visit Guyana to find out what was happening to the more than nine hundred members of Jonestown, many of whom were his constituents from the San Francisco area who'd followed the scandal-plagued Jones to South America. Ryan and his congressional delegation flew to Guyana on November 14. A few days later, they arrived in Jonestown along with various government officials and a group of reporters. There, Ryan met with Jones and interviewed many of his followers. Not surprisingly, some families and several individuals asked to leave with Ryan, while others apparently left on foot on their own. Jones was not happy.

Ryan wanted the entire group to fly out together, fearing retribution to any left behind, but that required a second plane and delayed the departure. The group eventually assembled at a local airstrip on the afternoon of November 18, but as Ryan's plane prepared to leave, a dump truck from Jonestown arrived with several armed men. They opened fire on one plane, while a cultist named Larry Layton on board the other pulled out a gun and began shooting. In the melee, Ryan and several others were killed and many wounded.

Meanwhile, back at the compound, Jones was hatching an unthinkable plan. He called his followers together and essentially ordered them to swallow a fruit drink that was apparently laced with cyanide. He rationalized that

Jim Jones's first church was in Indianapolis, Indiana.

the attack on the planes would bring harm to the residents of Jonestown. A few apparently objected, but in the end, more than nine hundred cultists, including more than two hundred children, were soon lying lifeless on the ground. Jones, too, was dead, with a gunshot wound to the head.

The FBI soon launched an extensive investigation in concert with other agencies, with their jurisdiction based on a congressional assassination law passed six years earlier. Working with authorities in Guyana, agents interviewed survivors of the mass murder/suicide, while fingerprint and forensic experts from our Disaster Squad identified the many victims and Jones himself. Agents across the nation also searched out and talked with members of the Peoples Temple in the United States for further insights.

In the end, along with helping to unravel the chain of events and bring closure to grieving families, the FBI was able to make a case against Larry Layton. Layton, the only member of the Peoples Temple tried in the United States for criminal acts at Jonestown, was ultimately extradited, convicted, and sentenced to life in prison.

Phineas Priesthood

The Phineas Priesthood is a secret group noted for one thing in particular: it has no members. On top of that, it has no headquarters, no offices, and no newsletter or website. Rather, it is composed of an untold number of people who adhere to certain, very controversial beliefs. However, there is an erroneous assumption that the group has some actual structure to it, as the Anti-Defamation League notes: "Many people mistakenly believe that there is an actual organization called the Phineas Priesthood, probably because there was a group of four men in the 1990s who called themselves Phineas Priests. The men carried out bank robberies and a series of bombings in the Pacific Northwest before being sent to prison. But there is no evidence that their organization was any larger than those four individuals."

So, this begs the question, from where do the "members" get their inspiration to commit outrageous, terrible crimes—including murder? The answer is in the pages of a 1990 book penned by Richard Kelly Hoskins. Its title: *Vigilantes of Christendom: The Story of the Phineas Priesthood*. Hoskins made his position very clear on a number of issues: abortion (wrong), same-sex relationships (wrong), and interracial relationships (wrong, too). Put simply, those who follow the teachings of the Phineas Priesthood are racist homophobes.

Phineas Priesthood devotees are not at all against engaging in violence to get their message across. In 1996, they were responsible for a wave of attacks on abortion clinics. One year later, a trio of men influenced by the Phineas Priesthood were convicted of bombing the Spokane, Washington, offices of the *Spokesman-Review* newspaper.

In November 2014, a copy of Richard Kelly Hoskins's book was found in the home of one Larry Steven McQuilliams. On November 28, 2014, McQuilliams went on a gun-toting rampage in Austin, Texas. He shot up a federal courthouse, tried to burn down the local Mexican consulate, and blasted a local police station. McQuilliams's assault on Austin and its people was brought to a swift and fatal end by Sergeant Adam Johnson, of the Austin Police Department Mounted Patrol.

For law enforcement officials, the Phineas Priesthood is perceived as being an extremely dangerous, secret group. This is primarily due to the lack of any kind of structure or even registered members—which makes those who act on its behalf incredibly difficult to identify and track. Unfortunately, and as a result of the beyond flexible nature of the group, it is typically the case that the first we know of an attack or killing caused by the Phineas Priesthood is when one of its deranged devotees claims responsibility.

Pickingill, George

Born in Hockley, Essex, England in 1816, George Pickingill was someone who lived most of his life in the Essex village of Canewdon, and who was described as a "cunning man." That's to say he was a practitioner of ancient witchcraft—primarily white witchcraft, but not always. Divination, benevolent spells, and folk medicine were Pickingill's chief tools of trade. Paganism was a big part of his life, too, as was a lifestyle that ultimately mutated into today's Wiccan religion.

Despite the fact that Pickingill was renowned at a local level as a man who performed magical rites and rituals, and who had the power to heal, it was not until decades later that the story of this extraordinary and mysterious figure reached the eyes and ears of the rest of the country. The person responsible for highlighting Pickingill's work and beliefs was Eric Maple, an expert on British folklore and witchcraft. In the 1960s, Maple wrote a number of articles for *Folklore*, the in-house publication of the London, England-based Folklore Society. Those articles included "Cunning Murrel," "The Witches of Canewdon," "The Witches of Dengie," and "Witchcraft and Magic in the Rochford Hundred." Collectively, Maple's work was considered to be "a perhaps unique contribution to the literature of English witchcraft. Totally jargon-free, they are the raw stuff of folklore, stories told by real people about still remembered (reputed) witches and their doings."

> **D**ivination, benevolent spells, and folk medicine were Pickingill's chief tools of trade. Paganism was a big part of his life, too, as was a lifestyle that ultimately mutated into today's Wiccan religion.

It was during the course of his extensive research that Maple came across the life and work of George Pickingill. By all accounts Pickingill was as feared just about as much as he was revered. He claimed the ability to control the minds of animals (both wild and domestic, and particularly horses), asserted that he had a band of small, wizened, goblin-like creatures that followed his every order, and regularly threatened to place supernatural curses upon the local village folk who he felt threatened by.

While some of the locals took the view that Pickingill was nothing more than a harmless, eccentric old man, the vast majority of the people in and around did not. For the rest of the village folk, he was not someone to cross paths with. There was a very good reason for that: Pickingill had apparently "cursed" farming machinery, provoked illness and disease in people he took a dislike to, and even provoked wild poltergeist-like activity in the homes of his enemies.

The most amazing and controversial claims surrounding Pickingill surfaced in the 1970s. That was when a man named E. W. "Bill" Liddell came forward, claiming to know a great deal about Pickingill and his links to secret groups, clandestine covens, and much more. As for how, exactly, Liddell knew all this, it came as a result of the fact that Pickingill was the first cousin of Liddell's paternal great-great-grandfather. According to Liddell, the Pickingills had an extraordinarily long lineage, one that extended back to at least the eleventh century, maybe even longer. Even back then, claimed Liddell, the Pickingills were immersed in the world of sorcery and worshipped a "horned god" of the type embraced by today's Wiccans.

Liddell also asserted that Pickingill had a deep-seated hatred of Christianity and was "England's most feared and vilified 'Satanist.'" The story becomes more and more complex, with Pickingill traveling to France, where he became a member of a local witchcraft cult. As a result of this, when he returned back home to Canewdon, Pickingill—who, by now, was a man with a well-known reputation for being an occultist—was asked to oversee the activities of a powerful coven in the area, one that had existed since the 1400s. Its name: the Seven Witches of Canewdon. Pickingill didn't stop there: he created what became known as the "Nine Covens." As the name suggests, it was a network of covens, all of which could be found in certain English counties—specifically, Norfolk, Hampshire, Sussex, Essex, and Hertfordshire. At least two of the covens, said Liddell, existed until the 1970s.

Pickingill was also someone who moved near-effortlessly in the world of secret societies: midway through the nineteenth century, Pickingill

St. Nicholas Church in Canewdon, Essex, England, is where one will find George Pickingill's final resting place.

began working with a band of Freemasons who believed that both Freemasonry and Rosicrucianism were offshoots of witch cults. According to two such Freemasons—W. J. Hughan and Hargrave Jennings—Pickingill even had personal input on the Societas Rosicruciana, a Rosicrucian edict that ensures its members must be Christian Masons. Pickingill was also associated with the Hermetic Order of the Golden Dawn—and, said Liddell, Pickingill had spent time with Aleister Crowley, although to what extent is presently unclear.

Pickingill was an enigma until the very end. It is, perhaps, apt to quote Eric Maple, who said this mysterious and feared figure left "a legacy of myth which is curiously alien to the general run of witch traditions. In all the stories told of Pickingill there is a subtle undercurrent of horror which one finds hard to pinpoint. Possibly it arises from the fact that many of those who recount the tales actually knew the man and experienced just such a quiet terror when he passed them in the village street."

Pitchfork Murder

February 14, 1945, was the date of a still unresolved murder in rural England that bore all the hallmarks of death at the hands of a secret society. Some suggested a band of witches were the culprits, and others said a secret sect of Druids. The victim was a farm worker, seventy-four-year-old Charles Walton, found dead with nothing less than a pitchfork sticking out of his chest. He was a resident of a small, picturesque village in Warwickshire, England, called Lower Quinton. Walton had lived in the village all his life, in a pleasant old cottage that stood across from the local church. It was a scene not unlike what one might expect to see on *Downton Abbey* or in the pages of a Jane Austen novel. Until, that is, murder, mayhem, and a secret cult came to Lower Quinton.

So far as can be ascertained, no one in the village had a grudge against Walton: he was known to all of the locals. He was an affable but quiet sort, and—somewhat intriguingly— had the ability to entice wild birds to eat seeds from his hands. He was also said to have the power to reduce a wild, aggressive dog to a man's best friend simply by speaking to it. On top of that, he had expert knowledge of local folklore and legend. Rumors suggest that perhaps Walton's slightly uncanny powers had ensured him a place in a secret witchcraft cult, one that he ultimately fell out of favor with, and, as a result, paid the ultimate price—his life.

> **H**e was lying dead on the grassy ground, with the pitchfork pinning him to the ground, and the hook having pierced his throat in savage and violent fashion.

What is known for sure is that on the day in question—the evening before Valentine's Day, no less—Walton was busily trimming hedges on what was known as Hillground: a large field at the foot of the Meon Hill. His tools were a hook and a pitchfork. It was while working on the hedges that someone stealthily intervened and took Walton's life—and in savage fashion. When his body was stumbled upon by a shocked local, all hell broke loose in the small village. He was lying dead on the grassy ground, with the pitchfork pinning him to the ground, and the hook having pierced his throat in savage and violent fashion. On top of that, a large cross had been cut into his chest.

It should be noted that Meon Hill has, for centuries, been associated with supernatural activity: sightings of blazing-eyed black dogs—not unlike the terrible beast in Sir Arthur Conan Doyle's *The Hound of the Baskervilles*—have been reported. Satan himself is said to have kicked a large rock from the top of the hill to the bottom of it, with the intention of flattening Evesham Abbey.

Such was the strange and sinister nature of Walton's death that the investigation wasn't just left in the hands of the local bobbies. None other than Scotland Yard's finest detectives were soon on the case, and they weren't just on the case; they took over the entire investigation, under the control of Detective Inspector Robert Fabian. Despite an extensive investigation, and suspicions that the guilty party was a man named Albert Potter—who was employing Walton on the day he met his grisly end—the matter was never resolved to the satisfaction of the police and the mystery remained precisely that: a mystery.

It's worth noting, however, that Detective Inspector Fabian later said of his investigation of the affair: "One of my most memorable murder cases was at the village of Lower Quinton, near the stone Druid circle of the Whispering Knights. There a man had been killed by a reproduction of a Druidical ceremony on St. Valentine's Eve."

He also offered the following, memorable words: "I advise anybody who is tempted at any time to venture into Black Magic, witchcraft, Shamanism— call it what you will—to remember Charles Walton and to think of his death, which was clearly the ghastly climax of a pagan rite. There is no stronger argument for keeping as far away as possible from the villains with their swords, incense and mumbo-jumbo. It is prudence on which your future peace of mind and even your life could depend."

It should also be noted that within Lower Quinton, the village folk are still very reluctant to speak about the decades-old affair. Tony Smith, the landlord of the village's College Arms pub, told the BBC: "I can't talk to you about that. After 17 years of running this place I know there are some things we don't talk about. Talking about it would upset people and there's no sense in alienating people in a small village like this. There are no relatives of Charles Walton left in the village and people that might have known what happened are all dead or gone."

A Mrs. Wakelon, who ran the village store, was equally reluctant to say much to the BBC: "People don't talk about it; it's a closed subject. Those that know about it are gone, except one who's in hospital and another that's in a nursing home. All the others have gone or passed away."

The manager of the local post office—who was only willing to be referred to by the BBC as Joyce—spoke in a similar vein and tones: "No one will talk to you about it. The family have all gone now, anyway. There are none of the Walton family left here now. I have no answers to your questions."

Death by pitchfork, rumors of a witchcraft cult, and a village still living in uneasy and closed-mouth fashion: the memories of the murder of Charles Walton show no signs of fading away anytime soon.

Planetary Defense Coordination Office

Significant numbers of eyebrows were raised in the domain of conspiracy-theorizing 2016 when NASA announced the establishment of a group within its ranks called the Planetary Defense Coordination Office—a body that would be tasked with "detecting and tracking near-Earth objects (NEOs), such

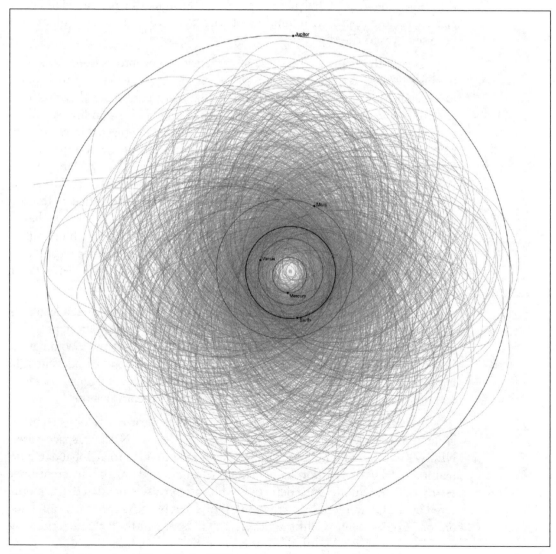

This graphic shows the orbits of all the NEOs that have so far been identified as potential threats to Earth.

as meteorites and asteroids, and particularly those of significant size and which could potentially provoke massive disaster should one or more slam into the Earth." NASA noted: "More than 13,500 near-Earth objects of all sizes have been discovered to date—more than 95 percent of them since NASA-funded surveys began in 1998. About 1,500 NEOs are now detected each year."

John Grunsfeld, the associate administrator for NASA's Science Mission Directorate in Washington, said: "Asteroid detection, tracking and defense of our planet is something that NASA, its interagency partners, and the global community take very seriously. While there are no known impact threats at this time, the 2013 Chelyabinsk super-fireball and the recent 'Halloween Asteroid' close approach remind us of why we need to remain vigilant and keep our eyes to the sky."

One of the reasons why those aforementioned eyebrows were raised was because NASA revealed its plans to work alongside FEMA—the Federal Emergency Management Agency—a body that many conspiracy theorists look at with suspicious eyes, chiefly because of the rumors surrounding so-called FEMA camps. The space agency said: "NASA has been engaged in worldwide planning for planetary defense for some time, and this office will improve and expand on those efforts, working with the Federal Emergency Management Agency (FEMA) and other federal agencies and departments. In addition to detecting and tracking potentially hazardous objects, the office will issue notices of close passes and warnings of any detected potential impacts, based on credible science data. The office also will continue to assist with coordination across the U.S. government, participating in the planning for response to an actual impact threat, working in conjunction with FEMA, the Department of Defense, other U.S. agencies and international counterparts."

Lindley Johnson, a longtime NEO program executive and then a lead program executive for the office, with the title of planetary defense officer, provided the following: "The formal establishment of the Planetary Defense Coordination Office makes it evident that the agency is committed to perform a leadership role in national and international efforts for detection of these natural impact hazards, and to be engaged in planning if there is a need for planetary defense."

As NASA explained: "Astronomers detect near-Earth objects using ground-based telescopes around the world as well as NASA's space-based NEOWISE infrared telescope. Tracking data are provided to a global database maintained by the Minor Planet Center, sanctioned by the International Astronomical Union. Once detected, orbits are precisely predicted and monitored by the Center for NEO Studies (CNEOS) at NASA's Jet Propulsion Laboratory in Pasadena, California. Select NEOs are further characterized by assets such as NASA's InfraRed Telescope Facility, Spitzer Space Telescope and interplanetary radars operated by NASA and the National Science Foundation. Such efforts are coordinated and funded by NASA's longtime NEO Observations Program, which will continue as a research program under the office."

NASA had much more to say, too: "The Planetary Defense Coordination Office is being applauded by the National Science Foundation (NSF), which supports research and education in science and engineering. 'NSF welcomes the increased visibility afforded to this critical activity,' said Nigel Sharp, program director in the agency's Division of Astronomical Sciences. 'We look forward to continuing the fruitful collaboration across the agencies to bring all of our resources—both ground-based and space-based—to the study of this important problem.'"

In terms of the work that the group would undertake, NASA explained that "long-term planetary defense goals include developing technology and techniques for deflecting or redirecting objects that are determined to be on an impact course with Earth. NASA's Asteroid Redirect Mission concept would demonstrate the effectiveness of the gravity tractor method of planetary defense, using the mass of another object to pull an asteroid slightly from its original orbital path. The joint NASA-European Space Agency Asteroid Impact and Deflection Assessment (AIDA) mission concept, if pursued, would demonstrate an impact deflection method of planetary defense. Even if intervention is not possible, NASA would provide expert input to FEMA about impact timing, location and effects to inform emergency response operations. In turn, FEMA would handle the preparations and response planning related to the consequences of atmospheric entry or impact to U.S. communities."

"FEMA is dedicated to protecting against all hazards, and the launch of the coordination office will ensure early detection and warning capability, and will further enhance FEMA's collaborative relationship with NASA," said FEMA administrator Craig Fugate.

The concept of a central office to coordinate asteroid detection and mitigation was under consideration as far back as 2010, when an Ad-Hoc Task Force on Planetary Defense of the NASA Advisory Council recommended that NASA "organize for effective action on planetary defense and prepare to respond to impact threats," and should "lead U.S. planetary defense efforts in national and international forums." In addition, a NASA Office of Inspector General 2014 report concluded that the NEO Observations Program would be more "efficient, effective and transparent" if it were organized and managed in accordance with standard NASA research program requirements.

And, as NASA also revealed: "The recently passed federal budget for fiscal year 2016 includes $50 million for NEO observations and planetary

> **The concept of a central office to coordinate asteroid detection and mitigation was under consideration as far back as 2010....**

defense, representing a more than ten-fold increase since the beginning of the current administration."

This is all well and good, but one has to wonder: if, one day a huge asteroid or meteorite does slam into the United States, and the country is plunged into a state of chaos, will we see FEMA finally making use of its long-rumored "camps" to house millions of Americans when chaos and anarchy break out?

Population Culling Group

Is a nefarious, secret, and deadly group hard at work to reduce the world's population—and to reduce it quickly, drastically, and to levels that will amount to nothing less than full-blown decimation? Certainly, one only has to take a look at the case of Adolf Hitler. He waged a determined war of extermination against the Jews during World War II. And, as a result, and with phenomenal, horrific speed, an entire race of people came close to being systematically wiped off the face of the planet. Could such a thing, one day, happen again? If it does, will it be due to the actions of a future Hitler, a madman with lunatic delusions of grandeur? Maybe not: conspiracy theorists maintain that the death knell for not just millions, but for billions, might come from none other than a secret cabal within the heart of the United Nations.

That planet Earth cannot adequately house an ever-growing population indefinitely is not a matter of any doubt. That the world's weather is changing—in ways that are seen as both hostile and suspicious—has given rise to the likelihood that global warming is the culprit. Humankind's ever-growing need for dwindling fossil fuels, combined with its exponentially increasing pollution of the planet's ecosystem, has almost irreversibly altered our future and has raised fears that our most precious commodity—water—will soon become scarce. And, as a result, some of us—maybe billions of us—will be culled to ensure the survival of the elite.

Many conspiracy theorists believe that things began in 1974, specifically on December 10 of that year, when a highly controversial report was prepared for the United States National Security Council. It was a report, and attendant project and study, overseen by one of the most powerful figures in global politics, Henry Kissinger, who held such positions as U.S. secretary of state and national security advisor to the presidential office. The report was titled *Implications of Worldwide Population Growth for U.S. Security and Overseas Interests.*

As the authors noted, in those particular countries where growth and development were far from being on par with the rest of the planet—such as Thailand,

Pakistan, Brazil, Ethiopia, Egypt, Turkey, and Nigeria—there was a distinct possibility that with falling food supplies, dwindling water and fuel, and more and more people, demands from the relevant populations for action to combat famine, would soon become civil unrest and then uncontrollable anarchy. There was another worry for Kissinger's people. If the economies of countries with exploding populations collapsed, the result might be that the United States would be unable to import from those same countries things that were essential to its own economy. In that scenario, everyone suffers. Or, maybe not: Kissinger was determined that the United States would not fall, even if other nations did. It was up to the United Nations and the United States to solve the problem.

Clearly, as the following extracts show, a great deal of thought had gone into how the rise of populations in the underdeveloped world could possibly bring the United States to its knees: "The U.S. economy will require large and increasing amounts of minerals from abroad, especially from less developed countries. That fact gives the United States enhanced interest in the political, economic, and social stability of the supplying countries. Wherever a lessening of population pressures through reduced birth rates can increase the prospects for such stability, population policy becomes relevant to resource supplies and to the economic interests of the United States."

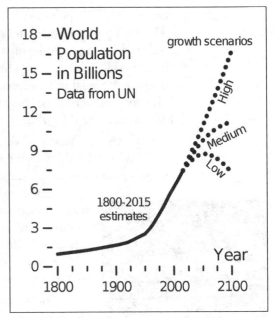

A graph developed by the United Nations shows three possible tracts for population growth in the future.

The document continues: "The location of known reserves of higher grade ores of most minerals favors increasing dependence of all industrialized regions on imports from less developed countries. The real problems of mineral supplies lie not in basic physical sufficiency, but in the politico-economic issues of access, terms for exploration and exploitation, and division of the benefits among producers, consumers, and host country governments."

Anticipating how things could turn very bad for the United States, there is the following: "Whether through government action, labor conflicts, sabotage, or civil disturbance, the smooth flow of needed materials will be jeopardized. Although population pressure is obviously not the only factor involved, these types of frustrations are much less likely under conditions of slow or zero population growth."

The brains behind the report then targeted the people themselves, their collective mindset, and how to get around increasing issues of concern. In a section titled "Populations with a High Proportion of Growth," it was noted: "The young people, who are in much higher proportions in many LDCs, are likely to be more volatile, unstable, prone to extremes, alienation and violence than an older population. These young people can more readily be persuaded to attack the legal institutions of the government or real property of the 'establishment,' 'imperialists,' multinational corporations, or other-often foreign-influences blamed for their troubles."

There were words of warning in the report, too: "We must take care that our activities should not give the appearance to the LDCs of an industrialized country policy directed against the LDCs. Caution must be taken that in any approaches in this field we support in the LDCs are ones we can support within this country. 'Third World' leaders should be in the forefront and obtain the credit for successful programs. In this context it is important to demonstrate to LDC leaders that such family planning programs have worked and can work within a reasonable period of time."

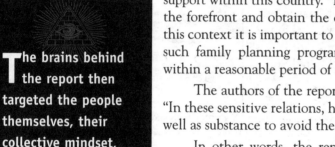

The brains behind the report then targeted the people themselves, their collective mindset, and how to get around increasing issues of concern.

The authors of the report make an interesting statement: "In these sensitive relations, however, it is important in style as well as substance to avoid the appearance of coercion."

In other words, the report does not deny that nations might be coerced, only that there is a concerted effort to "avoid the appearance" of such.

So much for the 1970s—when the program of planetary extermination, on an obscene scale, is reported to have begun—but what of today? According to some, today it's downright out of control: "A reasonable estimate for an industrialized world society at the present North American material standard of living would be 1 billion. At the more frugal European standard of living, 2 to 3 billion would be possible," stated the United Nations' Global Diversity Assessment, in shockingly matter-of-fact fashion.

Poro

A male-only secret group that has its bases of operations in the Ivory Coast, Liberia, and Sierra Leone, Poro has origins that extend back more than one millennium. *Sierra Leone Heritage* says of this ancient body: "A name used throughout Sierra Leone for the men's society that is responsible for organizing the initiation that prepares boys and young men for adult life. In the past it was described by Europeans as akin to freemasonry and credited with country-wide organization and political power to impose respect for its laws and decisions, even against the will and over the heads of the chiefs, the traditional rulers ... it has had to modify its practices to meet the demands of contemporary Sierra Leone society, but it remains a potent force in most country areas and its prohibitions are strictly observed."

Not unlike the very similar Sande Society—which is also widespread in Liberia, the Ivory Coast, and Sierra Leone and which prepares girls for womanhood—Poro is steeped in controversy.

Primrose League

Established in London, England, in the nineteenth century—specifically in 1883—the Primrose League was a quasi-official group of people who wished to secretly ensure that the powerful, conservative, right-wing figures within government maintained that power. It had four primary goals: "To Uphold and support God, Queen, and Country, and the Conservative cause; To provide an effective voice to represent the interests of our members and to bring the experience of the Leaders to bear on the conduct of public affairs for the common good; To encourage and help our members to improve their professional competence as leaders; To fight for free enterprise."

That all sounds well and good; however, it should be noted that much of the work of the Primrose League—as it sought to influence the public mindset on the matter of politics in the U.K.—was undertaken in a decidedly secret, cloak-and-dagger, and near-Machiavellian fashion. Concerned that the Conservatives might lose their influence and sway, a number of powerful men in London got together to bring to life what became known as the Primrose League. They included Sir Randolph Churchill, Sir John Gorst, Sir Henry Drummond Wolff, and Colonel Fred Burnaby. By 1910, the membership had reached an astonishing two million. All of the members had to make a specific pledge: "I declare on my honor and faith that I will devote my best ability to the maintenance of religion, of the estates of the realm, and of the imperial ascendancy of the British Empire; and that, consistently with my allegiance to the sovereign of these realms, I will promote with discretion and fidelity the above objects, being those of the Primrose League."

Primrose League badges.

Of course, most of the many men and women who pledged allegiance to the Primrose Club had no dark side attached to them. Rather, they were simply enthused by the idea of being able to help the Conservatives hold sway, and they did so in an open and enthusiastic fashion. But, just like so many societies, the Primrose League had a public face (which was the only face that even most of the members were aware of) and a far more intriguing private face. It's this shadowy face that we will focus our attentions upon.

It's important to note that the meetings of the Primrose Club were held at the prestigious Carlton Club, which is located on St. James's Street, London. The club's members, at the time, included prime ministers, high-ranking military and political figures, and shadowy characters linked to the growing world of espionage. It's notable that the Carlton Club remains, to this very day, a place where the elite of London meet and secretly plot. Its members include senior figures in the U.K.'s intelligence community: personnel within MI5 (the U.K.'s equivalent of the FBI), MI6 (the U.K.'s version of the CIA), and the Government Communications Headquarters (whose widespread surveillance programs very closely mirror those of the United States National Security Agency).

> **The group secretly hired people whose job it was to dig up dirt on politicians who were against the ideology of the Conservatives....**

Not only that, one of those who undertook a great deal of work for the Primrose League (undercover work, it should be stressed) was none other than the infamous occultist and "Great Beast" Aleister Crowley—who, during the course of his lifetime, had ties to more than a few secret societies. While still only in his early twenties, Crowley was, essentially, recruited into the Primrose League for one specific reason. It was a reason filled with controversy and potential hazards.

The group secretly hired people whose job it was to dig up dirt on politicians who were against the ideology of the Conservatives, to uncover scandal, and to ferret out just about anything and everything inflammatory that might be used to quiet potentially troublesome characters in the world of nineteenth-century U.K. politics. Aleister Crowley was one of those brought on board. By all accounts, he did a very good job of seeking out information on politicians involved in shady financial deals, and on well-known society figures engaged in affairs behind the backs of their wives. Less than subtle blackmail of those same figures very quickly became the order of the day. The Primrose League secretly flexed its muscles and issued dire warnings to those on whom it had extensive and damning dossiers, thanks in significant portions to Crowley's spying activities. Typically, those facing potential ruin—and specifically those opposed to Conservatism—quickly caved in. The result: the Primrose League became a major body in Victorian era politics—and, for those who incurred its secret wrath, a much feared one.

In 2004, the Primrose League—which, by that date, had long given up its more controversial activities of the nineteenth century—finally closed down, citing dwindling interest in the group and falling attendance at its meetings.

Project Blue Beam

Within the field of conspiracy theorizing, a great deal has been said and written about what has become known as Project Blue Beam. Allegedly, it is the work of a secret group of powerful figures in NASA, the United Nations, the Bilderbergers, the Trilateral Commission, and the Vatican. Project Blue Beam, so the story goes, will be at the forefront of a program to create an iron-fisted New World Order. It's a story that has its origins in the mid-1990s.

The source of the Project Blue Beam story was a journalist from Montréal, Québec, named Serge Monast. Although Monast began his career in regular journalism, by 1994 he was focused almost exclusively on conspiracy theories, including matters relative to Masonic-based conspiracy theories and the New World Order. It was at this time that Monast claimed to have uncovered secret information on Project Blue Beam and how it would be utilized to enslave the human race. Although the Project Blue Beam story is viewed by many researchers as a hoax, the fact that Monast died in a jail cell in December 1996, at the age of fifty-one, has led to suspicions that he was murdered. With that all said, what, exactly, is Project Blue Beam?

The Watcher Files notes: "The infamous NASA Blue Beam Project has four different steps in order to implement the new age religion with the antichrist at its head. We must remember that the new age religion is the very foundation for the new world government, without which religion the dictatorship of the new world order is completely impossible. I'll repeat that: Without a universal belief in the new age religion, the success of the new world order will be impossible! That is why the Blue Beam Project is so important to them, but has been so well hidden until now."

The Watcher Files adds that Project Blue Beam "involves a gigantic 'space show' with three-dimensional optical holograms and sounds, laser projection of multiple holographic images to different parts of the world, each receiving a different image according to predominating regional national religious faith. This new 'god's' voice will be speaking in all languages."

David Openheimer, who has studied Project Blue Beam, claims says: "The 'system' has already been tested. Holographic projections of the 'CHRIST IMAGE' have already been seen in some remote desert areas. These have only been reported in tabloid papers, so they are instantly rendered moot. They can also project images of alien craft, aliens, monsters, angels—you name it. Computers will coordinate the satellites and software will run the show-and-tell.

"Holography is based on very nearly identical signals combining to produce an image, or hologram, with depth perception. This is equally applicable to acoustic (ELF, VLF, LF) waves as it is to optical phenomena.

"Specifically, the 'show' will consist of laser projections of multiple holographic images to different parts of the planet, each receiving different images according to the predominating regional religious faith. Not a single area will be excluded. With computer animation and sound effects appearing to come from the depths of space, astonished followers of the various creeds will witness their own returned Messiah in spectacularly convincing lifelike realness.

> **W**ithout a universal belief in the new age religion, the success of the new world order will be impossible!

"The various images of Christ, Mohammed, Buddha, Krishna, etc., will merge into ONE after 'correct explanation' of the mysteries, prophecies and revelations are disclosed. This 'ONE GOD' will in fact function as the 'Anti-Christ,' who will 'explain' that the various scriptures 'have been misunderstood'—that the religious of old are responsible for turning brother against brother, nation against nation—that the religions of the world must be abolished to make way for the GOLDEN AGE (NEW AGE) of the One World Religion, representing the One God they see before them. Naturally, this superbly staged, full-scale production will result in social and religious disorder on a massive scale."

Time may tell if Project Blue Beam is the real deal.

Project Chatter

MKUltra was certainly the most infamous of all the CIA-initiated mind-control programs. It was, however, very far from being an isolated, secret group. Numerous and secret sub-projects, post-projects and operations initiated by other agencies existed from the 1950s to the 1970s. One was Project Chatter, which, in 1977, the Senate Select Committee on Intelligence and the Committee on Human Resources described thus: "Project Chatter was a Navy program that began in the fall of 1947. Responding to reports of amazing results achieved by the Soviets in using truth drugs, the program focused on the identification and the testing of such drugs for use in interrogations and in the recruitment of agents. The research included laboratory experiments on animals and human subjects involving *Anabasis aphylla*, scopolamine, and mescaline in order to determine their speech-inducing qualities. Overseas experiments were conducted as part of the project. The project expanded substantially during the Korean War, and ended shortly after the war, in 1953."

Then there were Projects Bluebird and Artichoke. Again, the Committee dug deep and uncovered some controversial and eye-opening data and testimony: "The earliest of the CIA's major programs involving the use of chemical and biological agents, Project Bluebird, was approved by the Director in 1950. Its objectives were: (a) discovering means of conditioning personnel to prevent unauthorized extraction of information from them by known means, (b) investigating the possibility of control of an individual by application of special interrogation techniques, (c) memory enhancement, and (d) establishing defensive means for preventing hostile control of Agency personnel."

The Committee added with respect to Bluebird: "As a result of interrogations conducted overseas during the project, another goal was added—the evaluation of offensive uses of unconventional interrogation techniques, including hypnosis and drugs. In August 1951, the project was renamed Artichoke. Project Artichoke included in-house experiments on interrogation techniques, conducted under medical and security controls which would ensure that no damage was done to individuals who volunteer for the experiments. Overseas interrogations utilizing a combination of sodium pentothal and hypnosis after physical and psychiatric examinations of the subjects were also part of Artichoke."

Interestingly, the Committee noted that: "Information about Project Artichoke after the fall of 1953 is scarce. The CIA maintains that the project ended in 1956, but evidence suggests that Office of Security and Office of Medical Services use of 'special interrogation' techniques continued for several years thereafter."

Psychic Spies

In a 1977 document titled *Parapsychology in Intelligence*, Kenneth A. Kress, an engineer with the CIA's Office of Technical Services, wrote: "Anecdotal reports of extrasensory perception (ESP) capabilities have reached U.S. national security agencies at least since World War II, when Hitler was said to rely on astrologers and seers. Suggestions for military applications of ESP continued to be received after World War II. For example, in 1952 the Department of Defense was lectured on the possible usefulness of extrasensory perception in psychological warfare."

Moving on to 1960: Ruth Montgomery was a well-known and controversial psychic, and the author of such books as *Aliens Among Us* and *A World Beyond*, who died in 2001. On June 14, 1960, Montgomery wrote an article entitled "Spying by Mind-Reading" that was published in the *New York Journal-American* newspaper.

Files declassified under the terms of the Freedom of Information Act reveal that Montgomery's eye-opening article led none other than FBI head honcho J. Edgar Hoover to ask "Is there anything to this?" in a memo that was sent to three of the FBI's most respected figures: Clyde Tolson, who had been the FBI's associate director; Alan Belmont, who held the position of assistant director of the Domestic Intelligence Division of the FBI; and Cartha DeLoach, who in 1948 became the liaison point between the FBI and the CIA.

Forty-eight hours later Belmont prepared a reply. It stated: "*The New York Journal-American* on 6-14-60 carried a column by Ruth Montgomery called 'Spying by Mind-Reading!' in which she stated the Army Intelligence Service was conducting research experiments in mental telepathy. She speculated that the ultimate achievement would be to develop a method whereby U.S. spies could 'receive' thoughts of plotters in the Kremlin.… Lieutenant Colonel Lee Martin, Chief of Investigations, Assistant Chief of Staff for Intelligence, advised liaison agent [Deleted] that the Army is conducting no such project as described in the article."

The CIA has been interested in the potential of psychic spies as a tool in warfare.

But, did this mean that no such research had ever been initiated by other branches of the military? When faced with yet further inquiries, Lt. Col. Martin seemingly backtracked to a degree. He admitted to the FBI that the denial to the Montgomery article about the Army's noninvolvement in such matters did not mean other agencies were not implicated. In fact, Hoover was told: "He [Lt. Col. Martin] did state that the U.S. Air Force had a contract in 1958 and 1959 with the Bureau of Social Science Research, Washington, D.C., which did research in the many phases of mental problems raised by the Korean War, with particular emphasis on brainwashing. This research did incidentally include mental telepathy or extra sensory perception; however, the results were inconclusive."

Hoover was further informed: "Our Laboratory experts advised that informed scientific opinion at the present time is that there is no basis in science for the validity of extra sensory perception as described in this article. It is true, of course, there are some areas and activities of the human mind which have not been explored or completely understood by psychologists for the purpose of explaining these little-understood functions of the mind."

As for the aforementioned Alan Belmont, having reviewed additional FBI files on "mental phenomena," he told Hoover the following: "In 1957, one William Foos, Richmond, Virginia, claimed that he could teach blind persons to see through the use of extra sensory perception. He claimed he could teach people to read a paper which was covered or to see through a wall. Recognizing the value of such activity to our counterespionage work, we thoroughly checked the claim and had to conclude that his alleged powers had no scientific basis. Other Government agencies such as Veterans Association, Central Intelligence Agency and Assistant Chief of Staff for Intelligence also checked on Foos and were highly skeptical of his work."

Nevertheless this did not stop the FBI from continuing to carefully, and secretly, watch Ruth Montgomery. Indeed, the Bureau noted that, according to Montgomery's insider sources, "top intelligence agents" were involved in classified ESP-themed operations in the early 1960s and cited Montgomery's words in an official memorandum for Hoover. It reads as follows: "The Army Intelligence Service is beginning to delve into an unknown reach of the mind which—should it eventually prove successful—could make spying the least hazardous branch of defense.... The project receives expert guidance within the department, but many of the officers have become so fascinated by the possibility [of ESP] that they have formed groups, outside of office hours, to try reading each other's minds."

Clearly, then, and despite what many have assumed and presumed, official U.S. government interest in extrasensory perception began way before remote viewing became fashionable within official circles. Precisely when such research actually began, however, is an issue just about as murky and as mysterious as the phenomenon itself.

Raëlians

The Raëlians are a UFO cult created by a man named Claude Maurice Marcel Vorilhon, a Frenchman born in Vichy in 1946. By all accounts, Vorilhon had a normal childhood. Things began to change, however, when he was fifteen. That was when Vorilhon dropped out of school, hitchhiked to Paris and began busking on the streets to make money. Finally, Vorilhon made a breakthrough: a man named Lucien Morisse was impressed by Vorilhon's ability to craft songs and play them in an entertaining, crowd-pulling fashion. Vorilhon soon found himself with a recording contract and, under the name of Claude Celler, he had a small degree of success in the music industry. Then, in 1971, he turned his attention to racing cars and sports cars and established a magazine dedicated to both: *Autopop*. Two years later, Vorilhon's life changed radically.

It was December 13, 1973, when Vorilhon suddenly, and quite out of the blue, felt a need to jump in his car and head off to Puy de Lasollas, close to the capital of Avergne, where there stands an ancient, dormant volcano. As to what happened next, we have to turn our attentions to acclaimed UFO investigator, Dr. Jacques Vallée: "The weather was foggy, overcast. He suddenly saw a blinking red light, and something like a helicopter came down and hovered two yards above the ground. It was the size of a small bus, conical on top. A stairway appeared, and a child-like occupant came out, smiling with a glow around his body."

The very human-looking extraterrestrial gave its name as Yahweh and entered into extensive dialog with amazed and astonished Vorilhon. Such was the sheer level of data imparted that Vorilhon wrote an entire book on his close encounter, titled (in English) *The Book Which Tells the Truth*. According to Vorilhon's cosmic source, the human race owed its origins to Yahweh's people: around 25,000 years ago ETs visited the Earth and, via highly sophisticated DNA manipulation, gave birth to the human race.

The aliens were known as the Elohim ("those who came from the sky") and during the early, burgeoning years of human development, they sent a number of ambassadors to our planet, chiefly as a means to try and ensure that early man lived a good and peaceful life. Among those ambassadors were Buddha, Jesus, and Moses. And, those same Elohim had a plan in mind for Vorilhon—one that has pretty much dominated the rest of his life.

One day, he was told, the Elohim would return to the Earth and show themselves—on a planet-wide scale, no less, and Vorhilon had been selected as their number one contact on Earth to pave the way for the return of the ancient alien race. The first thing Vorilhon was asked to do was to build a "res-

Raëlianism is a religion based on the belief that life on Earth was planted here deliberately by extraterrestrials.

idential embassy" for the aliens and also to create a group to which others of a like-mind would gravitate. Its name, in English, was "The Movement for Welcoming the Elohim, Creators of Humanity."

It was in September 1974 that things exploded big time for Vorilhon. That was the month in which he held a major conference in the city of Paris, at which he told the story of his by now extensive encounters, the alien Elohim, and their mission on Earth. It was a phenomenally successful conference which attracted more than 2,000 curious attendees. Vorilhon soon adopted another name: Raël, and Madech became the International Raëlian Movement. In no time, the group went global.

Raëlian teaching states that the human soul is nothing but a myth. The group's members are taught to believe that we are nothing more than flesh and blood, and that when life is over … well, it's over. However, the Raëlian ideology does offer a form of never-ending life: cloning. On December 26, 2002, the Raëlians announced the birth of the world's first human clone. It was an announcement that the church, the world of medicine, and even world politicians condemned—if the story was true, of course.

With human cloning now possible, announced the Raëlians, the next step was to perfect what they term "mind-transfer." Namely, at the time of death, a person's entire mind and life experiences would transfer into a newborn baby—and potentially *ad infinitum*. In that sense, the Raëlians believe that living forever is feasible—but only in physical, rather than spirit, form.

Ralstonism

Born in Massachusetts in 1852, Webster Edgerly was a social reform activist and a staunch supporter of a healthy, and highly alternative, diet, who was intent on perfecting the ultimate human being—in his eyes, at least. After he graduated from the Boston University School of Law in 1876, Edgerly became fascinated with the idea that via certain controversial and, at times, distinctly occult-based techniques largely of his own design, the latent powers of both the human mind and body could be elevated to near superhuman levels. As a result of this same fascination and obsession, Edgerly founded a now-obscure movement that was known as Ralstonism.

Edgerly eagerly proclaimed to anyone and everyone who would listen to him that: "We believe that Ralstonism, since it is becoming universal, is as necessary as food, light or water. This movement is the grandest, noblest, and already the most far-reaching power that has originated in the present age. Ralstonism is the grandest movement that man is capable of establishing."

And, quite literally, thousands of people did listen: astonishingly, at its height, Ralstonism attracted more than an incredible 800,000 followers. There was, however, a dark side to Ralstonism, which was largely known only to his devotees and which Edgerly did not broadcast publicly. It was Ralstonism's dirty little secret. Edgerly's intention was to have his followers become the founding members of what he firmly hoped would become a new order—possibly even a new breed of human—that would be wholly Caucasian and completely free from what Edgerly very disturbingly referred to as "impurities." That's right: Edgerly was a full-blown racist extremist.

Edgerly's fifty-plus books were mostly written under the pseudonym of Edmund Shaftesbury (he also used the name Everett Ralston when the mood took him) and encompassed such issues as diet, exercise, punctuation, sexual magnetism, "artistic deep breathing," facial expressions, and even, very oddly, ventriloquism!

Mind manipulation was at the forefront of Ralstonism, as it is in so many secret societies that wish to seek control of their followers.

Mind manipulation was at the forefront of Ralstonism, as it is in so many secret societies that wish to seek control of their followers. In his book *In Operations of the Other Mind*, Edgerly wrote: "Against the growing errors, vagaries, morbid theories, occult teachings, and wild beliefs that are darkening present-day life, depressing the mind, weakening the nerves, preying on the health and creating gloomy forebodings, this work comes as an inspiring guide and a practical instructor. It has been our wish and purpose to make this course of training one of the most important and valuable ever published. So, into the book we have put the great study, 'HOW TO EMPTY THE MIND.' Recall the countless times you have been mentally upset, worried, bothered with troubles. Think of what it would have meant—and will now mean—to know how to cast all such mental torture out of your mind. The relief and peace of mind this one study alone can bring you can be worth thousands of dollars."

From 1894 to 1895, Edgerly purchased huge areas of farmland along the northern slope of Hopewell Valley, New Jersey. It was there, in 1905, that Edgerly founded Ralston Heights. It was a large and imposing house built to his own specific design and that was destined to contain a whole community of Ralstonites who Edgerly enthusiastically envisaged becoming the heart and soul of a futuristic metropolis that would be christened the City of Ralston.

Interestingly, the rolling, curved contours of Edgerly's sprawling estate were specifically designed in accordance with his firm belief that sudden stops, as well as walking in straight lines, would result in dramatic and catastrophic leakage of "vital force" in his new race of people. Edgerly's plans were highly ambitious: it was his goal to expand Ralston Heights to the point where it was composed of literally hundreds of lots, at least sixteen small farms, no fewer than seven palaces, and the loftily named Temple of Ralston.

None of that came to pass, however; and that's certainly a good thing. Edgerly died on November 5, 1926, in Trenton, New Jersey, before his dreams could be fulfilled. As a result, Edgerly's wife sold the property within twelve months of his death, and the eccentric, unusual and controversial world of Webster Edgerly and Ralstonism came to a rapid close. Today, the Edgerly estate stands in ruins. Needless to say, had Edgerly achieved all that he set out to achieve—namely the creation of a race of elite, super-human Caucasians with the ability to control minds via occult means, the result would have been the rise of a truly formidable and sinister force of undoubtedly fascist-based proportions. Or, perhaps, a Master Race would have been a far more correct description of what Edgerly had in mind. Thankfully, and just like that other man who was intent on creating such a Master Race—Adolf Hitler—Edgerly was stopped in his tracks by the actions of the Grim Reaper.

RAND Corporation

When it comes to the matter of government interest in paranormal phenomena, certainly one of the most controversial aspects of the entire issue revolves around the ways and means by which official agencies have exploited—or have tried to exploit—religious iconography as a weapon of war, deception, and manipulation.

So the story goes today, darkly ambitious plans are afoot to unleash upon the entire planet a monstrous and malignant holographic hoax relative to the so-called Second Coming. Known to the wilder elements of conspiracy-theorizing as Project Blue Beam, it is said to be an operation designed to usher in a definitive New World Order-type society, in which the populace—duped into believing by a series of aerial holograms that the final battle between good and evil is taking place in the skies above—will give up their freedoms and allow a secret society of powerful figures to rule them with an iron fist born out of Old Testament wrath of God-style teachings.

Could such an astonishing scenario actually be true? Are there really cold-hearted people, buried deep within the corridors of power, who see the religious teachings and beliefs of the ancients as being viable ways of keeping all of us living in a state of never-ending, Hell-driven terror and martial law?

True or not, we do see prime evidence of official manipulation of religious iconography for military and psychological warfare purposes.

One of the most important, relevant, and earliest contributions to this particular debate is an April 14, 1950, publication of the RAND Corporation titled *The Exploitation of Superstitions for Purposes of Psychological Warfare.* Written by a RAND employee named Jean M. Hungerford, and prepared for the attention of intelligence personnel within the U.S. Air Force, the thirty-seven-page document is an extremely interesting one and delves into some highly unusual areas, one of which has a direct bearing upon the extraordinary data contained within this particular article.

Before we get to the matter of the document itself, a bit of background on the RAND group is required. Although not a secret society, as such, RAND is an organization that has fingers in numerous worldwide pies—as its very own website confirms: "The RAND Corporation is a nonprofit institution that helps improve policy and decision making through research and analysis. For

RAND Corporation headquarters in Santa Monica, California. RAND is a nonprofit group that influences policies worldwide regarding everything from education and health issues to environmental and military concerns.

more than six decades, RAND has used rigorous, fact-based research and analysis to help individuals, families, and communities throughout the world be safer and more secure, healthier and more prosperous. Our research spans the issues that matter most, such as energy, education, health, justice, the environment, and international and military affairs.

"As a nonpartisan organization, RAND is widely respected for operating independent of political and commercial pressures. Quality and objectivity are our two core values.

"RAND's research is commissioned by a global clientele that includes government agencies, foundations, and private-sector firms. Philanthropic contributions, combined with earnings from RAND's endowment and operations, make possible the RAND-Initiated Research program, which supports innovative research on issues that are crucial to the policy debate but that reach beyond the boundaries of traditional client funding."

All of which brings us back to the matter of RAND and religious manipulation.

Jean Hungerford stated: "Recently a series of religious 'miracles' has been reported from Czechoslovakian villages. In one instance the cross on the altar of a parish church was reported to have bowed right and left and finally, symbolically, to the West; the 'miracle' so impressed the Czechs that pilgrims began to converge on the village from miles around until Communist officials closed the church and turned the pilgrims away from approaching roads."

On another occasion, noted Hungerford, the Virgin Mary herself was said to have materialized—in a vision—and to have given a communist a resounding slap that knocked him unconscious! And then there was a story from Western Bohemia that made its way into Hungerford's report, which asserted that locals had seen the Virgin Mary parading along the streets of a small town—with the American flag in her hand, no less—as U.S. troops and tanks followed dutifully behind.

Of course, the overriding message behind these particular visitations of the Marian kind, and the attendant reported miracles, was acutely clear: God was (a) right behind Uncle Sam; and (b) hardly a noted supporter of communism. Whether or not this was all provoked by some top secret hand of the U.S. government—of which RAND had no personal awareness—is unknown.

But, as RAND noted in its report to the Air Force, the U.S. government had carefully and secretly monitored Moscow- and Czech-based radio broadcasts that discussed the claimed miracles in great depth. Most notably of all, the Russians and the Czechs exhibited deep, on-air anger and annoyance that the rumors in question were essentially casting a major slur on the entire Soviet Bloc and the communist way of life.

But, as RAND noted in its report to the Air Force, the U.S. government had carefully and secretly, monitored Moscow- and Czech-based radio broadcasts....

Hungerford noted something else that clearly demonstrated the large-scale extent to which American agents were dutifully monitoring this particular situation: "According to the Foreign Broadcast Information Services' daily reports of Soviet and Eastern European radio broadcasts, there were nine broadcasts concerning the 'miracles' between February 28 and March 19, seven from Czech transmitters and two from Moscow (including a review of a *New Times* article on the subject)."

Every response and reaction by the Soviets, it appears, was being carefully watched and analyzed by the U.S. government.

In closing on this particular matter, Hungerford detailed that the Soviets had their deep suspicions that this was all some sort of religious ruse perpetrated on them by intelligence agents of the United States. Concerning the report of the Virgin Mary waving the Stars and Stripes, a Prague-based radio broadcaster, whose words were transcribed and translated by the CIA, said: "It is obvious at first sight that this apparition bears the mark made in the United States. These despicable machinations only help to unmask the high clergy as executors of the plans of the imperialist warmongers communicated to them by the Vatican through its agents."

It is this affair, and, perhaps, this particular RAND-originated document of 1950 that galvanized America, and RAND itself, to further explore how, and under what particular circumstances, religion could be used as a tool of warfare, psychological manipulation, and control.

Report from Iron Mountain

Mercury Theatre on the Air performed Orson Welles's radio adaptation of H. G. Wells's classic sci-fi book *War of the Worlds* on October 30, 1938, specifically as a Halloween special. The program was broadcast from the twentieth floor of 485 Madison Avenue and was ingeniously presented in the form of a regular show that was repeatedly interrupted by a series of disturbing and escalating news stories detailing gigantic explosions on the planet Mars that were rapidly followed by frantic reports of the landing of an alien spacecraft near the town of Grover's Mill, New Jersey.

As the broadcast progressed, more Martian war machines landed and proceeded to wreak havoc throughout the continental United States. The secretary of the interior informed the pain-stricken populace of the grave nature of the ever-growing conflict, and the military launched a desperate counterattack against the burgeoning Martian assault. Frantic reports described thousands of people fleeing urban areas as the unstoppable Martians headed towards New York City. "Isn't there anyone on the air?" pleaded a desperate broadcaster in suitably dramatic and chilled tones.

Of course, Welles had merely intended the show to be an entertaining radio rendition of *War of the Worlds* and nothing more. However, those listeners who were unfortunate enough to have missed the beginning of the production—in which Welles was very careful to say that the broadcast was simply a piece of fictional entertainment and absolutely nothing else—really did believe that a Martian attack on the Earth had begun and that the end of civilization was possibly looming on the dark horizon.

Indeed, newspapers of the day stated that large-scale panic followed in the wake of the show, and although later studies suggested the hysteria was actually far less widespread than newspaper accounts initially suggested, many people were indeed caught up in the initial cosmic confusion.

It has been suggested by conspiracy theorists, such as the late William Cooper, that the *War of the Worlds* broadcast was actually a psychological warfare experiment secretly sponsored by a secret group within the U.S. government to try and accurately determine how the population might react to the presence of a hostile alien menace, albeit an entirely false and officially manufactured one, rather like a War on Terror for the *X-Files* generation.

Although the majority of those who have studied such claims have outright dismissed them, the scenario of government officials conspiring to unite (or, perhaps, enslave) humankind under one banner, as a result of an intergalactic alien threat, was discussed extensively in a controversial publication titled *Report from Iron Mountain*.

The late writer Philip Coppens stated: "In 1967, a major publisher, The Dial Press, released *Report from Iron Mountain*. The book claimed to be a suppressed, secret government report, written by a commission of scholars, known as the "Special Study Group," set up in 1963, with the document itself leaked by one of its members. The Group met at an underground

An illustration from a 1906 edition of H. G. Wells' *War of the Worlds.*

After the book's initial publication, it was reported that President Lyndon B. Johnson had deep suspicions that President John F. Kennedy had authorized the publication of the report.

nuclear bunker called Iron Mountain and worked over a period of two and a half years, delivering the report in September 1966. The report was an investigation into the problems that the United States would need to face if and when 'world peace' should be established on a more or less permanent basis."

And as the report itself noted: "It is surely no exaggeration to say that a condition of general world peace would lead to changes in the social structures of the nations of the world of unparalleled and revolutionary magnitude. The economic impact of general disarmament, to name only the most obvious consequence of peace, would revise the production and distribution patterns of the globe to a degree that would make the changes of the past fifty years seem insignificant.

"Political, sociological, cultural, and ecological changes would be equally far-reaching. What has motivated our study of these contingencies has been the growing sense of thoughtful men in and out of government that the world is totally unprepared to meet the demands of such a situation."

Upon its first appearance in 1967, *Report from Iron Mountain* ignited immediate and widespread debate among journalists and scholars with its disturbingly convincing conclusion: namely, that a condition of permanent peace at the end of the Cold War would drastically threaten the United States' economic and social stability.

Although subsequently identified as nothing more than an ingenious hoax written by Leonard Lewin, who had both conceived and launched the book with the help of a select body of players in the peace movement—including *Nation* editors Victor Navasky and Richard Lingeman, novelist E. L. Doctorow, and economist John Kenneth Galbraith—the controversy surrounding *Report from Iron Mountain* refuses to roll over and die.

Long out of print, the report suddenly began to reappear in bootlegged editions more than twenty years after its original publication, amid claims that its contents were all-too-real.

Colonel Fletcher Prouty, a national security aide in the Kennedy administration (and the model for Donald Sutherland's character X in Oliver Stone's hit movie *JFK*), continues to believe to this very day that the report is indeed authentic, and he specifically referred to it within the pages of his memoirs. Notably, in a 1992 Preface to Prouty's memoirs, no less a person than Stone himself cited *Report from Iron Mountain* as specifically raising "the key questions of our time."

After the book's initial publication, it was reported that President Lyndon B. Johnson had deep suspicions that President John F. Kennedy had authorized the publication of the report. Moreover, Johnson is famously alleged to have hit the roof upon learning of its publication.

In 1992, *Report from Iron Mountain* author Lewin filed a lawsuit for copyright infringement against Willis Carto, a white supremacist, for allegedly publishing the now-discontinued, bootleg editions of the book. Interestingly, Mark Lane, an author who has written extensively on the Kennedy assassination and who served as Carto's lawyer, stated that *Report from Iron Mountain* may indeed have been a real government document and, therefore, could not be seen to have any bearing upon current U.S. copyright laws.

Similarly, a May 1995 front-page article in the *Wall Street Journal* reported that extreme-right fringe groups continued to quote *Report from Iron Mountain* as "proof of a secret government plot to suppress personal liberties and usher in a New World Order dominated by the U.N."

Right Club

Just four months before the outbreak of World War II in September of 1939, a highly controversial and, at the time, secret, group was created in the heart of the United Kingdom. Its title was the Right Club. Its title was highly appropriate, given that it was composed of extreme right-wingers with fascist tendencies and intense anti-Semitic overtones. The Right Club was created by one Archibald Maule Ramsay, who, at the time, was a member of the British Parliament, specifically as a Scottish Unionist.

It was Ramsay's intention, with world war looming large on the horizon, to try and convince the British public that going head to head with Adolf Hitler would not be a good idea at all. Ramsay also did all that he could to whip up support for his party within the government, too. Ramsay had no qualms about his main goals: to (a) demolish the Conservative Party and oust the prime minister of the day, Neville Chamberlain, who went on to declare war on Germany on September 3, 1939; and (b) to free British politics of what he, Ramsay, termed "organized Jewry."

Disturbingly, when war broke out and the secrecy surrounding the group was replaced by open, public activity, Ramsay quickly gathered a great deal of support from hundreds of high-profile, powerful figures, including the Fifth Duke of Wellington and a then-serving member of Parliament, John Hamilton Mackie. He, too, like Ramsay, was a Scottish Unionist. Ramsay created what he termed *The Red Book*, a journal-type publication that listed all of the members and supporters of his group—many of whom insisted on absolute secrecy and anonymity, even though the existence of the group was now becoming known. Both the book and the flag of the Right Club prominently displayed the letters P and J. They were abbreviations of Perish Judah and were accompanied by a bird of prey killing a serpent. The message was clear: Ramsay viewed the Jewish people as nothing more than snakes that had to be snuffed out of existence.

With the Right Club up and running, it wasn't long before significant support for the group increased to a notable degree. The *Daily Worker* newspaper gave major space to Ramsay and his inflammatory, racist views. Of particular note—although certainly not in a positive way—Ramsay blustered to the *Daily Worker* that if it could not be achieved via the law of the land, he and his cohorts would take away what he perceived as Jewish control "with steel." While many rightly condemned Ramsay for his comments and plans, that didn't stop him from being profiled in numerous other publications, including the *Peeblesshire Advertiser* newspaper and the magazine *John Bull*. Attention towards the Right Club was clearly growing.

When war became a reality in September 1939, the Right Club did all it could to try and bring to a rapid end what it termed "the phony war."

When war became a reality in September 1939, the Right Club did all it could to try and bring to a rapid end what it termed "the phony war." Not only did the Right Club spend an inordinate amount of money distributing pamphlets encouraging people to denounce Prime Minister Chamberlain and the war effort, it also sought support for an "honorable negotiated peace" with Adolf Hitler. Certainly, Ramsey was—to his shame—doing his utmost to appease Hitler when he said: "This is a Jews' War. The stark truth is that this war was plotted and engineered by the Jews for world-power and vengeance."

The end, however, was not far away for the Right Club. It was largely due to the actions of a man named Tyler Kent. At the time, Kent was in the employ of the American Embassy in London, England. Kent, born in Manchuria and who was already suspected of being a Russian spy, gravitated towards Ramsay—to the extent that, with British authorities now keeping a very close eye on Ramsay, the latter decided to give *The Red Book* to Kent for safekeeping, and that was Ramsay's big mistake.

Not only was Kent suspected of having spied for the Russians but there were also concerns that with war now raging in Europe, Kent had turned his attentions in the direction of Adolf Hitler. Such was indeed the case. Kent carefully, and skillfully, stole an untold number of highly classified documents and memoranda between the U.S. president of the day, Franklin D. Roosevelt, and Winston Churchill, who in 1940 replaced Neville Chamberlain as prime minister.

It was Kent's intention to use damaging documentation to try and prevent the United States from entering the war, something that Ramsay was keen to see, too. It did not work out like that, however: agents of MI5—the British equivalent of the FBI—raided Kent's apartment on May 20, 1940, and found not only numerous U.S. embassy files but also Ramsay's *Red Book*. In no time at all, Ramsay and his followers were rounded up and arrested. After seven years in jail, Kent returned to the United States, eventually hooking up with elements of the Ku Klux Klan. He died in 1988. As for Archibald Maule Ramsay, he was detained by British authorities for the duration of the rest of World War II—a surefire, guaranteed way of keeping him from espousing his fascist ways and demanding an end to the hostilities. Ten years after the war was over, Ramsay was dead.

River Thames Mutilation Murder

In September 2001, an investigation began into one of the U.K.'s most mysterious—and still unresolved—murders. It all revolved around the shocking killing of a young boy who was suspected of being the victim of a mysterious and deadly cult. The date was September 21 when the body of a child was found in London's River Thames, near where the reconstruction of Shakespeare's Globe Theater now stands. To say that the child's body was found would, however, be something of an exaggeration. All that was recovered was the poor child's torso: his arms, legs, and head were missing. On top of that, his body was drained of blood. The police wasted no time in trying to get to the bottom of the mystery, which caught the attention of practically the entire U.K. population and the media.

It quickly became clear to the police that this was not a case of murder as such. Rather, it was a disturbing example of full-blown sacrifice. All of the child's limbs had been removed with what was obviously surgical expertise, and his stomach contents included the calabar bean, which is native to Africa. Notably, if ingested, the calabar bean can provoke seizures, respiratory failure, and even death. Very oddly, the boy's stomach also contained clay particles that were peppered with gold dust. The shocking story was widely reported by the U.K.'s press, amid rumors that perhaps an African secret society had killed the young boy—who the police dubbed Adam.

> The police wasted no time in trying to get to the bottom of the mystery, which caught the attention of practically the entire U.K. population and the media.

Forensic analysis of Adam's remains revealed that they contained close to three times higher than normal levels of lead and copper—which suggested

Adam originated in West Africa, and almost certainly Nigeria. That theory was bolstered even further when it was determined that the calabar bean particles found in Adam's stomach were of a kind that were only found in Nigeria's Edo State. The investigation was led by Detective Constable Will O'Reilly and Commander Andy Baker. In quick time they were able to determine that the shorts that were still attached to Adam's waist were available in only two countries: Austria and Germany. In addition, there was no doubt on the part of the investigators that this was indeed a case of human sacrifice.

One of those brought into the investigation was Dr. Richard Hoskins of Bath University, an authority on African voodoo cults and their practices. He said: "Adam's body was drained of blood, as an offering to whatever god his murderer believed in. The gold flecks in his intestine were used to make the sacrifice more appealing to that god. The sacrifice of animals happens throughout sub-Saharan Africa and is used to empower people, often as a form of protection from the wrath of the gods. Human sacrifice is believed to be the most 'empowering' form of sacrifice—and offering up a child is the most extreme form of all."

Within West African witchcraft cults, it is not at all uncommon for the victims' amputated limbs to be used as a form of medicine. The eyes, fingers, and sexual organs are also utilized as magical charms.

Despite the overwhelming mystery surrounding the case, a breakthrough was finally made. It all revolved around a woman named Joyce Osagiede. A citizen of Nigeria, she was detained at Scotland's Glasgow Airport by immigration officers—partly because she was acting in a highly erratic fashion. Significantly, she claimed knowledge of "extreme religious ceremonies" that her husband was involved in. Detective Constable Will O'Reilly and Commander Andy Baker wasted no time in checking out the woman's story. They discovered something notable.

Osagiede and her children were temporarily housed in a Glasgow apartment—in which the team found a pair of shorts identical to those that Adam was wearing at the time of his death. Osagiede was also found to have lived for a while in Germany, where such shorts, the police had confirmed, were available. In fact, it was also discovered that Osagiede was in Hamburg, Germany, at the time of Adam's murder. So, although she may very well have known something of the grisly affair, she certainly wasn't the murderer. British authorities quickly deported her back to Nigeria. That was not the end of the matter, however.

Years later, Osagiede decided to come clean on what she knew—or, rather, on what she claimed she knew. While living in Germany, asserted Osagiede, she took care of a young Nigerian boy whose mother was about to be sent back home, German authorities having refused to give her permission to stay. Osagiede added that she later handed the boy over to a man only known as Bawa, who was prepared to take him to London, England. Osagiede even had a name for the child: Ikpomwosa. She was certain that whatever cult Bawa was attached to, "They used [Ikpomwosa] for a ritual in the water."

There are, however, problems with this story. Osagiede has also claimed that the boy's name was Patrick Erhabor. And she later maintained that Bawa was actually one Kingsley Ojo, a bogus asylum-seeker who arrived in the U.K. in 1997. Ojo denies any involvement in the death of the child, and the police have found nothing that might suggest any involvement on his part. Nevertheless, as the BBC noted: "Ojo, who used three different identities, was arrested in London in 2002 by officers investigating the Adam case. In his flat they found in a plastic bag, a mixture of bone, sand and flecks of gold very similar to a concoction found in the dead boy's stomach. There was also a video marked 'rituals' which showed a B-movie in which an actor cuts off the head of a man. Ojo said the video and mixture belonged to other people in the house and detectives could not establish a link between him and the Adam case. In 2004, he

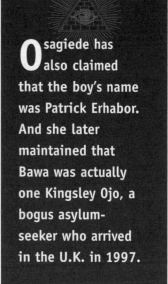

Osagiede has also claimed that the boy's name was Patrick Erhabor. And she later maintained that Bawa was actually one Kingsley Ojo, a bogus asylum-seeker who arrived in the U.K. in 1997.

was sentenced to four-and-a-half years in prison for people smuggling. While in prison he contacted officers and offered to help with the inquiry. But investigators concluded he was wasting police time and he was deported to Nigeria."

The police's latest word on this horrific saga: "The investigation remains ongoing and any new information provided to the team will be thoroughly investigated."

Robertson Panel

On December 2, 1952, the CIA's assistant director, H. Marshall Chadwell, noted in a classified report on UFO activity in American airspace: "Sightings of unexplained objects at great altitudes and traveling at high speeds in the vicinity of major U.S. defense installations are of such nature that they are not attributable to natural phenomena or known types of aerial vehicles."

Believing that something really might be afoot in the skies of America, Chadwell prepared a list of saucer-themed recommendations for the National Security Council:

1. The Director of Central Intelligence shall formulate and carry out a program of intelligence and research activities as required

to solve the problem of instant positive identification of unidentified flying objects.

2. Upon call of the Director of Central Intelligence, Government departments and agencies shall provide assistance in this program of intelligence and research to the extent of their capacity provided, however, that the DCI shall avoid duplication of activities presently directed toward the solution of this problem.

3. This effort shall be coordinated with the military services and the Research and Development Board of the Department of Defense, with the Psychological Board and other Governmental agencies as appropriate.

4. The Director of Central Intelligence shall disseminate information concerning the program of intelligence and research activities in this field to the various departments and agencies which have authorized interest therein.

Forty-eight hours later, the Intelligence Advisory Committee concurred with Chadwell and recommended that "the services of selected scientists to review and appraise the available evidence in the light of pertinent scientific theories" should be the order of the day. Thus was born the Robertson Panel, so named after the man chosen to head the inquiry: Howard Percy Robertson, a consultant to the Agency, a renowned physicist, and the director of the Defense Department Weapons Evaluation Group.

Chadwell was tasked with putting together a crack team of experts in various science, technical, intelligence and military disciplines and have them carefully study the data on flying saucers currently held by not just the CIA, but the Air Force too—who obligingly agreed to hand over all the UFO files, it had for the CIA's scrutiny. Or, at least, the Air Force *said* it was all it had.

Whatever the truth of the matter regarding the extent to which the U.S.A.F. shared its files with Chadwell's team, the fact that there was a significant body of data to work with was the main thing, and so the team—which included Luis Alvarez, physicist, and radar expert (and later, a Nobel Prize recipient); Frederick C. Durant, CIA officer, secretary to the panel, and missile expert; Samuel Abraham Goudsmit, Brookhaven National Laboratories nuclear physicist; and Thornton Page, astrophysicist, radar expert, and deputy director of Johns Hopkins Operations Research Office—quickly got to work.

The overall conclusion of the Robertson Panel was that while UFOs, per se, did not appear to have a bearing on national security or the defense of the United States, the way in which the subject could be used by unfriendly forces to manipulate the public mindset and disrupt the U.S. military infrastructure *did* have a bearing—and a major one, too—on matters of a security nature.

Back in 1952 a plan was formulated by the CIA, and presented to the National Security Council, on how to deal with a UFO threat. (Simulated UFO photograph.)

According to the panel's members: "Although evidence of any direct threat from these sightings was wholly lacking, related dangers might well exist resulting from: A. Misidentification of actual enemy artifacts by defense personnel. B. Overloading of emergency reporting channels with 'false' information. C. Subjectivity of public to mass hysteria and greater vulnerability to possible enemy psychological warfare."

There was also a recommendation that a number of the public UFO investigative groups that existed in the United States at the time, such as the Civilian Flying Saucer Investigators (CFSI) and the Aerial Phenomena Research Organization (APRO), should be watched carefully due to "the apparent irresponsibility and the possible use of such groups for subversive purposes."

The panel also concluded that "a public education campaign should be undertaken" on matters relative to UFOs. Specifically, agreed the members, such a program would "result in reduction in public interest in 'flying saucers' which today evokes a strong psychological reaction. This education could be accomplished by mass media such as television, motion pictures, and popular articles. Basis of such education would be actual case histories which had been

Well-known and well-respected radio broadcaster Arthur Godfrey was suggested as the man to recruit to handle communication efforts to manage public reaction.

puzzling at first but later explained. As in the case of conjuring tricks, there is much less stimulation if the 'secret' is known. Such a program should tend to reduce the current gullibility of the public and consequently their susceptibility to clever hostile propaganda.

"In this connection, Dr. Hadley Cantril (Princeton University) was suggested. Cantril authored *Invasion from Mars* (a study in the psychology of panic, written about the famous Orson Welles radio broadcast in 1938) and has since performed advanced laboratory studies in the field of perception. The names of Don Marquis (University of Michigan) and Leo Roston were mentioned as possibly suitable as consultant psychologists.

"Also, someone familiar with mass communications techniques, perhaps an advertising expert, would be helpful. Arthur Godfrey was mentioned as possibly a valuable channel of communication reaching a mass audience of certain levels. Dr. Berkner suggested the U.S. Navy (ONR) Special Devices Center, Sands Point, L. I. [Long Island], as a potentially valuable organization to assist in such an educational program. The teaching techniques used by this agency for aircraft identification during the past war [were] cited as an example of a similar educational task. The Jam Handy Co. which made World War II training films (motion picture and slide strips) was also suggested, as well as Walt Disney, Inc. animated cartoons."

Robbie Graham, a UFO researcher who has studied the many and varied intricacies of the Robertson Panel and its links to Disney and Ward Kimball, says: "The panel's singling-out of Disney made sense given the animation giant's then firmly established working relationship with the U.S. government: during World War II Disney made numerous propaganda shorts for the U.S. military, and in the 1950s corporate and government sponsors helped the company produce films promoting President Eisenhower's 'Atoms for Peace' policy, as well as the retrospectively hilarious Duck and Cover documentary, which depicted schoolchildren surviving an atomic attack by sheltering under their desks."

Graham continued: "That the Robertson Panel highlighted Disney is significant in that the Panel's general recommendation to debunk UFOs through media channels is known to have been acted upon in at least one instance: this being the CBS TV broadcast of *UFOs: Friend, Foe, or Fantasy?* (1966), an anti-UFO documentary narrated by Walter Cronkite. In a letter addressed to former Robertson Panel Secretary Frederick C. Durant, Dr. Thornton Page confided that he 'helped organize the CBS TV show around the Robertson Panel conclusions,' even though this was thirteen years after the Panel had first convened. In light of this case alone, it seems reasonable to assume that the government may at least have attempted to follow through on the Robertson Panel's Disney recommendation."

As for Ward Kimball, in 1979, he went public on certain aspects of Disney's links to the UFO conundrum and officialdom and stated that it wasn't just the CIA that Disney was working with when it came to UFOs. At some point during 1955 or 1956 Disney was contacted by representatives of the U.S. Air Force and asked to secretly cooperate on a documentary about the UFO controversy. As part of the deal, the Air Force offered to supply actual UFO footage, which Disney was told they could include in their film.

According to Kimball, at that time it wasn't at all unusual for either Walt Disney or his studio to go along with the government's wishes—or, perhaps, demands might be a far more accurate term to use. Kimball revealed how, during World War II, the military practically took over Disney's Burbank facilities, where dozens of hours of military training productions and war effort films featuring Disney characters, like Donald Duck, were made.

The studio began work on the requested UFO documentary and animators were asked to imagine what an alien would look like, while Walt Disney himself eagerly waited for the Air Force to deliver the promised film of actual UFOs. At the last moment, however, the Air Force mysteriously withdrew the offer of the footage, and the planned documentary was canceled.

But, what all this does demonstrate is that Disney had a link to UFOs, the CIA, and secret projects—and specifically, and collectively, in a fashion that revolved around manipulating and controlling public opinion on, and perception of, all things of the flying saucer variety.

Walt Disney, head of the famous animation and family movie studio, worked with the U.S. military to produce pro-America propaganda during World War II.

Copeland also commented on the CIA's involvement in the UFO issue and confirmed that ... the phenomenon could be manipulated and used as a tool of psychological warfare and propaganda....

In 1981, Kimball made a stealthy, and somewhat tentative, approach to a man named Miles Axe Copeland Jr., who, during World War II, served with the Strategic Services Unit (the remnants of the Office of Strategic Services) and later became a key and senior figure within the CIA. Copeland was also the father of none other than Stuart Copeland, drummer with the new-wave band the *Police*. But, Kimball's reason for hooking up with Miles Copeland wasn't to find a roundabout way to get Sting's autograph. No, he had something altogether different on his mind. Kimball wanted to talk about MKUltra, flying saucers, and Ron Hubbard. But why did Kimball seek out Copeland?

Miles Copeland, as a senior CIA operative, knew a great deal about MKUltra. As far as his bosses were concerned, maybe way too much, and Copeland had nothing positive to say about the program either. He went on record as stating that, in the buildup to the 1972 election, Democratic presidential candidate Edmund Muskie had been secretly targeted by a CIA goon-squad who knew far more than a few disturbing things about psychedelics and scrambled minds. The reason: Richard Nixon's people wanted the CIA to covertly but regularly slip Muskie LSD and provoke ongoing, increasingly erratic and emotional behavior in the man that, when seen by the public and commented upon by the media, would hopefully discredit him and push voters further towards Nixon. History has shown that Muskie did indeed suddenly begin to exhibit odd, over-the-top actions and rival George McGovern won the Democratic nomination. Copeland also maintained that when the MKUltra program became public knowledge in the 1970s, the Church Committee got no more than the barest glimpse at what was really, and deeply, afoot behind closed doors at Langley and elsewhere.

In addition, Copeland had notable things to say about L. Ron Hubbard's Church of Scientology, which, Copeland asserted, was created with the helping hand of our old friends at the CIA. Investigative writer Daniel Brandt says of this matter: "Toward the end of his career, Hubbard was certainly a renegade, far beyond anyone's capacity to control him. But in the 1950s and early 1960s, it's probable that he had support from U.S. intelligence. His early expertise in mind control is curious, as well as his lifetime interest in intelligence tradecraft. Copeland claims that his CIA colleague Bob Mandlestam made 'arrangements' with Scientology and Moral Re-Armament [an organization established in 1938 that encouraged spiritual, multi-faith development and which was infiltrated and manipulated by the CIA] about this time."

Copeland also commented on the CIA's involvement in the UFO issue and confirmed that, while certain elements of the agency never actually ruled out the possibility of a small number of alien intrusions in the skies of our world, far more pressing and intriguing to agency personnel was how the phenomenon could be manipulated and used as a tool of psychological warfare and propaganda—which is the exact area in which the CIA envisioned the Walt Disney Corporation, including Ward Kimball, playing a potential role. Thus, while we can never be one hundred percent sure, it seems fairly safe to conclude that Kimball had heard of Copeland's combined comments relative to LSD, MKUltra, UFOs, and L. Ron Hubbard, and sought him out for those specific reasons. And, it should be noted, Hubbard's Church of Scientology had a connection to Kenneth Goff (via its 1955 manual, *Brain-washing: A Synthesis of the Russian Textbook on Psychopolitics*).

Kimball had a great deal to say about Copeland—most of it pretty disturbing and whacked out. In a lengthy, typed letter, Kimball claimed to Copeland to be very disturbed by something that he had learned, from longtime friends in the CIA, as a result of the Church Committee's probing into MKUltra in the 1970s. After outlining to Copeland his work with Disney, the CIA, a mid-1950s post-Robertson Panel operation to confuse the Soviets on what the U.S. government knew about UFOs, and the manipulation by agency personnel of a number of UFO research groups across the country in the early years of the Cold War—all of which Kimball felt was fine, justified, and "not overstepping the mark"—Kimball then began spilling the beans on certain other things that, he stressed, he was not involved in but had merely heard about and which, if true, most assuredly *did* overstep the mark.

Those things included agency personnel using American citizens—members of the public, people in the UFO research arena, certain players in Scientology, patients in asylums, prisoners, and military personnel—in MKUltra-connected experiments to (a) "affect the public's views" on UFOs, as a means to "seeing how far they [the CIA] could go" in terms of harnessing, controlling, and altering human perception and belief via potent chemical cocktails; (b) "construct a UFO mythos" behind which such experimentation could be carefully concealed; and, perhaps most worrying of all, (c) develop a long-term plan to understand how chemical and subliminal manipulation, as well as the creation of new beliefs and the modification of old ones, could be used to create a subservient, docile populace that was envisioned as being part-*1984* and part-*Brave New World*.

Perhaps eerily anticipating what we are seeing today, more than three decades ago Kimball told Copeland that these plans included long-term operations to ensure that more and more of the American population became hooked on addictive, mood-altering, and mood-controlling drugs; attempts to drive American culture away from outdoors/social activity and more towards lethargy and solely indoors-based activities, such as being glued to the television 24/7; the creation of fear myths to keep the populace in a perpetual state of terror born out of nonexistent threats; a slow but deliberate erosion of civil liberties; and even plans for a manufactured UFO threat, one that might even take decades to carefully create, nurture, and instill in the minds of the people but which, in part, would include "MK techniques" with a "defined end."

Then, with a population pummeled and subdued by drugs, a significant lessening in outside excursions, mounting ill health of both a physical and psychological nature, and a growing number of spurious threats to national security—including, specifically, one of a flying saucer nature—it would be a case of nothing less than coldhearted checkmate, after which a brave new world of a bleak, totalitarian nature would take the place of the old world.

Romagna

Charles Godfrey Leland's 1892 book, *Etruscan Roman Remains in Popular Tradition*, tells an interesting story: "There is in Northern Italy a mountain district known as La Romagna Toscana, the inhabitants of which speak a rude form of the Bolognese dialect. These Romagnoli are manifestly a very ancient race, and appear to have preserved traditions and observances little changed from an incredibly early time. It has been a question of late years whether the Bolognese are of Etrurian origin, and it seems to have been generally decided that they are not. With this I have nothing whatever to do. They were probably there before the Etruscans. But the latter at one time held all Italy, and it is very likely that they left in remote districts those traces of their culture to which this book refers."

Leland continued that the title—Romagna—was designated to the area in question for one specific reason: centuries earlier it was a part of the Papal or Roman dominion. The specific area to which Leland was referring was situated between Forli and Ravenna. During the course of his research, Leland uncovered something both intriguing and, from his personal perspective, disturbing: "Among these people, *stregeria*, or witchcraft—or, as I have heard it called, 'la vecchia religione' (or 'the old religion')—exists to a degree which would even astonish many Italians. This *stregeria*, or old religion, is something more than a sorcery, and something less than a faith. It consists in remains of a mythology of spirits, the principal of whom preserve the names and attributes of the old Etruscan

During the course of his studies, Leland discovered that many of the peasant folk in the Romagna area had deep knowledge of what he referred to as "scores of these spells."

gods, such as *Tinia*, or Jupiter, *Faflon*, or Bacchus, and *Teramo* (in Etruscan *Turms*), or Mercury. With these there still exist, in a few memories, the most ancient Roman rural deities, such as Silvanus, Palus, Pan, and the Fauns. To all of these invocations or prayers in rude metrical form are still addressed, or are at least preserved, and there are many stories current regarding them."

Leland further noted that deeply connected to the acceptance of, and devotion to, such ancient gods, there was a local, secret tradition that taught that every living thing—man, animal, plant, flower, tree, and so on—contains a life-force, a supernatural essence that many would term the soul. The recycling of the soul—into new forms after death— was part and parcel of the old lore, too. Leland also learned that: "All kinds of goblins, brownies, red-caps and three-inch manikins, haunt forests, rocks, ruined towers, firesides and kitchens, or cellars, where they alternately madden or delight the maids—in short, all of that quaint company of familiar spirits which are boldly claimed as being of Northern birth by German archaeologists, but which investigation indicates to have been thoroughly at home in Italy while Rome was as yet young, or, it may be, unbuilt."

He added that linked to the acceptance of the *folletti*—also referred to as "minor spirits"— and their attendant observances and traditions were huge arrays of magical cures with appropriate incantations, spells, and ceremonies, to attract love, to remove all evil influences, or to ensure certain events occurred, such as to "win in gaming, to evoke spirits, to insure good crops or a traveler's happy return, and to effect divination or deviltry in many curious ways—all being ancient, as shown by allusions in classical writers to whom these spells were known, and I believe that in some cases what I have gathered and given will possibly be found to supply much that is missing in earlier authors."

During the course of his studies, Leland discovered that many of the peasant folk in the Romagna area had deep knowledge of what he referred to as "scores of these spells." He expanded on this by adding: "The skilled repe-

Charles Godfrey Leland was an American writer who became interested in folklore and wrote about an ancient people in northern Italy.

tition and execution of them is in the hands of certain cryptic witches, and a few obscure wizards who belong to mystic families, in which the occult art is preserved from generation to generation, under jealous fear of priests, cultured people, and all powers that be, just as gypsies and tramps deeply distrust everything that is not 'on the road,' or all 'honest folk,' so that it is no exaggeration to declare that 'travelers' have no confidence or faith in the truth of any man, until they have caught him telling a few lies."

Rosemary's Baby

Peter Beckman is, to put it mildly, a notable character. Having grown up in northern California, as a youngster he gravitated towards the arts and acting and was soon involved with local theater and production companies. In his early twenties, Peter attended the California Institute of Arts, where he studied screenwriting alongside Alexander Mackendrick, of *The Man in the White Suit* fame. His movie appearances include *Chud II*, Orson Welles's unfinished *The Other Side of the Wind*, and *Echo Park*.

Beckman is the voice of General Wolf in the SyFy Channel's series *Monster*; he worked as a voice artist on *Street Fighter 4* and *Street Fighter 5*; and he is the author of a highly entertaining paranormal-themed novel, *Dead Hollywood*. In addition, Beckman is the male voice in Josie Cotton's recordings of *Beyond the Valley of the Dolls* and *Faster Pussycat, Kill! Kill!* Beckman also had a starring role in the video for the Ramones' 1983 single, *Psycho Therapy*, in which he is kicked in the head, courtesy of a psychotic punk-rocker.

Many years ago, Beckman had a bizarre experience that was connected to the 1968 movie *Rosemary's Baby*, which was directed by Roman Polanski. It was based upon Ira Levin's novel of the same name, which was published one year earlier. It's a movie that revolves around a secret, satanic society and the lives of Rosemary and Guy Woodhouse. As for the baby of the movie's title, it's the offspring of none other than the Devil himself—and, of course, it is Rosemary who is destined to bring it into our world. A chilling story of a clandestine cult and its terrifying, manipulative actions, *Rosemary's Baby* has become—no pun intended—a cult classic.

In 2011, Peter told me: "I have always been fascinated by the Men in Black legend. But I had never really connected it with the experience I had back in 1969 or 1970—when I would have been about twenty or twenty-one—until you described a sequential series of events that are common, and you practically described what happened to me."

Peter continued that he and a friend, Stephen, "were big movie fans and great fans of Roman Polanski's movies. We loved *The Fearless Vampire Hunters* and *Rosemary's Baby*. This night we were listening to the soundtrack to *Rosemary's Baby* by Krzysztof Komeda. As one of the tracks ended, I noticed a kind of change in the air, a shift, a weird shift. It was a change in the mood of the place, and then the black mass track came on. Then things really changed. It seemed to me like we were in my living room, but also someplace else."

Then, something even weirder happened, as Peter notes: "There was a knock at the door. I remember the knock at the front door. I don't recall if it was me or Steve who said: 'Better let them in.' I opened it; we admitted two men into the house. After what we had just seen, in retrospect this seems amazing. They were dressed in square, Eisenhower-era cop clothing, or FBI clothing—which in 1969, 1970 was not that unusual. They came in and sat on the couch. They were pale and sickly; their clothes hung real loose and they looked as though they might expire at any moment. They appeared to have either trouble breathing, or trouble even being. I don't believe they said a thing. If they did, it has disappeared from memory. Very odd, indeed.

"I recall that, as I was waiting for them to speak, my mind was racing; should I try humor or invective? My general impression is that they were kind of confused, but just ever so slightly amused by the situation. It was as though they were waiting for us to speak. Their physical attitudes seemed to be waiting for some sort of answer, although no questions were asked. We were all waiting. This frightened me for an instant; then the whole scene felt absurd and humorous. After a couple of minutes, I started feeling funny about this, and I started saying something like: 'Can we see some ID? Did someone send you? What are you really here for?' But this did not affect them at all. When I thought: 'I want them to leave,' they seemed to pick up on this, and did leave."

And as Beckman also said, they didn't just leave, but vanished. As in literally.

As the following demonstrates, Peter Beckman and his friend, Stephen, were not the only ones involved in a strange situation related to *Rosemary's Baby* and black-clad figures at the door. In December 2014, I extensively interviewed a woman named Alison (who I first spoke with in 2011), who had a very bizarre experience in a motel in Orange County, California, one year earlier in 2010. At the time, Alison was in California on business. Her work was, and still is, in the field of acupuncture.

It was an hour or so before the witching hour when a loud knock on the door of her room had Alison in a sudden state of fear. This was hardly surpris-

A chilling story of a clandestine cult and its terrifying, manipulative actions, *Rosemary's Baby* has become—no pun intended—a cult classic.

ing: it was late at night, the sky was dark, and she was in bed watching none other than *Rosemary's Baby*. She lay frozen for a few seconds, then got up and tiptoed to the door and looked through the spyhole. She could see two young boys, dressed in black hoodies and black jeans. As if sensing that Alison was watching them, one asked, in a raised voice, if they could use the telephone. Particularly disturbing, both "boys" held their heads low, clearly making sure that Alison would not see their faces too well.

Alison was determined not to open the door, but she told me she felt weirdly compelled to do exactly that—as if her very own self-will was quickly being taken away from her. That was not a good sign. Alison, fortunately, managed to focus her mind and backed away from the door. As she did so, she instantly felt her mind return to normal, after which she tentatively moved closer to the door and peered through the spyhole, yet again.

This time, the pair in black was staring up at her, with their faces prominent. Alison was instantly filled with terror by the sight of their completely black eyes and utterly milk-white skin. She screamed, ran for the phone, and called the night manager. He was there in no time. The creepy kids, however, were gone. Alison, although she did not realize it at the time, had just had an experience with the notorious Black Eyed Children, which David Weatherly describes in his excellent book of the same name.

Is it only a coincidence that Peter Beckman, his friend Stephen, and Alison all experienced strange and malevolent figures in black at the door, and in situations linked to *Rosemary's Baby*—which has at its heart a secret, satanic cult? I rather think it's not a coincidence. Beckman and Stephen were listening to the soundtrack to the movie when the Men in Black appeared, and Alison was watching the movie itself when the Black Eyed Children manifested. What this all means, it's hard to know for sure. It would, however, be interesting to know precisely how many more people may have experienced similar, weird phenomena while watching certain and specific movies of the supernatural variety, and particularly those concerning secret, satanic cults and societies, and particularly so *Rosemary's Baby*.

Rosicrucian Order Crotona Fellowship

Established in the early part of the 1920s, the Rosicrucian Order Crotona Fellowship was deeply inspired by—as one might quickly deduce—Rosicrucianism. It was the creation of a man named George Alexander Sullivan. This was not, however, Sullivan's first immersion into the world of the Rosicrucians. A decade or so earlier, he ran what became known as the Order of Twelve, which also ran according to Rosicrucian principles. The Rosicrucian Order Crotona Fellowship first operated out of the English city of Liverpool, after which its base of operations was transferred to the town of Christchurch, in the south of England. It was there that Sullivan came into contact with one Gerald Gardner, the founder of today's Wicca movement.

The Rosicrucian Order Crotona Fellowship had fairly down-to-earth origins: its initial meetings were not held—as one might be inclined to imagine—in some ancient, underground chamber or something similar, but within the confines of nothing more than a pleasant, old, English pub. That situation changed, however, when the group moved to Christchurch in 1930 and put down roots. Six years later, the Ashrama Hall was built—a place destined to forever be associated with Sullivan's group and its practices and teachings.

Two years later, Sullivan and his followers added a new component to the Rosicrucian Order Crotona Fellowship: they created what became known as the Christchurch Garden Theater. It was not, however, your average theater. Rather, it staged plays written by Sullivan, under the alias of Alex Mathews, all of which were of a magical and mystical nature. The Rosicrucian Players, as they became known, included in their numbers the so-called New Forest Coven of witches, which also played a major role in the development of Wicca. Indeed, even Gerald Gardner himself became one of the players.

Not only that, Sullivan established the Rosicrucian Players with Mabel Emily Besant-Scott, a woman known affectionately as Mebs, and who happened to be a Rosicrucian, a Co-Freemason, and a Theosophist. Also on board were followers of Alice Bailey, who penned in excess of twenty books, all with Theosophy-based themes, including *Letters on Occult Meditation*, *A Treatise on Cosmic Fire*, and *The Problems of Humanity*.

> *S*ullivan and his followers added a new component to the Rosicrucian Order Crotona Fellowship: they created what became known as the Christchurch Garden Theater.

How Gardner came to be linked to the Rosicrucian players is an interesting story, as "Lady of the Abyss," of the *Witches of the Craft* website, notes: "In Highcliffe, Gardner came across a building describing itself as the 'First Rosicrucian Theatre in England.' Having an interest in Rosicrucianism, a prominent magico-religious tradition within Western esotericism, Gardner decided to attend one of the plays performed by the group; in August 1939, Gardner took his wife to a theatrical performance based on the life of Pythagoras. An amateur thespian, she hated the performance, thinking the quality of both actors and script terrible, and she refused to go again. Unperturbed and hoping to learn more of Rosicrucianism, Gardner joined the group in charge of running the theatre, the Rosicrucian Order Crotona Fellowship, and began attending meetings held in their local ashram."

Although not ultimately proved, there are rumors that, prior to 1940, Sullivan and at least some of his followers were practicing Co-Freemasonry, a form of Freemasonry that is open to both men and women alike. It was during this period that Sullivan met one Peter Caddy, a man who played a significant role in the development in the U.K. of organic gardening, and who was the founder of the spirituality-based Findhorn Foundation, a Scottish charitable trust that, today, runs the Findhorn Trust and an alternative health/medical facility.

In 1942, while only in his early fifties, Sullivan died, which led to the quick decline of the Rosicrucian Order Crotona Fellowship—which was never really a large scale society in the first place. The outcome was that it fell into obscurity—its lasting legacy being its connection to Gerald Gardner and the early years of Wicca.

Today, the records and books of the Rosicrucian Order Crotona Fellowship, which run to 140 titles—and which date from the sixteenth to the twentieth century—are housed in Southampton Library, England. Library staff note that: "The collection is one of only a few sources for the publications of the Rosicrucian Order's Crotona Fellowship. Pamphlets such as *Rosicrucian Philosophy: Pointers for Students* and *Secrets of the Rosicrucians* were published by the Crotona Press, as were plays by its founder, George Sullivan, writing as Alex Mathews e.g. *Twilight on the Threshold: a Mystic Play*. The books on mythology, hermeticism, freemasonry, mesmerism and alchemy give an indication of the range of interests of the Fellowship and there are also books by and about those associated with earlier Rosicrucian groups such as Francis Bacon and Robert Fludd."

RuSHA

High-ranking Nazis, such as Richard Walther Darre, Rudolf Hess, Otto Rahn, and Heinrich Himmler, are all credited with having an interest in the occult—albeit to varying degrees and at equally varying times. For example, Rahn was employed in a wing of the RuSHA Department of Nazi Germany's greatly feared SS—specifically to try and seek out the legendary Holy Grail, which, according to Christian teachings, was the dish, plate, or cup used by Jesus at the Last Supper and that was said to possess miraculous powers. Then, there's the matter of the RuSHA Department's secret role in the quest for the Spear of Destiny. RuSHA was the Rasse und Siedlungshauptamt der SS (in English: SS Race and Settlement Main Office). Although its primary mandate was to safeguard Germany's "racial purity," the organization also played a role in the quest to seek out ancient religious artifacts, including the aforementioned spear.

Trevor Ravenscroft's book *The Spear of Destiny* details a particular fascination Adolf Hitler had with the fabled spear, or, more correctly, the lance that is said to have pierced Jesus's body while he was nailed to the cross. Ravenscroft's book maintains that Hitler deliberately started World War II with the intention of capturing the spear, with which he was said to have been overwhelmingly obsessed. At the end of the war, we're told, the spear came into the hands of U.S. general George Patton. According to legend, losing the spear would result in nothing less than death—which was said to have been definitively fulfilled when Hitler committed suicide. Ravenscroft repeatedly attempted to define the strange powers that the legend says the spear serves. Notably, Ravenscroft found it to be a hostile and malevolent force, which he sometimes referred to as the Antichrist, although that is somewhat open to interpretation. He never actually

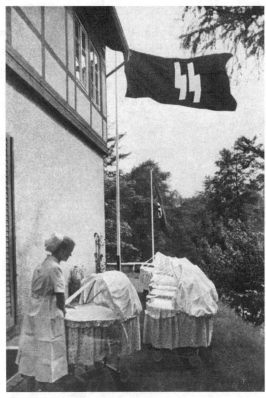

This photo from 1943 shows a nurse tending to babies who were part of the Lebensbornheim program of making certain that children of Nazi Germany were of "pure" Aryan blood.

referred to the spear as being spiritually controlled, but rather as intertwined with all of mankind's ambitions.

Interestingly, Dr. Howard A. Buechner, a professor of medicine at Tulane, and later Louisiana State University, wrote two books on the spear. Buechner was a retired colonel with the U.S. Army, served in World War II, and wrote a book about the Dachau massacre, to which he had personally been a witness. Buechner claimed he was contacted by a former German U-Boat submariner, the pseudonymous Captain Wilhelm Bernhart, who vigorously maintained to Buechner that the Spear of Destiny currently on display in the city of Vienna is nothing but a skilled, ingenious fake.

The real spear, Buechner was told by Bernhart, was clandestinely sent by Hitler to Antarctica, along with a whole host of other Nazi treasures, under the specific command of a Colonel Maximilian Hartmann. So the story went, the spear was said to have been recovered in 1979—by Hartmann himself. Bernhart presented Buechner with the logbook from this particularly secret expedition, along with photographs of the object recovered. Bernhart also claimed that after the Spear of Destiny was recovered from the ice in 1979, it was hidden somewhere in Europe by a secret society that had deep Nazi roots. After Buechner contacted most of the members of the alleged expedition, including senior Nazi officials and close associates, to find the spear, he came to accept the story as nothing less than startling fact.

Sacred Oak

Certainly one of the strangest of all the secret Germanic cults was one that, in times long gone, worshipped what has become known as the sacred oak. In 1922, Sir James George Frazer—a Scottish social anthropologist and a noted expert on secret societies, mythology, and religion—said: "In the religion of the ancient Germans the veneration for sacred groves seems to have held the foremost place, and according to Grimm the chief of their holy trees was the oak. It appears to have been especially dedicated to the god of thunder, Donar or Thunar, the equivalent of the Norse Thor; for a sacred oak near Geismar, in Hesse, which Boniface cut down in the eighth century, went among the heathen by the name of Jupiter's oak (*robur Jovis*), which in old German would be *Donares eih*, 'the oak of Donar.' That the Teutonic thunder god Donar, Thunar, Thor was identified with the Italian thunder god Jupiter appears from our word Thursday, Thunar's day, which is merely a rendering of the Latin *dies Jovis*."

As Frazer's words show, for the ancient Teutons, and as with the Greeks and Italians, the god of the oak and the god of the thunder were one and the same. Moreover, this same deity was regarded as "the great fertilizing power," a god who sent rain and caused the earth to bear fruit. Frazer continued that: "Adam of Bremen tells us that 'Thor presides in the air; he it is who rules thunder and lightning, wind and rains, fine weather and crops.' In these respects, therefore, the Teutonic thunder god again resembled his southern counterparts Zeus and Jupiter."

Sir James George Frazer was a Scottish social anthropologist who noted the importance of sacred trees and groves in ancient German culture.

Within the culture of the Slavs, the oak was perceived as the sacred tree of the thunder god known as Perun, who was the equivalent of both Zeus and Jupiter. Back to Frazer: "It is said that at Novgorod there used to stand an image of Perun in the likeness of a man with a thunder-stone in his hand. A fire of oak wood burned day and night in his honor; and if ever it went out the attendants paid for their negligence with their lives. Perun seems, like Zeus and Jupiter, to have been the chief god of his people; for Procopius tells us that the Slavs 'believe that one god, the maker of lightning, is alone lord of all things, and they sacrifice to him oxen and every victim.'"

As Frazer noted, the primary god of the Lithuanians was Perkunas—also known as Perkuns—specifically the god of thunder and lightning, and whose parallels to both Jupiter and Zeus are clear and obvious. According to Frazer, oaks were perceived as sacred trees to Perkunas, to the extent that, as Frazer revealed, "When they were cut down by the Christian missionaries, the people loudly complained that their sylvan deities were destroyed. Perpetual fires, kindled with the wood of certain oak-trees, were kept up in honor of Perkunas; if such a fire went out, it was lighted again by friction of the sacred wood."

Frazer's research also revealed that the men of the area made sacrifices to oak trees, as a means to ensure a flourish crop each year. The women did much the same to lime trees. It was Frazer's conclusion that oak trees were perceived as masculine, while lime trees were feminine. As far as those sacrifices were concerned, Frazer had much more to say: "In time of drought, when they wanted rain, they used to sacrifice a black heifer, a black he-goat, and a black cock to the thunder god in the depths of the woods. On such occasions the people assembled in great numbers from the country round about, ate and drank, and called upon Perkunas. They carried a bowl of beer thrice round the fire, then poured the liquor on the flames, while they prayed to the god to send showers. Thus the chief Lithuanian deity presents a close resemblance to Zeus and Jupiter, since he was the god of the oak, the thunder, and the rain."

Frazer's final words, demonstrating the widespread influence that such beliefs had on the people of the era and the area, were as follows: "From the foregoing survey it appears that a god of the oak, the thunder, and the rain was worshipped of old by all the main branches of the Aryan stock in Europe, and was indeed the chief deity of their pantheon."

Sacrifice on the Moors

Over the years far more than a few cases of distressing animal mutilations have been reported in the countryside of the United Kingdom. It's important to note that we're most definitely not talking about anything akin to the rumors of aliens mutilating and killing cattle in the United States for who knows what purposes. No, in the U.K., we're talking about something much more down to earth, but certainly no less disturbing.

In October 2005, for example, farmer Daniel Alford of Sampford Spiney, near Tavistock, Devon, England, made a shocking discovery on the wilds of Dartmoor: namely, six sheep, horrifically slaughtered, with their eyeballs removed and their necks viciously broken. More sinister is the fact that the corpses of the animals had been deliberately laid out, in what was perceived to be a pagan symbol, near a series of ancient standing-stones.

Alford was convinced this was the dark and horrific work of occultists, primarily because this was not the first occasion upon which he had made such a gruesome find. In January 2005, Alford had stumbled upon five sheep, killed in a similar fashion and spread out in a circle, only half a mile away. Interestingly, on both occasions the animal attacks had occurred at the height of a full moon.

Alford angrily said at the time: "This was a sacrifice—they had their necks broken. Initially, when you think of sacrifices you think sharp knives and slit throats. That wasn't the case here. If they had killed them and taken them, I would have accepted it more. Just to outright kill them and leave them is just a waste."

And as Alford perceptively and rightly noted: "You wouldn't just get kids catching sheep like that. Someone's got to know what they're on about." Alford was not wrong: somebody most definitely did know what they were doing, and the attacks were only destined to continue.

> **A**lford was convinced this was the dark and horrific work of occultists, primarily because this was not the first occasion upon which he had made such a gruesome find.

Equally of significance, in 2006, yet more unsettling sacrifices of sheep on Dartmoor occurred, again very near to Tavistock, and specifically on moorland at a location called Pork Hill. Once again, the necks of the animals had been broken, and their eyes had been taken. This time, however, there was another disturbing development: the tongues of the animals had also been removed.

Royal Society for the Prevention of Cruelty to Animals (RSPCA) inspector Becky Wadey commented: "These sheep must have been rounded up on the open moor by whoever carried out this barbaric attack. That would have required a number of people and potentially been quite a spectacle. The bodies were found on open, exposed ground very close to the road, so somebody must have seen something, even if they did not realise at the time that it was suspicious."

This is all very much the tip of a large iceberg. In fact, there are a number of additional cases of animal mutilation on Dartmoor, including one infamous case from 1977 that some flying saucer investigators, at the time, did link to the UFO phenomenon. Such slaughtering and accompanying sacrifice have also occurred in the English county of Staffordshire. We see no evidence of any link—at all—to UFOs. What we do see, however, is evidence that points in the direction of deeply warped, sick people who get their kicks out of sacrificing animals to achieve a certain goal via supernatural means. We're talking about money, power, and influence. More disturbing is the fact that many of these groups are interlinked. We're talking about a powerful network, an underground movement, that has tentacles all across the country and is highly active.

Sagan, Carl

Anative New Yorker, the late Carl Sagan was born in 1934 and developed a passion for the domain of outer space at a very early age. As a result of his work with NASA, he was awarded the space agency's medals for Exceptional Scientific Achievement and for Distinguished Public Service. Sagan remains well-remembered for his television series, *Cosmos: A Personal Voyage*, which aired on the Public Broadcasting Service in 1980. He died in 1996, at the age of just sixty-two, as a result of complications from myelodysplasia.

One of the strangest experiences in Carl Sagan's life occurred in late 1983. That was when he crossed paths with the FBI—albeit for a very alternative reason. Midway through November 1983, Sagan received in the mail a letter that spelled out the upcoming activities of a secret group that was intent on creating worldwide mayhem. It was written by someone who signed off as "M. Springfield," which soon became clear was an alias. It was on the morning of November 16 that the FBI office in Cleveland, Ohio, prepared the following document for the office of the director of the FBI in Washington, D.C.: "On November 15, 1983, Dr. Carl Sagan, Space Sciences Building, Cornell University, Ithaca, New York received a handwritten envelope postmarked Cleveland, Ohio, Nov 10 1983, containing a two page typewritten letter. Letter composed of cover page dated November 9, 1983 stating it was an open letter directed to various news publishers and identifying Sagan as an influential person to convince others veracity [sic] of message. Both message and cover letter bear typed name of author as M. Springfield."

The letter read as follows: "The message is so important that I want you to witness that you have received it before November 22, 1983. You have been chosen because of your standing in the community. I believe you are a person of integrity with the ability to convince others that this message is true. An Open Letter to All. Warning! Armageddon is coming!"

On November 22, 1983, Springfield told Sagan, terrorists would explode a bomb in either a warehouse or a market that was providing free food to impoverished people in San Salvador, but which, in reality was designed to divert people away from a planned attack on a nearby fuel storage installation. Then, suddenly moving on to a completely unconnected topic, Springfield added that if the next launch of the *Columbia* space shuttle went ahead on schedule, there would be a catastrophic explosion in the rocket, "due to a fuel leak."

Springfield had far more to say, all of it not just controversial but *beyond* controversial: "The American presidency will be Reagan-Bush-Bush and a democrat in 96 whose birthday is the same year as our first president. He will be our last." Springfield continued with a whole series of predictions: Poland would be free by 1990; New York and San Francisco would soon both disappear into the oceans; a Third World War would begin in 1998; and the world would be poisoned, the result being that life would be practically extinguished by the apocalyptic events.

The late Carl Sagan was an astrophysicist, astronomer, astrobiologist, and cosmologist who was well known for popularizing his field in the TV show *Cosmos*.

The FBI wasted no time in acting on Sagan's tip-off, as an FBI memo of November 18, 1983, shows: "A search of indices, State Law Enforcement Computer, and local directories, failed to locate a person identifiable with the author of captioned letter, described as 'M. Springfield.' Cleveland telephone directory shows a listing for an 'M. Springfield' which address is a large apartment complex. A suitable pretext telephone call to that address revealed that 'M. Springfield' at that address died in 1972 and widow now resides there. She had no knowledge of a letter sent to a Dr. Sagan."

Despite the fact that the FBI expressed concerns about "Springfield," the investigation stalled and was eventually closed down.

Sande Society

It goes by a number of names, including Bundo and Zadegi, but it is generally referred to as the Sande Society, a definitive secret cult that operates out of Sierra Leone, the Ivory Coast, and Liberia. Whereas many secret societies have exclusively male members—the Bohemian Club being a classic and highly visible example—the Sande Society is primarily female only, although there are exceptions to the rule. The work of the Sande Society primarily revolves around one thing: the transformation from childhood to adulthood. This involves controversial, painful, and occasionally dangerous mutilation and disfigurements of the genitals. The reasons, essentially, revolve around the importance of fertility and moral issues relative to relationships and sexual habits.

The Sande Society has a long history. Evidence of its existence in the late seventeenth century was confirmed by a man named Olfert Dapper, who spent time in Liberia and who in 1668, saw evidence of the group's practices. Dapper found data that pushed the barriers back to 1628. In all likelihood, however, the origins of the Sande Society are far older.

Initiation into the Sande Society is complex: when a girl reaches puberty, she is taken into the woods to begin the process. It's a long process too: girls are very often required to both live and work in the woods for a period of up to a year. The initiation is not just important to the girls, however. Unless a girl is initiated, she cannot marry, so it's vital for the girl's family that she embraces the world of the Sande Society.

Carol MacCormack, who has studied the beliefs and traditions of the Sande Society, says: "Shortly after entering the Bundu bush, girls experience the surgery distinctive of a Bundu woman in which the clitoris and part of the labia are excised. It is a woman, the *Majo* (Mende), or head of a localized Bundu chapter, who usually performs this surgery. [A] Bundu woman told me that excision helps women to become prolific bearers of children. A *Majo* reputed 'to have a good hand' will attract many initiates to her Bundu bush, increasing her social influence in the process. Informants also said the surgery made women clean."

When the girls have recovered from what is undeniably a traumatic and painful ordeal, there follows an extensive period of teaching, in all manner of issues, including sex and sexuality, healing and medicine, growing crops, cooking, and more. The completion of the mutilation of the genitals denotes the time when the girls are now ready for marriage and are no longer considered children, but adults. While many of us might consider the activities of the Sande Society brutal and harsh—not to mention potentially dangerous from a health perspective—for the initiates, it's all seen as a means to a positive end.

As Carol MacCormack points out: "There are pleasures to be enjoyed as well as ordeals, and the girls go gladly into the initiation grove. Food is plentiful since the initiation season occurs in the post-harvest dry season and each girl's family is obliged to send large

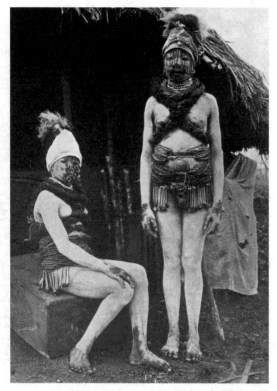

Sierra Leone initiates into the Sande Society have, in this photo, had their bodies smeared with animal fat and clay.

quantities of rather special food into the initiation grove on her behalf. There are also special Bundu songs, dances and stories to be enjoyed around the fire in the evening. The stories usually end with an instructive moral linked to Bundu laws given to the living by ancestresses of the secret society."

Santeria

The island of Puerto Rico is home to a number of different religions, one of them being Santeria—which is also practiced throughout much of the rest of the Caribbean. Its origins, however, can be found in the traditions of the Yoruba people of the Federal Republic of Nigeria, West Africa. While those who adhere to the teachings of Santeria believe in the existence of one overall god, they also believe there are numerous sub-gods too, which are collec-

A group of Santeria believers in Havana, Cuba, practice a ceremony that is a blend or Yoruba, Indian, and Roman Catholic traditions.

tively known as the Orishas. Those who are initiated into the religion—known as Santeros—are required to go through a week-long process of purification, which involves the application of both herbs and water to carefully and completely cleanse the body.

Not only that, a great deal of time and effort is expended by the Santeros when it comes to the appeasement of their many and varied sub-deities. One way in which this has been achieved (but far less so today) is by animal sacrifice—specifically, the killing of chickens and goats, which just happen to be the most favored delicacies of Puerto Rico's most famous and mysterious animal: the Chupacabra. There is a very good reason why I mention this, as will soon become clear.

Santeria has a long history on Puerto Rico: it took much of its inspiration from Nigerian slaves shipped over to the island in the eighteenth century. As for the matter of animal sacrifice, this was typically carried out by a Santero who was well versed in the many and varied intricacies of the religion. The reasons for such sacrifices were numerous and included a desire for physical well-being, riches, and good fortune. Just like each and every paranormal pact, this one came at a price: money, of course.

A Santero would rub the skin of a paying client with the body of the animal that was to be imminently sacrificed. Doing so, the followers of Santeria believed, transferred whatever ailed the person—or whatever they desire—into the body of the animal. The sacrificing of the animal was an act designed to ensure the wish reaches the Orishas, who granted them whatever it was that the person in question required. Sometimes, the corpse of the animal was destroyed; on other occasions it was eaten. As for the blood, it was served in a large vessel that was then offered to the gods.

Santeria has an offshoot known variously as Mayombe, Palo, or Palo Mayombe, but which, for the sake of ease, I will refer to as Palo. Its rituals—of supposedly being able to grant wealth, health, and power—are essentially identical to those of regular Santeria, but not always. While in Puerto Rico in May 2007 I spoke with a man named Sal, who knew a great deal about the dark world of Palo and who told me a profoundly disturbing story.

As well as sacrifices and the dishing up of dead bodies to ancient deities, wild alcohol- and cocaine-fueled orgies were the name of the game.

Sal said there existed on Puerto Rico what can only be described as a rogue form of Palo, one that was far removed from its conventional, original form, and which practiced highly controversial rituals. The group, he added, was one that pretty much no one in the regular Santeria community knew about or was linked to. The rituals of the group typically revolved around the sacrifice of chickens, goats, and peacocks. According to Sal, the group began its deadly activities in late 1994, or maybe early 1995, and was focused on providing a unique service, in return for a great deal of money: a guarantee of power and wealth.

This was, without doubt, very similar to the world of the Santeros, except for one thing. Sal said that many of the people who had sold their souls to this Palo offshoot were nothing less than major, household names: famous actors, politicians, musicians, authors, and even—he claimed—certain figures in the world of royalty.

Some of the rituals, Sal said, were held in a large and spacious house, one that was owned by a rich and influential figure in the equally rich and influential area of Condado, which is situated in Santurce, a district of San Juan. Other rituals were supposedly undertaken, in somewhat dicey fashion, deep in the heart of the El Yunque rainforest. As well as sacrifices and the dishing up of dead bodies to ancient deities, wild alcohol- and cocaine-fueled orgies were the name of the game. It's all very reminiscent of the Tom Cruise and Nicole Kidman movie of 1999, *Eyes Wide Shut.*

As for the Chupacabra connection to the story, Sal claimed that while the group was not responsible, per se, for creating the legend of the beast, the members most definitely exploited it to their great advantage and to the absolute hilt. By that, he meant—and particularly in relation to the events in El Yunque—when the group was busy killing chickens and goats in the rainforest, and then draining their blood and offering it up to the gods, it made a great deal of sense for them to spread tales of a Chupacabra or several on the loose. By doing so, their controversial actions remained buried under a mass of tales of an animal-killing, blood-drinking creature that may or may not actually exist.

Satanic Sacrifice

The 1980s saw a deeply disturbing and even dangerous phenomenon surface in the United Kingdom. It revolved around what became infamously known as Phantom Social Workers (PSW) or Bogus Social Workers (BSW). On numerous occasions, terrified parents throughout the United Kingdom were plagued by visits to their homes from women—occasionally accompanied by men—who claimed they were there to investigate reports of abuse to babies and children, whether mental, physical, or sexual. In many such cases, the claimed social workers acted in extremely strange and unsettling fashions, and they created atmospheres filled with dread and high strangeness.

Of one classic, early case of the modern era, investigator Peter Rogerson said the following, which accurately and concisely demonstrates the nature of Bogus Social Workers/Phantom Social Workers and their *modus operandi*: "A woman described as being her late 20s, 5' 7" (1.7m) in height, blonde, wearing a brown skirt suit, a white polo neck and carrying a briefcase called to a house near Blessington, Co. Wicklow, Ireland, claiming that she was a Public Health Nurse who had to take a baby boy away for vaccinations. She knew the boy's name and date of birth, but when the mother requested identification, the BSW upped sticks and left. The Eastern Health Board has issued warnings following the incident, advising people to be vigilant."

The reason why the authorities urged such vigilance was because the wave of BSW reports followed in the immediate wake of a satanic abuse scare that exploded across much of the U.K., including Rochdale, Nottingham, and Manchester. The primary theory was that some kind of secret satanic order was orchestrating the nightmarish events.

There were tales of babies being sacrificed, and even eaten, in abominable rituals to Satan and his demonic minions. Tales of aborted fetuses used in similar infernal rites, in darkened woods, and at the witching hour, abounded too. Major inquiries were launched, but nothing ever surfaced to suggest the hysterical rumors were anything other than that: hysterical rumors. It's hardly surprising, though, that the public and government agencies—and particularly so the police—were on edge.

Patrick Harpur, the author of an excellent piece of work, *Daimonic Reality*, said: "Reports poured in to the police, describing 'health workers' or 'social workers' who called to examine or take away children, but who hurriedly left when the householder became suspicious. The visitors were mostly one or two women, but sometimes a woman and a man. The women were typically in their late twenties or early thirties, heavily made up, smartly dressed and of medium height. They carried clipboards and, often, identification cards."

Tales of Satanic rites sometimes include horrifying claims of babies being killed and even eaten.

Harpur continued that by May 1990, the reports had grown in such numbers that the police believed no fewer than four groups of people were at work. He added: "They were thought to be gangs of pedophiles. But clearly there were signs that the matter was far from straightforward: the pedophile theory was weakened by the involvement of so many women, who are rarely implicated in pedophilia (except in cases of alleged satanic ritual abuse)."

Mike Dash, who has made a noteworthy contribution to the Bogus Social Worker controversy, has investigated yet another report from 1990; this one involving a woman named Elizabeth Coupland, of Sheffield, England. It was a winter's day when two women knocked on Coupland's door. Dressed in a fashion that suggested authority, the pair identified themselves as coming from the National Society for the Prevention of Cruelty to Children (NSPCC). Such was their manipulative skill, Coupland allowed the pair in, and even let them examine her children—one aged two and the other not even yet six months old.

According to Mike Dash: "The visitors soon left, and Coupland assumed that she would hear nothing more of the matter." Coupland was wrong, dead wrong. Dash notes that a couple of days later, one of the women returned, but this time with a man. Coupland was shell-shocked to learn that her children were to be taken away from her and to be placed into care. The terrified mother, now very suspicious, loudly said that she was going to call the police, at which point, says Dash, "the social workers beat a diplomatic retreat." It's hardly surprising—but disturbing—that the real NSPCC knew nothing of this highly worrying state of affairs.

Dash adds that these mysterious women have "continued to knock on the doors the length and breadth of Britain. They were in Edinburgh in 1995 and in Leicester a month later. They have called at homes in Bristol, Bath, Blackburn, Battersea and Barnsley." He observes, too, that not a single person has ever been charged in connection with any of these odd visits.

Thankfully, whatever the true nature of this sinister satanic order, they eventually faded away, vanishing as mysteriously as they first surfaced.

Scientology

Although the Church of Scientology, established by the late L. Ron Hubbard, is not a secret society as such, it most certainly operates in a fashion dictated by extensive secrecy. Both current and former members are dissuaded from speaking about their experiences with the church, and those who do so often find themselves on the receiving end of a distinct backlash. We can, however, learn a great deal about L. Ron Hubbard from his now-declassified FBI file.

An FBI document of 1951 reveals that in May of the same year, "Hubbard stated that while he was in his apartment on February 23, 1951, about two or three o'clock in the morning his apartment was entered. He was knocked out. A needle was thrust into his heart to produce a coronary thrombosis and he was given an electric shock. He said his recollection of this incident was now very blurred, that he had no witnesses and that the only other person who had a key to the apartment was his wife. It is further reported that he has been previously committed to a mental hospital."

Then we have the following from the FBI, also from 1951, that deals with Hubbard's pre-Scientology days, specifically those that revolved around his earlier brainchild, Dianetics:

"During March 1951, the Board of Medical Examiners, State of New Jersey, had a case against the HDRF [Hubbard Dianetics Research Foundation] scheduled for trial on the grounds that the organization was conducting a school, teaching a branch of medicine and surgery, without a license. In 1951 the HDRF established national headquarters at Wichita, Kansas, and sponsored the Allied Scientists of the World, which organization has as its avowed purpose 'to construct and stock a library … in an atomic proof area where the culture and technology of the United States could be stored in a state of use by science and preserve it in case of attack.'"

Further into the 1950s, we have this from the FBI on Hubbard: "He has been described as having 'delusions of grandeur,' and one newspaper item of divorce action quoted his wife as saying he was hopelessly 'insane.' Allegations have been made that organizations he was affiliated with were of particular interest to perverts, hypochondriacs and curiosity seekers. In 1951 the State of New Jersey reported it had a case against him for teaching medicine without a license and in 1952 the Post Office was investigating him for mail fraud."

Then there is this, from a May 22, 1953, FBI report: "People who were bothered with mental problems were being treated by this organization with the use of an apparatus involving two beer cans which were attached to an electric meter somewhat resembling a lie detector machine."

L. Ron Hubbard was a science fiction author who founded the Church of Scientology.

Consider, too, the following words of the FBI, from an April 14, 1967, document on Hubbard: "A perusal of the bankruptcy file … revealed that a warrant was issued on December 16, 1952, for L. Ron Hubbard to bring him forthwith before the court for examination in Ancillary Proceedings in Bankruptcy. The warrant was signed by Judge Allan K. Grim, executed by the U.S. Marshal and bail was allowed in $1,000. Hubbard, who is Chairman of the Board of Directors of Hubbard Dianetics of Kansas, wrongfully withdrew $9,286.99 from his bankrupt corporation. On December 17 and 19, 1952, he was examined before the bankrupt court and agreed with the Ancillary Receiver to make restitution. Judge Grim then discharged Hubbard. After the Kansas Corporation went bankrupt, he opened the 'Hubbard College' in Wichita, Kan., and when creditors began claiming against this establishment, he moved to Phoenix, Arizona. The file went on to say that it appears Hubbard displays a fine talent for profiting personally although his firms generally fail."

It's also worth noting the findings of Louis Proud, an investigative writer who has focused a great deal of his attention on Scientology. Proud says: "Because of L. Ron Hubbard's connection to the rocket scientist and occultist Jack Parsons … rumors abound that Scientology is in truth a 'black magic cult,' with those occupying the top echelons of the organization engaging in Crowleyian sex magick and other nefarious activities. At least some of these rumors stem from Scientology's heavy reliance on hypnosis—or, if not hypnosis itself, a state of consciousness very similar to hypnosis—as part of an allegedly therapeutic technique called 'auditing,' whereby 'engrams' (record-

Proud says: "Because of L. Ron Hubbard's connection to the rocket scientist and occultist Jack Parsons ... rumors abound that Scientology is in truth a 'black magic cult,'"

ings of experiences containing pain) are cleared from the 'reactive mind' (the unconscious) of the patient in order to liberate them from the influence of those engrams. (To be free of all engrams is to be considered 'clear')."

The words of L. Ron Hubbard Jr. should not be ignored either: "Hitler was involved in the same black magic and the same occult practices that my father was. The identical ones. Which, as I have said, stem clear back to before Egyptian times. It's a very secret thing. Very powerful and very workable and very dangerous. Brainwashing is nothing compared to it. The proper term would be 'soul cracking.' It's like cracking open the soul, which then opens various doors to the power that exists, the satanic and demonic powers. Simply put, it's like a tunnel or an avenue or a doorway. Pulling that power into yourself through another person—and using women, especially—is incredibly insidious.… It is the ultimate vampirism, the ultimate mind-fuck, instead of going for blood, you're going for their soul, and you take drugs in order to reach that state where you can, quite literally, like a psychic hammer, break their soul, and pull the power through."

Scotch Cattle

Quite possibly the strangest name ever dreamed up for a secret society, the Scotch Cattle quietly surfaced in South Wales, United Kingdom, in the 1800s, specifically the early 1820s. It was a society, and a name, dreamed up by coal miners—coal mining being a major industry in Wales at the time. There was nothing particularly positive about the Scotch Cattle, however. Its entire agenda was to threaten, intimidate, bully—and even beat to a near-pulp— miners who continued to work when their fellow striking miners had downed tools and were demanding higher wages and better working conditions. Those same threats and beatings were always undertaken late at night and became known, very appropriately, as The Midnight Terror.

The group's controversial actions were brought to light in the pages of an 1839 book, *Newport Rising*, written by Alexander Cordell. The book makes it clear that while some members of the Scotch Cattle were deeply driven by the cause to make things better for the mining community, others were simply thugs who enjoyed fighting and destroying peoples' property and personal belongings.

As for the odd name, *Welshnot* tells us: "But it's most likely linked to the menacing size and appearance of Highland breeds of cattle. The group used a bulls' head as its insignia—it was drawn on the Scotch Cattle's warning notices and daubed on the doors of homes they ransacked. The cattle theme extended to the group's structure with different pits/villages having their own 'herd' and the leader being known as the 'bull.' The secretive nature of Scotch Cattle makes it hard to estimate how many members it had or exactly how it was organized. One letter sent by the group boasted of 9,000 'faithful children', but this is liable to be an exaggeration."

Demonstrating the secret society nature of the group, we have this from *Historic Chronicles*: "The 'Scotch Cattle' existed as a secret society with its members sworn to allegiance under sufferance of death. Each valley town and village had its own cell (a pattern still adopted by current terrorist organizations) and a leader was elected, usually a person respected and feared for his aggressiveness and physical strength, known as the 'Bull' or in Welsh 'Tarw'. Their meetings were always held in complete secrecy, normally in dark secluded locations. Normally, this thuggery would be undertaken by a herd from another area to avoid recognition by local residents."

The Scotch Cattle finally fizzled out of existence in 1850—to the relief of many Welsh miners, but also to the anger of many more.

Second Coming

Born in 1908, Major General Edward Geary Lansdale served with the U.S. Office of Strategic Services during World War II. Then, in 1945, he was transferred to HQ Air Forces Western Pacific in the Philippines, and, in 1957, he received a posting to the Office of the Secretary of Defense, working as deputy assistant to the SoD for what were vaguely, but intriguingly, termed as Special Operations.

And, certainly, no such Cold War era operation got more special (and weird) than one that Lansdale pretty much singlehandedly coordinated. It was one, truly, of biblical proportions. Indeed, it was designed to try and convince the leadership and the people of Cuba of two startling things: (A) that the Second Coming of Jesus Christ had arrived; and (B) that he was a big fan of the U.S.A. It was a program that led Lansdale to create a small, secret group known as KF12 to study the feasibility of hoaxing a Second Coming. The group was not just filled with military elite, however. Historians, priests, psychologists, and experts in the fields of mythology and legend were secretly

A man in Norwich, England, warns passers-by that Jesus Christ will be returning, marking a time of atonement or judgment for all. The CIA wanted to spread the story that Cuban leader Fidel Castro would be out of power when Christ returned.

recruited into the elite group—essentially to provide input on how such a program should proceed, and what it would take to have people believe they were seeing the return of Jesus. As fantastic as it all sounds—a secret group faking a religious event—proof of its existence has been forthcoming.

Contained within the pages of a November 20, 1975, document titled *Alleged Assassination Plots Involving Foreign Leaders, Interim Report of the Select Committee to Study Government Operations with Respect to Intelligence Activities* is a fascinating statement from one Thomas A. Parrott, who served with the CIA for twenty-four years and who held the prestigious position of assistant deputy director for National Intelligence Programs. Commenting on some of Lansdale's more bizarre operations that were prompted by religion, ancient mythology, and legend, Parrott noted to the committee: "I'll give you one example of Lansdale's perspicacity. He had a wonderful plan for getting rid of [Fidel] Castro. This plan consisted of spreading the word that the Second Coming of Christ was imminent and that Christ was against Castro who was anti-Christ, and you would spread this word around Cuba, and then on whatever date it was, that there would be a manifestation of this thing, and at the time—this was absolutely true—and at the time just over the horizon there would be an American submarine that would surface off of Cuba and send up some star-shells, and this would be the manifestation of the Second Coming and Castro would be overthrown."

Star-shells, for those who may be wondering, are, essentially, pyrotechnic flares of the military designed to fill the skies at night with bright and widespread illumination. But, the ambitious plan that Lansdale had in mind involved much more than just dazzling the Cubans with mere flares. The feasibility was also looked into of using a U.S. Navy submarine to project images of Jesus Christ onto low-lying clouds off the coast of the Cuban capital of Havana.

The plan also involved—at the very same time—the crew of a U.S. military plane, camouflaged by the clouds and with its engine significantly muffled, using powerful loudspeakers to broadcast faked messages from an equally faked Christ to the people of Cuba, ordering them to overthrow their government and renounce communism.

Executed properly, such a highly alternative operation might very well have convinced the Cubans that Jesus Christ himself really was calling—and he was not bringing good news for Fidel Castro. Ultimately, while the whole thing was seen as undoubtedly ingenious in nature, it was also viewed as an operation that had a very big chance of failing catastrophically.

And if the Cubans got word there was a U.S. submarine in the very immediate area and took successful military action against it, the disastrous cost to American lives might have far outweighed anything that the operation could have achieved. Thus, this strange biblical charade of the Cold War was shelved.

Of course, this begs a very important, significant, and troubling question: if any sort of Second Coming really does occur at some point in the future of the human race, how will we know if it has its origins in Heaven or the murky and mysterious world of a secret group, deeply buried in the heart of officialdom? Maybe we actually won't know. Perhaps there are those in power who see the ingenious exploitation of religion as the ultimate tool of warfare, manipulation, and overwhelming control. One day, we may see the work of the secret KF12 group given a new face for the twenty-first century.

Secret City

Midway through 1947 a startling claim was made by a man named Howard Hill. The location of the revelation was the Los Angeles, California-based Transportation Club. According to Hill, he knew a great deal about a certain Dr. F. Bruce Russell—a physician from Ohio who had an overriding fascination for underground realms and archaeology. It was this fascination that ultimately led Russell to uncover something remarkable—according to the astounding words of Hill, at least. So the tale went, back in 1931 Russell and a friend and like-minded soul, Dr. Daniel S. Bovee, were trekking around Death Valley when they came upon an entrance to an amazing underworld. "Came upon" effectively means "fell into."

In Hill's story, the two men were checking out one particular area when the sandy ground beneath them gave way and they plunged into the depths of nothing less than an ancient, abandoned city.

> **E**ven more amazing, the city contained the skeletal remains of a number of giant humanoids—all around nine feet in height, no less.

Even more amazing, the city contained the skeletal remains of a number of giant humanoids—all around nine feet in height, no less. The bones of mammoths and saber-tooth tigers were also found. Not only that, the city—which extended in all directions in tunnel-style form—extended not for just a few miles, but for close to two hundred square miles. We're talking about a city easily rivaling anything of the likes that exist today. Or, so Howard Hill claimed. As for the age of the giants and the animals, Hill stated with confidence that they were likely around 80,000 years old. Although—and perhaps conveniently—he failed to explain how just such an estimate had been reached.

Hill's tale quickly caught the attention of the California-based media, although few within that same media had much time for such claims. The *San Diego Union*—on August 5, 1947—related the story to its readers without comment or opinion, but provided a few details on the clothing in which these massive men were dressed. The newspaper quoted Hill's words on this particular matter: "These giants are clothed in garments consisting of a medium length jacket and trouser extending slightly below the knees. The texture of the material is said to resemble gray dyed sheepskin, but obviously it was taken from an animal unknown today."

The Nevada-based *Hot Citizen* also covered the story, revealing even more of Hill's controversial assertions. Its staff quoted the following words from Hill: "A long tunnel from this temple took the party into a room where well-preserved remains of dinosaurs [and] imperial elephants and other extinct beasts were paired off in niches as if on display. Some catastrophe apparently drove the people into the caves."

For the most part, the media took a decidedly dim view of what Hill had to say—dismissing it as an entertaining, tall yarn of epic proportions and not much else. Maybe that's all it was, given that a third version of events surfaced—which contained all of the prime ingredients of the previous two: (a) Death Valley as the location; (b) a pair of adventurers who fall through the ground into an underground chamber that expands into tunnels and a city-style environment; and (c) the stumbling on of the remains of a long-gone civilization. In the third case, however, the two men were identified by Bourke Lee, a well-known figure in the region who, in 1930, penned a book titled *Death Valley*. It was followed, two years later, by *Death Valley Men*. In Lee's story, the men were Bill and Jack. Not a single surname was ever in sight, which does not bode particularly well. The saga, however, was essentially identical—aside from the bodies being of normal-sized, rather than giant-sized—even though Lee gave a date of the latter part of the 1920s.

Secret Society of Happy People

Almost certainly unique in the field of clandestine groups, the Secret Society of Happy People has just one goal in mind. The name of the group all but reveals its intent, namely, to promote happiness, and just about here, there, and everywhere. The origins of the group date back to the late 1990s, specifically to August 1998. It was the brainchild of Pamela Gail Johnson of Irving, Texas. The group's rallying cries are: "Don't even think of raining on my parade" and "Happiness Happens."

The Secret Society of Happy People would very probably have languished in relative obscurity, were it not for one particular thing. In December 1998, and with the Christmas holidays looming large, the society took issue with a certain advice columnist named Ann Landers. For reasons best known to herself, Landers told her readers that it would, perhaps, not be a good idea to send holiday newsletters to friends and family as the season grew ever nearer. Instead, Landers said that a card was enough. But it was far from being enough for the Secret Society of Happy People. Members loudly, and publicly, called for an apology from Landers, specifically to "the millions of people you made feel bad for wanting to share their happy news."

Despite being known for rarely changing her views or opinions on matters she felt were important, on this occasion Landers backed down. Because of the media publicity given to the affair, by the early 2000s the Secret Society of Happy People had followers in close to three dozen countries, spanning the globe.

But why was the Secret Society of Happy People created in the first place? According to Pamela Gail Johnson, she was sick and tired of those who

In December 1998, and with the Christmas holidays looming large, the society took issue with a certain advice columnist named Ann Landers.

seemed intent on making the lives of people miserable, and so she decided to do something about it—both whenever and wherever possible. She did so—and continues to do so—via sending out newsletters and blogging at her dedicated blog, "Ask Pamela Gail: Where Happiness Meets Reality."

The society also has a designated date—August 8—for what was originally termed Admit You're Happy Day, now known as Happiness Happens Day. And, then, there's HappyThon—a once-a-year event when members of the Secret Society of Happy People are encouraged to email, text, blog, and message as many people around the world as possible, and all with the specific and laudable intent of trying to make people happy. And, certainly, given the current state the world is in, we need it.

Secret Space Group

When, on July 20, 1969, NASA astronaut Neil Armstrong took his first steps on the surface of the Moon, it began a new era in the U.S. space program. Further manned missions continued until 1972. Plans were formulated to establish a permanent, manned base on the surface of the Moon. Then, in 1973, NASA launched its first space station, Skylab. Eight years later, the Space Shuttle was unveiled. Today, however, things are very different. NASA no longer has a manned space program. The only way for U.S. astronauts to head into Earth orbit, and spend time at the International Space Station, is to hitch a ride with the Russians. What went wrong? Some say that nothing went wrong. Rather, the theory is that although NASA's manned space program is largely no more, there exists—deep within the heart of the U.S. military—a secret group that is running a clandestine space program. We might even be talking about highly classified return missions to the Moon and possibly even secret flights to Mars.

UFO authority Richard Dolan says: "Over the years I have encountered no shortage of quiet, serious-minded people who tell me of their knowledge that there is such a covert program. Are there bases on the far side of the Moon? I do not know for sure, but I cannot rule it out."

One person who is convinced that there is a secret space group is Gary McKinnon, a British man who had a ufological Sword of Damocles hanging over his head for the better part of a decade after very unwisely deciding to hack the U.S. government for secrets of the UFO kind in 2001. According to McKinnon, while illegally surfing around classified systems of both NASA and the U.S. military, he came across a list titled "Non-Terrestrial Officers."

McKinnon said of this discovery: "It doesn't mean little green men. What I think it means is not Earth-based. I found a list of fleet-to-fleet transfers, and a list of ship names. I looked them up. They weren't U.S. Navy ships. What I saw made me believe they have some kind of spaceship, off-planet."

McKinnon was not the first to hint at the idea of a secret space group, however. As an experienced hacker of numerous computer systems, including those of NASA and the U.S. Department of Defense, a young Welshman named Matthew Bevan took the decision back in 1994 to uncover the long-rumored crashed UFO secrets of Wright Patterson Air Force Base in Dayton, Ohio. Stressing that Wright-Patterson was "a very, very easy computer system to get into," Bevan was utterly amazed to uncover astonishing information relating to a top secret project to design and build a truly extraordinary flying machine of UFO-like proportions.

British hacker Matthew Bevan claims he hacked into the computer system at Wright-Patterson AFB and discovered that the military was working on a UFO-like spacecraft.

"The files," Bevan said, "very clearly referred to a working prototype of an anti-gravity vehicle that utilized a heavy element to power it. This wasn't a normal aircraft; it was very small, split level, with a reactor at the bottom and room for the crew at the top."

Having accessed and carefully digested the fantastic information, Bevan duly exited the Wright-Patterson computer banks and began to doggedly search for alien answers, including in NASA's less-than-secure computer systems. Bevan got into the systems, carefully read the files, and escaped, all without any form of detection whatsoever.

Or so Bevan had assumed was the case. History, however, has shown that Bevan's initial assumptions were very wide of the mark. For approximately two years there was nothing but overwhelming silence. Then, on a particular morning in 1996, everything suddenly changed drastically in the life of Matthew Bevan. At the time when things began to go distinctly awry, he was working for an insurance company in Cardiff, Wales, and on the day in question he was summoned down to the managing director's office.

Upon entering the room, Bevan was confronted by a group of men in suits who seemed to practically ooze intimidation. Bevan recalled what happened next: "One of the men outstretched his hand and I shook it."

"Matthew Bevan?" the man asked.

"Yes," replied Bevan.

The man identified himself as being with Scotland Yard's Computer Crimes Unit: "I'm placing you under arrest for hacking NASA and Wright-Patterson Air Force Base.'" Bevan was in deep trouble. After being taken to Cardiff Central Police Station, the line of questioning became decidedly curious and worthy of an episode of *The X-Files*: "What does the term *Hangar 18* mean to you?" Bevan was immediately asked, in stern and intimidating tones.

"That's a hoarding place for alien technology," he replied, in a quite matter-of-fact fashion.

Bevan's recollections of that exchange were more than eye-opening. "Throughout the interview, they kept coming back to *Hangar 18*: Did I see anything on the Wright-Patterson and the NASA computers? Did I download anything? Well, when they asked me if I saw anything, I said: 'Yes, I saw emails talking about an anti-gravity propulsion system.'"

Needless to say, this did not go down too well, at all, with Scotland Yard's Computer Crimes Unit. Bevan correctly realized that he was in very hot water with the authorities, and a date was subsequently set for a hearing at London's Bow Street magistrate's court. But it was not just Bevan, his defense, and the prosecution who were present at the trial. There was also a man present representing the interests of the U.S. government and NASA.

A curious exchange occurred when the man took the stand—as Bevan remembered only too well. "As the hearing continued, the prosecution asked him what the American government thought about my motives regarding my hacking at NASA and at Wright-Patterson."

The man replied: "We now believe that Mr. Bevan had no malicious intentions and that his primary purpose was to uncover information on UFOs and *Hangar 18*."

Bevan said: "Well, everyone had a bit of a laugh at that point, even the judge; however, when the prosecution asked: 'Can you confirm if *Hangar 18* exists or if it's a myth?' the man said: 'I can neither confirm nor deny as I'm not in possession of that information.'"

The final outcome of the affair was that the case against Bevan completely collapsed. The magistrate overseeing the matter stated in no uncertain terms that a jail sentence was utterly out of the question and that any financial punishment he might be able to impose upon Bevan would be meager in the extreme. Coupled with the fact that neither NASA nor the American government as a whole was willing to divulge any and all information concerning the contents of the material on the Wright-Patterson computers to the British court, and the cost of prosecuting the case was perceived as being as high as $10,000 a day, the prosecution grudgingly elected to offer zero evidence.

Bevan's very last word on the matter: "Although I didn't print or download anything—I read it all online—I know what I read: America has a secret space plane."

Serpents, Sacrifice, and Secrets

Filey Brigg is an impressively sized, rocky peninsula that juts out from the coast of the Yorkshire, England, town of Filey. Local folklore suggests that the rocks are actually the remains of the bones of an ancient sea dragon. Unlikely, to say the least. But the story may have at least a basis in reality. In all likelihood, the story takes its inspiration from centuries-old sightings of giant monsters of the sea that called the crashing waters off Filey Brigg their home. One person who was able to attest to this was Wilkinson Herbert, a coastguard, who, in February 1934, had a traumatic, terrifying encounter with just such a sea dragon at Filey Brigg. It was—very appropriately—a dark, cloudy, and windy night when Herbert's life was turned upside down.

The first indication that something foul and supernatural was afoot came when Herbert heard the terrifying growling of what sounded like a dozen or more vicious hounds. The growling, however, was coming from something else entirely. As he looked out at the harsh, cold waves, Herbert saw—to his terror—a large beast, around thirty feet in length and equipped with a muscular, humped back, and four legs that extended into flippers. For a heart-stopping instant, the bright, glowing eyes of the beast locked onto Herbert's eyes. Not surprisingly, he said: "It was a most gruesome and thrilling experience. I have seen big animals abroad but nothing like this."

Further up the same stretch of coastland is the county of Tyne and Wear, and in the vicinity of the county's South Shields is Marsden Bay, an area that is overflowing with rich tales of magic, mystery, witchcraft, and supernatural, ghostly activity. Legend tells of a man named Jack Bates (a.k.a. "Jack the Blaster") who, with his wife, Jessie, moved to the area in 1782. Instead of setting up home in the village of Marsden itself, however, the Bates family decided that they would blast a sizeable amount of rock out of Marsden Bay and create for themselves a kind of grotto-style home.

It wasn't long before local smugglers saw Jack's cave-like environment as the ideal place to store their goods—something that led Jack to become one of their number. It was a secret working arrangement that existed until the year of Jack the Blaster's death, in 1792. The caves were later extended, to the point where they housed, rather astonishingly, a fifteen-room mansion. Today, the caves are home to the Marsden Grotto, one of the very few "cave pubs" in Europe.

Mike Hallowell is a local author-researcher who has uncovered evidence of a secret cult in the area that extends back centuries and which engages in controversial and dangerous activities. It all began with the Viking invasion of the U.K. in the ninth century and their beliefs in a violent, marauding sea monster known as the Shoney. Since the Shoney's hunting ground ranged from the coast of England to the waters of Scandinavia, and the monster had a reputation for ferociousness, the Vikings did all they could to placate it. That, primarily, meant providing the beast with certain offerings. We're talking, specifically, about *human* offerings.

> The first indication that something foul and supernatural was afoot came when Herbert heard the terrifying growling of what sounded like a dozen or more vicious hounds.

The process of deciding who would be the creature's victim was a grim one: the crews of the Viking ships would draw straws and he who drew the shortest straw would be doomed to a terrible fate. He would first be bound by hand and foot. Then, unable to move, he would have his throat violently slashed. After which, the body of the unfortunate soul would be tossed into the churning waters, with the hope that the Shoney would be satisfied and would not attack the Vikings' long-ships, as they were known. Sometimes, the bodies were never seen again. On other occasions they washed up on the shore of Marsden, hideously mutilated and savagely torn to pieces.

Incredibly, however, this was not a practice strictly limited to the long gone times when the Vikings roamed and pillaged in marauding fashion. Mike Hallowell was able to determine that belief in the Shoney never actually died out. As a result, the last such sacrifice was rumored to have occurred in 1928. Hallowell's sources also told him that the grotto's caves regularly, and secretly, acted as morgues for the bodies of the dead that the Shoney tossed back onto the beach, following each sacrifice.

And now the story becomes even more disturbing: as a dedicated researcher of the unknown, Hallowell began to dig ever deeper into the enigma of Marsden's dragon cult and even contacted local police authorities to try and determine the truth of the matter—and of the murders too, of course. It was at the height of his research that Hallowell received a number of anonymous phone calls, sternly and darkly warning him to keep away from Marsden and its tale of a "serpent sacrifice cult" and verbally threatening him as to what might happen if he didn't. To his credit, Hallowell pushed on, undeterred by the Men in Black-like threats. And, although much of the data is circumstantial, Hallowell has made a strong case that such a cult still continues its dark activities—and possibly in other parts of the U.K., too.

Shape-Shifting Pagans

The Reverend Sabine Baring-Gould (1834–1924) was someone who had a deep fascination for stories of strange creatures, including werewolves, ghouls, and a menacing phenomenon known as the *eigi einhamir*. In Baring-Gould's own words: "In Norway and Iceland certain men were said to be *eigi einhamir*, not of one skin, an idea which had its roots in paganism. The full form of this strange superstition was, that men could take upon them other bodies, and the natures of those beings whose bodies they assumed. The second adopted shape was called by the same name as the original shape, *hamr*, and the expression made use of to designate the transition from one body to another, was *at skipta homum*, or *at hamaz*; whilst the expedition made in the second form, was the *hamfor*. By this transfiguration extraordinary powers were acquired; the natural strength of the individual was doubled, or quadrupled; he acquired the strength of the beast in whose body he travelled, in addition to his own, and a man thus invigorated was called *hamrammr*."

But how exactly was transformation achieved? Baring-Gould researched this matter extensively and offered the following: "The manner in which the change was effected, varied. At times, a dress of skin was cast over the body, and at once the transformation was complete; at others, the human body was deserted,

American priest, hagiographer, and author the Reverend Sabine Baring-Gould wrote about shape shifters in Iceland and Norway.

and the soul entered the second form, leaving the first body in a cataleptic state, to all appearance dead. The second *hamr* was either borrowed or created for the purpose. There was yet a third manner of producing this effect—it was by incantation; but then the form of the individual remained unaltered, though the eyes of all beholders were charmed so that they could only perceive him under the selected form.

"Having assumed some bestial shape, the man who is *eigi einhammr* is only to be recognized by his eyes, which by no power can be changed. He then pursues his course, follows the instincts of the beast whose body he has taken, yet without quenching his own intelligence. He is able to do what the body of the animal can do, and do what he, as man, can do as well. He may fly or swim, if he is in the shape of bird or fish; if he has taken the form of a wolf, or if he goes on a *gandreid*, or wolf's-ride, he is fall of the rage and malignity of the creatures whose powers and passions he has assumed."

Shickshinny Knights of Malta

Established in 1956, the Shickshinny Knights of Malta were the brainchild of a man named Charles Pichel. Before we get to the matter of his religious order, a bit of background on Pichel himself is required. Born in New York in 1890, Pichel gravitated to Pennsylvania, and engaged in a wealth of dubious activity, including running narcotics and inventing schemes to defraud people of their hard-earned money. An ardent Roman Catholic, Pichel told anyone who would listen that he reached the rank of colonel in the U.S. Army, although such a claim has never been conclusively confirmed. His published writings include *History of the Sovereign Order of Saint John of Jerusalem, Knights of Malta, An Account of the Old Roman Catholic Church*, and *Samogitia: The Unknown in History*.

Pichel founded the group as a way to circumvent the expensive fee demanded for joining the Knights of Malta, so he created his religious, chivalric group, claiming it descended from White Russians (those opposed to the Communists).

Tony Buttigieg says of Pichel: "Pichel was not only an adherent of the Old Catholic Church but a fanatical anti-Communist who apparently actually came to believe that … his organization alone represented the true continuation of the ancient crusader order. He became increasingly eccentric (forming the Galactic Powers Task Force described above) and, in 1969, announced that he was forming the 'Maltese Cross Legionaries' to combat a secret alliance between the Holy See and the government of Malta to hand the island over to the Soviets."

As for his most famous—or, rather, infamous—creation, the Shickshinny Knights of Malta, Pichel came up with an ingenious way to entice people to join it. He claimed a direct connection between himself, his group, and the Russian Tradition of the Knights Hospitaller. The Russian Grand Priory of Malta notes that "on November 13, 1798 Tsar Paul I accepted the appointment to Grand Master of the Order of St. John of Jerusalem, Knights Hospitaller also called Knights of Rhodes and later of Malta.

"The solemn ceremony of handing over the crown and the decorations of the Grand Master took place on 29th November of that year in the Winter Palace. On that occasion the flag of the Order of St. John of Jerusalem

Emblem of the Shickshinny Knights of Malta, a chivalric group related to the older Knights of Malta.

was hoisted on the flagpole of Admiralty Palace and the Tsar ordered that the imperial coat of arms, namely the double-headed crowned eagle with spread wings, be added to the Order's emblem. That same day, the Emperor added to the existing Catholic Grand Priory of Russia (founded on the former Grand Priory of Catholic Poland, the Government of the Order of Malta Knights and all the European Knights who had reached St. Petersburg) a Grand Orthodox Priory with ten Commanderies, patronized by Russian nobility. Paul I also decreed that the title of Commander of the Order be inherited by the firstborn of those families and title of Protector by its descendants; this act, absolute and undisputable, would be the salvation of the Order."

As a result of Pichel's lies and manipulation, more than a few influential White Russians joined his group, as did powerful businessmen and members of European nobility. One of those was Peter II Karađorđević, the last king of Yugoslavia. Membership of the Shickshinny Knights of Malta also included various individuals attached to both the Minutemen and the John Birch Society. Things did not work out well for Pichel, however. Tony Buttigieg says: "In 1967 Pichel became allied with a group of Catholic traditionalists who denied the authority of the U.S. bishops and, in 1969, accused the Jesuits of manipulating the Papacy for their own ends. He also became associated with the 'alternative medicine' movement, sponsoring nature cures and promoting what he described as 'Cosmic Energy.' After the numerous divisions and quarrels among his adherents, his group ultimately fragmented and he died in very distressing circumstances in 1982 aged ninety-two."

Silver Legion of America

Better known as the Silver Shirts, the Silver Legion of America was a controversial group created in the 1930s that allied itself to the beliefs and ideology of the Nazis. Chris Valentine notes that the Silver Shirts were led by one William Dudley Pelley, who "built a Nazi bunker/compound expressly for the purpose of serving as the worldwide headquarters from which the Fascists' conquest of the world would come. The compound, called Murphy Ranch, was located in the hills of Los Angeles, California…. They were an underground group of fascists, estimated to have as many as 15,000 members back in 1934. A variation of Hitler's Brownshirts, the dress code for this group was a silver shirt and tie, blue trousers, and a hat. The shirts had the letter 'L' over the heart, which meant 'Loyalty' to the American Republic and 'Liberation' from materialism."

They were an underground group of fascists, estimated to have as many as 15,000 members back in 1934.

Holocaust Online says: "The Silver Shirts, Pelley pledged, would spearhead a new 'Christian Commonwealth' in the United States, which would register all Jews in a national census, then systematically reduce their role in business, government and cultural affairs, ultimately confining all Jews within one city in each state."

Joe Allen, who has carefully studied the history of Pelley's organization, said: "The Silver Shirts' menacing activities early on became the subject of congressional investigations. 'Arms Plot Is Laid to San Diego Nazis' was the headline of the *New York Times* on August 8, 1934. Two marines, Virgil Hayes and Edward T. Grey, infiltrated the Silver Shirts at the behest of Marine Corps intelligence and revealed the 'arms plot' to congressional investigators. Hayes testified before a congressional subcommittee in Los Angeles that the Silver Shirts had offered him money to purchase weapons stolen from military arsenals. When asked by the subcommittee investigator what the purpose of the Silver Shirts was, Hayes responded, 'To change the government, William Dudley Pelley, the national organizer told me…. He also planned to deport the Jews.' The investigator then asked him if they advocated violence to take control of the government. Hayes answered, 'Yes, I was commissioned as an instructor in military tactics with the Silver Shirts. I taught them the use of small arms and street fighting.'"

It is very disturbing to see just how quickly the Silver Shirts grew in the United States, and the extent to which they began to influence and attract like-minded individuals. Fully expecting the increasingly fascistic Germany to make its moves and to try and eventually dominate the planet, the Silver Shirts worked to ensure that they would be viewed by Hitler as allies, and that Murphy Ranch would become an integral part of the new world when Hitler invaded and conquered the United States—which, thankfully, did not happen, of course.

Things were taken to an even greater level when, in 1936, Pelley ran for the position of president of the United States. Pelley cared little about the democratic process behind American elections, however. If necessary, he told his followers, he would bypass convention and instigate a revolution, one that would involve the Silver Shirts taking over Congress, the White House, and the presidency itself. Pelley's crazed and inflated ego, combined with his unlikely plans for nationwide domination, put off some of his followers. Initially, they were willing to follow him, but, as his plans became far more grandiose, and on a par with what today we might call a supervillain from a James Bond movie, the Silver Shirts began to dwindle in number.

Matters all came crashing down for the Silver Shirts on December 7, 1941—the day on which the Japanese military launched a devastating, surprise attack on Pearl Harbor, Hawaii, a shocking event that killed thousands of Americans. As a direct result of the attack, police in the area of the Murphy Ranch stormed the facility and held the four dozen or so staff that were inside for a significant period of time. It was the beginning of the end. When war was declared on the Axis powers by President Franklin D. Roosevelt, support for the Silver Shirts crumbled.

Skinwalkers

For those who may not be fully aware of the disturbing phenomenon of the skinwalkers (or skin walkers), a bit of background data is in order. In her book *Real Wolfmen: True Encounters in Modern America*, Linda Godfrey says: "Most sources say the skin walker is the manifestation of a 'witch,' meant in the sense of a shaman or medicine person who has taken a dark path and uses magical power to hurt others. A skin walker may wear a coyote skin and can travel very speedily in animal shape."

The *Navajo Legends* website states: "To become a skinwalker requires the most evil of deeds, the killing of a close family member. They literally become humans who have acquired immense supernatural power, including the ability to transform into animals and other people. According to the Navajo skinwalker legend, these evil witches are typically seen in the form of a coyote, owl, fox, wolf, or crow—although they do have the ability to turn into any animal they choose."

Skinwalkers could take all kinds of forms, including owls, wolves, coyotes, and foxes like this one. Indeed, they could also take the form of other human beings.

As for my own involvement in the skinwalker issue, I can't claim it has been in-depth, as it most certainly has not been. Quite the opposite, in fact. But I do have one memorable and weird tale to tell, which dates back to August 2010. It was in the early part of the month that I set off for the California desert, specifically in the vicinity of Joshua Tree. The reason: to film an episode of VH1's series: *Real and Chance: The Legend Hunters*.

For those who may not know, Real and Chance (brothers Ahmad and Kamal Givens—Ahmad sadly having passed away in early 2015 from colon cancer) were two parts of the rap group The Stallionaires. They also starred in the VH1 show *Real Chance of Love*. But with the new show, Real and Chance were going to be in hot pursuit of monsters and marauding animals—including a Skinwalker.

When the production company asked me if I would be interested in hitting the road with Real and Chance, I said "Sure!" Across three days and two nights, Real, Chance, and I hung out with a woman who rescued wild and injured wolves, nursed them back to health in her sanctuary, and was not only terrified by the prospect of meeting a Skinwalker but would flatly refuse to even utter the "S word." We were taught to shoot by an old cowboy who answered only to the name of Doc. He made it very clear that if we were to encounter a Skinwalker we needed to proceed very carefully. Safety, he said, was paramount. Which basically meant we had a fine time preparing by blasting rocks and targets in the heart of the desert with our pistols. We also took part in Native American rituals designed to prepare us for, and protect us from, the potential and deep hazards ahead.

We headed out to a long-derelict ranch where, even as far back as the early 1980s, farm animals had been attacked and killed in violent fashion by something large, powerful, and dangerous, and we spent a night chasing something that stole a dead chicken (which had a tracking device attached to it) from under our very noses, and right around where the slaughtering had taken place some three decades earlier.

So, did we come face to face with a Skinwalker? Well, I can't say for certain. But what I can say is that we really did find ourselves confronted by a huge, dark wolf late on the final night of filming. It was an incredible beast, captured for onscreen posterity by VH1's camera crew. For several minutes, the animal loomed above us on a rocky outcrop that sat above a deep and shadow-filled cave. It stared intently at us, in eerie fashion. Then, without warning, it turned and vanished into the desert night.

As we continued to scour the area, Real, Chance and I checked out the entrance to the cave—where we found the remains of the chicken, minus the tracking device. Since a Skinwalker can take on the guise of a wolf, and have been reported in and around caves, this might make some think we really did encounter such a thing. Me? I don't know. What I do know, however, is that it was a very creepy ending to a highly entertaining few days in search of a monster in the California desert.

Skull and Bones

One of the most mysterious of all secret societies—one shrouded in intrigue and filled with influential figures—is Skull and Bones. It was formed in 1832 at Yale University, in New Haven, Connecticut, the origins of which date back to 1701. The founders of Skull and Bones were William Huntingdon Russell, a powerful businessman and a notable figure in the history of the Republican Party, and Alphonso Taft, who—under U.S. president Ulysses S. Grant—held the positons of both secretary of war and attorney general. As a result of significant differences between various debating groups at Yale, Taft and Russell elected to create their very own elite group: Skull and Bones, of course.

Kris Millegan, the editor of the *Conspiracy Theory Research List*, says: "According to information acquired from a break-in to the 'tomb' (the Skull and Bones meeting hall) in 1876, 'Bones is a chapter of a corps in a German University.... General Russell, its founder, was in Germany before his Senior Year and formed a warm friendship with a leading member of a German society. He brought back with him to college, authority to found a chapter here.' So class valedictorian William H. Russell, along with fourteen others, became the founding members of 'The Order of Scull and Bones,' later changed to 'The Order of Skull and Bones.'"

As a demonstration of how Skull and Bones developed a reputation as a powerful and shadowy order, we have the following from the October 1873 premier edition of *The Iconoclast*. Its staff held nothing back when it came to the matter of warning people of the power and influence that Skull and Bones wielded, and on an ever-growing basis, too: "Out of every class Skull and Bones takes its men. They have gone out into the world and have become, in many instances, leaders in society. They have obtained control of Yale. Its business is performed by them. Money paid to the college must pass into their hands, and

An 1879 photography of the Tomb, the meeting place of the Skull and Bones society at Yale University.

be subject to their will. No doubt they are worthy men in themselves, but the many, whom they looked down upon while in college, cannot so far forget as to give money freely into their hands. Men in Wall Street complain that the college comes straight to them for help, instead of asking each graduate for his share. The reason is found in a remark made by one of Yale's and America's first men: 'Few will give but Bones men and they care far more for their society than they do for the college....'"

The Iconoclast added: "Year by year the deadly evil is growing. The society was never as obnoxious to the college as it is today, and it is just this ill-feeling that shuts the pockets of non-members. Never before has it shown such arrogance and self-fancied superiority. It grasps the College Press and endeavors to rule it all. It does not deign to show its credentials, but clutches at power with the silence of conscious guilt."

Anthony C. Sutton is the author of a very revealing book, *America's Secret Establishment.* In its pages, Sutton says of Skull and Bones, "The order is not just another Greek letter fraternal society with passwords and handgrips common to most campuses. Chapter 322 is a secret society whose members are sworn to silence. It only exists on the Yale campus (that we know about). It has rules. It has ceremonial rites. It is not at all happy with prying, probing citizens—known among initiates as 'outsiders' or 'vandals.' Its members always deny membership (or are supposed to deny membership) and in checking hundreds of autobiographical listings for members we found only half a dozen who cited an affiliation with Skull & Bones. The rest were silent."

The membership of Skull and Bones is both illustrious and controversial and has included U.S. presidents William Howard Taft, George H. W. Bush, and George W. Bush, as well as Secretary of State John Kerry. *Time* magazine says of Skull and Bones: "Bonesmen have, at one time, controlled the fortunes of the Carnegie, Rockefeller and Ford families, as well as posts in the Central Intelligence Agency, the American Psychological Association, the Council on Foreign Relations and some of the most powerful law firms in the world."

Within the field of conspiracy theorizing, Skull and Bones is said to have played major roles in the November 22, 1963, assassination of President John F. Kennedy, the Iran-Contra scandal of the 1980s, and the "rigging" of the 2000 U.S. election.

Slenderman Cult

The Slenderman is a fictional character created in June 2009 by Eric Knudsen (using the alias of "Victor Surge," at the forum section of the *Something Awful* website), who took his inspiration from the world of horror fiction. The Slenderman is a creepy creature: tall, thin, with long arms, a blank (faceless, even) expression, and wearing a dark suit. It sounds almost like a nightmarish version of the Men in Black. While there is no doubt that Knudsen was the creator of what quickly became a definitive, viral meme, people have since claimed to have seen the Slenderman in the real world.

In other words, so the theory goes, it's a case of believing in the existence of the Slenderman and, as a result, causing it to actually exist—which is very much akin to the phenomenon of the Tulpa. An entity is envisaged in the mind, and the imagery becomes so powerful and intense that it causes that same, mind-based imagery to emerge into the real world, with some degree of independent existence and self-awareness. Such a scenario may well explain why people are now seeing something that began as a piece of fiction.

In a January 24, 2015, article that appeared in the U.K.-based *Birmingham Mail* newspaper (titled "Spooky Slender Men spotted in Cannock"), Mike Lockley wrote: "A paranormal probe has been launched in the Midlands following FOUR sightings of Slender Men—long, stick thin specters feared around the world. Each of the chilling close encounters took place in the Cannock area, and now X Files investigator Lee Brickley is trying to fathom why the ghoul has descended on the Staffordshire mining town. Slender Men have been a part of global folklore for centuries. They may be known by different names, but their harrowing, elongated appearance remains the same around the world."

In the words of the witness: "This character was tall, with very thin arms and legs, dressed in what I presumed were grey trousers and a tight long sleeved shirt of the same color. His hairless head was elongated and neck spindly, and his arms reached practically past

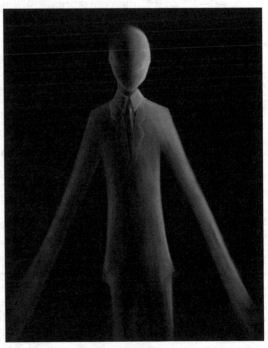

An artist's depiction of what Slenderman might look like.

his knees; I could not discern a facial feature. I realized he was around three meters tall."

Writer "Red Pill Junkie" notes that in 2014 "the creepy avatar took a much more sinister and serious spin when news broke about two teenage girls from southeastern Wisconsin [Morgan Geyser and Anissa Weier] who lured one of their 'friends' deep into the woods, stabbed her 19 times, and left her for dead. The heinous crime, the teens confessed to the authorities once their victim miraculously managed to pull herself out of the forest, had been planned as a ritual sacrifice to win the favor of Slenderman, with which they had acquired a disturbing obsession."

Let us hope that we hear no more of Slenderman-connected sacrifices.

Sonora Aero Club

Was a secret society, one that was obsessed with flight and fantastical flying contraptions, surfing the skies of the United States way back in the nineteenth century? It might sound wholly unfeasible to many, given that it was not until December 17, 1903, that the Wright brothers, Wilbur and Orville, made the first heavier-than-air flight at Kitty Hawk, North Carolina. Yet, as incredible as it may seem, the history books just might need revising— and revising to significant degrees, too. The story is a strange one and revolves around a man named Charles Dellschau.

John Lienhard says of Dellschau: "In 1850 Charles Dellschau immigrated from Prussia to Galveston, Texas. By the time the Civil War started he'd married a widow with a young daughter and was working as a butcher in Fort Bend County, near Houston. Other than service in the Confederate Army, he lived an unremarkable life. He had two more children of his own. His stepdaughter married the noted saddle-maker Stelzig. Then, in 1877, disaster struck 47-year-old Dellschau. In rapid succession his wife, then his six-year-old son, died. Dellschau moved into Houston to work for Stelzig as a clerk. Here he stayed until 1923 when he died at the age of 93."

There was, however, another side to Dellschau, a very strange and secret one. Just one year before the dawning of the twentieth century, Dellschau began to do something that many might find strange. Or, at the very least, a tad eccentric. He spent hours upon hours creating fantastic artwork showing equally fantastic flying machines, many of an airship-style nature.

Cynthia Greenwood, who is well versed in the saga of Dellschau, says: "His intricate collages show ship-like decks supported by striped balloon pontoons; they show bright-colored helicopters and evil-looking striped dirigibles outfitted for war; they show crews of dapper little gentlemen accompanied by the occasional cat. Many pages are bedecked with little newspaper clippings about aviation, and text in his weird Germanic lettering celebrates the pure, unexcelled marvelousness of the flying machines."

And, how do we know all this? Thanks to a strange set of circumstances, that's how. It was back in 1969 that a man named Fred Washington—who specialized in buying and selling used furniture—purchased a dozen old journals from a garbage collector. Washington did nothing more with them than find a place for them in his warehouse and leave them there. Things changed, however, when an art student named Mary Jane Victor came on the scene, not long after Washington made his purchase.

It was all down to random chance that Victor stumbled upon Dellschau's journals. A careful study of their contents by Victor revealed something amazing: they contained no fewer than close to 2,600 drawings of bizarre aircraft, the majority of which were done in watercolors and collages. In no time at all, Victor, realizing that her find was a significant one, contacted the art director of the William Marsh Rice University at Houston, Texas—Dominique de Menil, who quickly offered $1,500 for four of the journals. Dellschau was soon fairly big news.

> **I**t was all down to random chance that Victor stumbled upon Dellschau's journals. A careful study of their contents by Victor revealed something amazing....

Cynthia Greenwood says: "Taken at face value, Dellschau's collages document the feats of the Sonora Aero Club, a secretive group dedicated to the creation of 'aeros,' or flying machines. In code, and bad spelling in both English and German, Dellschau recounted how, in his youth 50 years before, he and fellow club members gleefully ruled the skies of Gold Rush California, piloting fantastical airships of their own invention."

A study of Dellschau's collective artwork and diaries reveals that his work spanned from 1899 to 1922. It told of a secret and groundbreaking organization called the Sonora Aero Club, a group to which Dellschau was closely allied. According to Dellschau's curious story, one particular member of the Sonora Aero Club had found a way to make heavier-than-air flight possible. It was all down to an "anti-gravity fuel" known as "NB Gas." As for the craft themselves, they were known by the club as "Aeros."

Those of a skeptical nature suggest that Dellschau's extensive body of artwork and words amounted to either (a) a huge and intricate fantasy of his own

Drawing of a UFO seen flying over the Sacramento, California, area in 1896. That year, reports of UFOs came rolling in from all across the United States.

making and for his own amusement and entertainment or (b) a deliberate hoax on his part. The fact is, however, that the latter part of the 1890s saw the birth of what became known as "phantom airships"—strange flying machines that captured the attention of the media and the American people, and which were somewhat of a precursor to the dawning of the flying saucer in 1947.

Lee Krystek says of the mysterious airships: "Eighteen ninety-six was marked by a strange occurrence, an amazing phenomenon that those that saw it probably never forgot. People, by the thousands, living across North America, from San Francisco to Chicago, observed strange lights in the sky. The lights, reportedly an airship, crossed the continent from west to east while the country watched."

Krystek adds: "Was there really a mysterious inventor who secretly built an airship and flew it around the country? Certainly the public had been primed to accept such a story. Science fiction in this era often used the 'mystery inventor' as a character. Jules Verne's *20,000 Leagues Under the Sea* featured a mystery inventor, Captain Nemo, who constructed a submarine. Verne's later book, *Robur the Conqueror*, featured a mystery inventor that built an airship and the similarities between the book and some of the airship stories are uncanny. *Robur* was published about ten years before the wave of airship sightings. If there was a real airship genius why didn't he ever make his invention public? Could he have really kept the construction of a flying machine out of the press? Was he really ten years ahead of his contemporary inventors?"

Perhaps, Charles Dellschau and the Sonora Aero Club were indeed the very mystery inventors to which Krystek referred.

Sons of Lee Marvin

While the term "secret society" is all but guaranteed to provoke imagery of powerful and dangerous groups engaged in all manner of clandestine operations, such is not always the case. Sometimes, a secret society is just a bit of fun—albeit in a very odd way. Take, for example, the Sons of Lee Marvin. That's right: we're talking about Lee Marvin, the late actor. *Dangerous Minds* says: "Back in the 1980s Tom Waits, Jim Jarmusch, John Lurie, and maybe one or two others started a facetious little organization called the Sons of Lee Marvin in honor of one of their favorite actors. As it is a secret society, details are scarce—Nick Cave is in the club, and the director John Boorman has been given an honorary membership. It is rumored that Thurston Moore, Iggy Pop, Josh Brolin, and Neil Young are also in the group. If you would like to join the Sons of Lee Marvin, here's all you have to do: 1. Be born with a penis. 2. Have 'a facial structure such that you could be related to, or be a son of, Lee Marvin.' 3. Develop an intense fondness for Lee Marvin, especially how his characters are 'outsiders and very violent' and 'have a very strong code.' 4. Achieve significant notoriety as an adorable bohemian/downtown musician or filmmaker. 5. Become close buddies with Jim Jarmusch."

Jarmusch, who was the prime mover in getting this very alternative secret society into existence, says, in decidedly tongue-in-cheek fashion: "I'm not at liberty to divulge information about the organization, other than to tell you that it does exist. I can identify three other members of the organization: Tom Waits, John Lurie, and Richard Bose. You have to have a facial structure such that you could be related to, or be a son of, Lee Marvin. There are no women, obviously, in the organization. We have communiques and secret meetings. Other than that, I can't talk about it."

Tom Waits, with good humor, says of the Sons of Lee Marvin: "It's a mystical organization and they have a New York chapter, and we met at one of the annual meetings. It's somewhere between the Elks Club and the Academy Awards."

If you're too young to know who Lee Marvin was, and you're wondering what all the fuss is about, here's a bit of background from *Biography.com*: "Actor Lee Marvin was born on February 19, 1924, in New York City. He eventually earned lead roles when his aggressive nature was perceived by such directors as Edward Dmytryk, Fritz Lang, and John Boorman. Marvin appeared in about 70 films between 1951 and 1986. He first branched out into sympathetic film roles in the early 1960s, partly thanks to his role in TV's *M Squad*. He died on August 29, 1987, in Tucson, Arizona.

Actor Lee Marvin is shown here in a still from the 1959 TV show *M Squad*. A secret society was named after him just for fun.

Sons of Satan

Since at least 1967, reports have surfaced throughout the United States of animals—but, chiefly, cattle—slaughtered in bizarre fashion. Organs are taken and significant amounts of blood are found to be missing. In some cases, the limbs of the cattle are broken, suggesting they have been dropped to the ground from a significant height. Evidence of extreme heat, which burns into the skin of the animals, has been found at mutilation sites. Eyes are removed, tongues are sliced off, and, typically, the sexual organs are gone. While the answers to the puzzle remain frustratingly outside of the public arena, theories abound. They include extraterrestrials, engaged in nightmarish experimentation of the genetic kind; military programs involving the testing of new bio-warfare weapons; and government agencies secretly monitoring the food chain, fearful that something worse than Mad Cow Disease may have infected the U.S. cattle herd—and, possibly, as a result, the human population, too. Then there is the matter of the Sons of Satan, a secret cult that engaged in the sacrifice of cattle to their lord and master, the Devil himself.

The story dates back to 1974 and an inmate of the Federal Penitentiary in Leavenworth, Kansas. The year had barely begun when one of the prisoners at Leavenworth—a man named A. Kenneth Bankston—penned a letter to a well-known UFO investigator, Jerome Clark. Bankston's reasoning for contacting Clark was simple enough: one year earlier, in 1973, Clark wrote an article on the cattle mutilation puzzle for *Fate* magazine. So Bankston was looking for someone with whom he could share his story—a story focused on the aforementioned Sons of Satan.

Given that the cattle mutilation hysteria was at its height in the mid-1970s, it's not at all surprising that others, besides Clark, were also writing about the grisly mystery. One of them was Kevin D. Randle, a noted UFO authority. Randle's article, "The Killer Cult Terrorizing Mid-America," appeared in *Saga*, just shortly after Clark's was published. Both men discussed the "cult" angle, which was gaining more and more interest.

Among those who were interested in the cattle mutilation problem—but who was not overly convinced that it had a connection to the UFO issue—was Dr. J. Allen Hynek, of the Center for UFO Studies. Hynek, at the time, was liaising with an agent of the Federal Bureau of Alcohol, Tobacco, and Firearms—Donald E. Flickinger—who had a personal interest in UFOs. Flickinger, when approached by Hynek, agreed to undertake an investigation into the cattle mutilation controversy. While Flickinger did not find any evidence suggestive of a UFO connection to the cattle killings, he did note that "a certain pattern existed" when it came to the nature of the attacks, the removal of organs, and the significant blood loss.

When Jerome Clark heard of Flickinger's studies, he provided the BATF agent with copies of A. Kenneth Bankston's correspondence. Bankston's story was as eye-opening as it was controversial. The Sons of Satan was a powerful, very well-hidden group that had seemingly endless funding and manpower and was led by a mysterious character, only referred to as "Howard." The secret group was determined to provoke "hell on earth." and the sacrificial rites were a way to ensure that Satan would aid in the group's efforts to create hellish mayhem.

U.S. authorities did not dismiss Bankston's story. In fact, the exact opposite was the order of the day. Flickinger wasted no time in calling the Minneapolis U.S. Attorney's Office. When the facts were outlined, the office agreed that an investigation should proceed—and proceed quickly. As a result, Bankston and another inmate, a man named Dan Dugan, who asserted he was a member of the Sons of Satan, were moved from Leavenworth to another prison. Whereas Leavenworth was a high-security facility, the situation at the new jail was far more relaxed.

Of course, one could make a very good case that Bankston and Dugan made the whole thing up, primarily as a means to make it appear they were trying to help clear up a very disturbing mystery—a mystery that the government dearly wanted clearing up. In other words, by helping the authorities, the pair hoped that as a "thank you" they would be moved from the oppressive environment at Leavenworth—which is exactly what happened.

It must be said, however, that this does not mean the story of Bankston and Dugan was without merit. The story was detailed, plausible, and—as far as the police were concerned—viewed as being far more likely than the sensationalized UFO explanation. Indeed, acting on the words of the two prisoners, law enforcement officials approached numerous Satanic cults in the United States, including Anton LaVey's Church of Satan. Despite such approaches, the secret order of the Sons of Satan was never found or exposed. Today, the cattle mutilation mystery continues—and also remains steadfastly unresolved.

Sorceresses

In 1939, Alfred Richard Allinson said: "For a thousand years the people had one healer and one only, the Sorceress. Emperors and kings and popes, and the richest barons, had sundry Doctors of Salerno, or Moorish and Jewish physicians; but the main body of every State, the whole world we may say, consult-

Sometimes called the wise woman or witch, the sorceress is a figure dating back through ancient times, through the Middle Ages, and beyond.

ed no one but the Saga, the Wise Woman. If her cure failed, they abused her and called her a Witch. But more generally, through a combination of respect and terror, she was spoken of as the Good Lady, or Beautiful Lady (Bella Donna), the same name as that given to fairies."

Allinson also said of these elite bands of sorceresses—who held their secrets close to their hearts—that their fate "resembled that which still often befalls [their] favorite herb, the belladonna, and other beneficent poisons she made use of, and which were antidotes of the great scourges of the Middle Ages. Children and ignorant passers-by cursed these somber flowers, without understanding their virtues, scared by their suspicious color. They shudder and fly the spot; yet these are the Comforting plants (Solanaceæ), which, wisely administered, have worked so many cures and soothed so much human agony."

Allinson noted that such plants were found growing "in the most sinister localities, in lonely, ill-reputed spots, amid ruins and rubbish heaps—yet another resemblance with the Sorceress who utilizes them."

He continued: "Where, indeed, could she have taken up her habitation, except on savage heaths, this child of calamity, so fiercely persecuted, so bitterly cursed and proscribed? She gathered poisons to heal and save; she was the Devil's bride, the mistress of the Incarnate Evil One, yet how much good she effected, if we are to credit the great physician of the Renaissance! Paracelsus, when in 1527, at Bâle, he burned the whole pharmacopúia of his day, declared he had learned from the Sorceresses all he knew."

And, finally, we have this from Allinson: "Had they not earned some reward? Yes! and reward they had. Their recompense was torture and the stake. New punishments were devised for their especial benefit, new torments invented. They were brought to trial en masse, condemned on the slightest pretext. Never was such lavish waste of human life. To say nothing of Spain, the classic land of the auto-da-fé, where Moor and Jew are always associated with Witches, seven thousand were burned at Trèves, and I know not how many at Toulouse; at Geneva five hundred in three months (1513); eight hundred at Wurzburg, in one batch almost, and fifteen hundred at Bamberg."

Soul Stealing

In early 2007, I conducted a series of extensive interviews with Ray Boeche, an Anglican priest and a former MUFON state director for Nebraska. The subject was Ray's 1991-onwards contact with a pair of U.S. Department of Defense physicists who were working on a classified program to contact what they termed Non-Human Entities, or NHEs. Many within the field of ufology might call them aliens or extraterrestrials. The group that Ray's informants were working for defined them as something else, something very different, and something deeply controversial and ominous: demons.

It was thanks to Boeche's revelations, in a roundabout way, that I was put on the trail of the so-called Collins Elite. The CE was (and, possibly, still is) a quasi-official think tank-type group in government that believes the UFO phenomenon does not originate within the heart of some faraway star system, but rather in the pits of Hell.

But what's interesting is that during the course of my research into the Collins Elite, I found evidence of what sounds suspiciously like yet another secret group in the U.S. government that was studying the Demonic UFO theory. This group, however, appears to have been operating at an even greater level of secrecy than the Collins Elite. Moreover, it appears that whatever this other group may have been, it took careful and stealthy steps to keep knowledge of its existence far away from the eyes and ears of the Collins Elite. Perhaps it's still doing that.

> **T**he CE [is] ... a quasi-official think tank-type group in government that believes the UFO phenomenon does not originate within the heart of some faraway star system, but rather in the pits of Hell.

That both groups seemed to cover very similar areas of research might make many wonder why they did not share their data, or even combine it into one, unified project. Within the world of officialdom, however, secrecy and a "need to know" (or, in this case, a definitive need not to know) reign supreme. So, in that sense, the idea of two groups following a near-identical agenda may not be so strange after all.

On the very matter of this other group—which I still have not been able to identify, unfortunately—I had the opportunity to conduct a face-to-face interview with a now-retired university professor in the field of theology who appears to have had direct contact with the group more than forty years ago.

"Two government people" had quietly consulted him, in 1972, at the professor's place of work, and the reasoning behind the consultation was simple, but disturbing, too. The two men identified themselves as employees of the

Department of Defense, said they were "knowing" of his work, and represented a group within government that believed that the many tales of extraterrestrial visitations that had surfaced since the 1940s were actually evidence of the presence of satanic forces engaging in worldwide deceit.

These forces had two goals: (A) encourage and entice the human race to follow their dark ways, and (B) ensnare the souls of one and all for reasons that not even the Bible touched upon, but that were apparently related to the "ingestion" of the human life-force in some not-exactly understood fashion.

What the professor described when I interviewed him was something chillingly like the scenes in the first *Matrix* movie, when Keanu Reeves's character, Neo, "wakes up" to find we're all living in a dream world. It's a world in which we are "grown" by machines that, essentially, farm us for energy. As the movie memorably suggests, we are the equivalent of batteries: a power-source, fuel, and nothing else.

The secret group had, by 1972, concluded that what has become known as Hell was not a fiery pit overseen by Satan, but some form of extra-dimensional realm inhabited by dark entities with a profound hatred of the human race, who "farm" our "soul-energy" upon death, for reasons that were hypothesized and suspected, but never ultimately proved.

Of course, 1972 was years before *The Matrix* hit the big screen. But, the only major differences were that (A) in the movie we are being milked by machines, whereas in the minds of the secret group, it was extra-dimensional entities that were doing the milking; and (B) in *The Matrix* it's our bodies that are being used, but for the group it was our life-force, our soul.

Space Shuttle *Challenger*

Shortly before midday on January 28, 1986, NASA suffered a terrible catastrophe: the destruction of the *Challenger* space shuttle. Worse still, all of the crew lost their lives in the fiery explosion that took out the shuttle. They were: pilot Michael J. Smith, payload specialists Gregory Jarvis and Christa McAuliffe, mission specialists Ellison Onizuka, Judith Resnik and Ronald McNair, and the commander of the flight, Dick Scobee. And, although the official verdict was that the *Challenger* disaster occurred as a result of wholly down-to-earth reasons, a wealth of conspiracy theories surfaced in the wake of the affair, all of which were carefully investigated by none other than the FBI. Before we get to the conspiracy theories, however, let's first take a look at what we know for sure, based upon NASA's careful study of all the evidence available.

The flight of *Challenger*—dubbed Mission 51-L—commenced at 11:38 A.M. EST. In no time whatsoever, it was all over. Just seventy-three seconds into the flight, a deadly explosion of oxygen and hydrogen propellants blew up the shuttle's external tank. The result, as NASA noted, was that this "exposed the Orbiter to severe aerodynamic loads that caused complete structural breakup. All seven crew members perished. The two Solid Rocket Boosters flew out of the fireball and were destroyed by the Air Force range safety officer 110 seconds after launch."

But, how did such a thing happen?

Although NASA's official conclusion was that the destruction of the *Challenger* and the deaths of the crew were the collective result of a terrible accident, in no time at all conspiracy theories surfaced, all of which suggested the event was not the accident that many concluded it to be. They were conspiracy theories that reached the very heart of the FBI. Interestingly, the FBI did not ignore or write off the claims. Instead, they launched concerted investigations to get to the truth. We know this, as the FBI's lengthy file on the

The crew of the *Challenger* included (back row, left to right) Ellison S. Onizuka, Sharon Christa McAuliffe, Greg Jarvis, and Judy Resnik, and front row (left to right) Michael J. Smith, Dick Scobee, and Ron McNair.

Challenger conspiracy has now been declassified, thanks to the provisions of the Freedom of Information Act.

One of those investigations revolved around the unusual and controversial claims that an ancient order—a secret society, one might say—of Japanese terrorists was behind the attack. It's a strange saga, made even stranger by the fact that, even today, nearly thirty pages of material on the affair remain classified—specifically for reasons having a bearing on the safety of the nation. It revolved around the claims of a woman who maintained two things: (a) that the destruction of the space shuttle was the work of Japanese terrorists, and (b) that her information on the matter was channeled into her mind by highly advanced extraterrestrials.

From practically the very beginning, the FBI's files detail the controversy surrounding the woman in question. The Bureau recorded, in its documents on the case, that the woman "claims to be in contact with certain psychic forces that provide her with higher information on selected subjects. She refers to these forces as 'Source' and when providing information from Source she often speaks in the collective 'we.' [She] claimed that she had come to Washington, D.C., to provide information concerning the *Challenger* Space Shuttle explosion on 1/28/86."

She did precisely that and provided the information on February 24, 1986.

Her claims were controversial: she maintained that the terrorist group in question had an ancient "ancestral lineage," and was partly composed of two workers at the Kennedy Space Center and one of the astronauts who died in the disaster: mission specialist Ellison Onizuka. As the FBI agents working on the case listened carefully—and, perhaps, a bit dubiously too—they were told that the group in question had a deep hatred of the United States and, by destroying the shuttle, wished to destabilize the U.S. space program and American morale. Whether the woman's story was true or not, it is a fact that the U.S. public was indeed shocked to the core, and the space shuttle program was put on hold for no fewer than thirty-two months.

When the agents asked the woman how the sabotage was achieved, they got a detailed answer: "The explosion was effected by a device placed inside the external fuel tank of the Shuttle. An individual whose description seems to match that of an engineer or technician placed this charge. The charge was triggered by a second saboteur using a hand-held transmitter while standing in the crowds watching the Shuttle lift-off. The individual matches the description of a guard or security person. The astronaut saboteur chose to die in the explosion as a sort of ritual death or 'cleansing.'"

As with all of the previous cases that the FBI had looked into, this one led nowhere—at least, that is the assumption, since no arrests were made. The odd affair came to a complete halt just weeks after it commenced.

The destruction of the *Challenger* space shuttle, on January 28, 1986 remains to this day one of the worst moments in NASA's history. Whether it was a moment provoked by nothing stranger than a terrible accident, or something filled to the brim with conspiracy theories and sinister, ruthless characters, very much depends on who you ask.

SS

Heinrich Himmler was acknowledged by many historians as being the driving force behind what became known as "Esoteric Hitlerism." Without doubt, he was a character of prime significance for the officially sanctioned research and practice of mysticism by the Nazis. He was a man who, perhaps more than any other high-ranking official in the Third Reich, was obsessed with the notion of pan-Aryan racialism and Germanic neo-Paganism, the occult, and astrology. In 1935, Himmler became a key player in the establishment of what became known as the Ahnenerbe, the ancestral heritage division of the SS—which was the paramilitary arm of the Nazi regime, created in 1925. Overseen by one Dr. Hermann Wirth, its chief motivation was research in the field of archaeology; however, its work also spilled over into areas such as demonstrating the supposed superiority of the Aryans and investigating the occult—the latter, primarily from the perspective of determining if it was a tool that could be useful to further strengthen the Nazi war machine.

The SS also had its very own mystical religion, vaguely based upon imagery taken from Germanic tribal faiths, that was then intertwined with certain aspects of Christianity—the prime purpose of which was to counter what the SS viewed as the Jewish-influenced religion of Christianity. Similarly, the official newspaper of the SS, *Das Schwarze Korps*, or *The Black Corps* (to give it its English translation), which was published from 1935 to 1945, ran articles that emphasized some of the occult-based beliefs of the organization, including the theory that the so-called Nordic supermen had their origins in the region of the North Pole that they believed was home to the original bloodline of the so-called Master Race.

In 1935, *Das Schwarze Korps* commissioned Heinar Schilling, a professor of Germanic history, to write for them a series of reports on the more significant aspects of early Germanic life. So popular did the reports become that they were ultimately bound together in 1937 in a book titled *Germanisches Leben*, which covered such issues as nature worship, Sun-based religions, and various Germanic cults, secret and otherwise.

SS officials, including Heinrich Himmler (front row, third from the left), are shown in this 1941 photo visiting a concentration camp.

It's known that the Germanic people of the late Bronze Age had adopted a four-spoke wheel as being symbolic of the Sun, and that this same symbol ultimately developed into the swastika of Nazi Germany; the notion was that the Nordics were the bringers of light—which is highly ironic in view of the fact that, in reality, they brought nothing but darkness to the world, and killed millions of people in the process.

The utilization of runic symbology, as well as the existence of the aforementioned officially sanctioned Nazi government department devoted to the study of the Germanic ancestral heritage (including paganism), has given much credence to the idea that there was a pagan component to Nazism, too. Certainly, at least as early as 1940, the occult scholar and folklorist Lewis Spence succeeded in identifying a distinctly neo-pagan undercurrent in Nazism, for which he largely blamed Alfred Rosenberg, and which he literally equated with Satanism.

STAC

As mentioned earlier in this book, in 1991 a Nebraskan priest named Ray Boeche was exposed to the bizarre world of a secret think tank-style group in the U.S. government referred to as the Collins Elite. It was the group's conclusion that the UFO phenomenon is not extraterrestrial in origin, but rather nothing less than full-blown demonic. The Collins Elite, however, was only one of several secret groups within the U.S. government that was investigating this particularly controversial issue at the time. Another was known as STAC—although, unfortunately, we don't presently know what those letters stand for, such is the high classification of the program. The two Department of Defense physicists whom Boeche met in 1991, and who revealed to him the work of the Collins Elite, also provided him with astonishing data on STAC—although Boeche was not given the name of this second group. Boeche's words, however, make it very clear that they were digging in very dangerous areas: "I found it interesting because they had contacted me at work; and I have no idea how they tracked me down there. But, they wanted to know if we could get together and have lunch to discuss something important. I met them for a brief period of time on that first meeting, and then they said: 'We'd like to get together and have a longer conversation.' I arranged a time and it was quite a lengthy discussion, probably three and a half hours, and that's how it all came about.

"After both meetings, when I was able to verify that the men held the degrees they claimed to hold, and were apparently who they claimed to be, I was intrigued and excited at the possibility of having stumbled on a more or less untouched area which could be researched. But I was also cautious in terms of 'why me?'

"I had no way of knowing before our face-to-face meeting if there was any legitimacy to this at all. I wasn't given any information at all before our meeting, just the indication that they were involved in areas of research I would find interesting, and that they had some concerns they wished to discuss with me. Both men were physicists. I'd guess they were probably in their early to mid-fifties, and they were in a real moral dilemma. Both of them were Christians, and were working on a Department of Defense project that involved trying to contact the NHEs [Non-Human Entities]. In fact, this was described to me as an 'obsessive effort' and part of this effort was to try and control the NHEs and use their powers in military weapons applications and in intelligence areas, such as remote viewing and psychotronic weapons.

"They came to believe that the NHEs were not extraterrestrial at all; they believed they were some sort of demonic entities, and that regardless of how benevolent or beneficial any of the contact they had with these entities *seemed* to be, it always ended up being tainted, for lack of a better term, with something that ultimately turned out to be bad. There was ultimately *nothing* positive from the interaction with the NHE entities. They felt it really fell more under the category of some vast spiritual deception instead of UFOs and aliens. In the course of the whole discussion, it was clear that they really viewed this as having a demonic origin that was there to simply try and confuse the issue in terms of who they were, what they wanted, and what the source of the ultimate truth is. If you extrapolate from their take that these are demons in the biblical sense of the word, then what they would be doing here is trying to create a spiritual deception to fool as many people as possible.

"From what they told me, it seemed like someone had invoked something and it opened a doorway to let these things in. That's certainly the impression they gave me. I was never able to get an exact point of origin of these sorts of experiments, or of their involvement, and when they got started. But I did get the impression that because of what they knew and the information that they presented, they had been involved for at least several years, even if the project had gone on for much longer. They were concerned that they had undertaken this initially with the best of intentions, but then as things developed they saw a very negative side to it that wasn't apparent earlier. So, that's what leads me to think they had a relatively lengthy involvement.

Demons have long been a part of cultures all over the world (architectural ornamentation seen here from Kiev, for example). What if they were real? What if they were connected to UFOs?

"Most of it was related to psychotronic weaponry and remote viewing, and even deaths by what were supposed to be psychic methods. The project personnel were allowed to assume they had somehow technologically mastered the ability to do what the NHEs could do: remote viewing and psychotronics. But, in actuality, it was these entities doing it all the time, or allowing it to happen, for purposes that suited their deception. With both psychotronic weapons and remote viewing, I was told that the DoD had not really mastered a technology to do that at all; they were allowed by the NHEs to think that this is what they had done. But the NHEs were always the causal factor.

"They showed me a dozen photos of three different people—four photos of each person, who had apparently been killed by these experiments. These were all post-mortem photographs, taken in-situ, after the experiments. The areas shown in all of the photographs were like a dentist's chair or a barber's chair, and the bodies were still in those positions, sitting in the chairs. Still there, with EEG and EKG leads coming off of them. They were all wired. It was a very clinical setting, and there was no indication of who they were. It was a very disturbing sort of thing, and I'm thinking in the back of my mind: if these are real, who would they have gotten for these experiments? Were they volunteers? Were they some sort of prisoners? I have no idea. Were they American? Were they foreign? There was no way to tell.

"They had read some of my stuff, and they knew that I'd become a pastor and that I had a Christian viewpoint from which I could examine these things, and they were concerned morally and ethically that they had allowed themselves to be duped into doing this research, and it had taken such a turn. My concern was always that: why come to me? Who am I? I can't do anything for you. I'm happy to evaluate it as best I can, but if you have this concern, why not go to a Christian leader with a lot more clout and public visibility than I've got? But that was their reason: they were aware of the research I had done on a lot of things, that I could approach it from a Christian viewpoint, and that it was more of a moral dilemma for them. They wanted the information out there. But, to me, I have to think: is any of this accurate? On one hand, is this a way to throw disinformation out? But, on the other hand, I think that even if they wanted to just spread disinformation, they could have done it with someone a lot more influential than me.

"I've been involved in this since 1965 and this is the most bizarre stuff I've ever run across. I didn't know what to make of it then and I don't know what to make of it now."

Star Wars Secret Group

To many, it might sound like the ultimate plotline of the equally ultimate conspiracy thriller: dozens of scientists and technicians—all working on highly classified programs, and all linked to one, particular company—dead under highly controversial and unusual circumstances. It's a controversy that ran from the early 1980s to 1991 and remains unresolved to this very day, and it all revolves around the top secret work of a company called Marconi Electronic Systems, but which, today, exists as a part of BAE Systems Electronics Limited. Its work includes the development of futuristic weaponry and spy satellite technology.

It was in March 1982 that Professor Keith Bowden, whose computer expertise made him a valuable employee of Marconi, lost his life in a car accident. His vehicle left a three-lane highway at high speed and slammed into a railway line. Death was instantaneous. In March 1985, Roger Hill, a draughtsman with Marconi, died of a shotgun blast. His death was deemed a suicide.

The list of Marconi-linked people who met bizarre and grim ends grew and grew—to the point where more than thirty controversial deaths were recorded—and finally came to a halt in the early 1990s, and more than a few of them were linked to research undertaken for U.S. president Ronald Reagan's Strategic Defense Initiative. It was far better known by its memorable nickname: "Star Wars." But there's something else worth noting on this particular matter, something controversial and disturbing, and it all revolves

A 1984 illustration showing how the satellites armed with lasers could disable hostile satellites and missiles in a modern-day space war.

around a man named Gordon Creighton, who is probably best known for his time spent as editor of *Flying Saucer Review* magazine. In August 2003, the U.K.'s *Times* newspaper wrote the following about Creighton, in his obituary: "Government service occupied most of the working life of Gordon Creighton, but he perhaps made his greatest mark as an authority on unidentified flying objects. His conviction that extraterrestrials were visiting Earth seemed oddly at variance with the more orthodox worlds of diplomacy and Whitehall.... His expertise took him into government research on maps in oriental and other languages with the Permanent Committee on Geographical Names, and he spent eight years as an intelligence officer on Russian and Chinese affairs at the Ministry of Defense. It is said that in the intelligence post he worked directly below the secret Whitehall department where the Air Ministry and the RAF were studying information on UFOs."

While it's true that Creighton firmly believed in the existence of a genuine UFO phenomenon, he was not at all sure—and particularly so in his later years—that the phenomenon was extraterrestrial. One of the things that both intrigued and worried

Al-Malik al-Aswad, the king of the Djinn, is shown at right in this illustration from the fourteenth-century Arabic *Book of Wonders*.

Creighton was the scenario of the UFO phenomenon being the product of nothing less than malevolent, dangerous Djinn.

In an article titled "A Short Course on the Djinn," Rosemary Ellen Guiley says: "In Arabian lore, djinn (also spelled jinn) are a race of supernaturally empowered beings who have the ability to intervene in the affairs of people. Like the Greek daimones, djinn are self-propagating and can be either good or evil. They can be conjured in magical rites to perform various tasks and services. A djinni (singular) appears as a wish-granting 'genie' in folk tales such as in *The Book of 1001 Nights* collection of folk tales."

Rosemary, a noted expert on the Djinn, also says: "In Western lore djinn are sometimes equated with demons, but they are not the same. They are often portrayed as having a demonic-like appearance, but they can also appear in beautiful, seductive forms. The djinn are masterful shape-shifters, and their favored forms are snakes and black dogs. They also can masquerade as anything: humans, animals, ghosts, cryptids, and other entities such as extraterrestrials, demons, shadow people, fairies, angels and more."

All of which brings us back to Gordon Creighton. When the Marconi controversy was at its height—and being reported on widely by the U.K. media—Creighton made brief references to the matter of the deaths and his suspicions that they were the work of deadly Djinn. Their purpose: to derail Reagan's Strategic Defense Initiative—"Star Wars." Yes, it sounds bizarre. That's because it was, and still is, bizarre.

According to Creighton, two things were going on. First, he was of the opinion that many of the Marconi scientists' deaths were indeed due to suicide. However, he qualified this by adding that he felt the unfortunate individuals were driven to commit suicide via what, in simplistic fashion, has popularly become known as mind control. Creighton was open-minded on who the guilty parties may have been, but he suggested maybe the Russians were involved—they would, of course, have had both a deep desire and a pressing need to derail "Star Wars." But, he said, the Russians weren't the only guilty parties.

There were, Creighton said, others who wanted to see the Strategic Defense Initiative extinct before it was even born. So Creighton said, those "others" were the Djinn. Rosemary Ellen Guiley says of the Djinn that they "… are born of smokeless fire (which in modern terms could be plasma). They live very long lives but they are not immortal. According to some accounts, they live with other supernatural beings in the Kaf, a mythical range of emerald mountains that encircles the Earth. In modern terms, they live in a parallel dimension."

As for why the Djinn wanted "Star Wars" terminated, it was all quite simple. Creighton assured me that while the Russians were a legitimate target of the SDI program, so was the intelligence behind the UFO phenomenon. It was a phenomenon, Creighton explained, that various government agencies (of more than a few nations) finally came to believe was not extraterrestrial, but Djinn-based—masquerading as ETs from the stars.

Of course, this begs an important question: if the Djinn exist as "plasma" and are the denizens of a dimension very different to our own reality, then how on earth could something like SDI cause them harm or death? Admittedly, Creighton was very hazy on this matter, but he suggested in concise words (maybe in too concise words) that the nature of the weapons systems could "disrupt the Djinn form." How that could happen exactly was an issue that Creighton remained hazy on, citing equally hazy "sources," in response to my questions.

Things got even stranger. Creighton asserted that elements of British Intelligence, at the height of SDI research in the 1980s, secretly consulted with experts on the Djinn. It was something that allegedly led to contact with such creatures and a form of Faustian pact between powerful figures here on Earth and the Djinn. The plan was to try and ensure a truce—albeit, probably, an uneasy truce—between the western world's military and the Djinn. The Djinn would agree to hold off on unleashing a "worldwide deception" and a "planetary invasion" if an agreement was made that SDI would not proceed. Western governments grudgingly agreed and were also forced to turn a blind eye to such things as Djinn-driven "alien abductions" and "cattle mutilations," added Creighton.

Creighton asserted that elements of British Intelligence, at the height of SDI research in the 1980s, secretly consulted with experts on the Djinn.

If you think things could not get any weirder, then you're wrong. Creighton made the astonishing claim that at least some of the Marconi deaths were the work of malevolent Djinn and also of British intelligence—both seeking to ensure that the aims of the pact (the end of SDI) were achieved. Yes, it's quite a story, one involving Russian assassins, U.K. assassins, and even Djinn assassins! It's no wonder that twenty-six years after I interviewed Creighton, I still ponder on his story.

But, pondering on it doesn't mean it's the absolute truth, or even anywhere near it. For example, assuming that Djinn are real, all-powerful, and manipulators of the human race, why would they even need to enter into some kind of Faustian agreement in the first place? Why not simply wipe out the SDI people directly and avoid any kind of negotiation with government officials? And, of course, the idea of Djinn and government officials negotiating on the SDI program sounds beyond surreal! I remain extremely doubtful regarding Creighton's claim that the ultimately ill-fated SDI program had the ability to wipe out plasma-based entities from some completely different realm of existence.

In conclusion, I would have to say that Gordon Creighton clearly believed that the UFO phenomenon was Djinn-based. I have no doubt of that. To what extent his theories concerning SDI, the Marconi deaths, and the Djinn had any merit, however, is anyone's guess. The whole thing lacks verification, and the bulk of the story came from Creighton himself and from certain unnamed "sources." Maybe it was just a theory on his part and nothing else.

On the other hand, could there be a nugget or several of truth in Creighton's thoughts and conclusions? Maybe. Over the years I've heard a few similar UFO-themed stories that substitute Djinn for demons, and I certainly don't dismiss some of those accounts. At the end of the day, however—and unless anything meaningful surfaces on this matter—the story remains very interesting, but highly controversial, and completely unproved. So far.

Stephenville UFO Group

When the Texas town of Stephenville was hit by a wave of incredible UFO activity in January 2008, it wasn't just the people of the area who quickly sat up and took notice of what was going on in the skies right above them. The local media caught wind of what was afoot, too. Then the story went national. And, following that, in no time at all, it was nothing less than global. The Lone Star State was subjected to a full-blown UFO invasion.

The U.S. military was soon caught up in the cosmic controversy, too—chiefly as a result of its curious and conflicting public statements on the affair. Key witnesses were interviewed on prime time television shows. The UFO research community hadn't seen anything like this in years—maybe decades, even—and no wonder: there were, after all, reports of an absolutely huge UFO overflying the town of Stephenville, of attempts by the military to intercept the massive "mothership"-like craft, of frightened and traumatized witnesses, of dark government conspiracies, and even of none other than the highest echelons of the United Nations taking a secret and deep interest in what was happening in and around Stephenville. The story received major media coverage: "Stephenville, Texas—In this farming community where nightfall usually brings clear, starry skies, residents are abuzz over reported sightings of what many believe is a UFO.

"Several dozen people—including a pilot, county constable and business owners—insist they have seen a large silent object with bright lights flying low and fast. Some reported seeing fighter jets chasing it. 'People wonder what in the world it is because this is the Bible Belt, and everyone is afraid it's the end of times,' said Steve Allen, a freight company owner and pilot who said the object he saw last week was a mile long and half a mile wide. 'It was positively, absolutely nothing from these parts.'" The Associated Press, January 14, 2008.

"Major Karl Lewis, a spokesman for the 301st Fighter Wing at the Joint Reserve Base Naval Air Station in Fort Worth, said no F-16s or other aircraft from his base were in the area the night of January 8, when most people reported the sighting. Lewis said the object may have been an illusion caused by two commercial airplanes. Lights from the aircraft would seem unusually bright and may appear orange from the setting sun. 'I'm 90 percent sure this was an airliner,' Lewis said. 'With the sun's angle, it can play tricks on you.' Officials at the region's two Air Force bases—Dyess in Abilene and Sheppard in Wichita Falls—also said none of their aircraft were in the area last week. The Air Force no longer investigates UFOs." CNN, January 15, 2008.

"Stephenville's latest close encounter is weirder than any light in the sky. Stephenville is under assault—not by Martians, but by people hunting them. The phones haven't stopped ringing at Steve Allen's trucking company in nearby Glen Rose. He's the guy who was out Jan. 7 watching the sunset at a friend's house near Selden when they all saw some weird flashing lights. Now he can't work for all the calls from London and around the world. Some of the callers are scarier than space aliens. 'I'll be OK,' he joked Tuesday, 'as long as I don't get abducted.'" *Star Telegram*, January 15, 2008.

"Dozens of eyewitnesses have reported seeing a mile-long UFO being pursued by fighter jets last week in the small town of Stephenville, Texas. 'It was very intense bright lights ... and they spanned a wide area,' said one woman. NBC News spoke with County

There were reports that a UFO mothership was flying over the town of Stephenville, Texas.

Constable Lee Roy Gaitan, who offered a somewhat different description. 'I saw two red glows,' he said. 'I never seen anything like that, never.'" *The Raw Story*, January 15, 2008.

"The U.S. military has owned up to having F-16 fighters in the air near Stephenville on the night that several residents reported unusual lights in the sky. But the correction issued Wednesday doesn't exactly turn UFOs into Identified Flying Objects. Several dozen witnesses reported that they had seen unusual lights in the sky near Stephenville shortly after dusk Jan. 8. One sighting included a report that the lights were pursued by military jets. Military officials had repeatedly denied that they had any flights in the area that night. But that position changed Wednesday with a terse news release: 'In the interest of public awareness, Air Force Reserve Command Public Affair realized an error was made regarding the reported training activity of military aircraft. Ten F-16s from the 457th Fighter Squadron were performing training operations from 6 to 8 P.M., Tuesday January 8, 2008, in the Brownwood Military Operating Area (MOA), which includes the airspace above Erath County.' Major Karl Lewis, a spokesman for the 301st Fighter Wing at the former Carswell Field, blamed the erroneous release on 'an internal communications error.' That still left unanswered the question of what F-16s might have been doing that would look like a line of silent, glowing spheres. Maj. Lewis said he could not give any details." *Dallas Morning News*, January 23, 2008.

"A lot has been said as of late on the apparent trend of UFO reports being treated with more respect by mainstream media. This trend seems to have begun with the O'Hare Airport sightings, and reached fruition with the recent Texas sightings near Stephenville. Now there is a report from researcher Michael Salla, who claims to have insider information that confirms a series of meetings on alien contact held in secret by a group sanctioned by the United Nations. These meetings are reported to have spanned three days, beginning on February 12. Supposedly, three United States Senators have asked for further meetings on the subject. The primary concern of these meetings was dealing with public reaction to an announcement that alien contact has, or will soon occur." *About.com*, March 4, 2008.

Although Ken Cherry has publicly revealed a great deal about what went on during those crazy days and nights of early 2008, he has not revealed everything....

From practically the day that the controversy kicked off, one man—more than any other—was at the forefront of trying to figure out what on earth was taking place in Stephenville. That man was a Texas-based UFO investigator named Ken Cherry, who today runs EPIC, the Extraordinary Phenomena Investigations Council.

As he dug into the mystery of Stephenville, Cherry quickly found himself plunged into a strange world filled with concerned eyewitnesses, insider whistleblowers, tales of coverups and conspiracies, and accounts of secret groups studying acquired alien technology at classified installations across the United States, and that was just the tip of the extraterrestrial iceberg.

Although Ken Cherry has publicly revealed a great deal about what went on during those crazy days and nights of early 2008, he has not revealed everything; at least, not in the way that you might expect. Today, close to a decade after the incredible events at Stephenville occurred, Cherry has chosen to take a new and alternative approach to reporting on the case.

He has penned a work of fiction on the affair, one that makes for highly entertaining and thought-provoking reading: *Marc Slade Investigates: The Stephenville UFO*. Taking this particular approach has allowed Cherry to use witness accounts, data from those aforementioned whistleblowers, and a variety of never-before-seen data, without compromising his sources and their identities. It's an approach that works very well. It's a book that is part science fiction, part thriller, and part conspiracy saga, all rolled into one—and in a fine and skillful fashion. The story is fast-paced and is filled with numerous twists and turns, characters who range from the shadowy to the sinister, and plotlines that will keep you guessing until the final few pages.

One of the primary reasons that led Cherry to present his story in a decidedly non-fiction fashion is because of issues relative to (a) data provided by whistleblower-style sources and (b) Cherry's personal safety. As Cherry dug further into the heart of the mystery, he discovered something astonishing; something that has a major bearing on the theme of the book you are right now reading. It was nothing less than an incredibly powerful and secret group—one that was deeply buried in the heart of the U.S. government and had links to both the military and the intelligence community. What Cherry discovered was both amazing and disturbing—to significant degrees.

He uncovered extensive data that revealed the Stephenville UFO wave had nothing whatsoever to do with extraterrestrial visitations. Rather, the UFOs were homegrown, the secret technology of Uncle Sam. According to Cherry's behind-the-scenes informants, the UFOs were actually highly advanced aircraft of a very strange style and extraordinary size. But why would this powerful secret group embark on a program to try and convince people that aliens had invaded Stephenville, Texas? The answer is very disturbing: Cherry was told that the overflights at Stephenville were designed to determine how the general public would react to not just close encounters, but *extremely* close encounters—as in right above our heads. In other words, the alien invasion was nothing less than a brilliant ruse to have the American public believe that aliens are among us, when they may actually not be.

There was an even more disturbing agenda on the part of this group; namely, that it might use a faked "UFO invasion" as a means to implement martial law, ensure the loss of civil liberties, and provoke unending surveillance of the entire U.S. population. Are shadowy and influential figures, attached to a powerful organization, working to deceive the public that aliens are invading? Incredibly, that's exactly what the presently available data—born directly out of the 2008 Stephenville affair—suggests.

Strathmore Secrets

Situated just west of Forfar, Scotland, Glamis Castle is referred to by Shakespeare in *Macbeth*; in the story, Macbeth kills King Duncan there in 1040. The castle is also where assassins murdered King Malcolm II in 1034. In addition, Glamis Castle was the childhood home of both Queen Elizabeth II and the Queen Mother, and the birthplace of Princess Margaret, and then there is the castle's very own monster—the story of which is carefully and secretly guarded by a powerful family.

Jonathan Downes, the director of the British-based Centre for Fortean Zoology—one of the few full-time groups dedicated to the search for unknown

Glamis Castle in Scotland was once the home of Queen Elizabeth II; it is also supposedly the residence of a monster.

creatures—notes that "the castle is the site of a well-known and semi legendary beast known as the Monster of Glamis. It's said that the creature was supposed to have been the hideously deformed heir to the Bowes-Lyon family and who was, according to popular rumor, born in about 1800, and died as recently as 1921."

Downes digs further into the puzzle: "Legend has it that the monster was supposed to look like an enormous flabby egg, having no neck and only minute arms and legs but possessed incredible strength and had an air of evil about it. Certainly, there is a family secret concerning the monster, which is only told to the male heir of the Bowes-Lyon family when they attain majority."

He continues: "But according to the author Peter Underwood, who has looked into this case, the present Lord Strathmore knows nothing about the monster, presumably because the creature has long been dead, but he always felt that there was a corpse or coffin bricked up behind the walls."

According to folklore and oral tradition, the existence of the terrifying creature was allegedly known to only four men at any given time, namely the Earl of Strathmore, his direct heir, the family's lawyer, and the broker of the estate. At the age of twenty-one each succeeding heir was told the truth of the terrible secret and shown the rightful—and horrendously deformed—Earl, and succeeding family lawyers and brokers were also informed of the family's shocking secret.

As no Countess of Strathmore was ever told the story, however, one Lady Strathmore, having indirectly heard of such tales, quietly approached the then-broker, a certain Mr. Ralston, who flatly refused to reveal the secret and would only say by way of a reply, "It is fortunate you do not know the truth for if you did you would never be happy."

So was the strange creature of the castle a terribly deformed soul with some bizarre genetic affliction or something else? While the jury, inevitably, remains steadfastly out, it's an intriguing fact that in 1912, in his book, *Scottish Ghost Stories*, Elliott O'Donnell published the contents of a letter that he had received from a Mrs. Bond who had spent time at Glamis Castle and who underwent an undeniably weird encounter while staying there.

In her letter to O'Donnell, rather notably, Mrs. Bond described a somewhat supernatural encounter with a beast that was possessed of nothing less than distinct ape-like qualities, rather than specifically human attributes.

Might it be the case, then, that the beast of Glamis was not simply a man with appalling genetic abnormalities but rather some terrifying ape-like beast—a definitive wild-man or ape-man, perhaps? Not surprisingly, the truth—whatever it may one day prove to be—remains hidden behind closed doors, just like the creature itself. And, of course, the Strathmores are saying absolutely nothing.

T—U

Taigheirm

Many people with an interest in the issue of powerful, secret societies will be familiar with the likes of the Bilderbergers, the Illuminati, and the Freemasons. Very few, however, will be conversant with an equally powerful body of people called the Taigheirm. Like so many other secret societies, the Taigheirm is populated by people who crave absolute power, massive wealth, and elite standing in society. It is, however, the way that the members of the Taigheirm achieve their goals that places them in their own near-unique category.

This centuries-old cult exists and operates in stealth in the highlands of Scotland and has done so since at least the seventeenth century; it uses ancient sacrificial rituals to get just about anything and everything it desires. It is rumored that numerous Scottish politicians, police officers, bankers, actors, doctors, judges, and landowners are just some of the Taigheirm's many and varied members.

Merrily Harpur is a British researcher who has carefully and deeply studied the history of the Taigheirm. She says that key to the success of the members is "an infernal magical sacrifice of cats in rites dedicated to the subterranean gods of pagan times, from whom particular gifts and benefits were solicited. They were called in the Highlands and the Western Isles of Scotland, the black-cat spirits."

The process of sacrifice was, and still is, gruesome in the extreme. Isolated and lonely places high in the mountains of Scotland are chosen, chiefly to

The Taigheirm rite was to kill black cats by slowly roasting them on a spit.

ensure privacy. Secrecy is paramount. Members arrive, in black cloaks and pointed hats, at the chosen spot in the dead of night, determined at all times to protect their identities and presence from outsiders. Then comes the main event. Huge spits are built, upon which cats are slowly roasted—and while they are still alive—for up to four days and nights, during which the operator of the spit is denied sleep or nourishment, aside from an occasional sip of water. Supposedly, when the ritual is at its height, from the terrifying paranormal ether huge black cats with glowing red eyes appear before the conjurer, demanding to know what it is that he or she wishes to have bestowed on them: money, influence, or something else. In return, and in a fashion befitting the likes of Faust, on his or her death the conjurer agrees to turn over their soul to those ancient, mighty gods worshipped by the Taigheirm.

Without doubt, the one person, more than any other, who was conversant with the terrible rituals of the Taigheirm was J. Y. W. Lloyd, who penned an acclaimed 1881 book, *The History of the Prince, the Lord's Marcher, and the Ancient Nobility of Powys Fadog and the Ancient Lords of Arwystli, Cedewen, and Meirionydd.* Lloyd became fascinated by the Taigheirm after reading Horst's *Deuteroscopy,* which was the first published work to expose the actions of this heartless group. Lloyd recorded that: "The midnight hour, between Friday and Saturday, was the authentic time for these horrible practices and invocations."

Horst, himself, presented a terrible image: "After the cats were dedicated to all the devils, and put into a magico-sympathetic condition, by the shameful things done to them, and the agony occasioned to them, one of them was at once put alive upon the spit, and amid terrific howlings, roasted before a slow fire. The moment that the howls of one tortured cat ceased in death, another was put upon the spit, for a minute of interval must not take place if they would control hell; and this continued for the four entire days and nights. If the exorcist could hold it out still longer, and even till his physical powers were absolutely exhausted, he must do so."

It was after that four day period, said Horst, that, "infernal spirits appeared in the shape of black cats. There came continually more and more of these cats; and their howlings, mingled with those roasting on the spit, were terrific. Finally, appeared a cat of a monstrous size, with dreadful menaces. When the Taigheirm rite was complete, the sacrificer [sic] demanded of the spirits the reward of his offering, which consisted of various things; as riches, children, food, and clothing. The gift of second sight, which they had not had before, was, however, the usual recompense; and they retained it to the day of their death."

As the nineteenth century reached its end, Lloyd came to believe that while the legend and cruel and cold reputation of the Taigheirm still existed, the group, as a fully functioning entity, no longer did. He recorded that one of the very last Taigheirm rituals was held on the Scottish island of Mull, in the early 1800s. Lloyd added that the folk of Mull "still show the place where Allan Maclean, at that time the incantor, and sacrificial priest, stood with his assistant, Lachlain Maclean, both men of a determined and unbending character."

Theirs was reportedly a frightening ritual held on a cold, winter's night and under a full moon. Lloyd noted: "Allan Maclean continued his sacrifice to the fourth day, when he was exhausted both in body and mind, and sunk in a swoon; but, from this day he received the second-sight to the time of his death, as also did his assistant. In the people, the belief was unshaken, that the second-sight was the natural consequence of celebrating the Taigheirm."

As the nineteenth century reached its end, Lloyd came to believe that while the legend and cruel and cold reputation of the Taigheirm still existed, the group, as a fully functioning entity, no longer did.

There is, however, intriguing data strongly suggesting that the Taigheirm are still with us, lurking in the shadows and still extending their power and influence. In 1922, Carl Van Vechten commented on post-nineteenth-century Taigheirm activity in a footnote contained in his book, *The Tiger in the House*. It reads: "The night of the day I first learned of the Taigheirm I dined with some friends who were also entertaining Seumas, Chief of Clann Fhearghuis of Strachur. He informed me that to the best of his knowledge the Taigheirm is *still* celebrated in the Highlands of Scotland."

Then there is the account of one Donald Johnson, a man born and bred in Scotland, but who, just like his late father, worked as a butler for a powerful and rich family that had its roots in the ancient English county of Staffordshire. According to Johnson, his father was invited by his employers to join an English offshoot of the Taigheirm in the winter of 1982—providing that he was willing to leave his old life and friends behind him and fully embrace the Taigheirm and its horrific teachings. Johnson Sr. was ready to do so, until, that is, he witnessed one of those monstrous sacrifices deep in the heart of England's Cannock Chase woods, and on a proverbial dark and stormy night, no less.

Johnson Sr.'s decision to walk away—quickly—was not at all appreciated by the Taigheirm, who reportedly made explicit threats about what might happen to him if he ever dared to go public with what he knew and had seen. Such was his fear, he stayed completely and utterly silent on the matter until he told his son, Donald, in 2010—the latter going public with the story in December of that year, out of fear for his own safety. The society of the Taigheirm, it seems, is still as much up to its terrible tricks as it was four centuries ago. Indeed, power, influence, and wealth are hard to give up or deny—even if one has to enter into Faustian pacts with ancient earth gods and supernatural black cats to achieve them.

Texas Taigheirm

In early 2008, rumors circulated to the effect that a U.S.-based equivalent of the ancient Scottish order of the Taigheirm was operating deep in the heart of Dallas, Texas. And, as was the case with the original Scottish members, those tied to this Lone Star State-based equivalent were using the rites and rituals to achieve two things: power and wealth. While such rumors were never conclusively proved to be real, the fact is that from 2008 to 2011, there were numerous cases of cat mutilation in the heart of Dallas, and they clearly weren't the work of coyotes or bobcats. There was method in the grisly, city-wide madness.

> It all began in the summer of 2008 when a pair of cats was found—"dissected" was how the local media reported on the affair—in the city's Lovers Lane.

It all began in the summer of 2008 when a pair of cats was found—"dissected" was how the local media reported on the affair—in the city's Lovers Lane. Almost one year later, a cat was found dead—with organs removed with surgical precision—in Dallas's Lakewood Heights. The unfortunate man who stumbled on the remains of the poor animal said: "The cat was literally cut in half at its midsection. There was no blood on our front lawn, so it appears that the mutilation probably occurred elsewhere and the remains were dumped on our lawn by the perpetrator."

Two more cats were found within days—also mutilated in fashions that suggested the culprits were all too human. As a result, the Dallas SPCA offered a $5,000 reward for anyone who could help solve the disturbing mystery. There was not even a single, solitary taker. A couple of weeks later, Dallas's Midway Hollow was targeted. The local police said: "We used to think it was a juvenile up to no good. But now we think it might be an older guy who lives nearby, snatches these cats, mutilates them, then takes them back to where he finds them."

Then, in August, NBC-DFW reported on the discovery of six dead and mutilated cats in the northwest part of Dallas.

Although 2010 was quiet, 2011 was anything but. It all began again in April of that year when a "surgically mutilated" cat was stumbled on in Wilshire Heights, Dallas. Yet again, a substantial reward was offered. There was, however, nothing but silence and not a single lead in sight.

Without doubt, the most controversial theory surfaced in May 2011. The story, from a local conspiracy theorist, Bob Small, was that the Taigheirm group was allied to the far more well-known Skull and Bones group, which was founded in 1832 at Yale University in New Haven, Connecticut. Small believed—and continues to believe—it's no coincidence that former President George W. Bush, himself a member of Skull and Bones, lives in Preston Hollow, Dallas, not at all any distance from where the cat killings took place from 2008 to 2011.

Thuggee

A secret group of ruthless assassins, stealthily roaming around India, slaughtering anyone and everyone who got in their way, stealing priceless artifacts, treasures, and money, and creating a reign of terror and murder that lasted for more than five hundred years? It sounds like the perfect plot for a historical murder mystery novel of bestselling proportions. It is, however, nothing less than coldhearted fact. Welcome to the world of the Thuggee, a band of elite, silent killers who pledged allegiance to no one but their fellow members—after whom the word "thug" is derived—and the sacred Hindu goddess, Kali, whose name translates as "lord of death."

The origins of the Thuggee are, very appropriately, steeped in fog-shrouded mystery and intrigue. Earliest references to this secret Indian order date back to the mid-fourteenth century. In 1356, one Ziau-d din Barni penned *The History of Firoz Shah*, which included the following brief words on the Thuggee: "In the reign of that sultan, some Thugs were taken in Delhi, and a man belonging to that fraternity was the means of about a thousand being captured. But not one of these did the sultan have killed. He gave orders for them to be put into boats and to be conveyed into the lower country, to the neighborhood of Lakhnauti, where they were to be set free. The Thugs would thus have to dwell about Lakhnauti and would not trouble the neighborhood of Delhi anymore."

Din Barni was in error: the Thuggee network went on to cause a great deal of trouble and death on a massive scale. Determined to ensure that their "fraternity" (as din Barni worded it) remained intact, they carefully and quietly increased their numbers and sought out appropriately secret locales—all across the cities and towns of ancient India—in which their plans for power and influence could grow. No one ever again, they vowed, would cross paths with the Thuggee and live to tell the tale.

Entry to the world of the Thuggee was usually dictated by two things: (a) a keen ability to kill swiftly, quietly, and without emotion; and (b) a family connection to an already-existing member of the group. Indoctrination sometimes began at a very early age, which saw young children taught to use a tool of strangulation called the Rumal. Little more than a tough length of cloth, it was most effective when the victim was sleeping. A Thuggee would creep up, under cover of darkness, and quickly tie the Rumal around the neck of the person, pulling it tight, and ensuring that death from strangulation came rapidly and quietly. Invariably, the victim would be relieved of his or her possessions.

Thugs strangle and rob an innocent traveler in this early nineteenth-century illustration.

Skilled in the field of not just assassination, but also deception and camouflage, the Thuggee often disguised themselves as members of the Indian Army and as priests. They soon found themselves in high demand—even by people in India's government, who wanted troublesome rivals dead, but with no way to link them to the murders. By the fifteenth century, the Thuggee were a full-blown society of secret assassins for hire—and for hire to just about anyone and everyone who could offer significant amounts of money in return for the deadly deed. Over the course of the next three hundred years, bands of Thuggee killed not just thousands of people across India, but *hundreds* of thousands. It was a reign of terror that was orchestrated and executed from within the hearts of ancient, underground chambers, bustling markets, and even the hearts of royal palaces. All of that came to a shuddering halt, however, in the early nineteenth century.

The 1800s had barely begun when the British government and military discovered the shocking scale and scope of the deadly, centuries-long activities of the Thuggee. Thus was begun an extensive operation to permanently wipe the Thuggee off the face of India. It was an ambitious program headed by Major General Sir William Sleeman of the British Army. Not only was the program ambitious, it was also highly successful. By the 1830s, the end of the reign of terror was in sight. Sleeman's men followed up on every lead, whisper, and piece of data available and, as a result, tracked down thousands of Thuggee, hanging one and all by the neck as a warning to others what awaited them. By the early 1840s, thanks largely to gangs of informers, the Thuggee were no more and the work of the British Army was finally over. The legend, however, remains. Indeed, to this day, the tales of the Thuggee continue to provoke chills and fear amongst the people of India, just as much as they did all those centuries ago.

Thule Society

The Thule Society has become notorious for its connections to the Nazis and the means by which it allegedly molded and influenced the belief systems of powerful figures in the Nazi Party. Even Adolf Hitler himself is a player in the controversial story.

Crystal Links provides the following data: "The Thule Society was a German occultist and volkisch group in Munich, named after a mythical northern country from Greek legend. The Society is notable chiefly as the organization that sponsored the Deutsche Arbeiterpartei (DAP), which was later reorgan-

The symbol of the Thule Society. Notice the stylized swastika, which is reminiscent of the Nazi symbol.

ized by Adolf Hitler into the National Socialist German Workers' Party (Nazi Party)."

They continue: "The Thule Society was originally a 'German study group' headed by Walter Nauhaus, a wounded World War I veteran turned art student from Berlin who had become a keeper of pedigrees for the Germanenorden (or 'Order of Teutons'), a secret society founded in 1911 and formally named in the following year. In 1917 Nauhaus moved to Munich; his Thule-Gesellschaft was to be a cover-name for the Munich branch of the Germanenorden, but events developed differently as a result of a schism in the Order.

"In 1918, Nauhaus was contacted in Munich by Rudolf von Sebottendorf (or von Sebottendorff), an occultist and newly elected head of the Bavarian province of the schismatic offshoot, known as the Germanenorden Walvater of the Holy Grail. The two men became associates in a recruitment campaign, and Sebottendorff adopted Nauhaus's Thule Society as a cover-name for his Munich lodge of the Germanenorden Walvater at its formal dedication on 18 August 1918."

Wulf Schwartzwaller—the author of *The Unknown Hitler*—said: "The Thule Society is known to be closely connected to the Germanenorden secret society. The Germanenorden was a secret society in Germany early in the 20th century. Formed by several prominent German occultists in 1912, the order, whose symbol was a swastika, had a hierarchical fraternal structure similar to freemasonry. It taught to its initiates nationalist ideologies of nordic race superiority, antisemitism as well as occult, almost magical philosophies.

"Some say that the Deutsche Arbeiter-Partei (later the Nazi Party) when under the leadership of Adolf Hitler was a political front, and indeed the organization reflected many ideologies of the party, including the swastika symbol. The Thule Society, another secret society with similar ideologies and symbols, was also closely linked to this."

And we have this from *The Forbidden Knowledge*: "The German Brotherhood of Death Society is the Thule Society. Adolf Hitler joined this society in 1919, becoming an adept under the leadership of Dietrich Eckhart. Later, the Thule Society selected Hitler to be their leader of the New World Order, as Eckhart revealed on his deathbed, saying, 'Follow Hitler; he will dance, but it is I who have called the tune. I have initiated him into the Secret Doctrine, opened his centers in vision, and given him the means to communicate with the powers.'"

In early 1920 Karl Harrer—a German politician and journalist—was ejected from the DAP, as Adolf Hitler became determined to distance the party's connections to the Thule Society. As a direct result of Hitler's actions, the Thule Society lost both its strength and its visibility, to the point that within half a decade it was no more.

Nevertheless, Rudolf von Sebottendorff—who had walked away from the Thule Society one year before Harrer was thrown out—had new and ambitious plans by 1933. They were plans designed to resurrect the Thule Society. Despite Hitler's personal distaste of the Thule Society, in a book titled *Bevor Hitler Kam* (in English, *Before Hitler Came*), Sebottendorff made it very clear that, in his opinion, the Thule Society played a key and instrumental role in bringing Hitler to power. In Sebottendorff's own words: "Thulers were the ones to whom Hitler first came, and Thulers were the first to unite themselves with Hitler."

Sebottendorff's words did not sit well with the Nazis. The result was that his book was banned, he spent time in prison, and he left Germany for Turkey. The Thule Society had finally run out of steam.

Trilateral Commission

In its very own words, "The Trilateral Commission was formed in 1973 by private citizens of Japan, Europe (European Union countries), and North America (United States and Canada) to foster closer cooperation among these core industrialized areas of the world with shared leadership responsibilities in the wider international system. Originally established for three years, our work has been renewed for successive triennia (three-year periods), most recently for a triennium to be completed in 2015.

"When the first triennium of the Trilateral Commission was launched in 1973, the most immediate purpose was to draw together—at a time of considerable friction among governments—the highest-level unofficial group possible to look together at the key common problems facing our three areas. At a deeper level, there was a sense that the United States was no longer in such a singular leadership position as it had been in earlier post-World War II years, and that a more shared form of leadership—including Europe and Japan in particular—would be needed for the international system to navigate successfully the major challenges of the coming years."

A Trilateral Commission Task Force Report, presented at the 1975 meeting in Kyoto, Japan, titled *An Outline for Remaking World Trade and Finance*, states: "Close Trilateral cooperation in keeping the peace, in managing the world economy, and in fostering economic development and in alleviating world poverty, will improve the chances of a smooth and peaceful evolution of the global system."

It is this "global system" issue that has led to claims and concerns that the Trilateral Commission is at the heart of a program to erode the idea of independent nations and usher in a single, planet-wide government.

Author Brad Steiger observes, "Conspiracy theorists estimate that the current membership of the Trilateral Commission includes approximately eighty Americans, ten Canadians, ninety Western Europeans, and seventy-five Japanese. Most conspiracists do not believe that the Trilateralists wish the destruction of the United States, but rather that it will surrender its independence and embrace the concept of a One World Government."

In 1990, Ron Paul (of the U.S. House of Representatives from 1976 to 1977, 1979 to 1985, and 1997 to 2013) said: "For years now, it's been claimed by many, and there's pretty good evidence, that those who are involved in the Trilateral Commission and the Council on Foreign Relations usually end up in positions of power, and I believe this is true. If you look at the Federal Reserve, if you look at key positions at the World Bank or the IMF, they all come from these groups. If you have national television on, you might see a big debate about the Far East crisis, and you have Brzezinski and Kissinger talking about how to do it. One says don't invade today, invade tomorrow, and the other says, invade immediately. That's the only difference you find between the Rockefeller trilateralists."

> **I**t is this "global system" issue that has led to claims and concerns that the Trilateral Commission is at the heart of a program to erode the idea of independent nations and usher in a single, planet-wide government.

UFO Assassins

Does there exist a secret cabal of assassins, a cabal that has one specific role, namely to terminate with extreme prejudice certain UFO researchers who get too close for comfort to the truth behind the phenomenon of flying saucers? Many might scoff at such a possibility. The facts, however, most assuredly do point in that direction. A perfect example is the strange and disturbing story that suggests one of those who uncovered the truth—and who paid with his life as a result—was none other than President John F. Kennedy, who was killed on November 22, 1963, at Dealey Plaza in Dallas, Texas. By whom? That's the big question. The answer may well be by that aforementioned cabal.

FBI special agent Guy Banister investigated a body of UFO reports for J. Edgar Hoover in the summer months of 1947. Then, in the early 1960s, we see him fingered as a central player in the Kennedy killing. Indeed, while working in New Orleans in 1963, Banister became deeply acquainted with none other than Lee Harvey Oswald—and under unclear, murky circumstances. It turns out that another individual had ties to 1947-era ufology and the death of JFK. That man was Fred Crisman, one of the key figures in the notorious UFO saga of Maury Island, Puget Sound, Washington State. It's a bizarre story involving an exploded UFO that predates, by a few days, Kenneth Arnold's famous flying saucer encounter of June 24, 1947. It's a case that involves the deaths of two members of the military—Lt. Frank Brown and Capt. William Davidson—and threats from a Man in Black-type character. Then there are claims of secret surveillance of the central players in the odd story.

Lee Harvey Oswald, accused of killing President Kennedy, is ushered into police custody in this photo. Did he act alone, or under the direction of a secret cabal?

As for Crisman, author Kenn Thomas tells us: "In 1968, New Orleans district attorney Jim Garrison subpoenaed Fred Crisman as part of his investigation into the JFK assassination, which became the subject of Oliver Stone's 1992 *JFK* movie. Garrison believed that Crisman was the infamous grassy knoll shooter, and he's the central figure in the 'Mystery Tramp' photo of the Dallas rail yard hobos."

It turns out that Garrison—played in the movie, *JFK*, by Kevin Costner—knew Guy Banister years before the Kennedy assassination, specifically in the 1940s. Garrison said in his book, *On the Trail of the Assassins*: "When he was in the police department, we had lunch together now and then, swapping colorful stories about our earlier careers in the FBI. A ruddy-faced man with blue eyes which stared right at you, he dressed immaculately and always wore a small rosebud in his lapel."

> **S**ome suggest Kilgallen's death on November 8, 1965, was not the result of an accidental overdose of booze and pills.

While there is a great deal of dispute about who shot JFK, there's no doubt about who killed Lee Harvey Oswald. It was Dallas strip club owner and Mob buddy Jack Ruby. Journalist Dorothy Kilgallen was deeply interested in the circumstances surrounding the JFK affair, and particularly so Ruby's links—to the extent that she managed to secure an interview with him. Back in 1955, the following words of Kilgallen appeared in the pages of the *Los Angeles Examiner*: "British scientists and airmen, after examining the wreckage of one mysterious flying ship, are convinced these strange aerial objects are not optical illusions or Soviet inventions, but are flying saucers which originate on another planet." Kilgallen claimed her information came from a British official of Cabinet rank.

Some suggest Kilgallen's death on November 8, 1965, was not the result of an accidental overdose of booze and pills. They see a far more sinister explanation: that Kilgallen's interest in UFOs had led her to uncover evidence of the cabal that killed Kennedy, and the list goes on. The late conspiracy theorist Bill Cooper made the wild and crazy claim that one of the Secret Service agents present in Dealey Plaza when Kennedy was killed—a man named William Greer—was responsible for the president's death. And how was death achieved? Via nothing less than a weapon employing extraterrestrial technology!

One day before his death, JFK spoke at the dedication ceremony of the Aerospace Medical Health Center at Brooks Air Force Base in San Antonio, Texas. The base had been chosen to conduct groundbreaking work in the field of space medicine—work involved figuring out how to keep astronauts free from deadly radiation, learning more about how gravity-free environments can affect the human body, and so on. While at Brooks, Kennedy met with personnel from Wright-Patterson Air Force Base, Ohio (the alleged home of the legendary Hangar 18). JFK also met with staff from Fort Detrick, Maryland. For years, rumors have circulated to the effect that Fort Detrick has been the home of classified research into alien viruses.

Still on the matter of Roswell, in 1997 one of the most controversial of all UFO books—ever—was published, titled *The Day After Roswell*. Penned by Bill Birnes (of *UFO Hunters* and *UFO Magazine*) and the late Lt. Col. Philip Corso, it told of Corso's alleged knowledge of alien technology, artifacts, and bodies in the hands of the U.S. military. At the time of his death in 1998, at the age of 83, Corso was planning another book, *The Day After Dallas*. No prizes for guessing the subject matter.

Moving on, back in the 1950s, U.S. senator Richard Russell paid a visit to the Soviet Union. At the time, Russell was the chairman of the Armed Services Committee. The date was October 4, 1955. Russell had a profound UFO encounter—which revolved around a pair of UFOs—while the train he was on was negotiating Russia's Trans-Caucasus area. Both the CIA and the Air Force took serious notice of what Russell had to say. Official records on the matter state that Russell "saw the first flying disc ascend and pass over the train."

We're also told: "One disc ascended almost vertically, at a relatively slow speed, with its outer surface revolving slowly to the right, to an altitude of about 6,000 feet, where its speed then increased sharply as it headed north. The second flying disc was seen performing the same actions about one minute later. The take-off area was about 1-2 miles south of the rail line … all three saw the second disc and all agreed that they saw the same round, disc-shaped craft as the first."

Senator Richard Russell was a member of the "Warren Commission" (actually, the President's Commission on the Assassination of President Kennedy) that sought to find answers to who killed JFK. The commission concluded that Oswald was the assassin. There's more about Oswald: in October 1962, he began working for a Texas company by the name of Jaggars-Chiles-Stovall. In his book, *Conspiracy*, Anthony Summers wrote that JCS's work "involved material obtained by the very U-2 planes Oswald had once watched in Japan, and only employees with a special security clearance were supposed to see it."

In 2013, the BBC noted: "The U-2 was one of the Cold War's most infamous aircraft, a plane designed to fly over unfriendly territory too high for enemy fighters or missiles, and take pictures of unparalleled detail—and, as it has just been revealed, helped spur the development of the secret Area 51 airbase."

There's no doubt that the threads are there to make a case that, sometimes, when people get too close to the truth behind the UFO enigma, death is looming large on the horizon.

UMMO

On February 6, 1966, a Mr. José Peña was said to have observed the flight of a large, white-colored flying saucer over Madrid, Spain. The UFO reportedly displayed a strange, prominent symbol on its underside. A similar craft, displaying the very same symbol, was supposedly seen in May 1967, in a suburb of Madrid, and quickly photographed. Such is the controversial nature of so many UFO-themed photos, it scarcely needs mentioning that the imagery remains highly inflammatory (despite having been shown to be a hoax) and is both championed and denounced.

Particularly intriguing is the fact that the controversy did not fade away. Actually, quite the opposite: it flourished for years, and thus was born the cult of UMMO—named after the planet from which the UFOs and their alien occupants supposedly originated. One of those who dug deep into the matter of the UMMO controversy was the late Jim Keith, the author of such books as *Saucers of the Illuminati*, *Black Helicopters over America*, and—with Kenn Thomas—*The Octopus*.

In his *Casebook on the Men in Black* book, Keith stated: "The UMMO case was created through a large number of contacts—UFO sightings, personal contacts, messages through the mail and telephone—alleged to be from space brothers from the planet UMMO," which, Keith added, was said to be "located 14.6 light years from our solar system."

Keith continued that much of the UMMO material was composed of "six-to-ten page letters containing diagrams and equations, delineating UMMO science and philosophy. Differing from most channeled and beamed by space beings, they were scientifically savvy, although according to Jacques Vallée, smacked more of Euro sci-fi than superior extraterrestrial knowledge."

But was the UMMO saga really evidence that extraterrestrials were amongst us? According to Jim Keith, the answer was: No. Keith cited the words of a Spanish journalist named Manuel Carballal. It was Carballal, Keith said, who wrote that researchers Cales Berche, Jose J. Montejo, and Javier Sierra had identified a well-known Spanish parapsychologist—who turned out to be none other than the aforementioned José Peña—as being the originator of the UMMO material.

Jim Keith expanded on this and stated that Peña "is later reported to have admitted his creation of the complex hoax, stating that it had been a 'scientific experiment' aimed at testing the gullibility factor amongst Spanish UFO researchers."

Notably, there were those who postulated that the story got even weirder and wilder, to the extent that the original UMMO hoax was, later, ingeniously hijacked and expanded upon by certain official intelligence services—and, chiefly, the former Soviet Union's KGB. The scenario involved intelligence-based personnel exploiting the original hoax as a cover for the dissemination of psychological warfare within the public UFO research community, as well as a means to secretly infiltrate and manipulate that same community to gather information.

Jacques Vallée noted of UMMO that "some of the data that was supposedly channeled from the UMMO organization in the sky was very advanced cosmology." Vallée added that portions of the material "came straight out of the notes" of none other than Andrei Sakharov, including certain "unpublished notes." Vallée commented further that there was a degree of thought suggesting "somebody had to have access to those notes, to inspire those messages, perhaps the KGB."

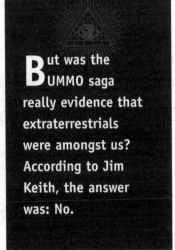

But was the UMMO saga really evidence that extraterrestrials were amongst us? According to Jim Keith, the answer was: No.

Andrei Sakharov—who died in 1989—was a scientist who played an instrumental role in the development of the Soviet Union's hydrogen bomb program. However, he ultimately became, in the words of the Nobel Peace Committee, a spokesperson for the conscience of mankind. Indeed, in 1975 Sakharov was awarded the prestigious Nobel Peace Prize.

That the KGB might have decided to use the UMMO affair to its own, secret advantage, and to try and infiltrate and manipulate ufology, is not so strange at all. In 1953, the Robertson Panel—a select group of consultants brought together by the CIA to look at the national security implications of the UFO issue—recommended that a number of public UFO investigative groups that existed at the time, such as Civilian Flying Saucer Investigators (CFSI) and the Aerial Phenomena Research Organization (APRO), should be watched carefully because of "the apparent irresponsibility and the possible use of such groups for subversive purposes."

Underground Secret Society

Before his death in late 2009, Mac Tonnies was digging deep into the strange and enigmatic world of what he termed the cryptoterrestrials. Tonnies's theory was that, perhaps, the intelligences behind the UFO phenomenon were not extraterrestrial or interdimensional, as many assume or believe them to be, after all. Rather, Tonnies was following the idea that the so-called "Grays" and many of the other bizarre humanoid creatures seen and presumed to have alien origins were from right here on Earth. Tonnies offered the theory (and he was very careful to admit it was just a theory) that his aliens of the terrestrial variety are, actually, a very ancient and advanced body of people, closely related to the human race, who have lived alongside us in secret—deep underground—for countless millennia.

In addition, Tonnies theorized that in today's world they may well be declining, in terms of both their numbers and their health. Tonnies also suggested that the cryptoterrestrials might make use of a great deal of subterfuge, camouflage, and deception to try and ensure they appear far more advanced than us, when—in reality—they may not be so far advanced, after all. Tonnies also had an interesting theory as to why the supposed aliens constantly warn abductees and contactees that we should not destroy, or pollute, our planet.

An alien "Gray," which, according to Mac Tonnies, actually comes from Earth and not some extraterrestrial source.

Let's face it, why would extraterrestrials from countless light-years away care even in the slightest about our small, insignificant world? A reasonable argument could be made that they wouldn't care. If, however, the extraterrestrials are actually cryptoterrestrials who—due to circumstances beyond both their and our control—are forced to secretly share the planet with us, then their desire to see the Earth preserved wouldn't just be a wish or a desire. It would, for their continued survival, be an overwhelming necessity.

Of course, such a theory is most assuredly not a new one: tales, stories, myths, and legends of advanced, humanoid entities living deep below the planet's surface have circulated not just for decades or hundreds of years, but for thousands of years. But, of the many reasons why Tonnies's book thrust the entire issue into the modern era, one in particular was his take on Roswell.

The fact is that none of us really knows what happened back in 1947 when something came down on the Foster Ranch in Lincoln County, New Mexico. There is nothing wrong with addressing, and contemplating, the merits—or the lack of merits—of the many and varied theories for what happened at Roswell, which is exactly what Tonnies chose to do.

In his 2009 book, *The Cryptoterrestrials*, Tonnies speculated on the possibility that the Roswell craft was built, flown, and disastrously crashed by ancient humanoids that lurk in the depths of the planet. Controversial? Definitely. But Tonnies made some interesting observations on this possibility. In his own words: "The device that crashed near Roswell in the summer of 1947, whatever it was, featured properties at least superficially like the high-altitude balloon trains ultimately cited as an explanation by the Air Force. Debunkers have, of course, seized on the lack of revealingly 'high-tech' components found among the debris to dismiss the possibility that the crash was anything but a case of misidentification; not even Maj. Jesse Marcel, the intelligence officer who advocated an ET origin for the unusual foil and structural beams, mentioned anything remotely resembling an engine or power-plant."

Tonnies continued in a fashion that emphasized that the cryptoterrestrials may not be as scientifically and technologically advanced as they might prefer us to think they are: "The cryptoterrestrial hypothesis offers a speculative alternative: maybe the Roswell device wasn't high-tech. It could indeed have been a balloon-borne surveillance device brought down in a storm, but it doesn't logically follow that it was one of our own."

Tonnies concluded: "Upon happening across such a troubling find, the Air Force's excessive secrecy begins to make sense."

Regardless of what you, I, or indeed any number of the well-known Roswell researchers—such as Bill Moore, Kevin Randle, Stan Friedman, or Don Schmitt—might think or conclude, the fact is that Tonnies's cryptoterrestrial theory is probably the only one that allows for the Roswell crash site to have been composed of very unusual, non-*Homo sapiens*, but, at the same time, incredibly simplistic technology.

The alien theory should, of course, require highly advanced technology to have been recovered—yet, we hear very little on this matter, aside from talk of fields full of foil-like material with curious properties. Accounts of the military coming across alien-created "power-plants" and "engines"—as Tonnies described them—are curiously 100 percent absent from the Roswell affair. It's that aforementioned foil and not much else.

Tonnies was not alone in talking about this particular theory. Walter Bosley, formerly of the U.S. Air Force Office of Special Investigations, has revealed an interesting and notable story told to him by his very own father, also of the U.S.A.F., who worked on issues connected to the U.S. space pro-

> **T**onnies continued in a fashion that emphasized that the cryptoterrestrials may not be as scientifically and technologically advanced as they might prefer us to think they are....

gram. According to the account related to Bosley, a very significant and highly anomalous event did occur some miles from the New Mexico town of Roswell. Not only did the crash have nothing to do with literal extraterrestrials, said Bosley's father, but it had nothing to do with us either.

In a briefing at Wright-Patterson Air Force Base, Bosley's father was told, essentially, the same thing upon which Mac Tonnies theorized—namely, that Roswell was the site of a the crash of a device piloted by a secret society of ancient humanoids that dwelled within the Earth, deep in hidden, cavernous abodes. Only occasionally did they ever surface, usually taking careful and stealthy steps to mask their presence—that is, until one of their fairly simple devices crashed outside of Roswell and revealed to a select few senior military personnel that we share our planet with something else, something from deep below.

Ustashi

When World War II began in September 1939, Adolf Hitler chose a highly alternative way to help fund the Nazi war machine. He and his cronies descended upon Europe's museums, palaces, churches, and cathedrals, and all with one specific goal in mind: namely, to loot them of just about as much gold, ancient artifacts, paintings, and priceless treasures as possible. From there, the Nazis then siphoned all of their bounties to a variety of banks, including the powerful Swiss National Bank, in exchange for money—money that would be used to build tanks, aircraft, ships, and weapons.

Despite the fact that the Swiss National Bank consistently denies any collaboration with the Nazis, the words of Stuart Eizenstat, who, during the presidential term of Jimmy Carter, held the position of Chief Domestic Policy Adviser, strongly suggest otherwise. In Eizenstat's own words: "The Swiss National Bank must have known that some portion of the gold it was receiving from the Reichsbank was looted from occupied countries, due to the public knowledge about the low level of the Reichsbank's gold reserves and repeated warnings from the Allies."

History has shown that much of this looting by the Nazis was undertaken by a secret group called the Ustashi, a group that specialized in securing the priceless treasures that Hitler demanded. More than $80 million was made available to the Ustashi, at least some of which is known to have reached the personal hands of powerful Swiss bankers. By early 1945, however, it became clear to the Ustashi that Hitler and the Nazis were on their last legs. The result: the Ustashi began to fall apart, with various members doing their own secret deals with Swiss bankers, as they fought to survive while the Nazis spiraled down to their end. Many of the Ustashi focused their activities on Italy, and particularly a certain Father Krunolav Dragonović, who ran Rome's San Girolamo pontifical college. Very disturbingly, senior staff in the Vatican were fully aware of this Faustian pact—yet did nothing to prevent it from going ahead.

> **Very disturbingly, senior staff in the Vatican were fully aware of this Faustian pact—yet did nothing to prevent it from going ahead.**

In the immediate postwar era, the U.S. government wasted no time in looking into the matter of the secret work of the Ustashi and its links with the Vatican. Emerson Bigelow was an agent of the U.S. Treasury who learned, in 1946, from insider sources at the Vatican that the Ustashi had secretly channeled no less than 200 million Swiss francs to the Vatican, to ensure it stayed out of the hands of those to whom it rightly belonged—namely, those from whom the Ustashi stole it. A further and near-identical amount, Bigelow learned, was held by the Institute for Works of Religion—the Vatican Bank. To this day, rumors continue to circulate that massive amounts of Nazi gold and treasures—stolen by the Ustashi and then transferred to the Vatican—remain hidden deep below the Vatican and the streets of Rome.

V. W. Z

Vampire Cults

It may surprise many to learn that the United States is teeming with people who are devoted to the worship of all things of a Vampire nature. And many of their practices are steeped in secrecy. Consider the following from the Vampire Society, a group with a large—and still growing—national membership: "The Vampire Society is a private and exclusive Society of real Vampires and their disciples. We are seeking others like us and those few who desire to become like us. The Vampire Society provides fellowship among Vampires and helps its Members in their search to understand why they are Vampires and where we came from. True Vampires are those who are possessed of full Vampire Blood. They are the Vampire of lore and legend, although the subject of much misunderstanding. Vampires can only be made of those with whom this Blood is shared."

The group continues that the "sharing of Vampire Blood" and the "making of a Vampire" is specifically achieved by well-guarded, occult means that known only to those who have reached the position of "Master Vampires."

The society continues: "Some say that Vampirism originated in the mating of angels with mortal women, spoken of in the Bible, in the book of Genesis. Vampires are their spiritual and physical descendants. The angelic bloodline became diluted with time and many today possess Vampire Blood without knowing it, although they know they are different."

A cult following all things vampiric has many adherents in the United States.

The Vampire Blood, the society notes, "is passed on genetically." Group members add that for those people "whose veins it courses," they typically demonstrate "characteristics of personality similar to Vampirism." This, the group explains, "is most widely expressed as gifts of psychic ability or paranormal powers, 'second sight' and telepathy, a hypnotic influence over others, clairvoyance, the ability to see spirits, a natural aversion to sunlight, an inborn ability to understand obscure occult subjects, an attraction to cemeteries, a desire to live in the past, and a feeling of being different and apart from others."

Then there is this from Temple of the Vampire, which also has a nationwide membership in the United States: "The Temple is the only authentic international organization in the world that represents the true Vampire religion. We have a worldwide membership and a dedicated Priesthood. The Temple of the Vampire has been in continuous existence since its creation in 1989 when we formed our organization in the United States. We did this to allow our membership to benefit from the legal protection of religion under the First Amendment of the U.S. Constitution."

The group has much more to say about its works and beliefs. Interestingly, the Temple of the Vampire owes much of its success not to vampires per se, but to the one thing that each and every one of us are tapped into: the worldwide web. The Temple of the Vampire notes this very clearly and openly: "Membership grew slowly but steadily for the first few years, but then with the explosion of electronic communications, membership has made rapid growth over the last decade. Most members have come to the Temple through word of mouth however it is increasingly common for new members to find the Temple through social networks on the Internet.

We are elitist for good reason and do not recognize any others who would make claims upon our heritage and authority, and we continue to grow internationally, offering members live support and training."

The Temple of the Vampire also notes that the classic creature of the night is "the next step in human evolution." And they have a challenge for you: "If you are ready, the Temple is here to empower you."

The group continues: "We believe the value of the individual is superior to that of any group or tribe or nation. In everything we do, we believe in challenging anything opposing individual freedom. The way we do this is by empowering individuals to achieve independent control over their lives through wealth, health, personal power, and unlimited life extension. We created a worldwide organization with proven methods for making this possible. For more than twenty-five years we have been active doing so.

"The Temple embraces only those aspects of the Vampire mythos that include a love and respect for all life, physical immortality, individual elegance, proven wisdom, civilized behavior, worldly success, and personal happiness. The Temple rejects those aspects of the Vampire mythos that are negative including any that are anti-life, anti-social, deathist, crude, gory, self-defeating, or criminal."

And, to demonstrate the regional—rather than solely national—nature of Vampire cults in the United States, consider the following from the Atlanta Vampire Alliance: "The mission of the Atlanta Vampire Alliance [AVA] is to promote unity in the greater Atlanta, Georgia real Vampire Community while being available to the newly awakened to encourage self-awareness and responsibility. We honor the traditions of history, respect and discretion regarding Community affairs while advocating the safety and wellbeing of our members. Emphasizing research and support of social gatherings we highlight the importance of education and strength of involvement as a cohesive force in our area. By taking an active role we will serve not only ourselves, but also our Community, and our City.

"We accept members from both sanguinarian and psychic backgrounds from the local Community. The [AVA] welcomes everyone to use our forums to contribute to the collective knowledge of our Community. We do not criticize other Houses, Orders, or paths but remain neutral and available to all who wish to belong. Additionally we offer an open hand to those who in the past have chosen to remain solitary in the Vampire Community. It is left to our members to discern which path is appropriate for them while we work in concert to support their journey of spiritual and intellectual growth."

Voodoo

While just about everyone has heard of Voodoo, not so many are aware of its origins and how it is defined. Author Brad Steiger says: "According to some of its more passionate adherents, Vodun/Vodoun is not a magical tradition, not an animistic tradition, not a spirit tradition neither, and it should be seen as a pagan religion. The deities of Voodoo are not simply spiritual energies and the path of Voodoo should not be followed for the sake of power over another. Although the Voodoo religion does not demand members proselytize, anyone may join. However, ninety-nine percent of its priesthoods are passed from generation to generation. The same individuals who esteem their Voodoo religion so highly insist that it is neither dogmatic nor apocalyptic. Whatever outsiders may make of their faith, the sincere Voodoo follower declares that it has no apocalyptic tradition that prophesies a doomsday or end-of-the-world scenario."

As far as what, precisely, Voodoo means, the closest English word is "spirit." And, despite what some have said, it's not a tradition that dates back a few centuries or thereabouts. A study of West African history and folklore reveals that Voodoo—in a very early incarnation—existed as far back as 8000 B.C.E.

Ancient Origins notes: "When African slaves were brought to the Americas to work on plantations, they brought Voodoo with them. Their white masters, however, had other plans regarding the religious practice of their slaves. A 1685 law, for instance, prohibited the practice of African religions,

The concept of Voodoo might bring to mind dolls used to control others magically, but its religion actually says it is wrong to have power over people.

and required all masters to Christianize their slaves within eight days of their arrival in Haiti. Although the slaves accepted Roman Catholicism, they did not give up their traditional beliefs either. Instead, the old and the new were syncretized, producing some unique results. Many of the Catholic saints were identified with traditional Voodoo lwas (spirits) or held a double meaning for the practitioners of Voodoo. For instance, in Haitian Voodoo, St. Peter is recognized as Papa Legba, the gatekeeper of the spirit world, whilst St. Patrick is associated with Dumballah, the snake lwa."

Now it's time to turn our attentions to the one place that so many associate with Voodoo, namely New Orleans, Louisiana. Severine Singh, who has made a deep study of Voodoo says: "New Orleans offered a perfect setting for the practice and growth of Voodoo. In 1809 many Haitians who had migrated to Cuba during the Haitian revolution found themselves cast out and came to New Orleans. They brought with them their slaves who incorporated their rites and beliefs to those of the existent slave population—Africans from Senegal, Gambia and Nigeria previously brought to Louisiana by the Companie des Indes. Voodoo in Louisiana was enriched and revitalized. It also incorporated the worship of the Snake Spirit (Damballah Wedo/Aida Wedo). To the Africans Voodoo was not only their religion, it was also their natural medicine, their protection and certainly a way of asserting and safeguarding a sense of personal freedom and identity."

And as Singh also reveals, "Today about 15% of the population of New Orleans practices Voodoo. Modern Voodoo has taken several directions: Spiritualist Reverends and Mothers who have their own churches, Hoodoos who integrate and work spells and superstitions, elements of European witchcraft and the occult, and traditionalists for whom the practice of Voodoo is a most natural and important part of their daily lives, a positive search for ancient roots and wisdom. The practice of Voodoo involves the search for higher levels of consciousness in the belief that—as indeed all of the ancient scriptures teach—it is we who must open the way towards the Gods, for when we call out from our hearts, the Gods hear and indeed are compelled to respond."

Voynich Manuscript

The *Voynich Manuscript* is an enigmatic book penned in the early part of the 1400s that has consistently defied the world's finest codebreakers who have spent decades trying to decipher the odd text. It takes its name from a man named Wilfrid Voynich, a dealer of books who obtained the manuscript back

A page of the *Voynich Manuscript* dates to the fifteenth century. The writing used is in an unknown language.

in 1912. As for the contents of the *Voynich Manuscript*, they include a great deal of material relative to botany—as well as close to thirty pages of imagery of the heavens: stars, planets and moons. But, as for why, and what the attendant text says, no one knows.

Rene Zandbergen, who has carefully and deeply studied the manuscript, says: "In 1639 the Prague citizen Georgius Barschius wrote to the Jesuit Athanasius Kircher in Rome that he owned a mysterious book that was written in an unknown script and was profusely illustrated with pictures of plants, stars and alchemical secrets. He hoped that Kircher would be able to translate this book for him, but Kircher could not. The book has come down to us and even now, almost four centuries later, the text on its well over 200 pages cannot be understood, and it ranks among the most famous historical riddles that just seems to be waiting for a solution.

It is not as if nobody has been able to propose any solution. Quite the contrary! Many different 'solutions' are proposed each year. The problem is that none of these have been sufficiently convincing."

As to how it fell into Voynich's hands, we have this from the man himself: "In 1912 I came across a most remarkable collection of preciously illuminated manuscripts. For many decades these volumes had lain buried in the chests in which I found them in an ancient castle in Southern Europe. While examining the manuscripts, with a view to the acquisition of at least a part of the collection, my attention was especially drawn by one volume. It was such an ugly duckling compared with the other manuscripts, with their rich decorations in gold and colors, that my interest was aroused at once. I found that it was written entirely in cipher. Even a necessarily brief examination of the vellum upon which it was written, the calligraphy, the drawings and the pigments suggested to me as the date of its origin the latter part of the thirteenth century. The drawings indicated it to be an encyclopedic work on natural philosophy.

"The fact that this was a thirteenth century manuscript in cipher convinced me that it must be a work of exceptional importance, and to my knowledge the existence of a manuscript of such an early date written entirely in cipher was unknown, so I included it among the manuscripts which I purchased from this collection. Two problems presented themselves—the text must be unraveled and the history of the manuscript must be traced. It was not until sometime after the manuscript came into my hands that I read the document bearing the date 1665 (or 1666), which was attached to the front cover. This document, which is a letter from Joannes Marcus Marci to Athanasius Kircher making a gift of the manuscript to him, is of great significance."

Notably, a theory exists that the manuscript was the work of a secret society based in Italy—one with a very long and clandestine lineage—that extended back to the time when the Roman Empire was at its height. It apparently still existed when the *Voynich Manuscript* was compiled, and was said to have been just one of dozens of such manuscripts—only one of which is, today, known.

It's intriguing to note that the National Security Agency has taken a very deep interest in trying to crack the code of the *Voynich Manuscript*. Via the terms of the Freedom of Information Act, the NSA has declassified into the public domain several important papers penned by those agency personnel who tried to tackle the mystery for themselves, one being "The Most Mysterious Manuscript in the World," written by Brigadier John H. Tiltman, a man who worked for the United Kingdom's equivalent to the NSA, the Government Communications Headquarters (GCHQ) at Cheltenham, England. As evidence of Tiltman's skills as a codebreaker, he was the first non-American to become a member of the NSA's Hall of Honor.

But, for all of the NSA's skills in codebreaking, cipher cracking, and spying, the *Voynich Manuscript* remains the mystery that it did when it fell into the hands of Wilfrid Voynich more than a century ago.

Vril Society

Toyne Newton says: "In his strange and fascinating book *The Coming Race* [actually *Vril, the Power of the Coming Race*, which was published in 1871), the British author Edward Bulwer Lord Lytton credits the Vril-ya, an intellectual super-race of subterranean peoples, as having mastered 'Vril-power,' their ultimate aim being to rise up from their underground realms and take control of the world."

For those who may be wondering what Vril really is, it's said to be a strange and supernatural force, known as Prana by those of a Hindu persuasion and as Vril by Tibetan lamas. Reportedly, there are no fewer than eight "levels" of Vril, the most significant being "Garima," which allegedly allows those who master it to manipulate nothing less than matter itself.

Although Lytton's book was presented in the form of a novel, there were many who came to believe that *Vril, the Power of the Coming Race* had a basis

Politician and author Edward Bulwer Lord Lytton was the author of *The Coming Race*.

in reality. Among those believers were no less than high-ranking Nazis. Willy Ley, a brilliant German expert in the field of rocketry who transplanted to the United States in 1937, took a great deal of interest in the way in which the Nazis were increasingly incorporating occult lore and teachings into their ideology. Ley said of one such group that it was "literally founded upon a novel. That group which I think called itself Wahrheitsgesellschaft—Society for Truth—and which was more or less localized in Berlin, devoted its spare time looking for Vril."

Echoes of Enoch says: "The Vril Society was formed by a group of female psychic mediums led by the Thule Gesellschaft medium Maria Orsitsch (Orsic) of Zagreb, who claimed to have received communication from Aryan aliens living on Alpha Cen Tauri, in the Aldebaran system. Allegedly, these aliens had visited Earth and settled in Sumeria, and the word Vril was formed from the ancient Sumerian word 'Vri-Il' ('like god'). A second medium was known only as Sigrun, a name etymologically related to Sigrune, a Valkyrie and one of Wotan's nine daughters in Norse legend.

"The Society allegedly taught concentration exercises designed to awaken the forces of Vril, and their main goal was to achieve *Raumflug* (Spaceflight) to reach Aldebaran. To achieve this, the Vril Society joined the Thule Gesellschaft to fund an ambitious program involving an inter-dimensional flight machine based on psychic revelations from the Aldebaran aliens.

"Members of the Vril Society are said to have included Adolf Hitler, Alfred Rosenberg, Heinrich Himmler, Hermann Goring, and Hitler's personal physician, Dr. Theodor Morell. These were original members of the Thule Society which supposedly joined Vril in 1919. The NSDAP (National Sozialistische Deutsche Arbeiter Partei) was created by Thule in 1920, one year later. Dr. Krohn, who helped to create the Nazi flag, was also a Thulist. With Hitler in power in 1933, both Thule and Vril Gesellschafts allegedly received official state backing for continued disc development programs aimed at both spaceflight and possibly a war machine."

The final words go to Lytton, who, back in 1871, said: "There is no word in the English language that I know of which is an exact synonym for 'VRIL.' I should call it electricity, except that it comprehends in its manifold branches other forces of nature, to which in our scientific nomenclature, differing names are assigned, such as magnetism, galvanism, etc. These people consider that in 'VRIL' they have arrived at the unity in natural energic agencies, which has been conjectured by many philosophers above ground, and which Faraday (an English experimental physicist who founded the science of electromagnetism) thus intimates under the more cautious term of correlation: 'I have long held an opinion,' he says, 'almost amounting to a conviction in common with many other lovers of natural knowledge, that the various forms under which the forces of matter are made manifest have one common origin; or, in other words, are so directly related, and mutually dependent, that they are convertible, as it were, into one another, and possess equivalents of power in their action.'"

Lytton continued: "These subterranean philosophers assert that, by one operation of VRIL, which Faraday would perhaps call 'atmospheric magnetism,' they can influence the variations of temperature—in plain words, the weather, that by other operations, akin to those ascribed to mesmerism, electro-biology, odic force, etc., but applied scientifically through VRIL conductors, they can exercise influence over minds, and bodies, animal and vegetable, to an extent not surpassed in the romances of our mysticism. To all such agencies they give the common name of VRIL."

Wackenhut Corporation

G4S Secure Solutions (U.S.A.) is an American security services company, and a wholly owned subsidiary of G4S plc. It was founded as The Wackenhut Corporation in 1954, in Coral Gables, Florida, by George Wackenhut and three partners (all of them former FBI agents). In 2002, the company was acquired for $570 million by Danish corporation Group 4 Falck (which then merged to form a British company, G4S, in 2004). In 2010, G4S Wackenhut changed its name to G4S Secure Solutions (U.S.A.) to reflect the new business model. The G4S Americas Region headquarters is in Jupiter, Florida.

After early struggles (including a fistfight between George Wackenhut and one of his partners), Wackenhut took sole control of his company in 1958, then choosing to name it after himself. By 1964, he had contracts to guard the Kennedy Space Center and the U.S. Atomic Energy Commission's nuclear test site in Nevada, which included Area 51. The following year, Wackenhut took his company public. In the mid-1960s, Florida governor Claude Kirk commissioned the Wackenhut Corporation to help fight a "war on organized crime," awarding the company a $500,000 contract. The commission lasted about a year but led to more than eighty criminal indictments, including many for local politicians and government employees.

Following the murder of a British tourist at a rest stop in 1993, Florida contracted with Wackenhut to provide security at all state rest stops.

The company's work includes: permanent guarding service, security officers, manned security, disaster response, emergency services, control room monitoring, armed security, unarmed security, special event security, security patrols, reception/concierge service, access control, emergency medical technicians (EMT) service, and ambassador service. Like other security companies, G4S targets specific sectors: energy, utilities, chemical/petrochemical, financial institutions, government, hospitals and healthcare facilities, major corporations, construction, ports and airports, residential communities, retail and commercial real estate, and transit systems.

> **Wackenhut then became the nation's second largest for-profit prison operator.**

Having expanded into providing food services for U.S. prisons in the 1960s, Wackenhut—in 1984—launched a subsidiary to design and manage jails and detention centers for the burgeoning private prison market. Wackenhut then became the nation's second largest for-profit prison operator. In April 1999, the state of Louisiana took over the running of Wackenhut's fifteen-month-old juvenile prison, after the U.S. Justice Department accused Wackenhut of subjecting its young inmates to "excessive abuse and neglect."

American journalist Gregory Palast commented on the case: "New Mexico's privately operated prisons are filled with America's impoverished, violent outcasts—and those are the guards."

The GEO Group, Inc. now runs former Wackenhut facilities in fourteen states, as well as in South Africa and Australia. Some facilities, such as the Wackenhut Corrections Centers in New York, retain the Wackenhut name, despite no longer having any open connection with the company.

Frequent rumors that the company was in the employ of the Central Intelligence Agency, particularly in the 1960s, were never substantiated; however, George Wackenhut, who was obsessive about high-tech security gadgets in his private life, never denied the rumors.

Weather Underground Organization

On January 29, 1975, an explosion rocked the headquarters of the U.S. State Department in Washington, D.C. No one was hurt, but the damage was extensive, impacting twenty offices on three separate floors. Hours later, another bomb was found at a military induction center in Oakland, California, and safely detonated. A domestic terrorist group called the Weather Underground claimed responsibility.

The Weather Underground Organization—originally called the Weathermen, taken from a line in a Bob Dylan song—was a small, violent offshoot of the Students for a Democratic Society (SDS), created in the turbulent '60s to promote social change.

When the SDS collapsed in 1969, the Weather Underground stepped forward, inspired by communist ideologies and embracing violence and crime as a way to protest the Vietnam War, racism, and other left-wing aims. "Our intention is to disrupt the empire … to incapacitate it, to put pressure on the cracks," claimed the group's 1974 manifesto, *Prairie Fire*. By the next year, the group had claimed credit for twenty-five bombings and would be involved in many more over the next several years.

The FBI doggedly pursued these terrorists as their attacks mounted. Many members were soon identified, but their small numbers and guerilla tactics helped them hide under assumed identities. In 1978, however, the Bureau arrested five members who were plotting to bomb a politician's office. More were arrested when an accident destroyed the group's bomb factory in Hoboken, New Jersey. Others were identified after two policemen and a Brinks driver were murdered in a botched armored car robbery in Nanuet, New York.

Key to disrupting the group for good was the newly created FBI-New York City Police Anti-Terrorist Task Force. It brought together the strengths of both organizations and focused them on these domestic terrorists. The task force and others like it paved the way for today's Joint Terrorism Task Forces—created by the Bureau in each of its field offices to fuse federal, state, and local law enforcement and intelligence resources to combat today's terrorist threats.

By the mid-1980s, the Weather Underground was essentially history. Still, several of these fugitives were able to successfully hide themselves for decades, emerging only in recent years to answer for their crimes. Once again, it shows that grit and partnerships can and will defeat shadowy, resilient terrorist groups.

Weathermen

In 2015, a strange and controversial story surfaced concerning a secret group known as the Weathermen. Their mandate is to clandestinely research, and ultimately perfect, weaponry that can provoke significant and drastic changes in the world's weather that will ensure massive starvation, flooding, tornadoes, and earthquakes, all as a means to ensure one sinister outcome: to depopulate human civilization until it reaches a point that it can be effectively controlled and enslaved by a looming New World Order. If such a scenario sounds likes science fiction, it's not. It's all too real.

April 28, 1997, was the date on which a startling statement was made by William S. Cohen—at the time, the U.S. secretary of defense in the Clinton administration. The location was the University of Georgia, which was playing host to the Conference on Terrorism, Weapons of Mass Destruction, and U.S. Strategy. As a captivated audience listened intently, Cohen revealed something that was as remarkable as it was controversial.

Hostile groups—that Cohen, whether by design or not, did not name—were actively "engaging in an eco-type of terrorism whereby they can alter the climate, set off earthquakes, volcanoes remotely through the use of Electro-Magnetic waves. So there are plenty of ingenious minds out there that are at work finding ways in which they can wreak terror upon other nations. It's real."

Cohen was not wrong: in 1996 the U.S. Air Force unveiled to the public and the media an astonishing document. It read like science fiction. It was, however, nothing less than amazing, controversial, science fact. The title of the document was *U.S.A.F. 2025.* It was basically a study of where the Air Force hoped to be—technologically and militarily speaking—in 2025.

Researched and written by the 2025 Support Office at the Air University, Air Education and Training Command, and developed by the Air University Press, Educational Services Directorate, College of Aerospace Doctrine, Research, and Education, Maxwell Air Force Base, Alabama, the document was "designed to comply with a directive from the chief of staff of the Air Force to examine the concepts, capabilities, and technologies the United States will require to remain the dominant air and space force in the future."

Beyond any shadow of doubt, the most controversial section of the entire *U.S.A.F. 2025* report was that titled "Weather as a Force Multiplier: Owning the Weather in 2025." Forget missiles, bombs, bullets, troops, and aircraft. The future, very possibly, lies in defeating the enemy via global weather manipulation.

"In 2025, U.S. aerospace forces can 'own the weather' by capitalizing on emerging technologies and focusing development of those technologies to war-fighting applications. While some segments of society will always be reluctant to examine controversial issues such as weather modification, the tremendous military capabilities that could result from this field are ignored at our own peril. Weather modification offers the war fighter a wide-range of possible options to defeat or coerce an adversary," the report states.

The authors also noted: "The desirability to modify storms to support military objectives is the most aggressive and controversial type of weather modification. While offensive weather modification efforts would certainly be undertaken by U.S. forces with great caution and trepidation, it is clear that we cannot afford to allow an adversary to obtain an exclusive weather modification capability."

It's very clear that a great deal of thought had gone into the production of this particular section of the report. It begins by providing the reader with a theoretical scenario, one filled with conflict, but which may very well be resolvable by turning the weather into a weapon: "Imagine that in 2025 the U.S. is fighting a rich, but now consolidated, politically powerful drug cartel in South America. The cartel has purchased hundreds of Russian- and Chinese-built fighters that have successfully thwarted our attempts to attack their production facilities. With their local numerical superiority and interior lines, the cartel is launching more than 10 aircraft for every one of ours. In addition, the cartel is using the French *système probatoire*

In 1997 Secretary of State William S. Cohen stated that terrorists were trying to control the weather and perform other acts of ecoterrorism.

d'observation de la terre (SPOT) positioning and tracking imagery systems, which in 2025 are capable of transmitting near-real-time, multispectral imagery with 1 meter resolution. The U.S. wishes to engage the enemy on an uneven playing field in order to exploit the full potential of our aircraft and munitions."

At this point, a decision is taken to focus carefully on making the local weather work for the United States and against the cartel: "Meteorological analysis reveals that equatorial South America typically has afternoon thunderstorms on a daily basis throughout the year. Our intelligence has confirmed that cartel pilots are reluctant to fly in or near thunderstorms. Therefore, our weather force support element (WFSE), which is a part of the commander in chief's (CINC) air operations center (AOC), is tasked to forecast storm paths and trigger or intensify thunderstorm cells over critical target areas that the enemy must defend with their aircraft. Since our aircraft in 2025 have all-weather capability, the thunderstorm threat is minimal to our forces, and we can effectively and decisively control the sky over the target."

The WFSE, the report notes, has the necessary sensor and communication capabilities to observe, detect, and act on weather modification requirements to support U.S. military objectives. These capabilities, we are told, "are part of an advanced battle area system that supports the war-fighting CINC. In our scenario, the CINC tasks the WFSE to conduct storm intensification and concealment operations. The WFSE models the atmospheric conditions to forecast, with 90 percent confidence, the likelihood of successful modification using airborne cloud generation and seeding."

The countdown to Weather War One may soon begin.

Welsh Secret Society

Back in 1993, Julian and Emma Orbach purchased a large piece of land in west Wales's Preseli Mountains. Ultimately, the then-soon-to-be camouflaged area became home to more than twenty like-minded people, all of whom wished to live outside of the confines of what passes for society. They constructed grass-covered, wooden buildings and became very much self-sufficient. In some respects, their story is not unlike that presented in M. Night Shyamalan's 2004 movie, *The Village*.

For all intents and purposes, they created a self-enclosed community, the existence of which very few, if indeed hardly any, had any inkling. That the secret village resembled something straight out of the Middle Ages or—as the media noted, when the story broke—Tolkein's *The Lord of the Rings*, only added to the engaging and near-magical nature of the area.

Astonishingly, the Orbachs, and the rest of their number, lived in blissful peace and stealth for no fewer than five years before anyone in authority even realized what was going on. In fact, the only reason why the story, and the facts behind it, ever surfaced was because, in 1998, a survey aircraft in the area happened to take aerial photographs of the village. This was most unfortunate for one and all who called the place their home, as their cover was finally blown. The result: it wasn't long at all before numerous tedious, humorless automatons of government descended on the colony, all determined to stick their meddling noses into the situation.

With no planning permission having ever been obtained for the village, the government was adamant that the buildings, along with each and every bit of the little, isolated locale, had to be destroyed. Or else. And, as a result, thus began a years-

> Astonishingly, the Orbachs, and the rest of their number, lived in blissful peace and stealth for no fewer than five years before anyone in authority even realized what was going on.

long campaign in which the unsmiling men in black suits sought to just follow orders, while those who called the Narnia-like area their home fought to remain there, untouched and unspoiled by officialdom and the aggravating presence of the Nanny State. At one point, bulldozers were even brought onto the scene, ready and waiting for the cold hearts of officialdom to give the green light to flatten the eight buildings that comprised the secret village.

Fortunately, it did not come to that. Finally, in 2008—which was a full decade after the existence of the village first became public knowledge, and fifteen years after the first steps to create it had been taken—the government caved in. It was a good day for the people of that little village.

The situation was helped by the fact that, come 2008, the government of the day was far more mindful of green issues than in previous years. So, the minions of officialdom agreed that providing the villagers followed certain rules and regulations—and could demonstrate that they were improving the biodiversity of the area and conserving the surrounding woodland—they could remain intact and free of bureaucratic busybodies. Sometimes, sanity and commonsense actually do prevail, even within government, as amazing as such a thing might sound.

Werewolf Cult of Australia

In November 2003, a very strange and controversial story surfaced in Australia's media. Certainly the most graphic example appeared in the pages of the Queensland-based *Sunday Mail* newspaper. In an article titled "Cult told my son he was a werewolf," readers were told the following: "A quasi-religious cult is using the Internet to recruit teenagers who are encouraged to act as werewolves, howl at the moon and eat raw meat. Counsellors at the Cult Information Hotline have received several complaints about the group, which has more than 50 members throughout Queensland. Counsellors and concerned parents said complaints had been made to police and government authorities about the activities of cult members in Housing Commission properties."

The article continued and revealed how a mother in the Australian city of Brisbane discovered—to her horror—that her teenaged son had become immersed in the world of the Australian werewolf. She wasted no time in contacting social workers attached to Queensland Health. One of those social workers, David Ward, offered his help to the young man and his mother and said: "My concern is these kids believe they can turn into werewolves and start eating raw meat, which makes them sick. The teenager I spoke to a couple of

A cult believing in the ability of people to become werewolves has emerged in Queensland, Australia.

times, who is living with this group, is just your average adolescent. There's a myth that says there must be something wrong with these children or they come from a broken home. This boy was going through normal adolescent stuff. They go through an identity crisis, where they wonder who they are, and they're vulnerable."

As for the boy's mother, she provided the following, on how her son became immersed in such a strange and secret society: "My son had been studying really hard at school, he was very quiet and I suggested he join a computer group." The boy decided to do exactly that, and was soon in the grip of werewolves, so to speak. The mother continued: "A young man then kept ringing us, wanting my son to come out and within three weeks he was part of the group. This fellow started to stalk us at night. He'd start howling like a werewolf at midnight outside our house, which frightened the other kids. My son left and moved into a house with this fellow and another bloke. They would dress up in costumes like wolves and take my son on a leash to South Bank."

The *Sunday Mail* stated that the young man's mother "still maintains weekly telephone contact with her son, who has joined other cult members, interstate. She said she had become concerned about his health after he joined the group several months ago."

Ward added: "The police can't do anything about these groups. It's not as if they're breaking the law. This mother will have to wait until her son comes to his senses. It could take two months, or two decades, depending on the person."

Wicca

The Church and School of Wicca says the following: "We are always happy to meet someone else who is interested in exploring Witchcraft, the Old Religion, and its way of life. Witchcraft (Wicca Craft), is also called Wicca, or alternatively, The Craft. This previously underground religion has much to teach every human about survival and about the ethical use of natural innate powers.

"The Craft is a way of life that investigates every potential that you have. The Craft draws its strength from the diversity of Nature itself; indeed it rejoices in diversity. Your views and interests are just as valid as those of anyone else, and we hope that you too will help to push back the artificial barriers that surround many religious dogmas.

They are also keen to stress: "Witches are not Satanists. The negativity in that offshoot of Christianity is not for harmonious thinkers such as Witches. Anyway, we at the Church see Satan as just one more juju-on-a-stick, created to serve the overworked Eternal Trinity of guilt, shame, and fear."

Wicca is a religion that has a huge and devoted following, as *The Truth* website makes abundantly clear. Wicca, it states, "is currently growing at an astounding pace. Wicca emerged as a faith in the middle of the twentieth century, but the origins of many Wiccan practices actually go back for thousands of years, and some researchers believe that certain aspects of Wicca can actually be traced all the way back to ancient Babylon. According to Wikipedia, Wicca 'is a modern pagan, witchcraft religion.' It has been estimated that the number of Americans that are Wiccans is doubling every 30 months, and at this point there are more than 200,000 registered witches and approximately

The religion of Wicca is one of the fastest growing in the United States.

8 million unregistered practitioners of Wicca, and it is important to remember that Wicca is just one form of witchcraft. There are many other 'darker' forms of witchcraft that are also experiencing tremendous growth."

Having addressed the matter of the beliefs of Wiccans and the huge popularity it has achieved, it's now time to take a look at its origins. They are steeped in intrigue. The Wiccan movement of today is a relatively recent phenomenon—in fact, it only dates back to the twentieth century. It is, however, inspired by ancient paganism. Owen Davies, an expert on matters of a pagan kind, says: "It is crucial to stress right from the start that until the 20th century people did not call themselves pagans to describe the religion they practiced. The notion of paganism, as it is generally understood today, was created by the early Christian Church. It was a label that Christians applied to others, one of the antitheses that were central to the process of Christian self-definition. As such, throughout history it was generally used in a derogatory sense."

> **The one person, more than any other, who introduced the modern-day phenomenon of Wicca to the world was Gerald Brosseau Gardner.**

The one person, more than any other, who introduced the modern-day phenomenon of Wicca to the world was Gerald Brosseau Gardner. An English archaeologist, anthropologist, and civil-servant with the British government, Gardner had a fascination for the worlds of magic, the occult, and witchcraft. In 1939, after spending much time in Ceylon and Malaya, Gardner returned to the United Kingdom and put down roots in the New Forest, a 219-square-mile area of dense woodland in southern England. Having done so, Gardner—having an interest in Rosicrucianism—joined the Rosicrucian Order Crotona Fellowship, a group created in the early 1920s by George Alexander Sullivan.

It was as a direct result of his links to the Rosicrucian Order Crotona Fellowship that Gardner came into contact with a shadowy witch cult—in the direct vicinity of the New Forest—called the New Forest Coven. Gardner did more than come into contact with the order, however: he was initiated into its fold. He came to accept many of the ancient teachings. In his own words: "The Gods are real, not as persons, but as vehicles of power. Briefly, it may be explained that the personification of a particular type of cosmic power in the form of a God or Goddess, carried out by believers and worshippers over many centuries, builds that God-form or Magical Image into a potent reality on the Inner Planes, and makes it a means by which that type of cosmic power may be contacted."

Incorporating both ritual- and ceremonial-magic into a new body that adhered to the teachings of Aleister Crowley and also aspects of Freemasonry, Gardner birthed what, today, is Wicca. According to Gardner, one of the most spectacular successes that he helped achieve was to prevent the hordes of Adolf Hitler from invading the U.K. In what was termed Operation Cone of Power, Gardner and his colleagues in the New Forest Coven performed a magical ritual—filled with supernatural energy invoked in the woods—that sent the following message to Berlin, Germany, and even to Hitler himself: "You cannot cross the sea, you cannot cross the sea, you cannot come, you cannot come."

That Hitler never did invade the U.K.—despite having overrun much of Europe—was seen as evidence by Gardner that the old magic could be utilized in a modern-day setting to achieve extraordinary goals. And, as a result, Wicca—with Gardner in the driver's seat—was born.

Women in Black

Within the world of UFO research, the Men in Black are about as legendary as they are feared. These pale-faced, ghoulish entities have for decades terrorized into silence both witnesses to, and researchers of, UFO encounters. Theories for who or what the MIB might be are legion. They include: extraterrestrials, government agents, demonic creatures, vampires, time travelers from the future, and interdimensional beings from realms that coexist with ours. There may very well be more than one explanation for the unsettling phenomenon.

While much has been written about the sinister and occasionally deadly actions of the MIB, very little has been penned on the subject of their equally bone-chilling companions: the *Women in Black*. Make no mistake: the WIB are all too real, and they are as ominous, predatory, and dangerous as their male counterparts. In the same way that the Men in Black don't always wear black, but sometimes wear military uniforms or specifically beige-colored outfits, so do the WIB, who are also quite partial to white costumes. In that sense, WIB is, just like MIB, a term that is somewhat flexible in terms of actual nature and description.

The WIB may not have achieved the iconic status of the MIB—until now—but these fearsome females, and their collective role in silencing those who immerse themselves in the UFO puzzle, as well as in the domains of the occult and the world of the paranormal, are all too terrifyingly real. Not only that, the WIB have a long and twisted history.

Years before they plagued and tormented flying saucer seekers, the Women in Black roamed the landscape by night, stealing babies and young children, and plaguing the good folk of nineteenth-century United States and United Kingdom. They were also up to their infernal tricks in the 1920s.

A definitive WIB surfaced in nothing less than a piece of publicity-based footage for a Charlie Chaplin movie, *The Circus*, which was made in 1928. The footage, undeniably genuine and shown not to have been tampered with, reveals what appears to be an old, short lady, wearing a long black coat and a black hat pulled low over her face, while walking through Los Angeles in west coast heat. If that was not strange enough, she is clearly holding to her ear what appears to be a cell phone and is talking into it as she walks. Weirder still, the Woman in Black sports an enormous pair of black shoes, which look most out of place, given her short stature. She also seems to be taking careful steps to avoid her face being seen clearly. Might she have been some kind of time-traveling Woman in Black, working hard—but spectacularly failing—to blend in with the people of Los Angeles, all those years ago?

Make no mistake: the WIB are all too real, and they are as ominous, predatory and dangerous as their male counterparts.

Fifteen years later, a terrifying WIB haunted the Bender family of Bridgeport, Connecticut. It so happens that a certain Albert Bender, of that very clan, near-singlehandedly began the Men in Black mystery. In the early 1950s, Bender, after establishing the International Flying Saucer Bureau, was visited and threatened with nothing less than death by a trio of pale, skinny, fedora-wearing MIB. They were visits that firmly set the scene for the decades of MIB-themed horror and mayhem that followed. Bender's visitors were not secret agents of government, however. He said they materialized in his bedroom—a converted attic in a creepy old house of *Psycho* proportions—amid an overpowering stench of sulfur. They were shadowy beings with demon-like, glowing eyes. We surely cannot blame the CIA, the FBI, or even the all-powerful NSA, for that!

In 1956, UFO sleuth Gray Barker penned a book on Bender's confrontations with the Men in Black. It was titled *They Knew Too Much about Flying Saucers* and became a classic. Six years later, Bender penned his very own book on his encounters with the MIB, *Flying Saucers and the Three Men*. It was these two books that brought the MIB into the minds and homes of flying saucer enthusiasts across the world, after which, Bender dropped each and every one of his ties to ufology. He was careful to avoid speaking about the subject ever again, and, thereon, focused his time on running the appreciation society of composer Max Steiner.

Back in the 1930s, however, the Bender family had a black-garbed woman in its midst that tormented both young and old in the dead of night. Predating Albert Bender's own experience with the MIB by years, the hideous silencer in black haunted the Benders near-endlessly. For the Bender family, long before the MIB there was a Woman in Black.

In the 1960s, the emotionless, evil-eyed WIB turned up in the small, doom-filled town of Point Pleasant, West Virginia, right around the time that sightings of the legendary flying monster known as Mothman were at their height. Claiming to be census takers, these pale-faced, staring-eyed WIB practically forced their way into the homes of frightened witnesses to Mothman. What began as seemingly normal questions about the number of people in the house, of the average income of the family, and of the number of rooms in the relevant property, soon mutated into something much stranger: persistent and intrusive questions about strange dreams, unusual telephone interference, and beliefs regarding the world of all things of a paranormal nature soon followed.

One of the WIB who put in an appearance at Point Pleasant claimed to have been the secretary of acclaimed author on all things paranormal, John Keel, author of *The Mothman Prophecies*. Just like her male counterparts, she turned up on doorsteps late at night, waiting to be invited in, before grilling mystified and scared souls about their UFO and Mothman encounters. She then vanished into the night after carefully instilling feelings of distinct fear in the interviewees. Only when dozens of such stories got back to Keel did he realize the incredible scale of the dark ruse that was afoot. Keel had to break the unsettling news to each and every one of the frightened souls who contacted him: "I have no secretary."

In the 1970s, wig-wearing and anemic-looking WIB made life hell for more than a few people who were unfortunate enough to cross their paths. Something similar occurred in England, Scotland, and Ireland during the 1980s: a weird wave of encounters with phantom social workers hit the U.K. They were out-of-the-blue encounters that eerily paralleled the incidents involving WIB-based census takers that manifested in West Virginia back in the 1960s.

Just as menacing, sinister, and unsettling as their American cousins, these particular WIB began by claiming that reports had reached them of physical abuse to children in the family home that had to be investigated. Worried parents, clearly realizing that these hag-like crones were anything but social workers, invariably phoned the police. The WIB, realizing when they had been rumbled, made hasty exits and always before law enforcement personnel were on the scene. Most disturbing of all, there was a near-unanimous belief on the part of the parents that the Women in Black were intent on kidnapping the children for purposes unknown, but surely no good.

Back to the United States, in early 1987, Bruce Lee, a book editor for Morrow, had an experience with a WIB-type character in an uptown New York bookstore. Lee's attention to the curious woman—short, wrapped in a

> **M**ost disturbing of all, there was a near-unanimous belief on the part of the parents that the Women in Black were intent on kidnapping the children for purposes unknown, but surely no good.

wool hat and a long scarf, and wearing large black sunglasses behind which could be seen huge, "mad-dog" eyes—was prompted by something strange and synchronistic. She and her odd partner were speed reading the pages of the then-newly published UFO-themed book, *Communion*, by Whitley Strieber. It was a book published by the very company Lee was working for. Lee quickly exited the store, shaken to the core by the appearance and hostile air that the peculiar pair oozed in his presence.

In 2001, Colin Perks, a British man obsessed with finding the final resting place of King Arthur, received a nighttime visit from a beautiful but emotionless Woman in Black—one with near-milk-white skin. She claimed to represent a secret arm of the British government that was intent on shutting down research into all realms of the paranormal. When Perks defiantly and defensively said he would not be stopped by veiled threats, the Woman in Black responded with a slight, emotionless smile and advised him he had just made a big mistake and that he should soon expect another visitor. That other visitor soon turned up late one dark night. It was a hideous, gargoyle-like beast with fiery, blazing red eyes that loomed large over Perks's bed in the early hours. Perks, forever thereafter blighted by fear and paranoia, came to believe his Woman in Black and the winged beast were one and the same: namely, a monstrous shapeshifter, a nightmarish thing intent on scaring him from continuing his dedicated research.

When paranormal activity occurs, when UFOs intrude upon the lives of petrified people, and when researchers of all things paranormal get too close to the truth for their own good, the WIB are ready to strike. They dwell within darkness, they surface when the landscape is black and shadowy, and they spread terror and negativity wherever they walk. Or, on occasion, silently glide. They are the Women in Black. Fear them. Keep away from them, and never, *ever*, let them in the house.

Wyrley Gang

I spent my childhood and teens living in a small village in central England called Pelsall, which is a very old village, to say the least. Its origins date back as far as 994 C.E. But more important and relevant than that, Pelsall is located only a five- or ten-minute drive from the site of what ultimately became one of the most controversial, weird, and—some even said—paranormal-themed events of the early twentieth century, and it all focused upon a man named George Edalji.

Edalji, the son of a priest, lived in the very nearby town of Great Wyrley and was thrust into the limelight in 1903 when he was convicted, sentenced, and imprisoned for maiming and mutilating horses in the area—reportedly in the dead of night, and, some believed, for reasons related to occult rite and ritual.

Collectively, the horse mutilations and deaths generated not only a great deal of concern at a local level, but also anger, fear, and a distinct distrust of the Edalji family, who the locals had frowned upon ever since they moved into the area years earlier. Notably, however, such was the publicity given to the case of George Edalji, and his subsequent lengthy prison sentence, even none other than the creator of Sherlock Holmes—Sir Arthur Conan Doyle—sat up and took notice.

Actually, Conan Doyle did far more than that. Believing that there had been a huge miscarriage of justice in the Edalji affair, he highlighted it, wrote about it, and even complained to the government of the day about it—events that, combined with the work of others, ultimately led to Edalji's release from prison. History has shown that the evidence against Edalji was decidedly flimsy and controversial, to say the least. Also controversial were the public statements of the local police, who frowned upon the fact that George's father, Shapurji, was from India.

That anonymous letters were flying around, and that there were other suspects under the microscope (such as a local butcher's boy, Royden Sharp), ensured that more than a few people—whether they cared to publicly admit it or not—were of the opinion that Edalji was a convenient scapegoat and nothing else. Whatever the truth, Edalji found himself sentenced to seven years of hard labor.

To his credit, Conan Doyle raised his doubts about the sentence given to Edalji, as his 1907 title, *The Story of Mr. George Edalji*, demonstrates. Given Conan Doyle's fame and standing, the nation's media took a great deal of interest in Doyle's investigation—as did the British government's Home Office. The result: a committee was created that concluded Edalji was wrongly convicted, after all. Mind you, there was not a bit of compensation forthcom-

Sir Arthur Conan Doyle—of Sherlock Holmes fame—wrote about the Edalji case because he believed a miscarriage of justice had been done.

ing. There was barely an apology, either. Edalji was a free man after three years, but he lived under the specter of the attacks until his death in 1953.

Particularly intriguing is a story that surfaced in 2015, suggesting that neither George Edlaji nor Royden Sharpe were the culprits. Sam Bakewell is the author of a currently unpublished manuscript that offers evidence suggesting that the attacks on the poor horses were undertaken on behalf of a secret society of occultists known as the Wyrley Gang, which believed sacrificial offerings—made to ancient "Earth Gods"—could provide them with power and influence on levels unparalleled. According to Bakewell, many of those same occultists had ties to the local police and, as a result, had a vested interest in deflecting the press, and even Conan Doyle, away from their activities and in the direction of George Edlaji—who became nothing less than a scapegoat in someone's infernal plot.

Zombie Army

In August 1964, a very strange yet fascinating document was secretly prepared for senior personnel in the U.S. Army and the Pentagon titled *Witchcraft, Sorcery, Magic, and Other Psychological Phenomena and Their Implications on Military and Paramilitary Operations in the Congo*. It was a document written by James Price and Paul Juredini, both of whom worked for the Special Operations Research Office (SORO), which was an agency that undertook top secret contract work for the military. The document, now in the public domain via the terms of the Freedom of Information Act, is a fascinating one in the sense that it focuses on how beliefs in paranormal phenomena can be successfully used and manipulated to defeat a potential enemy.

The bigger the belief in the world of the supernatural, noted Price and Juredini, the greater the chance was that a particularly superstitious foe could be terrorized and manipulated by the spreading of faked stories of paranormal creatures on the loose, of demons in their midst, and of ghostly, terrible things with violent slaughter on their monstrous minds.

Interestingly, one portion of the document deals with a classic aspect of the zombie of the modern era: its terrifying ability to keep on coming, even when its body is riddled with bullet upon bullet. In the example at issue, the authors reported that: "Rebel tribesmen are said to have been persuaded that they can be made magically impervious to Congolese army firepower. Their fear of the government has thus been diminished and, conversely, fear of the rebels has grown within army ranks."

A 1964 military document explored the potential of using paranormal forces in special operations, including the creation of zombie armies impervious to bullets.

That was not all: rumors quickly spread within the army to the effect that the reason why the rebels were allegedly so immune to bullets was because they had been definitively zombified.

Not in Romero-style, but by good old, tried-and-tested Voodoo techniques, the rebels, entire swathes of army personnel very quickly came to believe, had literally been rendered indestructible as a result of dark and malignant spells and incantations. On top of that, the minds of the rebels, controlled by a Voodoo master, had been magically distilled, to the point where they were driven by a need to kill and nothing else. Or so it was widely accepted by the Congolese military.

It transpired, as one might guess, that the stories were actually wholly fictional ones. They were ingeniously created and spread by none other than the rebels themselves, and with just one purpose in mind: to have the army utterly convinced that the rebels were unbeatable and indestructible.

Such was the ingrained fear that infected the army, the brilliant piece of disinformation was accepted as full-blown fact—as was the belief that fearless, and fear-inducing, zombies were roaming the landscape impervious, to bullets. The result: the rebels delivered the army a powerful blow of a terrifyingly psychological kind. While the bulletproof zombies of the Congo never really existed, for all of the stark fear and mayhem they provoked, they just might as well have been the real thing.

FURTHER READING

"1963: Hypnotist George Estabrooks Admits Creating Multiple Personality Assassins." http://ahrp.org/1963-hypnotist-george-estabrooks-admits-creating-multiple-personality-assassins/. 2016.

"22 Shocking Population Control Quotes from the Global Elite." http://www.fourwinds10.net/siterun_data/health/intentional_death/news.php?q=1291600521. 2014.

"About Brookings." http://www.brookings.edu/about#research-programs/. 2016.

"About CFR." http://www.cfr.org/about/. 2016.

"About the RAND Corporation." http://www.rand.org/about.html. 2016.

"About the Trilateral Commission." http://trilateral.org/page/3/about-trilateral. 2016.

Adachi, Ken. "Chemtrails." http://educate-yourself.org/ct/. 2014.

Addison, Charles G. *History of the Knights Templar*. Kemtpon, IL: Adventures Unlimited Press, 2015.

"Adolph Hitler and the Occult." http://www.crystalinks.com/hitleroccult.html. 2016.

"Aetherius Society." http://www.aetherius.org/. 2016.

"African Criminal Enterprises." https://www.fbi.gov/about-us/investigate/organizedcrime/african. 2016.

"AIDS as a Biological Weapon." http://iipdigital.usembassy.gov/st/english/texttrans/2005/01/20050114151424atlahtnevel8.222598e-02.html#axzz49rivnGUM. 2016.

"Air Force 2025." http://fas.org/spp/military/docops/usaf/2025/. 2016.

Alchemy Website. http://www.levity.com/alchemy/. 2016.

Alfred, Randy. "March 20, 1995: Poison Gas Wreaks Tokyo Subway Terror." http://archive.wired.com/science/discoveries/news/2009/03/dayintech_0320. March 20, 2009.

Allen, Joe. "It Can't Happen Here?" http://isreview.org/issue/85/it-cant-happen-here. 2016.

"American Nazi Party." https://en.wikipedia.org/wiki/American_Nazi_Party. 2016.

"American Protective Association." http://immigrationtounitedstates.org/340-american-protective-association.html. 2015.

"American Vision." https://en.wikipedia.org/wiki/American_Vision. 2016.

"Ancient Egyptian Arabic Order Nobles Mystic Shrine." http://www.aeaonms.org/. 2016.

"Animal Mutilation." https://vault.fbi.gov/Animal%20Mutilation. 2016.

"Army of God." http://www.historycommons.org/timeline.jsp?timeline=us_domestic _terrorism_tmln&haitian_elite_2021_organizations=haitian_elite_2021_army_ of_god. 2016.

"Aryan Nations." https://www.splcenter.org/fighting-hate/extremist-files/group/aryan-nations. 2016.

"Assassination of President Abraham Lincoln." http://memory.loc.gov/ammem/alhtml/ alrintr.html. 2014.

"Atlanta Vampire Alliance." http://www.atlantavampirealliance.com/. 2016.

The Atlantean Conspiracy. "Committee of 300." http://www.bibliotecapleyades.net/ sociopolitica/atlantean_conspiracy/atlantean_conspiracy08.htm. 2016.

"The Atticus Institute." http://www.metacritic.com/movie/the-atticus-institute. 2016.

"Aurum Solis: The Order of the Gold of the Sun." http://unmyst3.blogspot.com/2011/ 07/aurum-solis-order-of-gold-of-sun.html. July 2011.

Ausiello, Michael. "The Sept. 11 Parallel 'Nobody Noticed' ('Lone Gunmen' Pilot Episode Video)." http://www.freerepublic.com/focus/news/703915/posts. June 21, 2002.

Austin, Jon. "New Shock Claim JFK Was 'Murdered by CIA' Days after Demanding UFO Files and NASA Visit." http://www.express.co.uk/news/science/631341/ New-shock-claim-JFK-was-murdered-by-CIA-days-after-demanding-UFO-files-and-NASA-visit. January 4, 2016.

Baring-Gould, Sabine. *The Book of Werewolves*. New York: Causeway Books, 1973.

Begg, Paul. *Jack the Ripper: The Uncensored Facts*. London, U.K.: Robson Books, 1993.

———, Martin Fido, and Keith Skinner. *The Jack the Ripper A to Z*. London, U.K.: Headline Book Publishing, 1991.

Bekkum, Gary S. "Ingo Swann." http://ufoexperiences.blogspot.com/2006/08/ingo-swann .html. August 3, 2006.

Bellers, Veronica. "The Leopard Murders of Opobo." http://www.britishempire.co.uk/ article/sanders/sanderschapter19.htm. 2016.

"Benandanti—The Story." http://www.academia.edu/7974994/Benandanti_-_The_story. 2016.

Bernstein, Marc. D. "Ed Lansdale's Black Warfare in 1950s Vienam." http://www.histo rynet.com/ed-lansdales-black-warfare-in-1950s-vietnam.htm. February 16, 2010.

"Bilderberg." http://www.sourcewatch.org/index.php/Bilderberg. 2016.

"Black Helicopters Exist." http://www.theforbiddenknowledge.com/hardtruth/black_ helicopters_exist.htm. 2016.

Black, John. "Ahnenerbe: Nazis and the Search for Relics." http://www.ancient-origins .net/unexplained-phenomena/ahnenerbe-nazis-and-search-relics-00424. May 8, 2013.

"Black-eyed Children." http://www.leprechaunpress.com/. 2016.

Blackwood666. "Exposing the Order of Nine Angles." http://disinfo.com/2008/10/ exposing-the-order-of-nine-angles/. October 14, 2008.

"Blamed on Hypnosis." https://news.google.com/newspapers?nid=1798&dat=1971102 2&id=E_geAAAAIBAJ&sjid=HY0EAAAAIBAJ&pg=4117,3992185&hl=en. 2016.

"Bohemian." http://www.worldwidewords.org/qa/qa-boh1.htm. 2016.

"Bohemian Grove." http://bohemiangroveexposed.com/. 2016.

"A Brief History of Voodoo." http://www.neworleansvoodoocrossroads.com/historyand voodoo.html. 2016.

"Bush Wants Right to Use Military If Bird Flu Hits." http://www.freerepublic.com/focus/ news/1497126/posts?page=152. 2014.

"Camorra." http://www.britannica.com/topic/Camorra. 2016.

"The Carbonari—Secret Society—A Must Read." https://wesdancin.wordpress.com/ 2011/09/30/the-carbonari-secret-society-a-must-read/. September 30, 2011.

"Carbonari Society." http://www.globalsecurity.org/military/world/europe/carbonari.htm. 2016.

"Carl Sagan." https://vault.fbi.gov/Carl%20Sagan/. 2016.

Carter, John. *Sex and Rockets: The Occult World of Jack Parsons*. Los Angeles, CA: Feral House, 2005.

"Chalcedon Foundation." http://chalcedon.edu/. 2016.

Chapman, Douglas. "Sorcerous Scientist." *Strange Magazine*, No. 6, 1990.

Check, Christopher. "The Sad History of the Knights Templar." http://www.catholic .com/magazine/articles/the-sad-history-of-the-knights-templar. 2016.

"Chemtrail Conspiracy Theory." http://moonconspiracy.wordpress.com/chemtrail-con spiracy-theory/. 2014.

"Chemtrails." http://www.sheepkillers.com/chemtrails.html. 2014.

"Chemtrails Killing Organic Crops, Monsanto's GMO Seeds Thrive." http://www.geo engineeringwatch.org/chemtrails-killing-organic-crops-monsantos-gmo-seeds- thrive/. May 23, 2014.

"Chemtrails—Spraying in Our Sky." http://www.holmestead.ca/chemtrails/response- en.html. 2014.

Cherry, Ken. *Marc Slade Investigates: The Stephenville UFO*. Hamburg, NJ: Glannant Ty Media, 2015.

"Church of Light." https://www.light.org/index.cfm/. 2016.

"Church of Satan." http://www.churchofsatan.com/. 2016.

"CIA Agent Loses Part of the Bible." http://www.biblehistory.net/newsletter/BookOf- Daniel.htm. 2013.

"CIA Report on Noah's Ark." http://www.jasoncolavito.com/cia-report-on-noahs-ark .html. 2016.

Clelland, Mike. *The Messengers: Owls, Synchronicity and the UFO Abductee*. Richard Dolan Press, 2015.

Clemens, Martin J. "The Clapham Wood Mystery." http://mysteriousuniverse.org/20 16/02/the-clapham-wood-mystery/. February 11, 2016.

"The Clovelly Cannibals." https://sjhstrangetales.wordpress.com/2015/10/18/new-on- strangeblog-the-clovelly-cannibals/. October 18, 2015.

"Club of Rome." http://www.clubofrome.org/. 2016.

"The Club of Rome." http://www.jeremiahproject.com/newworldorder/club-of- rome.html. 2016.

Coleman, John. "'Committee of 300' aka ... Olympians." http://www.bibliotecapley ades.net/sociopolitica/esp_sociopol_committee300_11.htm. 2016.

"Committee of 300." http://www.whale.to/b/300.html. 2016.

"The Committee of 300 Governs the World via a Three City State Empire, in Which the Cities Pay No Taxes and Obey Their Own Laws." https://sites.google.com/site/nocancerfoundation/council-of-300. 2016.

Coppens, Philip. "Report from Iron Mountain." http://philipcoppens.com/ironmountain.html. 2016.

Corbett, James. "Lone Gunmen Producer Questions Government on 9/11." http://www.corbettreport.com/articles/20080225_gunmen_911.htm. February 25, 2008.

Corrales, Scott. "The Ummo Experience: Are You Experienced" http://www.strangemag.com/ummo.html. 2016.

Cosgrove Baylis, Sheila. "The Slender Man Phenomenon: Behind the Myth That Allegedly

Drove Girls to Stab Friend." http://www.people.com/article/slender-man-myth-wisconsin-girls-murder-friend. June 4, 2014.

"Council for National Policy." https://www.cfnp.org/. 2016.

"Council for National Policy." http://www.publiceye.org/ifas/cnp//. 2016.

"Council for National Policy." http://www.sourcewatch.org/index.php/Council_for_National_Policy. 2016.

"The Council on Foreign Relations." http://www.jeremiahproject.com/newworldorder/nworder06.html. 2016.

Crawford, Angus. "Torso Case Boy 'Identified.'" http://www.bbc.com/news/uk-21365961. February 7, 2013.

Crenshaw, Dennis, and P. G. Navarro. *The Secrets of Dellschau*. San Antonio, TX: Anomalist Books, 2009.

"Cult Told My Son He Was a Werewolf." http://www.religionnewsblog.com/4973/cult-told-my-son-he-was-a-werewolf. November 8, 2003.

Darling, David. "Jonathan Swift and the Moons of Mars." http://www.daviddarling.info/encyclopedia/S/Swift.html. 2016.

Dash, Mike. "The Monster of Glamis." http://www.smithsonianmag.com/history/the-monster-of-glamis-92015626/?no-ist. February 10, 2012.

———. *Thug: The True Story of India's Murderous Cult*. London, U.K.: Granta Books, 2005.

"Daughter Charged in Slaying of Scientist." *Washington Post*, February 2, 2002.

Davidson, Michael. "A Career in Microbiology can be Harmful to Your Health—Especially since 9-11." http://www.rense.com/general20/car.htm. February 15, 2002.

———, and Michael C. Ruppert, Michael C. "Microbiologist Death Toll Mounts as Connections to Dynocorp, Hadron, Promis Software & Disease Research Emerge." http://www.rense.com/general20/mic.htm. March 3, 2002.

Davies, Owen. *Paganism: A Very Short Introduction*. Oxford, U.K.: Oxford University Press, 2011.

"Dead Scientists: The Marconi Murders—Was There a Plot to Murder Marconi Scientists in the 1980s?" http://theunredacted.com/dead-scientists-the-marconi-murders/. 2016.

"Decided Ones of Jupiter." http://www.unexplainedstuff.com/Secret-Societies/The-Decided-Ones-of-Jupiter.html. 2016.

"The Depopulation/Genocide Conspiracy Articles." http://www.whale.to/b/population.html. 2016.

"Dianic Witchcraft." http://www.thissideofsanity.com/dianic/dianic.html. 2016.

Dowbenko, Uri. "Masonic Ritual Murders AKA Jack the Ripper." http://www.con spiracy archive.com/NWO/Masonic_Ritual_Murders.htm. 2016.

"Druids." http://www.crystalinks.com/druids.html. 2016.

Duffy, Jonathan. "Bilderberg: The Ultimate Conspiracy Theory." http://news.bbc.co.uk/ 2/hi/uk_news/magazine/3773019.stm. June 3, 2004.

"The Dulce Base." http://www.sacred-texts.com/ufo/dulce.htm. 2016.

"Ernest Hemingway." https://vault.fbi.gov/ernest-miller-hemingway/ernest-heming way-part-01-of-01/view. 2016.

"Fabian Society." http://www.fabians.org.uk/. 2016.

"The Fabian Society." https://fabiansociety.wordpress.com/. 2016.

Fairclough, Melvin. *The Ripper and the Royals*. London, U.K.: Gerald Duckworth & Co., 1992.

"Famous Sorcerers and Sorceresses of History." http://spellsofmagic.wikia.com/wiki/ Famous_Sorcerers_and_Sorceresses_of_History. 2016.

"Federal Emergency Management Agency." http://www.fema.gov. 2016.

Fido, Martin. *The Crimes, Detection & Death of Jack the Ripper*. London, U.K.: Wei- denfeld & Nicolson, Ltd., 1987.

"Filey Brigg." http://www.mysteriousbritain.co.uk/england/north-yorkshire/legends/filey -brigg.html. 2016.

Flock, Elizabeth. "Bohemian Grove: Where the Rich and Powerful Go to Misbehave." https://www.washingtonpost.com/blogs/blogpost/post/bohemian-grove-where- the-rich-and-powerful-go-to-misbehave/2011/06/15/AGPV1sVH_blog.html. June 15, 2011.

Frascella, Tom. "Carbonari Movement." http://www.sanfelesesocietynj.org/History%20 Articles/Carbonari%20Movement.htm. May 2012.

Frazer, James George. *The Golden Bough*. New York: Dover Publications, 2002.

Freeman, Mara. "Tree Lore: Oak." http://www.druidry.org/library/trees/tree-lore-oak. 2016.

Freemasonry." https://tshaonline.org/handbook/online/articles/vnf01. 2016.

Friedman, Herb. "The Death Card." http://www.psywarrior.com/DeathCardsAce .html. 2016.

"The Garduna." http://www.unexplainedstuff.com/Secret-Societies/The-Garduna.html. 2016.

Garrison, Jim. *On the Trail of the Assassins*. London, U.K.: Penguin Books, 1992.

"George Adamski." FBI File, Declassified under the Terms of the Freedom of Informa- tion Act. 2016.

"The George Edalji Case." http://www.birmingham.gov.uk/edalji. 2016.

"George Van Tassel." FBI File, declassified under the terms of the Freedom of Infor- mation Act. 2016.

"The Golden Dawn FAQ. " http://hermetic.com/gdlibrary/gd-faq.html. December 1999.

Gordon, Stan. *Silent Invasion*. Greensburg, PA: Stan Gordon, 2010.

"Gracchus Babeuf (1760–1797) and the Conspiracy of the Equals (1796)." https:// www.marxists.org/history/france/revolution/conspiracy-equals/. 2005.

Greenwood, Cynthia. "Secrets of the Sonora Aero Club." http://www.houston press.com/news/secrets-of-the-sonora-aero-club-6567727. December 10, 1998.

"Guild of St. Bernulphus." https://en.wikipedia.org/wiki/Guild_of_St._Bernulphus. 2016.

Gurney, Ian. "The Mystery of the Dead Scientists: Coincidence or Conspiracy?" http://www.rense.com/general39/death.htm. July 20, 2003.

Hall, Manly P. *The Secret Teachings of All Ages.* Wilder Publications, 2009.

"The Halliwell Manuscript." http://www.masonicdictionary.com/halliwell.html. 2016.

Harper, Mark J. "Dead Scientists and Microbiologists—Master List." http://www.rense.com/general62/list.htm. February 5, 2005.

Heidrick, Bill. "Ordo Templi Orientis: A Brief Historical Review." http://hermetic.com/heidrick/oto_history.html. 2016.

"Hekate." http://www.theoi.com/Khthonios/Hekate.html. 2016.

"The Hellfire Club." http://www.mysteriousbritain.co.uk/england/buckinghamshire/occult/the-hellfire-club.html. 2016.

"Heretic Among Heretics: Jacques Vallee Interview." http://www.ufoevidence.org/documents/doc839.htm. 2016.

"The Hermetic Brotherhood of Luxor." http://www.kheper.net/topics/Hermeticism/HBoL.html. 2016.

"Hermetic Order of the Golden Dawn." http://www.golden-dawn.com/eu/index.aspx. 2016.

"Hermetic Order of the Golden Dawn. " http://www.themystica.com/mystica/articles/h/hermetic_order_of_the_golden_dawn.html. 2016.

"The Hexham Heads." http://www.mysteriousbritain.co.uk/england/northumberland/legends/the-hexham-heads.html. 2016.

"The Hidden City of Death Valley." http://www.legendsofamerica.com/ca-deathvalley undergroundcity.html. 2016.

"History and Origins of Wicca." https://carm.org/religious-movements/wicca/history-and-origins-wicca. 2016.

"History of Freemasonry." http://www.msana.com/historyfm.asp. 2016.

"The History of Samhain And Halloween." http://www.paganspath.com/magik/samhain-history.htm. 2015.

Hodges, Dave. "Will Humanity Survive the Depopulation Agenda of the Global Elite?" http://www.thecommonsenseshow.com/2014/04/26/will-humanity-survive-the-depopulation-agenda-of-the-global-elite/. April 26, 2014.

Hoeck, Kenneth M. "The Jesuit Connection to the Assassination of Abraham Lincoln." http://www.truthontheweb.org/abe.htm. November 1999.

Holiday, F.W. *The Goblin Universe.* Woodbury, MN: Llewellyn Publications, 1986.

"Horsa Tradition." https://covenofthewolfa.wordpress.com/tag/horsa-tradition/. 2016.

Hoskins, Richard Kelly. *Vigilantes of Christendom: The Story of the Phineas Priesthood.* Lynchburg, VA: Virginia Publishing Company, 1990.

"How to Join the Sons of Lee Marvin in Five Easy Steps." http://dangerousminds.net/comments/how_to_join_the_sons_of_lee_marvin_in_five_easy_steps. 2016.

Howells, Martin, and Keith Skinner. *The Ripper Legacy.* London, U.K.: Sphere Books, Ltd., 1988.

"Hubbard Believed He Was Satan Incarnate!" http://www.bible.ca/scientologysatanism-Hubbard-jr.htm. 2016.

Hungerford, J.M. "The Exploitation of Superstitions for Purposes of Psychological Warfare." RAND Corporation. http://www.rand.org/pubs/research_memoranda/RM365.html. 1950.

Hymenaeus Beta XII. "Aleister Crowley." http://oto-usa.org/thelema/crowley/. 2015.

"'I AM' Activity." https://en.wikipedia.org/wiki/%22I_AM%22_Activity. 2016.

The Iconoclast. Vol. 1, No. 1, October 1873.

"Illuminati: Order of the Illumined Wise Men." http://www.bibliotecapleyades.net/esp_sociopol_illuminati.htm. 2016.

Illuminati Watcher. "Illuminati Symbolism of Princess Diana's Death in Selena Gomez 'Slow Down' Video." http://illuminatiwatcher.com/illuminati-symbolism-of-princess-dianas-death-in-selena-gomez-slow-down-video/. July 22, 2013.

"Improved Order of Red Men." http://www.stichtingargus.nl/vrijmetselarij/redmen_en.html. 2016.

"The Improved Order of Red Men." http://www.redmen.org/. 2016.

"Italian Organized Crime." https://www.fbi.gov/about-us/investigate/organizedcrime/italian_mafia. 2016.

"Jacobin Club." http://www.encyclopedia.com/topic/Jacobins.aspx. 2016.

"Jacobins." http://www.encyclopedia.com/topic/Jacobins.aspx. 2016.

Johnson, Robert. "Who Were the Gormogons?!" http://www.midnightfreemasons.org/2013/04/who-were-gormogons.html. 2015.

"John Birch Society." http://www.jbs.org/. 2016.

"John Whiteside Parsons." FBI file, declassified under the terms of the United States' Freedom of Information Act. 2016.

Juliano, Michael. "Exploring Devil's Gate, a Portal to Hell in Pasadena." http://www.timeout.com/los-angeles/blog/exploring-devils-gate-a-portal-to-hell-in-pasadena. October 9, 2014.

"Kabbalistic Order of the Rose and Cross." http://www.okrc.org/index.php/en-us/. 2016.

Kazlev, M. Alan. "Max Théon 1848–1927." http://www.kheper.net/topics/Theon/Theon.htm. September 23, 2005.

Keith, Jim. *Casebook on the Men in Black.* Lilburn, GA: IllumiNet Press, 1997.

Kelley, Ruth Edna. *The Book of Halloween.* CreateSpace, 2014.

"Kenneth Goff." https://en.wikipedia.org/wiki/Kenneth_Goff. 2016.

"Key Facts about Avian Influenza (Bird Flu) and Highly Pathogenic Avian Influenza A (H5N1) Virus." http://www.cdc.gov/flu/avian/gen-info/facts.htm. 2014.

"Kim Johnson's Chemtrail Analysis—Updated." http://www.nmsr.org/mkjrept.htm. October 31, 1999.

King, Jeffrey. "The Lone Gunmen Episode 1: Pilot." http://www.plaguepuppy.net/public_html/Lone%20Gunmen/The_Lone_Gunmen_Episode_1.htm. 2014.

Klickna, Cinda. "The Case of the Mad Gasser of Mattoon." http://illinoistimes.com/article-70-the-case-of-the-mad-gasser-of-mattoon.html. May 1, 2003.

Knight, Kevin. "The American Protective Association." http://www.newadvent.org/cathen/01426a.htm. 2012.

Knight, Stephen. *Jack the Ripper: The Final Solution.* London, U.K.: Grafton Books, 1989.

"The Knights Templar: History." http://www.theknightstemplar.org/history/. 2016.

"Know-Nothing Party." http://www.ohiohistorycentral.org/w/Know-Nothing_Party?rec =911. 2016.

Koenig, Peter-Robert. "The Ordo Templi Orientis Phenomenon." http://www.parareligion.ch/2016.

Kress, Kenneth. "Parapsychology in Intelligence." Central Intelligence Agency, 1977.

"Ku Klux Klan." http://www.history.com/topics/ku-klux-klan. 2016.

Kushner, David. "Cicada: Solving the Web's Deepest Mystery." http://www.rolling-stone.com/culture/features/cicada-solving-the-webs-deepest-mystery-20150115. January 15, 2015.

"Kwakwaka'wakw (Kwakiutl)." http://www.thecanadianencyclopedia.ca/en/article/kwakiutl/. 2016.

"L. Ron Hubbard—Church of Scientology FBI Files." http://www.paperlessarchives.com/hubbard.html. 2016.

"League of Just Men." http://www.globalsecurity.org/military/world/europe/league-of-just-men.htm. 2016.

Leiderman, Daniel. "Night Battles: How the Benandanti Fought Witches during the Sabbath." http://www.deliriumsrealm.com/night-battles-benandanti/ 2016.

Leland, Charles Godfrey. "Etruscan Roman Remains in Popular Tradition." http://sacred-texts.com/pag/err/index.htm. 2016.

"The Lemuria Connection." http://www.lemurianconnection.com/category/about-mt-shasta/. 2009.

Lendman, Stephen. "'The True Story of the Bilderberg Group' and What They May Be Planning Now." http://www.globalresearch.ca/the-true-story-of-the-bilderberg-group-and-what-they-may-be-planning-now/13808. June 1, 2009.

"The Leopard Society in 'Vai Country', in Bassaland." http://www.liberiapastandpresent .org/RitualKillings1900_1950b.htm. 2016.

Lewin, Leonard. *Report from Iron Mountain.* Carson City, NV: Bridger House Publishers Inc. 2008.

Liberty, Equality, Fraternity. "Exploring the French Revolution." http://chnm.gmu.edu /revolution/searchfr.php?function=find&x=0&y=0&keyword=constitution+1793. 2016.

"Liberty Lobby." http://www.publiceye.org/rightwoo/rwooz9-05.html. 2013.

Lienhard, John H. "Charles Dellschau." http://www.uh.edu/engines/epi1308.htm. 1998.

Linsboth, Christina. "Turning Lead into Silver—Experiments in Alchemy at the Imperial Court." http://www.habsburger.net/en/chapter/turning-lead-silver. 2016.

London Daily Post, September 3, 1724.

"Macumba." http://www.occultopedia.com/m/macumba.htm. 2016.

"Macumba, Another Source of African Spirituality." http://www.aaregistry.org/historic_events/view/macumba-another-source-african-spirituality. 2013.

"Majestic 12." http://www.crystalinks.com/mj12.html. 2016.

"Majestic 12." https://vault.fbi.gov/Majestic%2012. 2016.

Marinacci, Michael. "Krishna Venta and the WKFL Fountain of the World." http://califias.blogspot.com/2014/12/krishna-venta-and-wkfl-fountain-of-world.html. December 18, 2014.

Mastin, Luke. "Famous Witches—George Pickingill (c.1816–c.1909)." http://www.witchcraftandwitches.com/witches_pickingill.html. 2009.

———. "The Enigma of the Green Man." http://www.greenmanenigma.com/theories.html. 2011.

McNeill, Emma. "Return of the Bogus Social Workers." http://subscribe.forteantimes.com/blog/return-of-the-bogus-social-workers/. 2016.

Melanson, Terry. "The Vril Society, the Luminous Lodge and the Realization of the Great Work." http://www.conspiracyarchive.com/NWO/Vril_Society.htm. 2001.

Melton, John Gordon. "I AM Movement." http://www.britannica.com/topic/I-AM-movement. 2016.

Mendryk, Harry. "Speaking of Art, Jack Kirby's 'The Face On Mars.'" http://kirbymuseum.org/blogs/simonandkirby/archives/4555. September 1, 2012.

"Mermaids and Mermen." http://www.paranormaldatabase.com/reports/mermaid.php. 2016.

Michael, D. N. "Proposed Studies on the Implications of Peaceful Space Activities for Human Affairs." http://ntrs.nasa.gov/archive/nasa/casi.ntrs.nasa.gov/19640053196.pdf. December 1960.

"Military Use of Remote Viewing & the CIA FOIA Documents." http://www.remote-viewed.com/remote_viewing_history_military.htm. 2016.

Millegan, Kris. "The Order of the Skull and Bones: Everything You Always Wanted to Know, But Were Afraid to Ask." http://www.conspiracyarchive.com/NWO/Skull_Bones.htm. 1996.

"Minutemen." http://www.ushistory.org/people/minutemen.htm. 2016.

Molloy, Mark. "Who Is Behind Cicada 3301? A Brief History of the Hardest Puzzle on the Internet." http://www.telegraph.co.uk/technology/internet/12103306/Cicada-3301-Who-is-behind-the-hardest-puzzle-on-the-internet.html. January 16, 2016.

Montgomery, Ruth. "Spying by Mind-Reading." *New York Journal American*. June 14, 1960.

"Moor Sheep 'Killed by Occultists.'" http://news.bbc.co.uk/2/hi/uk_news/england/devon/4357188.stm. October 19, 2005.

"Navajo Skinwalker Legend." http://www.navajolegends.org/navajo-skinwalker-legend/. 2016.

"Nazi War Crimes Trials: The RuSHA Trial,(October 1947–February 1948)." https://www.jewishvirtuallibrary.org/jsource/Holocaust/rushacase.html. 2016.

Newton, Toyne. *The Demonic Conspiracy*. Poole, U.K.: Blandford Press, 1987.

O'Brien, Chris. *Stalking the Herd*. Kempton, IL: Adventures Unlimited Press, 2014.

"An Octopus Named Wackenhut." http://www.bibliotecapleyades.net/esp_sociopol_wackenhut.htm. 2016.

"Of the Bloody Sacrifice: And Matters Cognate." http://www.sacred-texts.com/oto/aba/chap12.htm. 2016.

Openheimer, David. "What Is the Blue Beam Project?" http://www.bibliotecapleyades.net/sociopolitica/esp_sociopol_bluebeam04.htm. April 16, 2000.

"Operation Often: Satanism in the CIA." http://coverthistory.blogspot.com/2007/12/operation-often-satanism-in-cia-this.html. December 17, 2007.

"Operation Paperclip." http://www.operationpaperclip.info/. 2016.

"Order of Nine Angles." http://theisticsatanism.wikia.com/wiki/Order_of_Nine_Angles . 2016.

"Ordo Aurum Solis." http://www.aurumsolis.org/index.php/en-us/. 2016.

"Ordo Aurum Solis—History—Denning and Phillips." http://www.liquisearch.com/ordo _aurum_solis/history/denning_and_phillips. 2016.

"Ordo Templi Orientis." http://oto-usa.org/. 2016.

"Origins of the Mafia." http://www.history.com/topics/origins-of-the-mafia. 2016.

"The Origins of Voodoo, the Misunderstood Religion." http://www.ancient-origins .net/history-ancient-traditions/origins-voodoo-misunderstood-religion-002933. April 21, 2015.

"Patriot Act." https://en.wikipedia.org/wiki/Patriot_Act. 2016.

Peabody, David. "Exploding the Ripper Masonic Link." http://www.mqmagazine.co .uk/issue-2/p-45.php. *MQ Magazine*, July 2002.

"Peacock Symbolism and Meaning." http://www.whats-your-sign.com/peacock-symbol ism.html. 2016.

"Philip K. Dick." FBI file, declassified under the terms of the United States' Freedom of Information Act. 2016.

"Philip K. Dick Contacted FBI to Warn of Secret Neo-Nazi Plot to Start World War III." http://disinfo.com/2010/02/philip-k-dick-contacted-fbi-to-warn-of-secret-neo-nazi-plot-to-start-world-war-iii/. February 16, 2010.

"Phineas Priesthood." https://www.splcenter.org/fighting-hate/extremist-files/ideology /phineas-priesthood. 2016.

Pike, John. "La Cosa Nostra." http://fas.org/irp/world/para/lcn.htm. October 3, 1998.

Pinch, Dr. Geraldine. "Ancient Egyptian Magic." http://www.bbc.co.uk/history/ancient/ egyptians/magic_01.shtml. February 17, 2011.

"Planetary Defense Coordination Office." https://www.nasa.gov/planetarydefense/over view. February 3, 2016.

"Poro." http://www.sierraleoneheritage.org/glossary/word.php?id=poro. 2016.

Posner, Sarah. "Just Who Is the Council for National Policy, and Why Isn't It Paying Taxes?" http://www.alternet.org/story/21372/secret_society. February 28, 2005.

"President Abraham Lincoln's Assassination and Freemasonry." http://freemasonry-watch.org/lincoln.html. 2016.

Price, James R., and Paul Jureidini. "Witchcraft, Sorcery, Magic, and Other Psychological

"Phenomena and Their Implications on Military and Paramilitary Operations in the Congo." https://www.researchgate.net/publication/235137065_witchcraft_sorcery _magic_and_other_psychological_phenomena_and_their_implications_on_mili tary_and_paramilitary_operations_in_the_congo. 2016.

"The Primrose League." http://www.theodora.com/encyclopedia/p2/the_primrose_lea gue.html. 2011.

"Princess Diana's Death and Memorial: The Occult Meaning." http://vigilantcitizen .com/vigilantreport/princess-dianas-death-and-memorial-the-occult-meaning/. 2016.

"Project Blue Beam." http://www.thewatcherfiles.com/bluebeam.html. 2016.

"Project MKNAOMI." https://en.wikipedia.org/wiki/Project_MKNAOMI. 2016.

Proud, Louis. "Does Scientology Have Its Roots in 'Black Magic'?—Part One." http://mysteriousuniverse.org/2015/11/does-scientology-have-its-roots-in-black-magic-part-one/. November 27, 2015.

———. "Does Scientology Have Its Roots in 'Black Magic'?—Part Two." http://mysteriousuniverse.org/2015/12/does-scientology-have-its-roots-in-black-magic-part-two/. December 1, 2015.

"The Raelian Movement." http://www.rael.org/. 2016.

Randles, Jenny. "The Strange Affair of APEN." http://magonia.haaan.com/2009/apen/. *NUFON*. No. 3, summer, 1976.

Reade, W. Windwood. *The Veil of Isis; or, Mysteries of the Druids.* Los Angeles, CA: Newcastle Publications Company, Inc. 1992.

Redfern, Nick. Interview with Colin Perks, May 14, 2001.

———. Interview with Frank Wiley, June 3, 2004.

———. Interview with Jenny Randles, March 28, 1997.

———. Interview with Mac Tonnies, March 14, 2004, and July 7, 2009.

———. Interview with Matthew Bevan, April 12, 1998.

———. Interview with Ray Boeche, January 22, 2007.

———. Interview with Rob Lea, 2000.

———. *Men in Black: Personal Stories and Eerie Adventures.* Bracey, VA: Lisa Hagan Books, 2015.

———. "The Odd World of Webster Edgerly." Mystic Utopian Supermen. New Brunswick, NJ: Global Communications, 2008.

———. *Women in Black: The Creepy Companions of the Mysterious M.I.B.* Bracey, VA: Lisa Hagan Books, 2016.

Rense, Jeff. "Cattle Mutilations Explained? End of the Beef Industry?" http://www.rense.com/general32/beef.htm. July 2, 2003.

"Report of Scientific Advisory Panel on Unidentified Flying Objects Convened by Office of Scientific Intelligence, CIA. January 14–18, 1953." http://www.cufon.org/cufon/robert.htm. 2016.

"The Right Club." http://spartacus-educational.com/2WWrightclub.htm. 2016.

"The RIIA & CFR." http://www.bibliotecapleyades.net/sociopolitica/atlantean_conspiracy/atlantean_conspiracy13.htm. 2016.

Roberts, Andy. *UFO Down!* Woolsery, U.K.: CFZ Press, 2010.

"Rosemary's Baby (1968)." http://www.filmsite.org/rosem.html. 2016.

"Rosicrucian Collection, Special Collections, Hartley Library: Home." http://library.soton.ac.uk/rosicrucians. 2016.

"Rosicrucian Order Crotona Fellowship." https://witchesofthecraft.com/tag/rosicrucian-order-crotona-fellowship/. 2016.

Ross, Colin A. "BLUEBIRD: Deliberate Creation of Multiple Personality by Psychiatrists." http://www.wanttoknow.info/bluebird10pg. 2016.

Ruggiero, Jennifer. "Hamatsa." http://www.pantheon.org/articles/h/hamatsa.html. 2016.

Rumbelow, Donald. *The Complete Jack the Ripper.* London, U.K.: Penguin Books, 1988.

"Sande Society." http://academics.smcvt.edu/africanart/Sonja_Cole/Sande_Society_Temp.htm. 2016.

"Santeria, A Syncretistic Caribbean Religion: Beliefs and Practices." http://www.religioustolerance.org/santeri3.htm. 2016.

Sayer, Ian & Botting, Douglas. *Nazi Gold: The Sensational Story of the World's Greatest Robbery—and the Greatest Criminal Cover-Up*. Edinburgh, Scotland: Mainstream Publishing, 2003.

Scarborough, Samuel. "The Influence of Egypt on the Modern Western Mystery Tradition: The Hermetic Brotherhood of Luxor." *Journal of the Western Mystery Tradition*, No. 1, Autumnal Equinox, 2001.

Schaeffenberg, A.V. "The Life of William Dudley Pelley." http://come-and-hear.com/supplement/life-of-pelley/index.html. 2016.

"School of Wicca." http://wicca.org/. 2016.

Schwarz, Rob. "Agharta and the Golden City of Shambhala." http://www.strangerdimensions.com/2013/01/18/agharta-and-the-golden-city-of-shambhala/. January 18, 2013.

"Scotch Cattle: The Welsh Mob Who Took No Bull." http://www.welshnot.com/scotch-cattle-wales-weirdest-terrorists/. 2016.

"Secret Eco-Village Hidden in Wales Wins Permission to Stay after 10-Year Fight." http://www.telegraph.co.uk/news/uknews/2973146/Secret-eco-village-hidden-in-Wales-wins-permission-to-stay-after-10-year-fight.html. September 17, 2008.

Shapiro, Joshua. "The Montauk Project and the Philadelphia Experiment." http://www.v-j-enterprises.com/montauk.html. 2016.

"Shickshinny Knights of Malta." http://en.metapedia.org/wiki/Shickshinny_Knights_of_Malta. 2016.

"Silver Shirts." http://holocaustonline.org/silver-shirts/. 2016.

Six, Janet. "Hidden History of Ralston Heights." *Archaeology*. Volume 57, Number 3, May/June 2004.

Snyder, Michael. "From 7 Billion People to 500 Million People—The Sick Population Control Agenda of the Global Elite." http://endoftheamericandream.com/archives/from-7-billion-people-to-500-million-people-the-sick-population-control-agenda-of-the-global-elite. October 27, 2011.

"The Sons of Lee Marvin: An Iconic Brotherhood of Famous Look-alikes." https://selvedgeyard.com/2009/05/16/the-sons-of-lee-marvin/. May 16, 2009.

"Space Shuttle Challenger." https://vault.fbi.gov/Space%20Shuttle%20Challenger%20/. 2016.

Special Branch. "The Aetherius Society." 1962 file, declassified under the provisions of the U.K. Freedom of Information Act.

Steiger, Brad. "Ancient Secret Societies, UFOs, and the New World Order." http://www.bibliotecapleyades.net/sociopolitica/sociopol_brotherhoodss30.htm. January 29, 2008.

———. *Conspiracies and Secret Societies*. Canton, MI: Visible Ink Press, 2013.

———. "Three Tricksters in Black." *Saga's UFO Report*, winter 1974.

———. "Who Really Killed Abraham Lincoln?" http://www.rense.com/general80/slin.htm. February 11, 2008.

"The SS (Schutzstaffel): Background & Overview." http://www.jewishvirtuallibrary.org/jsource/Holocaust/SS.html. 2016.

Stephey, M. J. "A Brief History of the Skull and Bones Society." http://content.time.com/time/nation/article/0,8599,1881172,00.html. February 23 2009.

"A Study of Assassination." http://nsarchive.gwu.edu/NSAEBB/NSAEBB4/ciaguat2.html. 2016.

Sutton, Anthony C. *America's Secret Establishment*. Walterville, OR: Trine Day, 2004.

Sutton, William Josiah. *The Illuminati 666*. Fort Oglethorpe, GA: Teach Services, Inc., 1996.

Swann, Ingo. *Penetration—the Question of Extraterrestrial and Human Telepathy*. Ingo Swann Books, 1998.

Swartz, Tim R. "Richard Shaver's Inner Earth Mysteries." http://www.ufodigest.com/news/0507/innerearth2.html. 2016.

Swift, Jonathan. *Gulliver's Travels*. Mineola, NY: Dover Publications, 1996.

"Taigheirm." http://www.paranormality.com/occult_taigheirm.shtml. 2016.

"Temple of the Vampire." http://www.vampiretemple.com/. 2016.

"Testimony for Under Secretary of State, Stuart E. Eizenstat, House Banking Committee: On the U.S. Government Supplementary Report on Nazi Assets." http://archives.financialservices.house.gov/banking/6498eiz.shtml. June 4, 1998.

"Theodor Fritsch." http://en.metapedia.org/wiki/Theodor_Fritsch. 2016.

Thomas, Dave. "The Chemtrail Conspiracy." http://www.csicop.org/sb/show/chemtrail_conspiracy. *Skeptical Briefs*, Volume 18.3, September 2008.

Thomas, Kenn. "Casolaro's Octopus." http://www.theforbiddenknowledge.com/hardtruth/casolaro_octopus.htm. June 7, 2001.

———. *Maury Island UFO*. Lilburn, GA: IllumiNet Press, 1999.

———, and Jim Keith. *The Octopus*. Portland, OR: Feral House, 1996.

Thompson, Geoff. "US Involved in Bird Flu Conspiracy: Indonesia." http://www.abc.net.au/am/content/2008/s2167325.htm. February 20, 2008.

"Thule Society." http://www.crystalinks.com/thule.html. 2016.

"Thule Society." http://www.theforbiddenknowledge.com/hardtruth/thulesociety.htm. 2016.

"The Thule Society." http://www.bibliotecapleyades.net/sociopolitica/sociopol_thule01.htm. 2016.

Tonnies, Mac. *The Cryptoterrestrials*. San Antonio, TX: Anomalist Books, 2010.

"Triads and Organized Crime in China." http://factsanddetails.com/china/cat8/sub50/item300.html. 2016.

"Trilateral Commission." http://www.bibliotecapleyades.net/sociopolitica/atlantean_conspiracy/atlantean_conspiracy16.htm. 2016.

"Uncovering Warwickshire's Sinister Secret." http://www.bbc.co.uk/coventry/features/weird-warwickshire/1945-witchcraft-murder.shtml. September 24, 2014.

Valentine, Chris. "Silver Shirts, Murphy Ranch, and William Dudley Pelley." http://oddculture.com/silver-shirts-murphy-ranch-and-william-dudley-pelley/. 2015.

"The Vampire Society." http://thevampiresociety.yolasite.com/. 2016.

"The Vril Society." http://www.echoesofenoch.com/Musium13%20vril_society.htm. 2016.

Walters, Jonah. "A Guide to the French Revolution." https://www.jacobinmag.com/2015/07/french-revolution-bastille-day-guide-jacobins-terror-bonaparte/. 2016.

"Water Dowsing." http://water.usgs.gov/edu/dowsing.html. May 2, 2016.

"Watergate Investigations Reveal Nixon's Plans to Use Holograms to Simulate 'the Second Coming' over Havana, Cuba." https://www.reddit.com/r/conspiracy/comments/3x1lmm/til_watergate_investigations_reveal_nixons_plans/?. 2016.

W. E. B. "The Council on Foreign Relations (CFR) and The New World Order." http://www.conspiracyarchive.com/2013/12/21/the-council-on-foreign-relations-cfr-and-the-new-world-order/. December 21, 2013.

"Weather Underground." http://www.pbs.org/independentlens/weatherunderground/movement.html. 2016.

Weigel, David. "Ron Paul on the Trilateral Commission." http://www.slate.com/blogs/weigel/2011/12/23/ron_paul_on_the_trilateral_commission.html. December 23, 2011.

"What Is Germanenorden?" http://www.liquisearch.com/what_is_germanenorden. 2016.

"Where Does the Order of the Aurum Solis From?" http://www.aurumsolis.info/index.php?option=com_content&view=article&id=2229:where-does-the-order-of-the-aurum-solis-from&catid=1633&Itemid=2768&lang=en-us. 2016.

Wiener, James. "The Merovingians: The Kings and Queens of the Franks." http://etc.ancient.eu/2013/06/09/the-merovingians-the-lords-and-ladies-of-the-dark-ages/. June 9, 2013.

Williams, Matthew. "UK Hacker Says He Found Anti-Gravity Engine File at W/P AFB." February 7, 1999.

"The Witches of the New Forest." http://inewforest.co.uk/witches/. 2016.

Wunrow, Rose. "The Psychological Massacre: Jim Jones and Peoples Temple: An Investigation." http://jonestown.sdsu.edu/?page_id=29478. 2016.

Wylie, J. A. "History of the Jesuits." http://www.reformation.org/jesuits.html. 2016.

Zandbergen, Rene. "The Voynich Manuscript." http://www.voynich.nu/. 2016.

Zeller, Benjamin E. "Anatomy of a Mass Suicide: The Dark, Twisted Story behind a UFO Death Cult." http://www.salon.com/2014/11/15/anatomy_of_a_mass_suicide_the_dark_twisted_story_behind_a_ufo_death_cult/. November 15, 2014.

Zetter, Kim. "April 13, 1953: CIA OKs MK-ULTRA Mind-Control Tests." http://www.wired.com/2010/04/0413mk-ultra-authorized/. April 13, 2010.

INDEX

Note: (ill.) indicates photos and illustrations.

SECRET SOCIETIES: THE COMPLETE GUIDE TO COVERT GROUPS AND THEIR HISTORIES, RITES, AND RITUALS